HMH SCIENCE DIMENSIONS™

Teacher Edition • Grade 2

Houghton Mifflin Harcourt™

Acknowledgments for Covers

All photos ©HMH unless otherwise noted

Back Cover: *sand castle* ©koya79/Dreamstime

Printed in the U.S.A.

ISBN 978-0-544-71337-6

4 5 6 7 8 9 10 0877   25 24 23 22 21 20 19 18 17

4500661349   B C D E F G

Teacher Edition Contents

About the Program

Units

Resources

Michael A. DiSpezio

Global Educator
North Falmouth, Massachusetts

Michael DiSpezio has authored many HMH instructional programs for Science and Mathematics. He has also authored numerous trade books and multimedia programs on various topics and hosted dozens of studio and location broadcasts for various organizations in the U.S. and worldwide. Most recently, he has been working with educators to provide strategies for implementing the Next Generation Science Standards, particularly the Science and Engineering Practices, Crosscutting Concepts, and the use of Evidence Notebooks. To all his projects, he brings his extensive background in science, his expertise in classroom teaching at the elementary, middle, and high school levels, and his deep experience in producing interactive and engaging instructional materials.

Marjorie Frank

Science Writer and Content-Area Reading Specialist
Brooklyn, New York

An educator and linguist by training, a writer and poet by nature, Marjorie Frank has authored and designed a generation of instructional materials in all subject areas, including past HMH Science programs. Her other credits include authoring science issues of an award-winning children's magazine, writing game-based digital assessments, developing blended learning materials for young children, and serving as instructional designer and co-author of pioneering school-to-work software. In addition, she has served on the adjunct faculty of Hunter, Manhattan, and Brooklyn Colleges, teaching courses in science methods, literacy, and writing. For *HMH Science Dimensions*, she has guided the development of our K-2 strands and our approach to making connections between NGSS and Common Core ELA/literacy standards.

Michael R. Heithaus, PhD

Dean, College Of Arts, Sciences & Education
Professor, Department Of Biological Sciences
Florida International University
Miami, Florida

Mike Heithaus joined the FIU Biology Department in 2003, has served as Director of the Marine Sciences Program and Executive Director of the School of Environment, Arts, and Society, which brings together the natural and social sciences and humanities to develop solutions to today's environmental challenges. He now serves as Dean of the College of Arts, Sciences & Education. His research focuses on predator-prey interactions and the ecological importance of large marine species. He has helped to guide the development of Life Science content in *HMH Science Dimensions*, with a focus on strategies for teaching challenging content as well as the science and engineering practices of analyzing data and using computational thinking.

Cary I. Sneider, PhD

Associate Research Professor
Portland State University
Portland, Oregon

While studying astrophysics at Harvard, Cary Sneider volunteered to teach in an Upward Bound program and discovered his real calling as a science teacher. After teaching middle and high school science in Maine, California, Costa Rica and Micronesia, he settled for nearly three decades at Lawrence Hall of Science in Berkeley, California, where he developed skills in curriculum development and teacher education. Over his career Cary directed more than 20 federal, state, and foundation grant projects, and was a writing team leader for the Next Generation Science Standards. He has been instrumental in ensuring *HMH Science Dimensions* meets the high expectations of the NGSS and provides an effective three-dimensional learning experience for all students.

Program Advisors

Paul D. Asimow, PhD
*Eleanor and John R. McMillan Professor
    of Geology and Geochemistry*
California Institute of Technology
Pasadena, California

Dr. Eileen Cashman, PhD
Professor
Humboldt State University
Arcata, California

Mark B. Moldwin, PhD
*Professor of Space Sciences and
    Engineering*
University of Michigan
Ann Arbor, Michigan

Kelly Y. Neiles, PhD
Assistant Professor of Chemistry
St. Mary's College of Maryland
St. Mary's City, Maryland

Dr. Sten Odenwald, PhD
Astronomer
NASA Goddard Spaceflight Center
Greenbelt, Maryland

Bruce W. Schafer
*Director of K-12 STEM Collaborations,
    retired*
Oregon University System
Portland, Oregon

Barry A. Van Deman
President and CEO
Museum of Life and Science
Durham, North Carolina

Kim Withers, PhD
Assistant Professor
Texas A&M University-Corpus Christi
Corpus Christi, Texas

Adam D. Woods, PhD
Professor
California State University, Fullerton
Fullerton, California

Classroom Reviewers

Michelle Barnett
Lichen K-8
Citrus Heights, California

Brandi Bazarnik
Skycrest Elementary
Citrus Heights, California

Kristin Wojes-Broetzmann
Saint Anthony Parish School
Menomonee Falls, Wisconsin

Andrea Brown
*District Science and STEAM Curriculum
    TOSA*
Hacienda La Puente Unified School
    District
Hacienda Heights, California

Denice Gayner
Earl LeGette Elementary
Fair Oaks, California

Emily Giles
Elementary Curriculum Consultant
Kenton County School District
Ft. Wright, Kentucky

Crystal Hintzman
*Director of Curriculum, Instruction and
    Assessment*
School District of Superior
Superior, Wisconsin

Roya Hosseini
Junction Avenue K-8
Livermore, California

Cynthia Alexander Kirk
Classroom Teacher, Learning Specialist
West Creek Academy
Valencia, California

Marie LaCross
Fair Oaks Ranch Community School
Santa Clarita, California

Emily Miller
Science Specialist
Madison Metropolitan School District
Madison, Wisconsin

Monica Murray, EdD
Principal
Bassett Unified School District
La Puente, California

Wendy Savaske
Director of Instructional Services
School District of Holmen
Holmen, Wisconsin

Tina Topoleski
District Science Supervisor
Jackson School District
Jackson, New Jersey

Educator Advisory Panel Members

Dr. C. Alex Alvarez
Director of STEM and Curriculum
Valdosta City Schools
Valdosta, Georgia

Kerri Angel
Science Teacher
Department Chair
Churchill County School District
Churchill County Middle School
Fallon, Nevada

Maria Blue
Teacher
Emblem Academy, Saugus Union
   School District
Saugus, California

Regina Brinker
STEM Coordinator
Livermore Valley Joint Unified School
   District
Livermore, California

Andrea Brown
*District Science and STEAM Curriculum
   TOSA*
Hacienda La Puente Unified School
   District
Hacienda Heights, California

Conni Crittenden
4th and 5th Grade Classroom Teacher
Williamston Community Schools
Williamston, Michigan

Ronald M. Durso, EdS
District Science Supervisor
Fair Lawn Public Schools
Fair Lawn, New Jersey

Cheryl Frye
NGSS/STEM Coordinator
Menifee Union School District
Menifee, California

Brandon A. Gillette, PhD
Middle School Science
The Pembroke Hill School
Kansas City, Missouri

Susan L. Kallewaard, MA Ed, NBCT
5th Grade Teacher
Haverhill Elementary School
Portage, Michigan

John Labriola
*Middle School Science Teacher, Science
   Content Coordinator*
Charities Middle School
Wood River Junction, Rhode Island

Gilbert J. Luna
K-12 Science Curriculum Specialist
Vancouver Public Schools
Vancouver, Washington

Jennifer Su Mataele
PreK-12 Technology, STEAM TOSA
Hacienda La Puente Unified School
   District
Hacienda Heights, California

Shawna Metcalf
Science Teacher Specialist
Glendale Unified School District
Glendale, California

Erica Rose Motamed
Science Teacher
Lake Center Middle School
Santa Fe Springs, California

Monica Murray, EdD
Principal
Bassett Unified School District
La Puente, California

Stefanie Pechan
*5th Grade Teacher, STEM Coordinator,
   PAEMST*
Robert Down Elementary
Pacific Grove, California

Christie Purdon
K-12 Science Coordinator
Blue Valley School District
Overland Park, Kansas

Stephen J. Rapa
Science Department Chair
Worcester Public Schools
Worcester, Massachusetts

Alison L. Riordan
Science Curriculum Coordinator, K-12
Plymouth Public Schools
Plymouth, Massachusetts

Greta Trittin Smith
Academic Coach--Science
Garvey School District
Rosemead, California

Marsha Veninga
8th Grade Science Teacher
Bloomington Junior High School,
   Bloomington District 87
Bloomington, Illinois

HMH SCIENCE DIMENSIONS™
ENGINEERED for the NEXT GENERATION

Program Overview
GRADES K–5

NEXT GENERATION
SCIENCE
STANDARDS*

*Next Generation Science Standards and logo are registered trademarks of Achieve. Neither Achieve nor the lead states and partners that developed the Next Generation Science Standards was involved in the production of, and does not endorse, this product.

HMH SCIENCE DIMENSIONS™

Spark your Students' Curiosity in Science

Kids are born scientists. They want to know **WHY**: Is the sun a star? How do magnets work? It's our job to encourage their curiosity, creativity, and exploration while preparing them for careers in science, technology, engineering, and math.

At **Houghton Mifflin Harcourt®** we've created a brand new K–12 science curriculum based off of the Next Generation Science Standards (NGSS)* to raise the level of science literacy and achievement in our students.

A brand-new K–12 program, built from the ground up specifically for NGSS that:

- engages students
- promotes active learning and deeper thinking
- sparks an interest in science and science-related careers

- creates enduring understanding
- builds problem-solving skills
- creates lifelong learners

…better than any other program.

An **all-new**, complete solution for NGSS: Digital, print, and hands-on

HMH Science Dimensions™ is thoughtfully crafted to incorporate the Three Dimensions of Learning and Performance Expectations (PEs) of NGSS* into every lesson, every activity, every video—every piece!

What sets **HMH Science Dimensions** apart?

Three-Dimensional Learning. Designed—not aligned—around the Three Dimensions of Science Learning: Disciplinary Core Ideas (DCIs), Crosscutting Concepts (CCCs), and Science and Engineering Practices (SEPs)

Professional Support from HMH®. Simplifying your transition to an NGSS curriculum every step of the way

Active Learning. Activities, investigation, and evidence-gathering at the foundation of every lesson

Integrated Engineering & STEM. Developing students who are experts in the engineering design process

Digital-First Flexibility. Immersive learning experiences that engage students in doing science

Embedded Assessment. Preparing students to succeed on high-stakes performance-based assessments

© Houghton Mifflin Harcourt • Image Credits: (tr) ©Fuse/Corbis/Getty Images

*Next Generation Science Standards and logo are registered trademarks of Achieve. Neither Achieve nor the lead states and partners that developed the Next Generation Science Standards was involved in the production of, and does not endorse, this product.

Three-Dimensional Learning Made Simple

HMH Science Dimensions expertly weaves the Three Dimensions of Learning into each lesson in order to meet the Performance Expectations (PEs). This braided approach takes the burden off of you while ensuring a **quality 3D learning experience** for your students.

3D Learning Objectives

Each lesson has unique interrelated 3D Learning Objectives that can be found in the Teacher Edition. The objective is generated from the Science and Engineering Practices, Crosscutting Concepts, and Disciplinary Core Ideas associated with the Performance Expectations correlated to the unit. These **custom stepping-stone objectives** ensure that the lessons cover 100% of the NGSS* material associated with the PEs.

Grade 2 Teacher Edition

Clearly Labeled NGSS References

- The NGSS labeling in the Teacher Edition clearly identifies all the PEs, SEPs, DCIs, and CCCs of NGSS, including the math and ELA connections. This helps educators **identify the standards** that are being covered in any given lesson.

- Additionally, throughout the **HMH Science Dimensions** Teacher Edition, you will find features to help you orient toward the critical dimensions of the **EQuIP Rubric**. These features will demonstrate the best practices of NGSS summarized by this evaluation instrument.

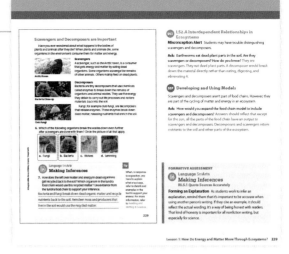

Grade 5 Teacher Edition

Follow the NGSS Story Through the Entire Curriculum!

- The **HMH Science Dimensions** Trace Tool to the NGSS helps you make sense of the standards, understand how they connect and spiral from one grade to another, and **identify HMH resources** to support your NGSS-based instruction.

- You can **trace the standards** by PEs, SEPs, CCCs, or DCIs. When you click on a standard, you can view where in the program that standard is covered.

- But the **Trace Tool** is more powerful than a typical correlation—it also shows you **how each standard** and **dimension spirals** throughout the entire K–12 sequence. It's a snap to see what students should know already, and what you're preparing them for.

English Language Arts and Math Connections

Strong math and reading skills are essential to ensuring STEM learning and science literacy. **HMH Science Dimensions** offers Common Core **Math and ELA connections** throughout the curriculum.

Do the Math
Above and Beyond

Elevation is the height above Earth's surface. The data in the table shows how much of Earth's surface you can see from different elevations.

Elevation (height)	Approximate Distance Seen
1 m	3.5 km
100 m	35.5 km
200 m	50.5 km
300 m	62.0 km
400 m	71.5 km
500 m	80.0 km

9. Use the data to make a bar graph above.

10. Select the best answer for the question. Why can you see more of Earth's surface the higher you are?

a. You can see over the clouds.

b. The air is cleaner so you can see farther.

c. You can see around the curved surface of Earth.

Grade 5 Print
Student Edition
"Do the Math"

Unmatched Professional Support to Help You Transition with Ease

HMH Science Dimensions invests as much in teachers as it does in students. With a thoughtfully structured Teacher Edition, professional development courses focused on NGSS* best practices, and professional learning videos built directly into the core curriculum, teachers have more support than ever. An NGSS curriculum requires a significantly different approach to teaching science, and although this new approach may be challenging, its **rewards** are immediate. HMH provides the support you need to make the transition to a **student-centered**, NGSS style of teaching.

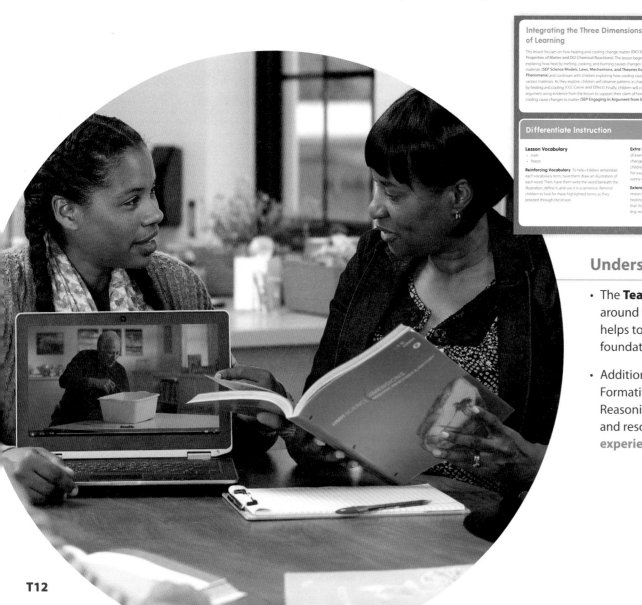

Grade 2
Teacher Edition

Integrating the Three Dimensions of Learning

This lesson focuses on how heating and cooling change matter (DCI Structure and Properties of Matter and DCI Chemical Reactions). The lesson begins with children exploring how heat by melting, cooking, and burning causes changes to various materials. (SEP Science Models, Laws, Mechanisms, and Theories Explain Natural Phenomena) and continues with children exploring how cooling causes changes to various materials. As they explore, children will observe patterns in changes caused by heating and cooling (CCC Cause and Effect). Finally, children will construct an argument using evidence from the lesson to support their claim of how heating and cooling cause changes to matter (SEP Engaging in Argument from Evidence).

▶ **Professional Development** Go online to view **Professional Development videos** with strategies to integrate CCCs and SEPs, including the ones used in this lesson.

Build on Prior Knowledge

Children should already know and be prepared to build on the following concepts:
- A state of matter is an observable property of matter.
- Matter can be a solid. A solid keeps its shape. It will not change its shape unless you do something like cut, bend, or break it.
- Matter can be a liquid. A liquid does not have its own shape. A liquid takes the shape of its container.

Differentiate Instruction

Lesson Vocabulary
- melt
- freeze

Reinforcing Vocabulary To help children remember each vocabulary term, have them draw an illustration of each word. Then, have them write the word beneath the illustration, define it, and use it in a sentence. Remind children to look for these highlighted terms as they proceed through the lesson.

Extra Support Supply children with additional images of examples of solids and liquids and how these materials change from solid to liquid or from liquid to solid. Provide children with context of how these changes take place. For example, a solid ice pop melting into a puddle on a sunny day, or a pond freezing to ice in the winter.

Extension Children who want to find out more can do research on gases and how liquids change to gases by heating. Children should use their data to make a poster that illustrates the three states of matter of one material (e.g. water) and how it changes states.

ELL Strategy Be sure to point out all labels, pictures, captions, and headings throughout lesson to assist children with strategies to summarize chunks of content. Discuss with children real-life connections to content and provide hands-on examples of materials when possible to best support the needs of these learners.

Understand Where Your Instruction Fits

- The **Teacher Edition** (online and print) is organized around the familiar **5E instructional model**. This helps to lower the learning curve and provide a solid foundation upon which to build an NGSS curriculum.

- Additional Collaboration, Differentiate Instruction, Formative Assessment, and Claims, Evidence, and Reasoning suggestions provide a wealth of support and resources to help you **enrich the learning experience** for everyone.

Getting Started is included with Purchase!

Professional Learning for *HMH Science Dimensions*
Our mission is to advance yours.

- **A STRONG START** The *Getting Started with* **HMH Science Dimensions** *Course* provides you with an overview of the program from both a teacher's and student's perspective.

- **DEEPEN MASTERY** To accelerate your learning from the *Getting Started Course,* **Follow-Up Courses** focus on planning, monitoring student progress, supporting English learners and assessment.

- **COACHING** Our **Team** and **Individual Coaching** will ensure you are confident and prepared to deliver instruction that addresses the needs of the changing science classroom. HMH Coaches work side by side with you, supporting 3D Learning, student engagement, differentiated support, science literacy, literacy across the curriculum, 21st century skills and STEM applications.

- **NEED MORE HELP?** When implementing *HMH Science Dimensions*, you may have questions regarding instruction, pedagogy, and best practices. **AskHMH™** provides access to program experts who can support you.

hmhco.com/professionalservices

See NGSS in Action

Embedded professional development videos help teachers better prepare for this new approach to science education. Just-in-time videos featuring our **dynamic consulting authors** guide teachers through the key approaches that ensure NGSS success.

» **FOUNDATION** videos help educators and parents better understand the NGSS, as well as the background that led up to their development.

» **ENGINEERING** videos support educators as they incorporate the design process into their classrooms.

» **CHALLENGING Content** videos for Grades 4–12 help educators know how to address specific content areas that students tend to struggle with in an NGSS curriculum.

» **HANDS-ON Activity** videos for Grades K–2 model what the hands-on activities within the curriculum should look like when implemented. These help ensure a more successful implementation of an NGSS solution.

Michael DiSpezio, Author

0:06 / 3:23

Professional Development Video

Build Student Confidence with Authentic Investigations

Students are more engaged and learn more meaningfully through investigative inquiry. *HMH Science Dimensions* is built on this approach. Your students will learn to conduct hands-on investigations, define questions and objectives, make claims, and identify evidence—in short, to **take charge** and **fully engage** in their learning!

Every Lesson Is an Activity

- Each lesson begins with **Can You Explain It?**— a **problem to solve or discrepant event to explain**. This lesson-leading feature provides intrinsic motivation to spark curiosity and serves as the context for the three-dimensional learning and hands-on activities throughout the lessons. Students are motivated to think critically and construct explanations of *how* and *why*.

- The program is built around **active learning**. Rather than receive content passively, students are asked to **solve problems** or explain phenomena, by stating **claims**, gathering **evidence**, and providing explanations through **reasoning**.

In a tundra ecosystem, organisms must be able to survive under extremely cold and dry conditions. Even though plant life may be scarce at times, there is still enough energy and matter to support many organisms.

CAN YOU EXPLAIN IT?

Why do you think the owls have left the area?

Grade 5 Online Student Edition

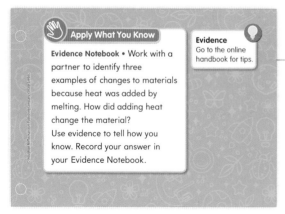

Apply What You Know

Evidence Notebook • Work with a partner to identify three examples of changes to materials because heat was added by melting. How did adding heat change the material? Use evidence to tell how you know. Record your answer in your Evidence Notebook.

Evidence
Go to the online handbook for tips.

Grade 2 Print Student Edition

Science Notebooking to Strengthen Writing Skills

Many of the lessons in *HMH Science Dimensions* support the use of **Evidence Notebooks. Helpful prompts** have been inserted throughout the lessons to guide students on when to use these notebooks. Students will love creating their own study guides that can be taken into the next grade, and teachers will love the extra writing practice!

Drive Student Learning with Hands-On Investigations

- **Hands-On Activities** are integrated into many of the lessons. These are built with teachers' busy schedules in mind. Each activity uses **easily sourced materials**.

- Students get to actively "do science;" they **think critically** about their observations, practice gathering evidence, and defend their claims.

Grade 2 Print Student Edition

Cultivate Collaboration

Working as a team is an essential part of developing **21st-century skills**. *HMH Science Dimensions* provides ample opportunities for students to participate in groups to complete activities and partner with their peers to discuss their findings.

Grade 5 Print Student Edition

Save Prep Time with Equipment Kits

- **Equipment Kits** provide the **consumable** and **non-consumable** materials you need to complete most of the hands-on activities so you have all the materials you need right at your fingertips.

- The **Safety Kit** provides the materials you need to address **classroom safety** while performing the program activities.

T15

The Students of Today Will Solve the Technology Challenges of Tomorrow!

NGSS* has raised the engineering design process to the same level as scientific inquiry. In ***HMH Science Dimensions***, science, technology, engineering, and math are considered an **integral** part of the curriculum. Lessons are designed for students to explore science the same way real-life scientists do. Watch your students' eyes **light up** as they brainstorm solutions, share their ideas, and experiment to find solutions.

Elevate Engineering

In **HMH Science Dimensions**, engineering and STEM are carried throughout every unit and not just treated as an ancillary. This approach elevates engineering design to the same level as scientific literacy. Each Unit includes a **Performance Task**, offering students multiple opportunities throughout the program to apply the **engineering design process** by defining a problem and designing a solution.

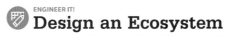

ENGINEER IT!
Design an Ecosystem

You work for company that is building an animal theme park. After studying the animals in their natural ecosystem, your team needs to choose an animal to bring back to live in the park. Your team has access to an empty room with a sprinkler for precipitation and temperature control. There are skylights in the ceiling to allow sunlight in. There is no floor, so the ground is covered in soil.

FIND A PROBLEM: What problem do you need to solve?

This reptile terrarium has everything the lizard needs to survive.

Before beginning, look at the checklist at the end of this project to be sure you are meeting all the requirements.

RESEARCH: Study the animal you plan to bring to the lab and write down your observations. Use online or library resources for research. Use multiple sources and cite them.

BRAINSTORM: Brainstorm three or more ideas with your team to solve the problem. Keep in mind the criteria and constraints.

Criteria	Constraints
☐ Animal must survive	☐ Your animal will not have access to the natural outdoors
☐ The landscape must mimic the animals natural ecosystem	☐ Limited to one room to build your ecosystem
☐ A food web must be present to meet your animal's nutrition needs	☐ Room is about the size of your classroom
☐ The animal needs enough room to exercise and move freely	☐ Room is 6 meters by 6 meters

270

Grade 5 Print Student Edition

Provide Extra Support for Students Who Need It

The **Science and Engineering Practices Online Handbook** will help students achieve a higher level of understanding and skill as they build their experience applying the **Science and Engineering Practices** of NGSS.

Science and Engineering Leveled Readers

Grade 2
Teacher Guide
English and Spanish

Why Is Weather Important?

Making Crayons

What Do We Know About Matter?

Build Literacy and Science Content Knowledge

* The program includes print and online access to **Science and Engineering Leveled Readers** for Grades K–5. These colorful, fun, and interesting Readers provide three levels of readability for students: **On-Level, Extra Support,** and **Enrichment**.

* The accompanying **Teacher Guide** provides **activities** and **support** for before reading, during reading, and during response to reading.

*Next Generation Science Standards and logo are registered trademarks of Achieve. Neither Achieve nor the lead states and partners that developed the Next Generation Science Standards was involved in the production of, and does not endorse, this product. **T17**

Engage with Meaningful Technology

HMH Science Dimensions is a truly digital-first program. The curriculum leverages the advantages of technology while prioritizing a **student-centered learning model**. Students can view videos and animations, interact with instructional images and text, enter responses, pursue their intellectual interests by choosing lesson paths, and enjoy simulation-based learning. All of these features help you maintain an **integrated three-dimensional approach** to learning science.

Grade 2 Online
Student Edition

Immersive Digital Curriculum

Online lessons are enriched above and beyond the print lessons with educational videos, learning interactivities, and places to save student work as **responses** and **technology-enhanced item choices**. Vocabulary is highlighted and clickable, with point-of-use pop-up definitions.

Maximize Student Choice

The **Take It Further** feature at the end of each lesson maximizes the opportunity for students to elaborate further on what they have learned so far. By leveraging the power of technology, students can continue to go in depth on **topics of their choice**, to learn more and create stronger, more personal links to their learning.

Grade 5
Online Student Edition

Deepen Understanding with Open-Ended Simulations

Unique **You Solve It** simulations provide completely **open-ended opportunities** for students to demonstrate their ability to problem solve and perform at the level described by the NGSS* Performance Expectations. The program encourages students to explore multiple answers to a problem and learn to develop explanations and defend their answers.

Grade 5 *You Solve It*

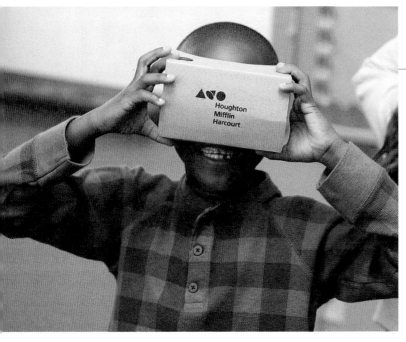

Explore Immersive Virtual Worlds

- As a Google® content partner, HMH has developed field trips for Google Expeditions.

HMH Field Trips
powered by

Using a simple Google Cardboard™ device and a smartphone, students are swept away into **3D, 360-degree experiences** in fascinating locations, directly tied to science content!

- An HMH **Teacher Guide** provides ideas for incorporating the Expeditions into your lessons, as well as tips on how to **guide** and **customize** the experience.

The Ultimate Online and Offline Program Experience

- Teachers can look forward to accessing **HMH Science Dimensions** on **Ed: Your Friend in Learning**. Ed is a new online learning system that combines the best of technology, HMH content, and instruction to personalize the teaching and learning experience for every teacher and student. Ed is designed to be a friend to learners while supporting teachers and simplifying their instructional practice.

your friend in learning

- Additionally, program content can be accessed offline through the **HMH Player**® app. This allows for **maximum compatibility** in 1:1 or **Bring Your Own Device** learning environments and with the wide variety of technology that students have at home.

Making 1:1 Learning a Reality

*Next Generation Science Standards and logo are registered trademarks of Achieve. Neither Achieve nor the lead states and partners that developed the Next Generation Science Standards was involved in the production of, and does not endorse, this product. **T19**

Let Students Show What They Know

For the first time ever, through NGSS,* science standards now include specific **measureable learning outcomes**. These Performance Expectations guide test developers and teachers in understanding how to measure student learning. *HMH Science Dimensions* offers flexible assessment tools in a variety of formats to help you assess both formative and summative student learning according to NGSS.

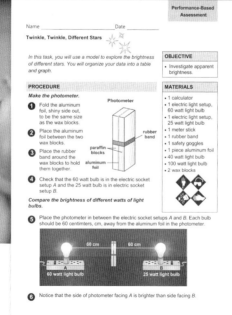

Performance-Based Assessment

Name _____ Date _____

Twinkle, Twinkle, Different Stars ✨

In this task, you will use a model to explore the brightness of different stars. You will organize your data into a table and graph.

OBJECTIVE
- Investigate apparent brightness.

PROCEDURE

Make the photometer.

1 Fold the aluminum foil, shiny side out, to be the same size as the wax blocks.

2 Place the aluminum foil between the two wax blocks.

3 Place the rubber band around the wax blocks to hold them together.

4 Check that the 60 watt bulb is in the electric socket setup A and the 25 watt bulb in electric socket setup B.

Compare the brightness of different watts of light bulbs.

5 Place the photometer in between the electric socket setups A and B. Each bulb should be 60 centimeters, cm, away from the aluminum foil in the photometer.

6 Notice that the side of photometer facing A is brighter than side facing B.

MATERIALS
- 1 calculator
- 1 electric light setup, 60 watt light bulb
- 1 electric light setup, 25 watt light bulb
- 1 meter stick
- 1 rubber band
- 1 safety goggles
- 1 piece aluminum foil
- 40 watt light bulb
- 100 watt light bulb
- 2 wax blocks

Grade 5 Performance-Based Assessment

Authentic Performance Assessment

Performance-Based Assessments help you ensure that your students can perform the science and engineering practices called for by NGSS. And they also guide students toward making connections across Performance Expectations.

T20

Assess on All Dimensions

- Formal assessment questions **aligned to multiple dimensions** provide you with a complete picture of student understanding.

- A unique **3D Evaluation Rubric** helps you evaluate open-ended student responses and identify the underlying cause of student misunderstanding so that you can target remediation where it's most needed.

Performance-Based Assessment
Teacher Resources

Task 1 Performance Rubric	
Rating Scale	
3 Outstanding	1 Needs Improvement
2 Satisfactory	0 Did Not Demonstrate Skill

Skills	Rating
DCI.5-ESS1.A.1 The Universe and Its Stars The student demonstrates differences in apparent brightness of the sun and other stars.	
SEP.3-5.G.1 Engaging in Argument from Evidence The student uses data to explain that the sun appears to be larger and brighter than other stars because of its distance from Earth.	
CCC.3-5.C.1 Scale, Proportion, and Quantity The student demonstrates that stars vary in size and distance from the Earth.	
Additional: SEP.3-5.C.1 Planning and Carrying Out Investigations The student conducts an investigation to show that the difference in apparent brightness of stars is due to their relative distances from Earth.	
Additional SEP.3-5.C.2 Planning and Carrying Out Investigations The student makes measurements demonstrating the differences in apparent brightness of the sun and stars.	
Total	

Grade 5 Online Student Edition

Reflect on Evidence Gathered

At the end of a lesson, the **Lesson Self-Check** encourages students to reflect on the evidence they gathered throughout the lesson. They have another chance to respond to the discrepant phenomenon or central question of the lesson with **open-ended response** questions.

Prepare for High-Stakes Tests

Technology-enhanced assessment items prepare your students for modern **computer-based high-stakes tests**. Parallel print assessments ensure that your students are challenged in the same way both on- and offline.

Kindergarten Online Assessment

NGSS and *HMH Science Dimensions*

2-PS1 Matter and Its Interactions

	Print and Digital Resources	
	Supporting Learning Experiences	**Assessment & Performance**
Performance Expectation **2-PS1-1** Plan and conduct an investigation to describe and classify different kinds of materials by their observable properties.	Unit 2 Lesson 1 and **Hands-On Activity**	Unit 2 Unit Project **Unit Performance Task** Assessment Guide and Online Lesson Quizzes Unit Test **Performance-Based Assessment** End-of-Year Test (or End-of Module Test)
Disciplinary Core Idea	**PS1.A Structure and Properties of Matter** Different kinds of matter exist and many of them can be either solid or liquid, depending on temperature. Matter can be described and classified by its observable properties.	
Science and Engineering Practice	**Planning and Carrying Out Investigations** Plan and conduct an investigation collaboratively to produce data to serve as the basis for evidence to answer a question.	
Crosscutting Concept	**Patterns** Patterns in the natural and human designed world can be observed.	
Performance Expectation **2-PS1-2** Analyze data obtained from testing different materials to determine which materials have the properties that are best suited for an intended purpose.	Unit 2 Lesson 1 and **Hands-On Activity**	Unit 2 Unit Project **Unit Performance Task** Assessment Guide and Online Lesson Quizzes Unit Test **Performance-Based Assessment** End-of-Year Test (or End-of Module Test)
Disciplinary Core Idea	**PS1.A Structure and Properties of Matter** Different properties are suited to different purposes.	
Science and Engineering Practice	**Analyzing and Interpreting Data** Analyze data from tests of an object or tool to determine if it works as intended.	
Crosscutting Concepts	**Cause and Effect** Simple tests can be designed to gather evidence to support or refute student ideas about causes. **Influence of Engineering, Technology, and Science on Society and the Natural World** Every human-made product is designed by applying some knowledge of the natural world and is built using materials derived from the natural world.	

2-PS1 Matter and Its Interactions
continued

	Print and Digital Resources	
	Supporting Learning Experiences	**Assessment & Performance**
Performance Expectation **2-PS1-3** Make observations to construct an evidence-based account of how an object made of a small set of pieces can be disassembled and made into a new object.	Unit 2 Lesson 2 and **Hands-On Activity**	Unit 2 Unit Project **Unit Performance Task** Assessment Guide and Online Lesson Quizzes Unit Test **Performance-Based Assessment** End-of-Year Test (or End-of Module Test)
Disciplinary Core Idea	**PS1.A Structure and Properties of Matter** Different properties are suited to different purposes. A great variety of objects can be built up from a small set of pieces.	
Science and Engineering Practice	**Constructing Explanations and Designing Solutions** Make observations (firsthand or from media) to construct an evidence-based account for natural phenomena.	
Crosscutting Concept	**Energy and Matter** Objects may break into smaller pieces and be put together into larger pieces, or change shapes.	
Performance Expectation **2-PS1-4** Construct an argument with evidence that some changes caused by heating or cooling can be reversed and some cannot.	Unit 2 Lesson 3 and **Hands-On Activity** Lesson 4 and **Hands-On Activity**	Unit 2 Unit Project You Solve It (digital only) **Unit Performance Task** Assessment Guide and Online Lesson Quizzes Unit Test **Performance-Based Assessment** End-of-Year Test (or End-of Module Test)
Disciplinary Core Idea	**PS1.B Chemical Reactions** Heating or cooling a substance may cause changes that can be observed. Sometimes these changes are reversible, and sometimes they are not.	
Science and Engineering Practices	**Engaging in Argument from Evidence** Construct an argument with evidence to support a claim. **Science Models, Laws, Mechanisms, and Theories Explain Natural Phenomena** Scientists search for cause and effect relationships to explain natural events.	
Crosscutting Concept	**Cause and Effect** Events have causes that generate observable pattern.	

2-LS2 Ecosystems: Interactions, Energy, and Dynamics

	Print and Digital Resources	
	Supporting Learning Experiences	**Assessment & Performance**

Performance Expectation
2-LS2-1
Plan and conduct an investigation to determine if plants need sunlight and water to grow.
	Unit 3
	Lesson 1 and **Hands-On Activity**
		Unit 3
		Unit Project
		Unit Performance Task
		Assessment Guide and Online
		   Lesson Quizzes
		   Unit Test
		   Performance-Based Assessment
		   End-of-Year Test (or End-of Module Test)

Disciplinary Core Idea	**LS2.A Interdependent Relationships in Ecosystems** Plants depend on water and light to grow.	
Science and Engineering Practice	**Planning and Carrying Out Investigations** Plan and conduct an investigation collaboratively to produce data to serve as the basis for evidence to answer a question.	
Crosscutting Concept	**Cause and Effect** Events have causes that generate observable patterns.	

Performance Expectation
2-LS2-2
Develop a simple model that mimics the function of an animal in dispersing seeds or pollinating plants.
	Unit 3
	Lesson 2 and **Hands-On Activity**
		Unit 3
		Unit Project
		Unit Performance Task
		Assessment Guide and Online
		   Lesson Quizzes
		   Unit Test
		   Performance-Based Assessment
		   End-of-Year Test (or End-of Module Test)

Disciplinary Core Ideas	**LS2.A Interdependent Relationships in Ecosystems** Plants depend on animals for pollination or to move their seeds around. **ETS1.B Developing Possible Solutions** Designs can be conveyed through sketches, drawings, or physical models. These representations are useful in communicating ideas for a problem's solutions to other people.	
Science and Engineering Practice	**Developing and Using Models** Develop a simple model based on evidence to represent a proposed object or tool.	
Crosscutting Concept	**Structure and Function** The shape and stability of structures of natural and designed objects are related to their function(s).	

2-LS4 Biological Evolution: Unity and Diversity

	Print and Digital Resources	
	Supporting Learning Experiences	**Assessment & Performance**
Performance Expectation **2-LS4-1** Make observations of plants and animals to compare the diversity of life in different habitats.	Unit 3 Lesson 3 and **Hands-On Activity** Lesson 4 and **Hands-On Activity**	Unit 3 Unit Project You Solve It (digital only) **Unit Performance Task** Assessment Guide and Online Lesson Quizzes Unit Test **Performance-Based Assessment** End-of-Year Test (or End-of Module Test)
Disciplinary Core Idea	**LS4.D Biodiversity and Humans** There are many different kinds of living things in any area, and they exist in different places on land and in water.	
Science and Engineering Practices	**Planning and Carrying Out Investigations** Make observations (firsthand or from media) to collect data which can be used to make comparisons. **Scientific Knowledge is Based on Empirical Evidence** Scientists look for patterns and order when making observations about the world.	

2-ESS1 Earth's Place in the Universe

	Supporting Learning Experiences	**Assessment & Performance**
Performance Expectation **2-ESS1-1** Use information from several sources to provide evidence that Earth events can occur quickly or slowly.	Unit 5 Lesson 1 and **Hands-On Activity** Lesson 2 and **Hands-On Activity**	Unit 5 Unit Project **Unit Performance Task** Assessment Guide and Online Lesson Quizzes Unit Test **Performance-Based Assessment** End-of-Year Test (or End-of Module Test)
Disciplinary Core Idea	**ESS1.C The History of Planet Earth** Some events happen very quickly; others occur very slowly, over a time period much longer than one can observe.	
Science and Engineering Practice	**Constructing Explanations and Designing Solutions** Make observations from several sources to construct an evidence-based account for natural phenomena.	
Crosscutting Concept	**Stability and Change** Things may change slowly or rapidly.	

NGSS and *HMH Science Dimensions*

2-ESS2 Earth's Systems

	Print and Digital Resources	
	Supporting Learning Experiences	**Assessment & Performance**

Performance Expectation
2-ESS2-1
Compare multiple solutions designed to slow or prevent wind or water from changing the shape of the land.
	Unit 5
	Lesson 3 and **Hands-On Activity**
		Unit 5
		Unit Project
		You Solve It (digital only)
		Unit Performance Task
		Assessment Guide and Online
		  Lesson Quizzes
		  Unit Test
		  Performance-Based Assessment
		  End-of-Year Test (or End-of Module Test)

Disciplinary Core Ideas	**ESS2.A Earth Materials and Systems** Wind and water can change the shape of the land. **ETS1.C Optimizing the Design Solution** Because there is always more than one possible solution to a problem, it is useful to compare and test designs.	
Science and Engineering Practice	**Constructing Explanations and Designing Solutions** Compare multiple solutions to a problem.	
Crosscutting Concepts	**Stability and Change** Things may change slowly or rapidly. **Influence of Engineering, Technology, and Science on Society and the Natural World** Developing and using technology has impacts on the natural world. **Science Addresses Questions About the Natural and Material World** Scientists study the natural and material world.	

2-ESS2 Earth's Systems continued

	Print and Digital Resources	
	Supporting Learning Experiences	**Assessment & Performance**

Performance Expectation
 	
2-ESS2-2
 	
Develop a model to represent the shapes and kinds of land and bodies of water in an area.
	Unit 4
	
	Lesson 2 and **Hands-On Activity**
		Unit 4
		Unit Project
		You Solve It (digital only)
		Unit Performance Task
		Assessment Guide and Online
		  Lesson Quizzes
		  Unit Test
		Performance-Based Assessment
		End-of-Year Test (or End-of Module Test)

Disciplinary Core Idea	**ESS2.B Plate Tectonics and Large-Scale System Interactions** Maps show where things are located. One can map the shapes and kinds of land and water in any area.
Science and Engineering Practice	**Developing and Using Models** Develop a model to represent patterns in the natural world.
Crosscutting Concept	**Patterns** Patterns in the natural world can be observed.

Performance Expectation
 	
2-ESS2-3
 	
Obtain information to identify where water is found on Earth and that it can be solid or liquid.
	Unit 4
	
	Lesson 1 and **Hands-On Activity**
		Unit 4
		Unit Project
		You Solve It (digital only)
		Unit Performance Task
		Assessment Guide and Online
		  Lesson Quizzes
		  Unit Test
		Performance-Based Assessment
		End-of-Year Test (or End-of Module Test)

Disciplinary Core Idea	**ESS2.C The Roles of Water in Earth's Surface Processes** Water is found in the ocean, rivers, lakes, and ponds. Water exists as solid ice and in liquid form.
Science and Engineering Practice	**Obtaining, Evaluating, and Communicating Information** Obtain information using various texts, text features (e.g., headings, tables of contents, glossaries, electronic menus, icons), and other media that will be useful in answering a scientific question.
Crosscutting Concept	**Patterns** Patterns in the natural world can be observed.

NGSS and *HMH Science Dimensions*

K-2 ETS1 Engineering Design

	Print and Digital Resources	
	Supporting Learning Experiences	**Assessment & Performance**
Performance Expectation **K-2-ETS1-1** Ask questions, make observations, and gather information about a situation people want to change to define a simple problem that can be solved through the development of a new or improved object or tool.	Unit 1 Lesson 1 and **Hands-On Activity**	Unit 1 Unit Project **Unit Performance Task** Assessment Guide and Online 　Lesson Quizzes 　Unit Test **Performance-Based Assessment** 　End-of-Year Test (or End-of Module Test)
Disciplinary Core Ideas	**ETS1.A Defining and Delimiting Engineering Problems** A situation that people want to change or create can be approached as a problem to be solved through engineering. Asking questions, making observations, and gathering information are helpful in thinking about problems. Before beginning to design a solution, it is important to clearly understand the problem.	
Science and Engineering Practices	**Asking Questions and Defining Problems** Ask questions based on observations to find more information about the natural and/or designed world(s). Define a simple problem that can be solved through the development of a new or improved object or tool.	

K-2 ETS1 Engineering Design
continued

	Print and Digital Resources	
	Supporting Learning Experiences	**Assessment & Performance**

Performance Expectation
K-2-ETS1-2
Develop a simple sketch, drawing, or physical model to illustrate how the shape of an object helps it function as needed to solve a given problem.
	Unit 1
	Lesson 1 and **Hands-On Activity**
		Unit 1
		Unit Project
		Unit Performance Task
		Assessment Guide and Online
		    Lesson Quizzes
		    Unit Test
		Performance-Based Assessment
		    End-of-Year Test (or End-of Module Test)

Disciplinary Core Idea	**ETS1.B Developing Possible Solutions** Designs can be conveyed through sketches, drawings, or physical models. These representations are useful in communicating ideas for a problem's solutions to other people.
Science and Engineering Practice	**Developing and Using Models** Develop a simple model based on evidence to represent a proposed object or tool.
Crosscutting Concept	**Structure and Function** The shape and stability of structures of natural and designed objects are related to their function(s).

Performance Expectation
K-2-ETS1-3
Analyze data from tests of two objects designed to solve the same problem to compare the strengths and weaknesses of how each performs.
	Unit 1
	Lesson 2 and **Hands-On Activity**
		Unit 1
		Unit Project
		You Solve It (digital only)
		Unit Performance Task
		Assessment Guide and Online
		    Lesson Quizzes
		    Unit Test
		Performance-Based Assessment
		    End-of-Year Test (or End-of Module Test)

Disciplinary Core Idea	**ETS1.C Optimizing the Design Solution** Because there is always more than one possible solution to a problem, it is useful to compare and test designs.
Science and Engineering Practice	**Analyzing and Interpreting Data** Analyze data from tests of an object or tool to determine if it works as intended.

Program Scope and Sequence

	Grade K-2	Grade 3-5
Engineering and Design	**GK Unit 1** Engineering and Technology* **G1 Unit 1** Engineering and Technology* **G2 Unit 1** Engineering Design Process*	**G3 Unit 1** Engineering * **G4 Unit 1** Engineering and Technology* **G5 Unit 1** Engineering and Technology*

Physical Science	**GK Unit 2** Forces and Motion
	 G1 Unit 2 Sound
	     Unit 3 Light
	 G2 Unit 2 Matter
		G3 Unit 2 Forces
		     Unit 3 Motion
		 G4 Unit 2 Energy
		     Unit 3 Waves and Information Transfer
		 G5 Unit 2 Matter

Life Science	**GK Unit 3** Plants and Animals
	 G1 Unit 4 Plant and Animal Structures
	     Unit 5 Living Things and Their Young
	 G2 Unit 3 Environments for Living Things
		G3 Unit 4 Life Cycles and Inherited Traits
		     Unit 5 Organisms and Their Environments
		     Unit 6 Fossils
		 G4 Unit 4 Plant Structure and Function
		     Unit 5 Animal Structure and Function
		 G5 Unit 3 Energy and Matter in Organisms
		     Unit 4 Energy and Matter in Ecosystems

Earth and Space Sciences	**GK Unit 4** Sun Warms Earth
	     Unit 5 Weather
	     Unit 6 Earth's Resources
	 G1 Unit 6 Objects and Patterns in the Sky
	 G2 Unit 4 Earth's Surface
	     Unit 5 Changes to Earth's Surface
		G3 Unit 7 Weather and Patterns
		 G4 Unit 6 Changes to Earth's Surface
		     Unit 7 Rocks and Fossils
		     Unit 8 Natural Resources and Hazards
		 G5 Unit 5 Systems in Space
		     Unit 6 Earth's Systems
		     Unit 7 Earth and Human Activities

*Engineering strand is embedded throughout other units and strands.   Included in this Teacher Edition

Trace Tool to the NGSS
Go online to view how the standards apply to your grade level, and to trace connections to prior and subsequent grades.

Grade 6-8

Engineering and Design

Module A Engineering and Science*
Unit 1 Introduction to Engineering and Science
Unit 2 The Practices of Engineering

Physical Science

Module I Energy and Energy Transfer
Unit 1 Energy and Matter
Unit 2 Energy Transfer

Module J Chemistry
Unit 1 The Structure of Matter
Unit 2 States of Matter and Changes of State
Unit 3 Chemical Processes and Equations
Unit 4 The Chemistry of Materials

Module K Forces, Motion, and Fields
Unit 1 Forces and Motion
Unit 2 Electric and Magnetic Forces

Module L Waves and Their Applications
Unit 1 Waves
Unit 2 Information Transfer

Life Science

Module B Cells and Heredity
Unit 1 Cells
Unit 2 Organisms as Systems
Unit 3 Reproduction, Heredity, and Growth

Module C Ecology and the Environment
Unit 1 Matter and Energy in Living Systems
Unit 2 Relationships in Ecosystems
Unit 3 Ecosystem Dynamics

Module D The Diversity of Living Things
Unit 1 The History of Life on Earth
Unit 2 Evolution
Unit 3 Human Influence on Inheritance

Earth and Space Sciences

Module E Earth's Water and Atmosphere
Unit 1 Circulation of Earth's Air and Water
Unit 2 Weather and Climate

Module F Geologic Processes and History
Unit 1 The Dynamic Earth
Unit 2 Earth Through Time

Module G Earth and Human Activity
Unit 1 Earth's Natural Hazards
Unit 2 Resources in Earth's Systems
Unit 3 Using Resources
Unit 4 Human Impacts on Earth Systems

Module H Space Science
Unit 1 Patterns in the Solar System
Unit 2 The Solar System and Universe

Pacing Guide

The following Pacing Guide recommends days for the core instructional elements of each unit. You have options for covering lesson materials: you may choose to follow the comprehensive path or you may choose the core path. You may also customize your Pacing Guide based on your classroom schedule and needs.

An alternative Detailed Pacing Guide that provides further depth on how to manage class time is available online.

Pressed for time? Follow the faster-paced core path.

	Core	Comprehensive 30 minute class	Customize Your Pacing Guide
Unit 1 Engineering Design Process			
Unit 1 Project		3 days	
Lesson 1 **Engineer It** · What Is a Design Process?	5 days	7 days	
Lesson 2 **Engineer It** · How Can We Compare Design Solutions?	5 days	7 days	
You Solve It		1 day	
Unit 1 Performance Task		2 days	
Performance-Based Assessment		2 days	
Unit 1 Review and Unit 1 Test	2 days	2 days	
Total Days for Unit 1	12 days	24 days	

	Core	Comprehensive 30 minute class	Customize Your Pacing Guide
Unit 2 Matter			
Unit 2 Project		3 days	
Lesson 1 **Engineer It** · What Are Properties of Matter?	5 days	7 days	
Lesson 2 How Are Objects Put Together?	5 days	7 days	
Lesson 3 Do Heating and Cooling Change Matter?	5 days	7 days	
Lesson 4 How Does Matter Change?	5 days	7 days	
You Solve It		1 day	
Unit 2 Performance Task		2 days	
Performance-Based Assessment		2 days	
Unit 2 Review and Unit 2 Test	2 days	2 days	
Total Days for Unit 2	22 days	38 days	

Pacing Guide

	Core	Comprehensive 30 minute class	Customize Your Pacing Guide
Unit 3 Environments for Living Things			
Unit 3 Project		3 days	
Lesson 1 What Do Plants Need?	5 days	7 days	
Lesson 2 **Engineer It** · How Do Plants Depend on Animals?	5 days	7 days	
Lesson 3 What Plants and Animals Live in Water Habitats?	5 days	7 days	
Lesson 4 What Plants and Animals Live in Land Habitats?	5 days	7 days	
You Solve It		1 day	
Unit 3 Performance Task		2 days	
Performance-Based Assessment		2 days	
Unit 3 Review and Unit 3 Test	2 days	2 days	
Total Days for Unit 3	22 days	38 days	

	Core	Comprehensive 30 minute class	Customize Your Pacing Guide
Unit 4 Earth's Surface			
Unit 4 Project		3 days	
Lesson 1 Where Is Water Found on Earth?	5 days	7 days	
Lesson 2 **Engineer It** · How Can We Map Land and Water?	5 days	7 days	
You Solve It		1 day	
Unit 4 Performance Task		2 days	
Performance-Based Assessment		2 days	
Unit 4 Review and Unit 4 Test	2 days	2 days	
Total Days for Unit 4	12 days	24 days	
Unit 5 Changes to Earth's Surface			
Unit 5 Project		3 days	
Lesson 1 What Changes on Earth Happen Slowly?	5 days	7 days	
Lesson 2 What Changes on Earth Happen Quickly?	5 days	7 days	
Lesson 3 **Engineer It** · How Can We Prevent Wind and Water from Changing Land?	5 days	7 days	
You Solve It		1 day	
Unit 5 Performance Task		2 days	
Performance-Based Assessment		2 days	
Unit 5 Review and Unit 5 Test	2 days	2 days	
Total Days for Unit 5	17 days	31 days	

Cary I. Sneider, PhD

Change is rarely welcomed with open arms. A few weeks ago I was helping a colleague facilitate a team of teacher-leaders develop a district plan to implement the Next Generation Science Standards (NGSS). During a break two of the teachers asked to speak with me. They were upset and nearly in tears. One of the teachers explained that they had spent the past 20 years developing the best possible science program for their school. The kids and parents loved it. The principal was proud of what they had accomplished. But now they would be asked to start all over because they would be assigned to teach science units they had never taught before.

It helped that the district leaders were listening and willing to consider some changes that these teachers recommended, although the leaders were quite firm about implementing the NGSS. It was also helpful for these teachers to learn that they would be helping other teachers by sharing the great ideas and resources that they had developed for their own students, so their creativity and hard work wouldn't be wasted. Even more important, I believe, was the gradual realization, over the next couple of days, that the profound changes called for by the NGSS

were not simply a change in when different science topics would be taught but rather a change in how they would be taught—in ways that these excellent teacher-leaders valued and had established with their own students.

> **"...the profound changes called for by the NGSS were not simply a change in when different science topics would be taught but rather a change in how they would be taught."**

What follows is a brief summary of the ways that the NGSS is similar to but also different from science as it has been taught for the past 20 years. I won't compare it with "traditional" science education, because the method of having students read and answer questions at the end of the chapter is (thankfully) rarely done these days. But the changes called for by the NGSS can be surprising even for teachers who are comfortable with a hands-on inquiry approach that has come to characterize the best of science teaching. And I'll admit some of these changes have been hard for me to get used to, after nearly 50 years as a science educator and as a member of the NGSS writing team.

Disciplinary Core Ideas

With respect to the Disciplinary Core Ideas (what we used to call the "content") of the new standards, at least 80% are unchanged. Students still need to learn about Newton's Laws of Motion and the Periodic Table of Elements. Some topics in the Earth and space sciences have been updated—such as by the addition of a greater focus on human impacts on the environment—so that topics that many teachers introduced as a way to enrich the curriculum with contemporary issues are now mainstream.

Crosscutting Concepts

Crosscutting Concepts should also be familiar to teachers who appreciate the nature of scientific thinking. The purpose of these seven concepts is to help students see the commonalities among the science and engineering fields. They include the idea that patterns we observe in nature are clues to some underlying process. For example, the monthly pattern of moon phases can best be understood in terms of systems and system models by manipulating a model of the Earth-sun-moon system. The crosscutting concept of cause and effect grows from our human instinct to know why things occur as they do, and the concepts of energy and matter are fundamental to all fields of science and engineering. The crosscutting concept of structure and function is useful in understanding how the structure of molecules affects the macroscopic behavior of a substance, as well as understanding how the structure of an organ enables it to carry out its function in the body. As students mature they are more able to study the world by applying the concepts of scale, proportion, and quantity. And finally, the need to explain stability and change is at the

> **"Technology in the NGSS is portrayed as the application of science to the development of various products, processes, and systems to meet human needs..."**

root of our conservation laws in physics, chemical reactions in chemistry, and the theory of evolution in biology. By introducing these Crosscutting Concepts at appropriate times, teachers can help their students gain perspective on the study of various topics in science and see how they all—in a very important sense—reflect the same scientific way of thinking.

Emphasizing Technology and Engineering

Despite these similarities, the NGSS is very different from what has come before. One way it differs from prior standards is in the prominent role of technology and engineering. Although the idea that students should learn about technology and engineering has been around since the beginning of the standards movement[1], they have rarely been woven into the natural sciences as they are in the NGSS. Technology in

[1] American Association for the Advancement of Science. (1990). *Project 2061: Science for all Americans.* London: Oxford University Press.

the NGSS is portrayed as the application of science to the development of various products, processes, and systems to meet human needs, such as the application of wave phenomena to communication technologies. Engineering is positioned both as a core idea about defining and solving problems and as a means of applying the natural sciences to a wide variety of issues of both societal and environmental importance. And along with engineering comes a new set of skills for students to learn, such as defining problems by identifying criteria and constraints, applying tradeoffs to find the best acceptable solution, and learning to appreciate failure as a valuable aspect of the iterative design process.

Science and Engineering Practices

Some of the practices of science and engineering in the NGSS will be familiar to teachers, and some will seem quite different. What is especially different is that all of these practices are useful for scientific inquiry and engineering design. Table 1 illustrates why they are called practices of science and engineering.

It has taken me some time to fully appreciate what it means to help students develop skills in using these practices, since most of my career has focused on teaching concepts. I empathized with the two teachers whom I referred to in my opening paragraph because I've been in a similar position. My favorite subject is astronomy, and I've developed some really effective ways for students to use models so they can understand phenomena such as moon phases and seasons. I hated to give those methods up! But if students are to learn to develop and use models, then they are the ones who need to figure out how to use models to explain the phenomena. Telling them how to use the models just doesn't cut it. I should add that it's fine to illustrate how to use a model so they can learn how it's done, but at some point the students need to pick up the pieces as a means for figuring out why the moon goes through phases and how phases are different from eclipses. Another way to think about this is to consider who is doing the science. If the teacher is doing all of the explaining and asking all of the questions, the teacher—not the student—is doing the science.

Performance Expectations

Perhaps the most unusual aspect of the NGSS is the way these three dimensions are assembled—in single statements called Performance Expectations (PEs). They are called that because the NGSS is a set of assessment

> **"Perhaps the most unusual aspect of the NGSS is the way these three dimensions are assembled—in single statements called Performance Expectations."**

Table 1. Science and Engineering Practices

Practices	Science	Engineering
1. Asking Questions and Defining Problems	A basic practice of science is to ask questions about the world that can be answered by gathering data.	Engineering begins by defining a problem in terms of criteria for a successful solution, and constraints or limits.
2. Developing and Using Models	Science often involves the construction and use of models to help answer questions about natural phenomena.	Engineering makes use of models to analyze existing systems or to test possible solutions to a new problem.
3. Planning and Carrying Out Investigations	Scientific investigation can be controlled experiments to test predictions, attempts to identify correlations, or taxonomic identifications of species.	Engineers use investigations both to gain data essential for their design and to test the designs they develop.
4. Analyzing and Interpreting Data	Scientific investigations generally produce data that must be analyzed in order to derive meaning.	Engineers analyze and interpret data to determine how well each meets specific design criteria.
5. Using Mathematics and Computational Thinking	In science, mathematics and computers are used for a range of tasks from constructing models to analyzing data, and expressing relationships between variables.	In engineering, mathematics and computers are integral parts of the engineering design process.
6. Constructing Explanations and Designing Solutions	The goal of science is to explain phenomena in the natural world.	The goal of engineering is to solve meaningful problems.
7. Engaging in Argument From Evidence	In science, reasoning, argument, and participating actively in a community of peers are essential for finding explanations for natural phenomena.	In engineering, reasoning and argument are essential for finding the best possible solutions to problems.
8. Obtaining, Communicating and Presenting Information	A major practice of science is to communicate ideas and results of scientific inquiry and to obtain and evaluate findings reported by others.	Engineering needs to start by finding out how similar problems have been solved in the past and communicating ideas clearly and persuasively.

> **"The NGSS describes which practices students of various ages are expected to use in order to demonstrate their understanding of a specific core idea and crosscutting concept."**

standards. That is, they describe what students should be able to do at the end of instruction—not just what they know, but what they can do with what they know. That means achievement of these standards cannot be assessed with a multiple-choice test alone. Performance assessments of some sort will be necessary. The challenge for curriculum developers and teachers is to figure out what experiences they can provide so that their students will be able to meet these Performance Expectations not just at the end of class, but several months or even years later.

If all this seems daunting, keep in mind that the NGSS requires students to learn fewer core ideas than prior standards do so that teachers have time to teach those that remain in depth. When our writing team circulated drafts for public comment, we were told that there were too many standards to reasonably expect students to learn; so in the final round we cut the number of standards by one third. We did not "cheat" by combining standards—we actually cut the number of core ideas.

Another major advantage of the NGSS is that the standards are specific. I recall a project a few years ago, when I was helping to facilitate a team of teachers and other instructional leaders in the state of Washington to revise the state's standards. The Director of Science and I were meeting groups at various locations in the state to gather feedback on a draft. I recall one teacher who stood up to complain that the state test had questions that were impossible to anticipate because the standards were too vague. "Just tell us what the tests will be about," he said, "and we can help our students succeed!" The Next Generation Science Standards will not be subject to that objection. The NGSS describes which practices students of various ages are expected to use in order to demonstrate their understanding of a specific core idea and crosscutting concept. Each PE is followed by an additional clarification of the specific experiences that are referred to in the PE and also a list of performances that would not be assessed at that grade level.

So, to sum up: The great majority of core ideas in the NGSS are the same core ideas we've been teaching for years, with the addition of a few updates, especially related to societal and environmental issues. Although crosscutting concepts may sound new, they represent well-known features of scientific thinking. A new feature of the NGSS is that technology and engineering are woven deeply into the fabric of the document so that students are expected to develop skills that are quite new to most science teachers. And finally, the core ideas are fewer in number than prior standards in order to allow teachers more time to teach to mastery. The standards are also more specific to enable students to have greater success on tests by making it easier to align curriculum, instruction, and assessment. These last qualities alone are a reason for science teachers to cheer the NGSS.

Building an NGSS Curriculum

It's especially important for curriculum developers to keep in mind that the NGSS is sparse for a reason and to avoid including lessons just because they were there before and teachers expected to see them. Studies that have attempted to explain why U.S. students do poorly on international examinations have faulted textbooks in this country for being "a mile wide and an inch deep."[2] In light of that finding, I've been very impressed with the new *HMH Science Dimensions* textbook series. As a consulting author I've been pleased to see it develop as an entirely new curriculum that sticks to the PEs at each grade level, with rich science content and activities involving practices and core ideas but without extraneous material that would take up valuable instructional time.

It's hard to say what impact the NGSS will have, but I'm hopeful. For the past two years I've worked with middle school teachers in one school district in Oregon, which was one of the first states to adopt the NGSS. The teachers were given the task of designing units to match the sequence of PEs that their state recommended. I asked the teachers who had the most experience teaching a unit to design it for the district, even if they were not going to be teaching it in the fall. Initially some of the teachers protested having to spend a week during the summer preparing lessons they would not be teaching. One veteran teacher saved the day by saying, "Let's think of this as a barn raising. We'll all pitch in to help one group of teachers, and later they'll pitch in to help us."

Change is rarely embraced, but in the long run it has the advantage of keeping us on our toes. Science teachers are among the most creative people I know. With the support of their school and district leaders I know they will rise to the challenge, even if it means giving up some of their most treasured lessons. Their students will certainly be the beneficiaries of renewed instructional ideas and materials, especially as those students become the ones doing the science in the classroom.

> **"Science teachers are among the most creative people I know. With the support of their school and district leaders I know they will rise to the challenge."**

---

[2] Schmidt, W. H., McKnight, C., & Raizen, S. (Eds.). (1997). A splintered vision: An investigation of U.S. science and mathematics education (Vol. 1). Dordrecht, The Netherlands: Kluwer Academic Publishers.

Evidence Notebooks

by Michael A. DiSpezio

In **HMH Science Dimensions** you'll discover references to a brand-new type of tool—the Evidence Notebook—designed to support and reinforce the three-dimensional learning so central to NGSS pedagogy. Evidence Notebook may be a new term to you. So what is it and how does it differ from a traditional lab notebook or science journal? Great questions. As you are about to discover, the Evidence Notebook is a critical part of an NGSS approach to effective science education.

Think back to science notebooks that you maintained throughout your student experience. There's a good chance that these were a linear chronology of your learning accomplishments. In the earlier grades, they were bound records of classroom experience. For the most part, these entries were limited to lab observations; data collection tables; and answers to specific, prepackaged questions. By the time you reached middle school, the role of the lab notebook often segued into worksheet-and-lab-report repository.

Typically, all notebooks were organized in the same manner. There was little opportunity for individuality, personal voice, or indication of a student's interests. Often, they were used as summative assessment based on the expected homogenization of entries.

With the Next Generation Science Standards' revolutionary approach to pedagogy, the role and organization of what had been a record-keeping device has evolved. No longer a landscape on which to record prescriptive responses, the Evidence Notebook assumes the role of conceptual "scratch-pad." Like computer RAM, this is where the higher processing occurs.

With this evolution to a much more interactive role for the Evidence Notebook, let's examine the nuts and bolts of creating and maintaining it. The first thing to consider is that the notebook is student directed. Remember, it's primarily for the students—not for you! With that in mind, it is organized according to each student's learning style, personal interests, questions, observations, and interaction with the three dimensions of science.

Using Evidence Notebooks, students can

- assume an increased role and responsibility for their own learning

- direct or create their own learning path by recording, selecting, and pursuing questions of interest

- organize their thinking

- record and analyze observations

- compare/contrast passive information to higher-level thinking and critical analysis

- better commit ideas to long-term memory through the writing process

- perfect language skills in an authentic learning experience

- communicate understanding and competency

- record and evaluate evidence both from within the classroom and outside of the classroom in a Claims/Evidence/Reasoning model

EVIDENCE NOTEBOOK

Beyond the Classroom Walls

The Evidence Notebook travels both literally and figuratively beyond the physical school boundary. Not limited to recording classroom experiences and prescribed assignments, it assumes the role of interactive diary. Students record relevant thoughts and observations of the world around them in their notebooks. For example, if studying runoff, they might write about or photograph neighborhood gullies or storm-drainage systems. Entries can then be examined in a context of active learning using these meaningful examples from students' immediate world.

Spreading It Out

One way in which students might organize their notebooks is based upon right- and left-side pages of a spread. The left side of the page spread might incorporate the higher-level thinking process associated with an investigation. The posed question, evolving thoughts, and critical-thinking analysis would form this page's content. The facing right-hand page might include more of the prescribed and quantitative thought processes, such as the steps, data collection, and observations.

Claims/Evidence/Reasoning Connection

Claims/Evidence/Reasoning, or CER for short, is a strategy for getting students to go beyond memorization and construct explanations. The Evidence Notebook is the ideal landscape on which to address all three of the CER components. First, students can record and further distill their claims into testable hypotheses. Then, based upon a student-directed investigation, they can collect and record data as evidence. Finally, the students can illustrate the logic they used in arriving at a reasoned explanation.

Evidence for Assessment

Don't overlook the role that the Evidence Notebook can play in formative assessment. By reviewing student notebooks, the instructor gains insight into each student's qualitative thinking. The instructor can then offer targeted feedback to help students improve their Evidence Notebook's organization and entries.

"The Evidence Notebook travels both literally and figuratively beyond the physical school boundary."

From Data to Thinking About Data

As you know, "thinking about one's thinking" is a key element to successful learning. However, prior to Evidence Notebooks, students lacked a classroom tool adapted to metacognition. Now, within Evidence Notebooks, students can record and analyze their thinking processes. By reflecting on how best they learn, they can assume more control of personal learning. Not only does this awareness result in richer understanding, but it also evolves the organization and content of the Evidence Notebook to its most effective design.

Organizing the Evidence Notebook

By now, perhaps you are wondering what makes up the specific content and organization of an effective Evidence Notebook? The definitive answer is "it depends." That's because it varies from student to student. Although all notebooks should have a sequential format, the nature of each notebook's specific content and organization depends upon individual learning styles.

That said, effective Evidence Notebooks may include

- student interests and related questions

- a record of prior knowledge

- evidence collected from student-directed explorations

- short essays that address concepts and a student's personal thinking process

- graphic organizers such as concept maps and Venn diagrams

- drawings and embedded digital photographs

- observations that go beyond the classroom's physical boundaries

- reflections on understanding

- thinking and processes that address claims, evidence, and reasoning

21st Century Tools

Exploit the technology! As the installed base of tablets and PCs broadens, there are increasing opportunities for creating electronic Evidence Notebooks. Strategies in *HMH Science Dimensions* print and digital student editions offer the opportunity for open-ended student input. Students can also construct an Evidence Notebook using appropriate apps and software. In addition to accepting written input, electronic versions can include embedded media such as digital photos, video clips, and sound files.

Dynamic, Not Static

Unlike its traditional counterpart, the Evidence Notebook is not a static record. It is a work in progress on which understanding is continually constructed. Students update its content on a daily basis, not just around investigations and lab reports. So remind students to keep it current and use it as a foundation on which to construct understanding.

How *HMH Science Dimensions* Supports an Evidence Notebook

Throughout both the Interactive Online Student Edition and the student text of *HMH Science Dimensions* are Evidence-Notebook writing prompts. They are designed to introduce and reinforce the skills that you've just read about. But these should be considered only the beginning. Let your imagination run wild, but most of all, encourage your students to use this important tool in ways that foster their own learning and understanding of science and engineering and their connections to everyday life.

By Marjorie Frank

As educators, we often think in terms of disciplines: I teach English. I'm a science teacher. I'm a math coach. While these may be useful distinctions, they obscure an important consideration: Our brain has no such distinctions.

The Brain and Learning

No special region is active during science class and inactive during English or math. Or, vice versa. Yet, we often operate as if it were. Most science teachers don't focus deeply on reading or writing skills; English and math teachers aren't greatly concerned with science concepts. Yet, the cognitive processes in all these—and other—disciplines are pretty much the same. We just talk about them differently . . . and sometimes, we don't even do that. For example, citing evidence to support a claim is central to science. Explaining how an author uses evidence to support particular points is central to English language study. How different are these phenomena, really?

Which Standards?

Here's a short activity to test this idea. The sentences below are from science and English language arts standards. Except for giveaway words such as science and nonfiction, which I've deleted, the standards are reproduced here verbatim. See if you can tell which are science standards and which are ELA standards. [Answers are at the end of this article.]

1. Obtain information using various texts, text features (e.g. headings, tables of contents, glossaries, electronic menus, icons), and other media that will be useful in answering a question.

2. Ask questions based on observations to find more information. . . .

3. Write arguments to support claims . . . using valid reasoning and relevant and sufficient evidence.

4. Construct an argument with evidence to support a claim.

5. Ask questions to clear up any confusion. . . .

6. Know and use various text features (e.g. headings, tables of contents, glossaries, electronic menus, icons) to locate key facts or information. . . .

7. Obtain and combine information from books and/or other reliable media to explain phenomena or solutions . . . to a design problem.

8. Integrate information from several texts on the same topic. . . .

This confluence of interdisciplinary realities is embodied in the Next Generation Science Standards.

Curriculum Crossover in NGSS

Released in April 2013, the Next Generation Science Standards are, I believe, the only standards to date that recognize and embrace the natural crossover of disciplines. If you were to print the standards, each page would include a set of Science and Engineering Practices, a set of Disciplinary Core Ideas, a set of Crosscutting Concepts, and sets of ELA and Mathematics standards—formalizing what is true naturally: they all work together.

> **"Much of the time, you may be engaging in cross-disciplinary practices without even realizing it. "**

Much of the time, you may be engaging in cross-disciplinary practices without even realizing it. In English class, your students participate in exchanges that require close reading of a text. They cite evidence from the reading to support their responses to questions. Is this really different from asking students to cite evidence in support of a science claim? In science class, your students communicate solutions to a design problem via posters or verbal presentations. Is this all that different from reporting on a topic or engaging in collaborative discussions? Perhaps the expression a distinction without a difference applies here.

If your students are doing science, and I do mean doing science, they are likely to be engaging in crossover English language arts skills coincidentally.

HMH Science Dimensions takes the coincidence out of the crossover.

HMH Science Dimensions and Integrated Learning

The instructional design and lesson plans of the student-facing materials for all levels of **HMH Science Dimensions** facilitate English language arts in ways that are both subtle and explicit. Prompts throughout a lesson lead learners to collaborate, ask questions, summarize, explain, analyze. Frequent opportunities connected to students' Evidence Notebooks integrate writing into the process. You need only scroll through a digital lesson or page through the print to find evidence of these approaches.

Something else you'll find in the student-facing materials for young learners is a system of light-bulb icons and headings that identify an extensive structure of online handbooks containing tips and strategies for developing science, math, and language arts skills. Some of the language skills that receive attention include asking and answering questions, doing research, collaborating, using visuals, and describing problems.

For the youngest learners is a robust feature in the student-facing materials called Read, Write, Share! Here, children are guided to practice asking and answering questions, collaborating, drawing, writing, and presenting ideas to others. And throughout the teacher-facing materials you will find suggestions for collaboration, a quintessentially language-based endeavor.

For older learners you'll find a lesson feature called Language SmArts. These are activities that integrate language arts skills into the science learning process. Some Language SmArts activities appear in the student-facing materials; others appear only in the teacher-facing components. Examples of activities include those connected to making inferences, conducting research, and using visuals in multimedia displays among others. In all cases, they represent another way in which **HMH Science Dimensions** helps facilitate the alignment of English language arts and the Next Generation Science Standards.

In the end, if your goal is to help learners draw upon their full complement of natural abilities to gain ownership of science, you can relax knowing that you've come to the right place: **HMH Science Dimensions**.

"...all levels of *HMH Science Dimensions* facilitate English language arts in ways that are both subtle and explicit."

Answers:

1. NGSS standard; **2.** NGSS standard; **3.** English language arts standard; **4.** NGSS standard; **5.** English language arts standard; **6.** English language arts standard; **7.** NGSS standard; **8.** English language arts standard.

by Michael R. Heithaus, PhD

Improving STEM education at every level—from K–12 through university—is a national priority. Distinction in STEM fields is critical to ensuring the ability of the United States to compete in international markets and to actualize intellectual goals, and jobs in STEM fields are projected to grow at higher rates than in other professions. Yet at the university and career levels, there is seemingly not enough interest or achievement in STEM fields. How we prepare students for college and career is a growing concern. The Next Generation Science Standards are built to ensure readiness.

What Is College and Career Readiness?

At the simplest level, being college ready means that students are able to succeed in college classes without remediation. Being career ready means that graduates are prepared to obtain and succeed in entry-level positions. Sounds simple, but as STEM fields evolve and change, so do requirements related to content-area knowledge. For that reason, NGSS and **HMH Science Dimensions** focus on students demonstrating that they have mastered important skills more than specific knowledge or facts. Through formative assessments, evidence notebooks, and summative assessments, including critical performance-based assessments, teachers are supplied with the tools they need to understand student performance. Strategies throughout this Teacher Edition provide means of addressing many deficiencies.

When students have mastered skills and understand the underlying connections between STEM fields and other curriculum areas, they will not only have the background knowledge they need but also be prepared to fill in gaps in their understanding independently, without the need for remediation or extensive on-the-job training. And although college and career readiness might seem like qualities for students to master in high school, NGSS brings a greater coherence across grade levels: students from primary grades through high school have the opportunity to work on these skills and learn to apply them in everyday life.

According to the NGSS, career and college-ready students should be able to

- make sense of the world and approach novel problems, phenomena, and information using a blend of science and engineering practices, disciplinary core ideas, and crosscutting concepts

- use valid research strategies

- be self-directed in planning, monitoring, and evaluation

- flexibly apply knowledge across disciplines (through continued exploration of Science and Engineering Practices, Crosscutting Concepts, and Disciplinary Core Ideas)

Not included in this list are some other skills that students should master to succeed in today's college classroom and workplace. First, students need to be

- comfortable working in diverse groups and with peers with different perspectives

- able to support their claims with logical arguments while being respectful and constructive in dealing with those who don't agree

- able to think critically and creatively

- able to communicate effectively in multiple settings and via diverse media

New Teaching Methods and A New Role for Teachers

The new focus on skills rather than content knowledge alone has led to big changes, backed by research, in how we teach science at universities and in K–12 classrooms. We know that active learning from student-centered activities that include group work and problem solving enhance student success.

There is no question that implementing NGSS requires teachers to shift both what and how they teach. For much of the instruction, the teacher's role in the classroom is different. Because NGSS integrates the practices of science and engineering with content-area knowledge, there is an increasing focus on students being scientists in the discovery process and leading their own investigations. Does this mean teachers are less important? Not by a long shot. In fact, teachers are probably more important than ever! It will take a bit of work to adapt your course to active learning and to integrate NGSS-style learning, but believe me, it will be worth it for you and your students.

Some things to keep in mind:

- Think about questions. Asking the right questions can be critical to getting students on—or back to—the right track to discovering material for themselves and making connections between concepts that are critical to NGSS. Pose questions to get students to think deeply about the nature and strength of evidence used to support a claim.

- Facilitate team learning. Science and engineering are all about teams, and students need to be comfortable working in groups with peers. Team learning can help students at very different levels benefit from the same course of investigation. I have found that strong students gain better mastery of concepts when they help students who are having trouble. On the flip side, some students actually learn better from a peer than a teacher! Pay attention to group dynamics, but facilitate cooperative teams wherever you can.

- Moderate discussions and peer critiques purposefully.

- Remember that NGSS can help improve math skills. Throughout **HMH Science Dimensions**, you'll find opportunities to practice age- and discipline-appropriate math practices to support science investigations and learning. Find ways to bring

> **"There is no question that implementing NGSS requires teachers to shift both what and how they teach. For much of the instruction, the teacher's role in the classroom is different."**

math into investigations. Math is critical to science and engineering, and science and engineering can make math more accessible and exciting to students!

- Help students make connections continuously. The **HMH Science Dimensions** Teacher Edition provides many strategies to assist students in making those connections. There is plenty of evidence that having multiple opportunities to associate pieces of information in different contexts facilitates retention. NGSS is built so that particular standards can be blended with others and integrated throughout a year and across grade levels. Online resources facilitate this blending—and you will find them already integrated in **HMH Science Dimensions!**

- Collaborate! Whether you teach kindergarten or college, you are not alone in applying NGSS innovations in science education. When you talk to your colleagues and look online for best ideas and practices, you are serving as a role model for your students.

As you move into teaching NGSS and preparing students for college and career, look for the many strategies and opportunities for assessment embedded in both the student-facing materials and the Teacher materials of your **HMH Science Dimensions** program. These will facilitate implementation of best practices in NGSS pedagogy. Even if your students won't be entering STEM fields, solid science education at this point will help students prepare for the coming years by inculcating the critical thinking skills necessary for science literacy and making informed, reasonable, evidence-backed decisions in all facets of life.

"Whether you teach kindergarten or college, you are not alone in applying NGSS innovations in science education."

STEM

NGSS has a sharp emphasis on teaching all standards to all students. One of the challenges of teaching using NGSS pedagogy is reteaching. The three dimensions of science would seem to present challenges that you haven't encountered before. But there is good news: two of the dimensions are self-reteaching!

Both the Science and Engineering Practices and the Crosscutting Concepts are revisited time and again throughout the year. Strategies for teaching these occur within the teacher margin materials.

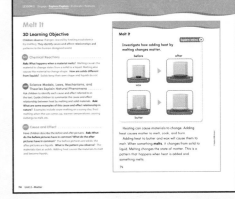

While you may need to remind children (about CCCs) or monitor closely (for SEPs), multiple exposures to a concept in different contexts have been shown to be the most effective reteaching possible.

And for reteaching Disciplinary Core Ideas, **HMH Science Dimensions™** has you covered.

Key Science concepts are recontextualized in the *Science and Engineering Readers*. These readers present the same concepts at two different levels and provide additional concepts and advanced reading for children who are easily mastering the concepts.

Sciencesaurus provides a quick, in depth, visual reference at suitable readabilities for students. The engaging writing and illustrations help to present the content in another context and in slightly different ways so as to reinforce key DCIs and recontextualize the Science Dimensions student-facing materials. Recontextualization and easier reading are both shown to improve comprehension of difficult, but important, science concepts.

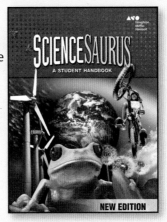

The *Interactive Worktext* and the *Interactive Online Student Edition* present the same content in different ways. The *Interactive Online Student Edition* provides additional interactions and voice over to reinforce and reteach the content in ways that enable children with reading deficits to learn the core science concepts. It also provides children with immediate feedback on many interactivities to reinforce learning.

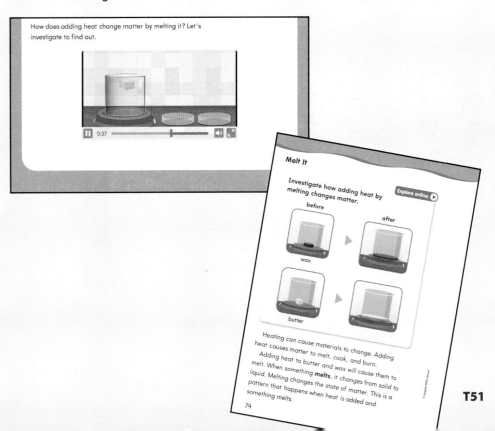

HMH Science Dimensions™ and the EQuIP Rubric

The **EQuIP Rubric** is an instrument for evaluating a curriculum's conformance with the contours of an authentic NGSS program. As such, one needs to bear in mind the known limitations and proper usages of the rubric:

• The rubric is intended to be applied to lessons or units, not to entire curricula.

• The rubric itself indicates that it is unlikely that a single lesson will lead to mastery of a Performance Expectation. High-Quality Units may do so.

• The evaluation process is intended to be done in a group, not by an individual.

• The rubric requires familiarity with the Performance Expectation and its supporting Dimensions of Learning. The **HMH Science Dimensions™ Trace Tool to the NGSS** can help provide this orientation.

Throughout the **HMH Science Dimensions Teacher Edition**, you will find features to help you orient toward the critical dimensions of the EQuIP Rubric. Using the book, you are well beyond the evaluation phase of considering a program, but these features will demonstrate the best practices of NGSS summarized by the evaluation instrument. Highlights of critical EQuIP Rubric evaluation points are summarized in the reduced pages you see here.

Unit Planning Pages

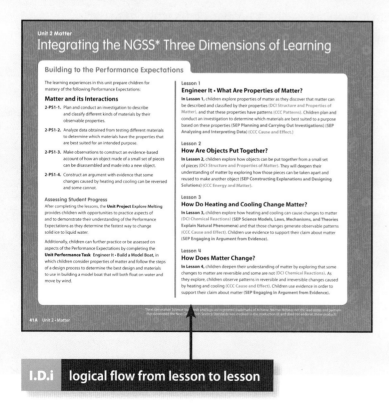

I.D.i logical flow from lesson to lesson

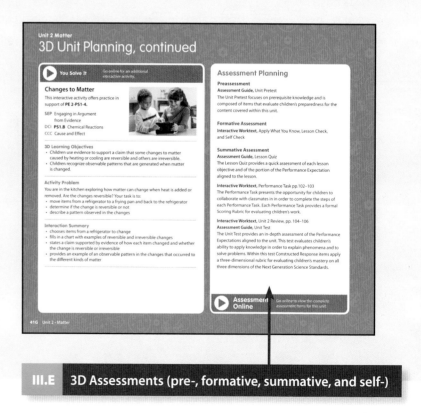

III.E 3D Assessments (pre-, formative, summative, and self-)

Lesson Planning Pages

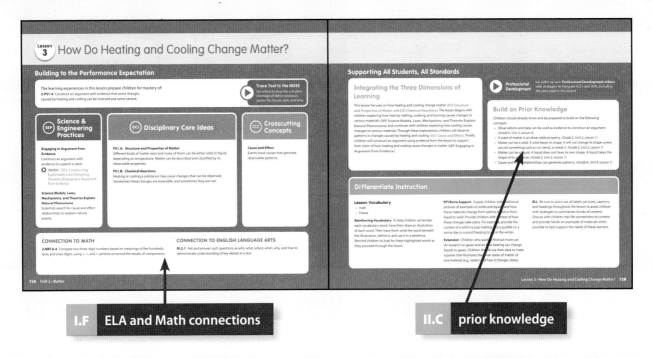

I.F ELA and Math connections

II.C prior knowledge

Lesson Opener Pages

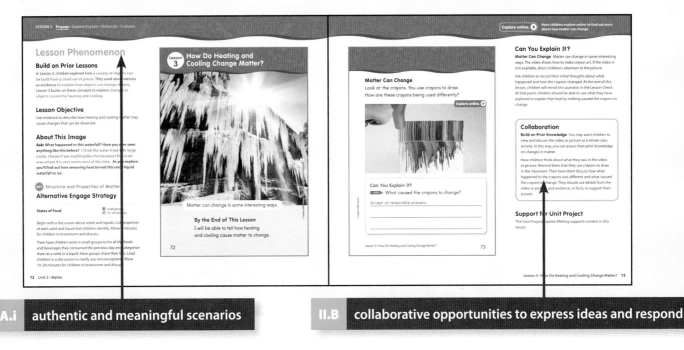

II.A.i authentic and meaningful scenarios

II.B collaborative opportunities to express ideas and respond

HMH Science Dimensions™ and the EQuIP Rubric

Lesson Pages

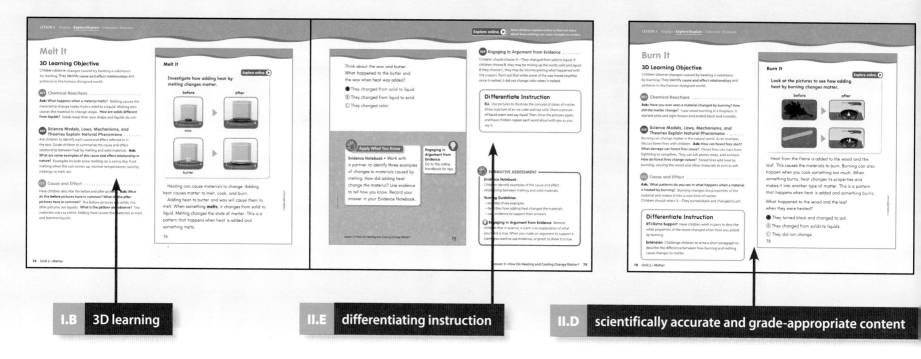

I.B 3D learning

II.E differentiating instruction

II.D scientifically accurate and grade-appropriate content

Lesson Pages

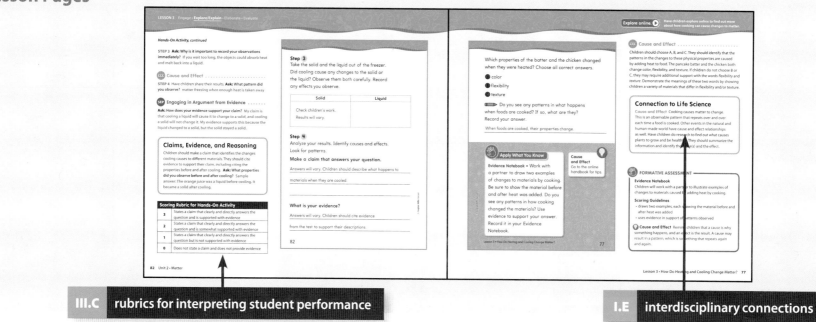

III.C rubrics for interpreting student performance

I.E interdisciplinary connections

Lesson Closer Pages

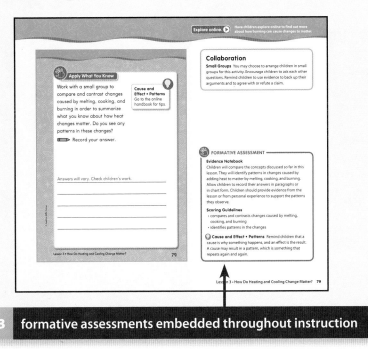

Explore online. ▶ Have children explore online to find out more about how burning can cause changes to matter.

Apply What You Know

Work with a small group to compare and contrast changes caused by melting, cooking, and burning in order to summarize what you know about how heat changes matter. Do you see any patterns in these changes?

Cause and Effect • Patterns Go to the online handbook for tips.

✏ Record your answer.

Answers will vary. Check children's work.

Collaboration

Small Groups You may choose to arrange children in small groups for this activity. Encourage children to ask each other questions. Remind children to use evidence to back up their arguments and to agree with or refute a claim.

FORMATIVE ASSESSMENT

Evidence Notebook
Children will compare the concepts discussed so far in this lesson. They will identify patterns in changes caused by adding heat to matter by melting, cooking, and burning. Allow children to record their answers in paragraphs or in chart form. Children should provide evidence from the lesson or from personal experience to support the patterns they observe.

Scoring Guidelines
• compares and contrasts changes caused by melting, cooking, and burning
• identifies patterns in the changes

Cause and Effect • Patterns Remind children that a cause is why something happens, and an effect is the result. A cause may result in a pattern, which is something that repeats again and again.

Lesson 3 • How Do Heating and Cooling Change Matter? 79

III.B formative assessments embedded throughout instruction

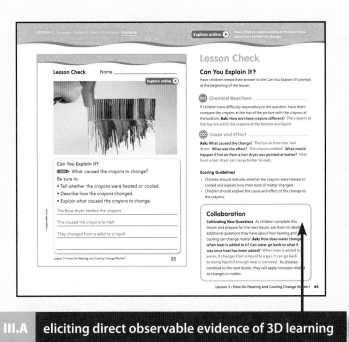

LESSON 3 · Engage · Explore · Explain · Elaborate · Evaluate

Explore online. ▶ Have children explore online to find out more about how matter can change.

Lesson Check   Name _____

Explore online. ▶

Can You Explain It?
✏ What caused the crayons to change?
Be sure to:
• Tell whether the crayons were heated or cooled.
• Describe how the crayons changed.
• Explain what caused the crayons to change.

The blow dryer heated the crayons.

This caused the crayons to melt.

They changed from a solid to a liquid.

Lesson 3 • How Do Heating and Cooling Change Matter? 85

Lesson Check

Can You Explain It?
Have children reread their answer to the Can You Explain It? prompt at the beginning of the lesson.

DCI Chemical Reactions
If children have difficulty responding to the question, have them compare the crayons at the top of the picture with the crayons at the bottom. **Ask: How are these crayons different?** The crayons at the top are solid; the crayons at the bottom are liquid.

CCC Cause and Effect
Ask: What caused the change? The hot air from the hair dryer. **What was the effect?** The crayons melted. **What would happen if hot air from a hair dryer was pointed at butter?** Heat from a hair dryer can cause butter to melt.

Scoring Guidelines
• Children should indicate whether the crayons were heated or cooled and explain how their state of matter changed.
• Children should explain the cause and effect of the change to the crayons.

Collaboration

Cultivating New Questions As children complete this lesson and prepare for the next lesson, ask them to identify additional questions they have about how heating and cooling can change matter. **Ask: How does water change when heat is added to it? Can water go back to what it was once heat has been added?** When heat is added to water, it changes from a liquid to a gas. It can go back to being liquid if enough heat is removed. As children continue to the next lesson, they will apply concepts related to changes in matter.

Lesson 3 • How Do Heating and Cooling Change Matter? 85

III.A eliciting direct observable evidence of 3D learning

Unit Interleaf Pages

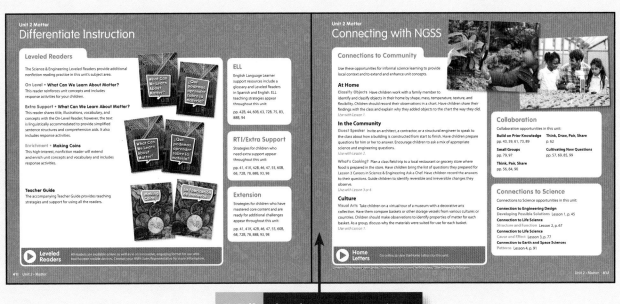

Unit 2 Matter
Differentiate Instruction

Leveled Readers

The Science & Engineering Leveled Readers provide additional nonfiction reading practice in this unit's subject area.

On Level • What Can We Learn About Matter?
This reader reinforces unit concepts and includes response activities for your children.

Extra Support • What Can We Learn About Matter?
This reader shares title, illustrations, vocabulary, and concepts with the On-Level Reader; however, the text is linguistically accommodated to provide simplified sentence structures and comprehension aids. It also includes response activities.

Enrichment • Making Coins
This high-interest, nonfiction reader will extend and enrich unit concepts and vocabulary and includes response activities.

Teacher Guide
The accompanying Teacher Guide provides teaching strategies and support for using all the readers.

▶ **Leveled Readers** All readers are available online as well as in an innovative, engaging format for use with touchscreen mobile devices. Contact your HMH Sales Representative for more information.

ELL
English Language Learner support resources include a glossary and Leveled Readers in Spanish and English. ELL teaching strategies appear throughout this unit:
pp. 42B, 44, 60B, 63, 72B, 75, 83, 88B, 94

RTI/Extra Support
Strategies for children who need extra support appear throughout this unit:
pp. 41, 41K, 42B, 46, 47, 55, 60B, 68, 72B, 78, 88B, 93, 98

Extension
Strategies for children who have mastered core content and are ready for additional challenges appear throughout this unit:
pp. 41, 41K, 42B, 46, 47, 55, 60B, 68, 72B, 78, 88B, 93, 98

41I Unit 2 • Matter

Unit 2 Matter
Connecting with NGSS

Connections to Community

Use these opportunities for informal science learning to provide local context and to extend and enhance unit concepts.

At Home
Classify Objects Have children work with a family member to identify and classify objects in their home by shape, mass, temperature, texture, and flexibility. Children should record their observations in a chart. Have children share their findings with the class and explain why they added objects to the chart the way they did.
Use with Lesson 2.

In the Community
Guest Speaker Invite an architect, a contractor, or a structural engineer to speak to the class about how a building is constructed from start to finish. Have children prepare questions for him or her to answer. Encourage children to ask a mix of appropriate science and engineering questions.
Use with Lesson 2.

What's Cooking? Plan a class field trip to a local restaurant or grocery store where food is prepared in the store. Have children bring the list of questions they prepared for Lesson 3 Careers in Science & Engineering Ask a Chef. Have children record the answers to their questions. Guide children to identify reversible and irreversible changes they observe.
Use with Lesson 3 or 4.

Culture
Visual Arts Take children on a virtual tour of a museum with a decorative arts collection. Have them compare baskets or other storage vessels from various cultures or countries. Children should make observations to identify properties of matter for each basket. As a group, discuss why the materials were suited for use for each basket.
Use with Lesson 1.

Collaboration
Collaboration opportunities in this unit:

Build on Prior Knowledge pp. 43, 59, 61, 73, 89   **Think, Draw, Pair, Share** p. 62

Small Groups pp. 79, 97   **Cultivating New Questions** pp. 57, 69, 85, 99

Think, Pair, Share pp. 56, 84, 90

Connections to Science
Connections to Science opportunities in this unit:

Connection to Engineering Design
Developing Possible Solutions Lesson 1, p. 45
Connection to Life Science
Structure and Function Lesson 2, p. 67
Connection to Life Science
Cause and Effect Lesson 3, p. 77
Connection to Earth and Space Sciences
Patterns Lesson 4, p. 91

▶ **Home Letters** Go online to view the Home Letters for this unit.

Unit 2 • Matter 41J

II.A.ii developing connections

T55

© Houghton Mifflin Harcourt

Physical Science
Unit 2 • Matter 39

© Houghton Mifflin Harcourt

xi

Life Science
Unit 3 • Environments for Living Things 107

Earth and Space Sciences

Unit 4 • Earth's Surface...........................183

© Houghton Mifflin Harcourt • Image Credits: © Arpad Benedek/E+/Getty Images

Safety in Science

Doing science is fun. But a science lab can be dangerous. Know the safety rules and listen to your teacher.

- ⊘ Do not eat or drink anything.
- ⊘ Do not touch sharp things.
- ✔ Wash your hands.
- ✔ Wear goggles to keep your eyes safe.
- ✔ Be neat and clean up spills.
- ✔ Tell your teacher if something breaks.
- ✔ Show good behavior.

© Houghton Mifflin Harcourt

xv

Use the following discussion points to emphasize key safety rules for science hands-on activities.

Ask: What safety gear are the children in the picture using? They are wearing goggles and gloves. **Ask:** How does the gear keep them safer? The goggles protect their eyes from harmful things. The gloves protect their skin.

Show children an ordinary pair of glasses (or sunglasses). Then show them safety goggles. **Ask:** What is different about the safety goggles? The safety goggles are made of sturdy material and have protection all around the sides of the lenses.

Ask: What would you do if you spilled some water? Tell the teacher, and help clean up the spill. **Ask:** What could happen if the spill wasn't cleaned up? Water could make the floor slippery and increase the risk of falls.

Ask: Why is it important to wash your hands when you're done? Washing hands helps keep you from getting sick, and keeps you from rubbing things into your eyes.

Ask for a volunteer. Tell him or her to walk up to and point at a piece of safety equipment in the classroom. Then tell the class when and how to use it.

Safety in Science

Children should circle the pictures of hands being washed, and gloves and goggles being worn. Remind students that following these rules can help them stay safe. If children chose the picture of the child pouring water without wearing goggles, look at the lab safety rules again and remind them that wearing goggles is a rule that helps keep eyes safe. **Ask: Why is it important to wear goggles?** Goggles keep things from getting into your eyes.

Children should place an x on the children not wearing goggles and the child using scissors the wrong way. If children didn't choose those pictures, remind them that one of the safety rules is to not touch sharp things.

Safety in Science

Circle the pictures where a safety rule is being followed. Place an X on the pictures where a safety rule is not being followed.

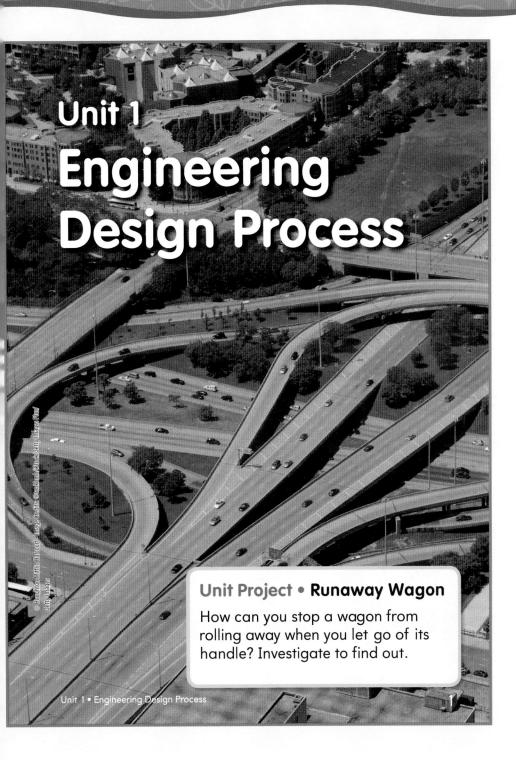

Unit 1
Engineering
Design Process

Unit Project • Runaway Wagon

How can you stop a wagon from rolling away when you let go of its handle? Investigate to find out.

Unit 1 • Engineering Design Process   1

Unit 1 • Engineering Design Process

Unit Overview

In this unit, children will…
- ask questions, make observations, and gather information to define a problem.
- use a design process to solve a problem.
- compare the strengths and weaknesses of multiple design solutions.

About This Image

Guide children in a discussion about the picture on this page.

Ask: Have you ever seen a set of highway ramps like this before? Why do you think engineers designed the highway roads using ramps like this? Engineers designed highway roads using ramps to make it easier for people to enter or exit the roads. These designs also make it safer for traffic to flow. **Ask:** Why are ramps good to use when two roads meet? Ramps allow cars to switch roads without having to stop. One road has to travel over the other road, and ramps make that possible.

Unit Project • **Runaway Wagon**

Have children plan and conduct an investigation that identifies the best way to keep a wagon from rolling away when you let go of its handle. Children may work in pairs or small groups, and should follow all steps of a design process as outlined in the first lesson of this unit. At the conclusion of the Unit Project, have children meet as a class to review and compare the strengths and weaknesses of each design in order to determine which design works best to keep a wagon from rolling away.

To begin, share details about wagons or challenge children to use online resources to find pictures of different wagons. More support for the Unit Project can be found on pp. 3I–3L.

Unit 1 At a Glance

The learning experiences in this unit prepare children for mastery of:

Performance Expectations

K-2-ETS1-1. Ask questions, make observations, and gather information about a situation people want to change to define a simple problem that can be solved through the development of a new or improved object or tool.

K-2-ETS1-2. Develop a simple sketch, drawing, or physical model to illustrate how the shape of an object helps it function as needed to solve a given problem.

K-2-ETS1-3. Analyze data from tests of two objects designed to solve the same problem to compare the strengths and weaknesses of how each performs.

Explore online. ▶

In addition to the print resources, the following resources are available online to support this unit.

Unit Pretest

Lesson 1 Engineer It • What Is a Design Process?
- Interactive Online Student Edition
- Lesson Quiz

Lesson 2 Engineer It • How Can We Compare Design Solutions?
- Interactive Online Student Edition
- Lesson Quiz

You Solve It Sort It Out

Unit Performance Task

Unit Test

Unit 1 At a Glance

© Houghton Mifflin Harcourt • Image Credits: ©tankbmb/iStock/Getty Images Plus/ Getty Images

2

Unit Vocabulary

engineer a person who uses math and science to define and solve problems (p. 6)

design process a set of steps that helps an engineer define a problem and plan, test and share a solution (p. 6)

solution an answer to a problem (p. 6)

strength a good feature (p. 24)

weakness a flawed feature (p. 24)

Vocabulary Game • Guess the Word

Materials
- 1 set of word cards

How to Play
1. Work with a partner to make word cards.
2. Place the cards face down in a pile.
3. One player picks the top card but does not show it.
4. The other player asks questions to guess the word.
5. When the word is guessed correctly, the other player takes a card.

Unit Vocabulary

The Next Generation Science Standards emphasize explanation and demonstration of understanding versus rote memorization of science vocabulary words. Keep in mind that these vocabulary words are tools for clear communication. Use these words as a starting point, not an end goal, for children to build deeper understanding of science concepts.

Children can explore all vocabulary words in the **Online Glossary**.

Vocabulary Strategies

- Have children review the vocabulary words. Then have children work in pairs to share an example of each word and explain why they think it's an example. Have pairs record their examples to refer back to during the unit.
- Have children think about how each word relates to an engineering design process. Have children work in pairs and share their ideas with a partner.

Differentiate Instruction

RTI/Extra Support Pronounce each word, and have children repeat it after you. Have children find each highlighted word within the unit content. Have children work in pairs and explain to a partner what they think each word means based on the surrounding context of imagery and text.

Extension Have children select two vocabulary words and work in small groups to illustrate and explain the words to a first-grade child.

Vocabulary Game • Guess the Word

Preparation Assemble vocabulary game cards. Assign partners for children. Provide instructions for how to play the game. Allow children to rotate through all five cards during gameplay.

Integrating the NGSS* Three Dimensions of Learning

Building to the Performance Expectations

The learning experiences in this unit prepare children for mastery of the following Performance Expectations:

Engineering Design

K-2-ETS1-1 Ask questions, make observations, and gather information about a situation people want to change to define a simple problem that can be solved through the development of a new or improved object or tool.

K-2-ETS1-2 Develop a simple sketch, drawing, or physical model to illustrate how the shape of an object helps it function as needed to solve a given problem.

K-2-ETS1-3 Analyze data from tests of two objects designed to solve the same problem to compare the strengths and weaknesses of how each performs.

Assessing Student Progress

After completing the lessons, the **Unit Project** Runaway Wagon provides children with opportunities to practice aspects of and to demonstrate their understanding of the Performance Expectations as they plan and conduct an investigation that identifies the best way to keep a wagon from rolling away after letting go of its handle.

Additionally, children can further practice or be assessed on aspects of the Performance Expectations by completing the **Unit Performance Task** Engineer It • Build a Water Bottle Holder, in which children define a problem to solve and then develop possible solutions that take into account the structure and function of their water bottle holder.

Lesson 1
Engineer It • What Is a Design Process?

In Lesson 1, children focus on how to define and solve a problem. The lesson begins with children exploring the five steps of a design process engineers use to solve problems. Children will ask questions, make observations, and gather information (**SEP Asking Questions and Defining Problems**) (**DCI Defining and Delimiting Engineering Problems**). The lesson continues with children using drawings and models to solve a real-life problem (**SEP Developing and Using Models**) (**DCI Developing Possible Solutions**). Children will explore how to improve their designs and how the structure of their design is related to its purpose (**CCC Structure and Function**). Finally, children will communicate their results.

Lesson 2
Engineer It • How Can We Compare Design Solutions?

In Lesson 2, children focus on comparing solutions to a problem. Children first analyze the strengths and weaknesses of a design (**SEP Analyzing and Interpreting Data**) for a stop sign. Then children follow the steps of a design process as a child who has a backpack with uncomfortable straps identifies it as a problem and then builds, tests, and compares the strengths and weaknesses of four possible design solutions (**DCI Developing Possible Solutions, DCI Optimizing the Design Solution**) using materials with different characteristics (**CCC Structure and Function**). Children apply the steps of a design process to build and test designs for bridges and towers (**DCI Developing Possible Solutions, DCI Optimizing the Design Solution**). Children analyze and compare their solutions (**SEP Analyzing and Interpreting Data**), relate the shape and stability of their structures to their functions (**CCC Structure and Function**), and use what they find out in order to improve their designs (**SEP Analyzing and Interpreting Data**).

Standards Supported by This Unit

Explore online.
Online only.

Next Generation Science Standards	Unit Project	Lesson 1	Lesson 2	Unit Performance Task	You Solve It
SEP Asking Questions and Defining Problems	•	•		•	•
SEP Developing and Using Models	•	•			•
SEP Analyzing and Interpreting Data	•		•		
DCI ETS1.A Defining and Delimiting Engineering Problems	•	•	•		•
DCI ETS1.B Developing Possible Solutions	•	•	•	•	•
DCI ETS1.C Optimizing the Design Solution	•		•		
CCC Structure and Function	•	•	•	•	•

NGSS* Across the Grades

Before	Grade 2	After
Engineering Design	**Engineering Design**	**Engineering Design**
K-2-ETS1-1	**K-2-ETS1-1**	**3-5-ETS1-1** Define a simple design problem reflecting a need or a want that includes specified criteria for success and constraints on materials, time, or cost.
K-2-ETS1-2	**K-2-ETS1-2**	**3-5-ETS1-2** Generate and compare multiple possible solutions to a problem based on how well each is likely to meet the criteria and constraints of the problem.
K-2-ETS1-3	**K-2-ETS1-3**	**3-5-ETS1-3** Plan and carry out fair tests in which variables are controlled and failure points are considered to identify aspects of a model or prototype that can be improved.

 **Trace Tool to the NGSS™** Go online to view the complete coverage of these standards across this grade level and time.

3D Unit Planning

Lesson 1 Engineer It • What Is a Design Process? pp. 4–19

Overview

Objective Ask questions, make observations, and gather information to define a problem to be solved through a design process.

SEP Asking Questions and Defining Problems
SEP Developing and Using Models
DCI **ETS1.A** Defining and Delimiting Engineering Problems
DCI **ETS1.B** Developing Possible Solutions
CCC Structure and Function

Math and **English Language Arts** standards and features are detailed on lesson planning pages.

	Print and Online Student Editions	Explore online.
ENGAGE	Lesson Problem pp. 4–5 Can You Solve It? Ramps	Can You Solve It? Video
EXPLORE/ EXPLAIN	What Engineers Do Step 1–Define a Problem Step 2–Plan and Build Step 3–Test and Improve Step 4–Redesign Step 5–Communicate Hands-On Activity Engineer It • Build a Better Lunchbox pp. 9–10	Hands-On Worksheet
ELABORATE	Take It Further, p. 14 Engineer It • Make Your Lunchbox Better Take It Further pp. 15–16 Careers in Science & Engineering • Mechanical Engineer	Take It Further Engineer It • Make Your Lunchbox Better
EVALUATE	Lesson Check p. 17 Self Check pp. 18–19	Lesson Quiz

Hands-On Activity Planning

Engineer It • Build a Better Lunchbox

Objective Children observe and gather information in order to plan and build a solution to design a better lunchbox.

👥 small groups
🕐 1 class period

Suggested Materials
- a lunchbox
- a water bottle
- aluminum foil
- waxed paper
- paper towels
- cotton batting

Preparation/Tip

Pre-assemble material bundles for small groups.

Lesson 2 Engineer It • How Can We Compare Design Solutions? pp. 20–33

Overview

Objective Analyze and compare multiple design solutions.

SEP Analyzing and Interpreting Data
DCI **ETS1.A** Defining and Delimiting Engineering Problems
DCI **ETS1.B** Developing Possible Solutions
DCI **ETS1.C** Optimizing the Design Solution
CCC Structure and Function

Math and **English Language Arts** standards and features are detailed on lesson planning pages.

Print and Online Student Editions	Explore online.
ENGAGE	**Lesson Problem** pp. 20–21 **Can You Solve It?** How We Use a Design Process Every Day	▶ Can You Solve It? Video
EXPLORE/ EXPLAIN	**One Problem, Many Solutions** **Build and Test a Solution** **Compare Design Solutions** **Hands-On Activity** Engineer It • Compare Strengths and Weaknesses of Design Solutions pp. 27–28	**Hands-On** Worksheet **You Solve It** Sort It Out
ELABORATE	**Take It Further** pp. 29–30 People in Science & Engineering • Gustave Eiffel	Take It Further Blast to the Past
EVALUATE	**Lesson Check** p. 31 **Self Check** pp. 32–33	Lesson Quiz

Hands-On Activity Planning

Engineer It • Compare Strengths and Weaknesses of Design Solutions

Objective Children will plan two solutions to a problem, and then compare the strengths and weaknesses of the solutions.

👥 small groups
🕐 1 class period

Suggested Materials
- uncooked spaghetti
- marshmallows
- masking tape
- scissors
- string

Preparation/Tip

Preassemble materials bundles for each group of children. Include 20 pieces of spaghetti, 1 meter of kitchen string, 1 meter of masking tape, scissors, and one marshmallow. Blocks, a small book, and a sheet of paper are alternative materials that can be used for this activity.

3D Unit Planning, continued

 You Solve It   Go online for an additional
interactive activity.

Sort It Out

This interactive activity offers practice in support
of **PE K-2-ETS1-2.**

SEP Asking Questions and Defining Problems
SEP Developing and Using Models
DCI **ETS1.A** Defining and Delimiting
          Engineering Problems
DCI **ETS1.B** Developing Possible Solutions
CCC Structure and Function

3D Learning Objectives

- Children execute the steps of the engineering design process to build a sieve that
  can sort materials at an afterschool activity center.
- Children compare their designs with another group to evaluate and improve the
  design.

Activity Problem

You are an engineer who needs to solve the problem of how to sort the toy balls
and craft materials that are all mixed together. You need to design a sieve that will
separate the mixture into layers when you shake it. How can you best separate the
materials into layers using a variety of screens?

- Describe your problem.
- Choose the material you will use for your sieve, and choose the layers of your sieve
  to make a drawing of your design.
- Test your design to see if it works.
- Compare it to another group and improve your design.

Interaction Summary

- Children will describe the problem and plan a design for their sieves. Then they will
  choose screens to sort the materials, placing them from top to bottom.
- Children will test their design to see how well it sorts the mixture and compare
  their results with other groups before improving and retesting their design.
- Children should be able to describe their problem, evaluate their design and
  another group's design, and improve their design based on their tests.

Assessment

Preassessment

Assessment Guide, Unit Pretest
The Unit Pretest focuses on prerequisite knowledge and is
composed of items that evaluate children's preparedness
for the content covered within this unit.

Formative Assessment

Interactive Worktext, Apply What You Know, Lesson Check,
and Self Check

Summative Assessment

Assessment Guide, Lesson Quiz
The Lesson Quiz provides a quick assessment of each lesson
objective and of the portion of the Performance Expectation
aligned to the lesson.

Interactive Worktext, Performance Task pp. 34–35
The Performance Task presents the opportunity for children
to collaborate with classmates in order to complete the steps
of each Performance Task. Each Performance Task provides a
formal Scoring Rubric for evaluating children's work.

Interactive Worktext, Unit 1 Review, pp. 36–38
Assessment Guide, Unit Test
The Unit Test provides an in-depth assessment of the
Performance Expectations aligned to the unit. This test
evaluates children's ability to apply knowledge in order to
explain phenomena and to solve problems. Within this test,
Constructed Response items apply a three-dimensional rubric
for evaluating children's mastery on all three dimensions of the
Next Generation Science Standards.

 **Assessment Online**   Go online to view the complete
assessment items for this unit.

Teacher Notes

_____

_____

_____

_____

_____

_____

_____

_____

_____

_____

_____

_____

Differentiate Instruction

Leveled Readers

The Science & Engineering Leveled Readers provide additional nonfiction reading practice in this unit's subject area.

On Level • How Do Engineers Solve Problems?
This reader reinforces unit concepts and includes response activities for your children

Extra Support • How Do Engineers Solve Problems?
This reader shares title, illustrations, vocabulary, and concepts with the On-Level Reader; however, the text is linguistically accommodated to provide simplified sentence structures and comprehension aids. It also includes response activities.

Enrichment • Ben's Engineering Project
This high-interest, nonfiction reader will extend and enrich unit concepts and vocabulary and includes response activities.

Teacher Guide
The accompanying Teacher Guide provides teaching strategies and support for using all readers.

ELL

English Language Learner support resources include a glossary and Leveled Readers in Spanish and English. ELL teaching strategies appear throughout this unit:

pp. 4B, 6, 20B, 23

RTI/Extra Support

Strategies for children who need extra support appear throughout this unit:

pp. 3, 4B, 7, 20B, 26

Extension

Strategies for children who have mastered core content and are ready for additional challenges appear throughout this unit:

pp. 3, 4B, 7, 20B, 26

Leveled Readers

All readers are available online as well as in an innovative, engaging format for use with touchscreen mobile devices. Contact your HMH Sales Representative for more information.

Connecting with NGSS

Connections to Community

Use these opportunities for informal science learning to provide local context and to extend and enhance unit concepts.

At Home

What Does It Solve? Have children identify ways to solve a problem at home. Children should identify the problem and solution and explain how the solution solves the problem. Children should make a poster to show the problem and the solution.
Use with Lesson 1 or 2.

In the Community

Guest Speaker Invite an engineer to speak to the class about the field in which they work and how they identify and solve problems. Have children prepare questions for the engineer to answer.
Use with Lesson 1 or 2.

Problem Solvers Identify a problem in your community that is appropriate for children. For example, there might be a street with too much traffic. If reasonable and safe, take children on a field trip to observe the problem; otherwise, provide children with information about the problem. Have children brainstorm possible solutions and identify which solution is likely to be the most successful. You may want to work as a class to draft a letter to community leaders explaining your solution.
Use with Lesson 1 or 2.

Culture

Transportation Explain to children how transportation has changed over time, moving from simple types to more complex ones such as going from horses, to trains, and to cars. Have children research other countries or cultures to see what types of transportation they use and how their modes of transportation have changed over time.
Use with Lesson 1 or 2.

Home Letters
Go online to view the Home Letters for this unit.

Collaboration

Collaboration opportunities in this unit:

Build on Prior Knowledge
pp. 5, 21

Think , Pair, Share
p. 22

Small Groups
p. 16

Cultivating New Questions
pp. 17, 31

Connections to Science

Connections to Science opportunities in this unit:

Connection to Earth and Space Sciences
Stability and Change Lesson 1, p. 15
Connection to Physical Science
Structure and Properties of Matter Lesson 2, p. 23

Unit Project

👥 small groups 🕐 1 class period

Runaway Wagon

Have children work in collaboration with one another to brainstorm design solutions to solve the problem of the runaway wagon. Provide guidance for groups that may have strayed off topic. Be sure to review each group's plans before children begin. This Unit Project supports content in Lessons 1 and 2.

3D Learning Objective

SEP Asking Questions and Defining Problems
Use a design process to define and solve a problem.
Construct an argument using evidence to support a claim.

Skills and Standards Focus

This project supports building children's mastery of **Performance Expectations K-2-ETS1-1, K-2-ETS1-2, and K-2-ETS1-3.**

SEP	Asking Questions and Defining Problems
SEP	Developing and Using Models
SEP	Analyzing and Interpreting Data
DCI	**ETS1.A** Defining and Delimiting Engineering Problems
DCI	**ETS1.B** Developing Possible Solutions
DCI	**ETS1.C** Optimizing the Design Solution
CCC	Structure and Function

Suggested Materials

- wagons or toy wagons
- rope, string, or twine
- blocks and boxes of various sizes
- playground balls
- heavy objects

Preparation

Acquire enough wagons or toy wagons to have one for each pair or group of children. Provide ample space for children to work in. Provide a variety of materials, but encourage children to use other materials they find in the classroom. Before beginning the project, review the steps of an engineering design process.

Unit 1
Engineering Design Process

Unit Project • Runaway Wagon
How can you stop a wagon from rolling away when you let go of its handle? Investigate to find out.

Unit 1 • Engineering Design Process

Differentiate Instruction

RTI/Extra Support Discuss with children that the wagon rolls because of its wheels. Guide children to identify solutions that prevent the wheels from turning.

Extension Challenge children to find a solution that would work when the wagon is facing uphill, downhill, and on a level surface.

Unit 1 Project

Name _____

Unit 1 Project
Runaway Wagon

Have you ever let go of a wagon? Did it roll away? Ask a question and define a problem on the lines below. Then follow a design process to solve the problem.

Children should write a question and problem related
_____

to a wagon rolling away.
_____

_____

Materials

Draw and label the materials you will need.

> Children should draw and label materials. The following are possible materials children can use for this project: a wagon, blocks, bricks, books, rope.

© Houghton Mifflin Harcourt Publishing Company

Unit 1 Project

Runaway Wagon

 **SEP** Asking Questions and Defining Problems . . . .

 **DCI** Defining and Delimiting Engineering Problems. . . . .

Pose the unit project question to children. **Ask: What is the first step in a design process?** Define a problem. Have children pose a question and define a problem with the wagon. Discuss all ideas as a class. Refer children to Lesson 1 Engineer It • What Is a Design Process?

In the sample investigation shown, children follow a design process to solve the problem of a wagon rolling away.

ESSENTIAL QUESTIONS Prepare children for their project by asking the following questions.

- What is a design process?
- What are the steps of a design process?
- What evidence can you observe to show that a solution is effective?

Ask: What is an engineer? Why is it important for an engineer to follow a design process? An engineer designs solutions. It is important for an engineer to follow a design process so that the problem is clearly defined and the solution fixes the problem.

Plan and Build

Provide children with a variety of materials. You may choose to provide toy wagons for children to use as models. If wagons aren't available, toy cars can be used to simulate the wagon since they have wheels.

(ccc) Structure and Function . . . .

Ask: What causes the wagon to roll away? the wheels **How does each design solution solve this problem?** Sample answer: My first solution uses rope to tie the handle to something that won't move. My second solution blocks the wheels. Both solutions keep the wagon from rolling away. **Which properties of the materials you chose helped to solve this problem?** Sample answer: The rope is strong and flexible so I can tie it. The boxes are solid and will not roll away so they can block the wheels.

Test and Improve

Have children predict which solution will work better. Observe children as they test their solutions and assist as needed. Remind children to record the results of each test. Have children discuss their data in order to write about improvements needed. Remind children to compare their solutions in order to determine which one worked best.

(SEP) Developing and Using Models . . . .

Ask: Why is it important to test each of your solutions? Sample answer: So I can make sure each works and to record data that will help me compare strengths and weaknesses. **What will you do after you test the solutions?** I will try to improve them.

(ccc) Structure and Function . . . .

Encourage children to think about the structure of the materials they chose as they improve their solutions.

Ask: Which materials can you use to make your solution work better? Explain why it would improve your solution. Sample answer: I can use a thicker rope. It will work better because it is stronger and won't break.

Plan and Build Draw and label at least two design solutions for the problem. Build your solutions.

> Drawings may vary but should show two possible solutions with labels.

Test and Improve

Test each solution. Record your results. Use your data to improve at least one of your solutions. Write about your improvements.

Answers may vary but should reflect observations made about

the solutions.

Unit 1 Project • Page 2 of 3

3K Unit 1 • Engineering Design Process

© Houghton Mifflin Harcourt Publishing Company

Redesign Choose one solution and redesign it.
Draw a model of your redesigned solution.

> Drawings may vary but should show a drawing of the children's redesigned solution.

Communicate
Explain how your solution solves the problem.

Answers may vary but should describe how the children's solution

solves the problem.

Claims, Evidence, and Reasoning
Make a claim that answers your question.

Answers should reflect children's solutions for how to stop a wagon

from rolling away.

Review your design process. What evidence from the investigation supports your claim?

Answer should cite evidence from children's proposed solutions.

Discuss your reasoning with a partner.

© Houghton Mifflin Harcourt Publishing Company

Redesign

DCI Developing Possible Solutions . . . .

Have children analyze the results of their tests. **Ask: Which solution worked better? Can you improve either one by redesigning it?** Answers will vary. Refer children to Lesson 2 Engineer It • How Can We Compare Design Solutions? if they need help with this step.

Communicate

DCI Optimizing the Design Solution . . . .

Have children share their solutions with the class. Discuss the strengths and weaknesses of each solution. **Ask: Which solution do you think will work best? Why?** Answers will vary.

Claims, Evidence, and Reasoning

Children should describe how they can solve the problem of the wagon rolling away and cite evidence, including how the design stops the wagon from rolling away.

SEP Analyzing and Interpreting Data. . . . .

Review with children what it means to make a claim. Guide them to understand that their data will be used as evidence to support their claim. **Ask: What can you use as evidence?** the data collected, such as the drawings and writings. **Ask: What claim can you make?** The rope stopped the wagon from rolling away. **How does your evidence support your claim?** When the wagon was tied to the door, it did not roll away.

Scoring Rubric for Unit Project	
3	Plans and builds a solution for the wagon rolling away, and provides evidence to support the solution
2	Plans and builds a solution for the wagon rolling away, and provides some evidence to support the solution
1	Plans and builds a solution for the wagon rolling away, but does not provide evidence to support the solution
0	Does not plan or build a solution

Lesson 1 · Engineer It • What Is a Design Process?

Building to the Performance Expectations

The learning experiences in this lesson prepare children for mastery of:

K-2-ETS1-1 Ask questions, make observations, and gather information about a situation people want to change to define a simple problem that can be solved through the development of a new or improved object or tool.

K-2-ETS1-2 Develop a simple sketch, drawing, or physical model to illustrate how the shape of an object helps it function as needed to solve a given problem.

 Trace Tool to the NGSS
Go online to view the complete coverage of these standards across the lesson, unit, and time.

 **Science & Engineering Practices**

Asking Questions and Defining Problems
- Ask questions…to find more information…designed world(s).
- Define a simple problem…of a new or improved object or tool.

 VIDEO SEP: Asking Questions and Defining Problems

Developing and Using Models
Develop a simple model…

 VIDEO SEP: Developing and Using Models

DCI Disciplinary Core Ideas

ETS1.A: Defining and Delimiting Engineering Problems
- A situation that people want to change or create can be approached as a problem to be solved through engineering.
- Asking questions, making observations, and gathering information are helpful in thinking about problems.
- Before beginning to design a solution, it is important to clearly understand the problem.

ETS1.B: Developing Possible Solutions
- Designs can be conveyed through sketches, drawings, or physical models. These representations are useful in communicating ideas for a problem's solution to other people.

 CCC Crosscutting Concepts

Structure and Function
The shape and stability of structures of natural and designed objects are related to their function(s).

 VIDEO CCC: Structure and Function

CONNECTIONS TO MATH

MP.2 Reason abstractly and quantitatively.

MP.4 Model with mathematics.

MP.5 Use appropriate tools strategically.

2.MD.D.10 Draw a…bar graph…up to four categories. Solve simple…problems…

CONNECTIONS TO ENGLISH LANGUAGE ARTS

RI.2.1 Ask and answer such questions as…understanding of key details in a text.

W.2.6 With guidance…use a variety of digital tools…in collaboration with peers.

SL.2.5 Create…add drawings or other visual displays…to clarify ideas…feelings.

Supporting All Students, All Standards

Integrating the Three Dimensions of Learning

This lesson focuses on how to define and solve a problem. The lesson begins with children exploring how engineers use five steps of a design process to solve problems. Children will use prior knowledge to ask questions, make observations, and gather information **(DCI Defining and Delimiting Engineering Problems)** **(SEP Asking Questions and Defining Problems)**. The lesson continues with children solving a real-life problem using drawings and models **(DCI Developing Possible Solutions)** **(SEP Developing and Using Models)**. Children will explore how to improve upon their designs and how the structure of their design is related to its purpose **(CCC Structure and Function)**. Finally, children will communicate their results.

Professional Development

Go online to view **Professional Development videos** with strategies to integrate CCCs and SEPs, including the ones used in this lesson.

Build on Prior Knowledge

Children should already know and be prepared to build on the following concepts:
- Problems can be solved through asking questions, analyzing information, and using models. *(Grade 1, Unit 1, Lesson 2)*
- Engineers build things to find solutions to problems. *(Grade 1, Unit 1, Lesson 1)*
- Technology is used to help solve problems. *(Grade 1, Unit 1, Lesson 1)*
- An object's structure is related to how it functions. *(Grade 1, Unit 1, Lesson 1)*

Differentiate Instruction

Lesson Vocabulary
- engineer
- design process
- solution

Reinforcing Vocabulary To help children remember each vocabulary word, have them draw an illustration of each word. Then have them write the word beneath the illustration, define it, and use it in a sentence. Remind children to look for these highlighted words as they proceed through the lesson.

RTI/Extra Support Supply children with flash cards that identify each step of a design process. Have children place the steps in order. Next, provide children with illustrations that align with the steps of a design process. Ask children to connect the correct step with each illustration.

Extension Challenge children to apply a design process to a problem in their own lives. Children should choose a problem that can reasonably be solved using materials that are available in the classroom. Have them make a poster or slide show to communicate their results.

ELL Be sure to point out all labels, pictures, captions, and headings throughout the lesson to assist children with strategies to summarize chunks of content. Discuss with children real-life connections to content, and provide hands-on examples of materials when possible to best support the needs of these learners.

Lesson Problem

Lesson Objective

Ask questions, make observations, and gather information to define a problem to be solved through a design process.

About This Image

Ask: What do you think is happening in this picture? Sample answer: There are robots competing or playing a game. How do you think these robots were built? Sample answer: Children drew pictures of what they wanted the robots to look like and then got materials together to build them. As you explore, you will find out how a design process can be used to solve many problems.

 Defining and Delimiting Engineering Problems

Alternative Engage Strategy

How Was It Made?	👥 pairs ⏱ 15–25 minutes

Hold up a stapler. **Ask: What is this? What problem does it solve? How does it work? Why is it shaped this way? What types of things were used to make it?**

Allow children to brainstorm answers. Record these ideas for the class to see. Then have children work in pairs to choose any object in the classroom and brainstorm what the object is and how its design helps solve a problem. Allow each pair to present their object to the class.

Lesson 1 **Engineer It • What Is a Design Process?**

Children used a design process to put together these robots.

By the End of This Lesson

I will use the steps of a design process to define and solve a problem.

4

Ramps

Look at the pictures to explore how people use ramps.

A ramp is a flat surface with one end higher than the other. People use ramps to solve problems.

Can You Solve It?

 How can a ramp solve a problem?

Accept all reasonable answers.

_____

_____

_____

Can You Solve It?

Ramps Ramps can be used to solve problems. The videos show some different ramps and how they are used. If the videos are not available, have children discuss how the ramps are being used in the pictures.

Ask children to record their initial thoughts about how a ramp can solve a problem. At the end of this lesson, children will revisit this question in the Lesson Check. At that point, children should be able to explain how ramps can help us move objects up and down.

Collaboration

Build on Prior Knowledge You may want children to view and discuss the videos or pictures as a whole-class activity. This will allow you to assess their prior knowledge about ramps and how they are used. Have children think about what they saw in the videos or in the pictures. Then have them discuss how ramps are used. They should use details from the videos or pictures, along with evidence, to support their answer.

Support for Unit Project and Performance Task

The **Unit Project** Runaway Wagon and **Unit Performance Task** Engineer It • Build a Water Bottle Holder supports content in this lesson.

What Engineers Do

3D Learning Objective

Children will explore **how an engineer defines a problem and solves it** by using steps in a design process.

DCI **Defining and Delimiting Engineering Problems** . . . .

Ask: What do engineers do? Engineers use a design process to solve many kinds of problems. **How does a design process help engineers?** A design process helps engineers to define a problem and test solutions. **How do you think a design process would help you?** It would help me find a solution to a problem. **Why is it important to understand a problem before designing a solution?** It is important to understand the problem so the most appropriate solution can be designed.

SEP **Asking Questions and Defining Problems** . . . .

Ask: Engineers ask questions and make observations when they encounter a problem. Why do engineers do this ? Engineers ask questions and make observations to help them better understand the problem.

Differentiate Instruction

ELL Children may be unfamiliar with the words *design* and *process*. Explain that a design is a drawing of an object and a process is a way of doing something. Then introduce the phrase *design process*. In pairs, have children discuss what they think it means. Have each pair write and draw to show their understanding of what a design process is.

What Engineers Do

Explore the steps of a design process that an engineer follows.

Explore online. ▶

1. Define a Problem
2. Plan and Build
3. Test and Improve
4. Redesign
5. Communicate

An **engineer** uses math and science to define and solve problems, such as how to get to the top of a tall building or how to cross a river. Engineers may solve different problems, but they always use a similar set of steps, called a design process. A **design process** helps engineers define a problem and plan, test, and share a solution with others. A **solution** is an answer to a problem.

✏️ **What does an engineer do?**

Sample answer: An engineer uses math and science

to define and solve problems.

6

Step 1–Define a Problem

Look at the picture to explore how to define a problem.

Explore online. ▶

Emma observes her dad trying to put a box into his car. The box is too heavy for him to lift. Emma thinks this is a problem that needs a solution. She has defined a problem, which is the first step of a design process.

✏️ **What is the first step of a design process?**

Sample answer: The first step of a design process

is to define a problem that needs a solution.

 Apply What You Know

Evidence Notebook • Work with a partner to define a problem within your classroom. Record it in your Evidence Notebook.

💡 **Asking Questions and Defining Problems** Go to the online handbook for tips.

Lesson 1 • Engineer It • What Is a Design Process? 7

© Houghton Mifflin Harcourt

Step 1—Define a Problem

3D Learning Objective

Children explore how to **observe a situation** in order to define a problem.

 Defining and Delimiting Engineering Problems. . . . .

Ask: What is the problem? Emma's dad cannot lift a heavy box into his car. **Why is it important for Emma to observe?** Observing helps Emma understand the problem better.

Differentiate Instruction

RTI/Extra Support Discuss what defines a problem. Then have children give examples of problems.

Extension Ask children what kinds of problems they have solved at home. Discuss the types of problems and how they discovered them.

✋ **FORMATIVE ASSESSMENT**

Evidence Notebook
Children define a problem in the classroom. Make sure children use evidence to support the problem they observe.

Scoring Guidelines
- describes a reasonable problem within the classroom
- makes connections to personal experiences
- provides evidence to support why the situation is a problem

💡 **Asking Questions and Defining Problems** Have children describe the problem. Then have them tell how something new or better can solve the problem.

Step 2—Plan and Build

3D Learning Objective

Children explore **how drawings and models** help when planning and building solutions. Children observe how **a model is based on a proposed object** and how **the structure of its design is based on its function**.

 **Structure and Function** . . . .

Ask children to look at Emma's model in the picture. **Ask: Why do you think Emma built a model from paper? How will that help Emma with her plan?** Although Emma's father will not use paper as a ramp, it allows Emma's father to see how using a ramp can help solve the problem of putting the heavy box into the car.

DCI Developing Possible Solutions . . . .

SEP Developing and Using Models . . . .

Ask: Why is it important to make drawings or models? Drawings or models can help you see if your solution solves the problem.

 FORMATIVE ASSESSMENT

Evidence Notebook

Have children work through the second step of a design process. Make sure they use evidence to support their plan to solve the problem.

Scoring Guidelines

• identifies the second step of a design process
• plans and builds a solution to a classroom problem
• provides evidence to support the answer

💡 **Developing and Using Models** A model is something that you draw or build. A model can show what a tool or object looks like.

Step 2–Plan and Build

Explore online. ▶

Look at the picture to explore how to plan and build a design solution.

How does Emma help her dad with the problem with the box? She knows a ramp can help move objects. Emma makes a plan. She draws a model to show how the ramp will work. Then she builds her model using paper. Emma has done the second step of a design process—plan and build.

✏️ **What takes place in Step 2 of a design process?**

Sample answer: The second step of a design process is to plan and

build a solution.

 Apply What You Know

Evidence Notebook • Think back to the classroom problem you defined. Work with a small group to plan and build a solution. Record your plan in your Evidence Notebook.

💡 **Developing and Using Models** Go to the online handbook for tips.

© Houghton Mifflin Harcourt

8

Hands-On Activity 🔍

Engineer It • Build a Better Lunchbox

Name _____

Materials _____

_____

Ask a Question

Sample answer: How can we build a better lunchbox? _____

Test and Record Data Explore online. ▶

Step 1 Define a Problem

What is wrong with the lunchbox? Which materials could help you solve the problem? Record your observations.

Lunchbox	Materials
Observations will vary. Check children's work.	

Step 2 Plan

Plan a solution. Draw and add labels.

Drawings may vary but should show a possible solution with labels.

Lesson 1 • Engineer It • What Is a Design Process?   9

© Houghton Mifflin Harcourt

Hands-On Activity 👥 small groups ⏱ 1 class period

Engineer It • Build a Better Lunchbox

3D Learning Objective

SEP **Asking Questions and Defining Problems** . . . .

Children observe and gather information in order to plan and build a solution to designing a better lunchbox. As children are new to the design process, this activity has been stepped out to cover the first two steps in order to provide them with a deeper understanding. The remaining three steps can be found on the first page of the Take It Further section, where children can complete the design process of building a better lunchbox. You may wish to do this activity separately or save it and do it in conjunction with the Take It Further section.

Suggested Materials a lunchbox, water bottle, aluminum foil, waxed paper, paper towels, cotton batting

Preparation
Pre-assemble materials bundles for small groups.

Activity
As a class, view the video. Then, discuss the question that will need to be answered. Have children record the question.

DCI **Defining and Delimiting Engineering Problems** . . . .

STEP 1 Discuss the picture, and have children identify the problem with the lunchbox. Have them ask questions about how they can make the lunchbox better.

DCI **Developing Possible Solutions** . . . .

STEP 2 Be sure children clearly understand the problem before they begin designing their solutions. Monitor children as they draw their plans. Guide them to include labels in their design.

Hands-On Activity, continued

SEP **Developing and Using Models** . . . .

STEP 3 Allow children time to build their solution using the suggested materials. Monitor children as they are building their models and offer guidance as needed.

STEP 4 **Ask:** How were your designs different? How were they the same? Did they both solve the problem? Answers will vary.

Claims, Evidence, and Reasoning

Children should write a claim that describes how they can build a better lunchbox. They should cite evidence to support their claim about an improved lunchbox design, including how the changes make the lunchbox better.
Ask: Is there only way one to solve a problem? Explain.
Sample answer: No, there are many ways to solve a problem. Each group came up with a different solution to the lunchbox problem.

Scoring Rubric for Hands-On Activity	
3	States a claim supported with evidence about how to build a better lunchbox
2	States a claim somewhat supported with evidence about how to build a better lunchbox
1	States a claim that is not supported by evidence
0	Does not state a claim and does not provide evidence

Step 3 Build

Follow your plan. Use your materials.
Build your solution.

Step 4

Share your solution with a partner. Compare your design solutions. How does each one solve the problem? Record your ideas.

Your Solution	Both	Your Partner's Solution
Answers will vary.	Check children's work.	

Make a claim that answers your question.

Answers should reflect children's solutions for how they can

build a better lunchbox.

What is your evidence?

Answers should cite evidence from children's proposed solutions.

10

Step 3—Test and Improve

Step 3–Test and Improve

Look at the pictures to explore how to test and improve a design solution.

Explore online. ▶

Will Emma be able to solve the problem? She tests her ramp to see if the block gets in the truck. The ramp is not strong or stable enough to support it. How can Emma improve it? She uses more stable materials to rebuild. She has done the third step of a design process—test and improve.

✏️ **What is the next step after plan and build?**

test and improve _____.

🖐️ **Apply What You Know**

Evidence Notebook • Test and improve your solution to the classroom problem. Use your observations as evidence and record them in your Evidence Notebook.

© Houghton Mifflin Harcourt

3D Learning Objective

Children explore **how to test and improve upon models in order to see if their solution is viable.** Children use their observations to identify **the strength and stability of materials used.**

 Defining and Delimiting Engineering Problems. . . . .

Ask: What is the next step after plan and build? The next step is test and Improve. **Why is it important to test a solution?** It is important to test a solution to see how well it works. **Why is it important to improve a solution?** It is important to improve a solution to make it work better.

 Structure and Function. . . . .

Discuss Emma's model in the picture. **Ask: How can Emma make the ramp stronger and more stable?** She can use cardboard instead of paper.

 FORMATIVE ASSESSMENT

Evidence Notebook
Children review the information in their Evidence Notebook about the classroom problem they defined earlier. Allow children to work with a partner to complete Step 3 of a design process. Monitor children, and provide support as needed. Have children use their observations of their tests as evidence.

Scoring Guidelines
- tests and improves the solution to the classroom problem
- uses observations as evidence and records it in their Evidence Notebook

Step 4—Redesign

3D Learning Objective

Children explore how **redesigning a model** can make for a better solution to a problem.

DCI Developing Possible Solutions. . . . .

Ask: What happens during Step 4 of a design process? A model gets redesigned to fix any problems. Then the new design is tested to see how it works.

SEP Developing and Using Models. . . . .

Remind children that redesigning is an important part of a design process. **Ask:** What if Emma's redesign still does not fix the problem? What should she do? Emma should try to redesign her solution until she finds one that works.

CCC Structure and Function . . . .

Ask: Emma figured out that cardboard was a better material to use for a ramp. How does this help solve her father's problem? She can explain to her father that using a ramp made of stronger material would hold the heavy box better than a ramp made of lighter material.

 FORMATIVE ASSESSMENT

Evidence Notebook
Children review their information about the classroom problem identified earlier. Monitor children and provide support as needed. Guide children to use evidence to support their claims.

Scoring Guidelines
• explains the effectiveness of the solution to the problem
• describes a redesign for the solution
• provides evidence to support their claims

Step 4–Redesign

Look at the picture to explore how to redesign a solution.

Explore online. ▶

Emma improves her ramp by redesigning it. She uses cardboard, which is stronger and more stable. She tests the new ramp. It works on the first try! Sometimes engineers must redesign a solution more than once until it works. Emma has done the fourth step of a design process.

 What happens during Step 4 of a design process?

Sample answer: Old models are changed to make them better.

Improved or new designs are tested to see how they work.

 Apply What You Know

Evidence Notebook • Did your solution work? Can you improve it? Redesign your solution. Use your observations as evidence and record them in your Evidence Notebook.

12

© Houghton Mifflin Harcourt

Step 5—Communicate

Look at the picture to explore how to communicate about a design solution.

Explore online. ▶

Emma found a design that works. How does Emma communicate, or share, what she did with others? First, she photographs the ramp. Then, she describes the ramp, the materials she used, and how she designed it. Emma has completed the last step of a design process.

✏️ **What are some ways to communicate the results of a design process?**

Sample answer: writing, drawing, and taking photographs

✋ Apply What You Know

Evidence Notebook • Communicate your results. Write a summary of how you solved a problem in your classroom by following a design process. Use evidence to support your summary. Compare your solutions with your classmates'.

Step 5—Communicate

3D Learning Objective

Children explore the importance of **communicating their design solutions to others**.

DCI **Developing Possible Solutions. . . . .**

Ask: What happens during Step 5 of a design process? You communicate the results of a design process by writing, drawing, taking photographs, or recording a video. **Why is it important to communicate your solutions to others?** By sharing your solutions, you can help others that are trying to solve similar problems. Also, people can use your design ideas to inspire solutions to different problems. **What can Emma do when she encounters another problem?** She can use a design process to help her solve her new problem.

✋ FORMATIVE ASSESSMENT

Evidence Notebook
Children work with their partners to communicate the results of the designs they made to solve a classroom problem. Guide children to include a summary of how they used all five steps of a design process. Remind children to use evidence to support the information in the summary. Have children compare their solutions with their classmates.

Scoring Guidelines
• effectively communicates how a design process was followed to solve a classroom problem
• provides evidence to support the claim about the solution
• compares solutions with their classmates

Take It Further

Engineer It • Make Your Lunchbox Better

The steps in this activity are continued from the Hands-On Activity as another path in the Take It Further.

3D Learning Objective

Children explore how to **test and improve, redesign, and then communicate the results of a model used to solve a problem.** Children observe how the materials chosen relate to how well the design works.

SEP **Developing and Using Models** . . . .

STEP 1 Have children test their designs. **Ask:** How well does your lunchbox design work? How can you improve the design? Children should include specific details regarding how their designs can be improved.

STEP 2 **Ask:** How could you redesign your solution so that it works better? Children should explain the changes they made to their plan in order to fix any problems with their designs.

CCC **Structure and Function** . . . .

Discuss the structure of children's lunchbox designs. **Ask:** How does the structure of the lunchbox you designed relate to how well it works? Children should include an explanation of how the materials used helped make the lunchbox work better.

Do the Math! • Make a Bar Graph

STEP 3 **Ask:** What material was used most in this class to redesign the lunchbox? Check children's graphs.

Ask: Why did some materials work better than others? Children should explain that some materials work better than others based on how and what they are being used for.

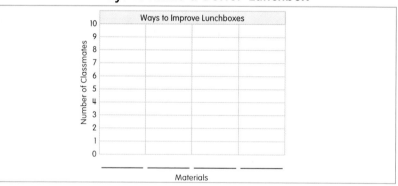

Take It Further
Engineer It • Make Your Lunchbox Better   **Explore online.** ▶

Step ① **Test and Improve**
Test your solution. Record the results. Identify ways to improve your design.

Results will vary. Check children's work.

_____

_____

Step ② **Redesign**
Define a different way to solve the problem. How does its structure relate to its function?

Step ③ **Communicate**
Do the Math! • Complete a bar graph to show the materials that you and your classmates used.

Ways to Make a Better Lunchbox

Ways to Improve Lunchboxes

Number of Classmates

10
9
8
7
6
5
4
3
2
1
0

Materials

© Houghton Mifflin Harcourt

14

Take It Further

Careers in Science & Engineering •
Mechanical Engineer

Explore more online.
• Engineer It • Make Your Lunchbox Better

Mechanical engineers invent machines and make them work better. They use a design process to do their jobs.

Explore online. ▶

Some mechanical engineers look for ways to improve machines so they are easier to use.

One engineer uses a computer to plan and build a model. Another engineer tests the model to see how it works.

Lesson 1 • Engineer It • What Is a Design Process?   15

Take It Further

Careers in Science & Engineering •
Mechanical Engineer

Children investigate how mechanical engineers use a design process to invent machines and make them work better.

DCI Defining and Delimiting Engineering Problems. . . . .

SEP Asking Questions and Defining Problems . . . .

Ask: What problem is the engineer in the second picture trying to solve? how to improve machines so they are easier to use

SEP Developing and Using Models . . . .

Ask: Which step of a design process is the engineer in the third picture performing? He is performing Step 3, Test and Improve. What do engineers do after they test and improve a solution to a problem? They redesign their solution.

Connection to Earth and Space Sciences

Stability and Change Changes to Earth's surface can be slow or rapid. Erosion is a slow change, while a flood is a quick change. Discuss with children that a water engineer works with flood prevention, among other water-related projects. Explain that this job is important in keeping people and communities safe from flooding. They may plan and build dams and drains. They may design ways to prevent river bank or beach erosion. Have children work in small groups to discuss ways a water engineer could help their area.

Take It Further, continued

Read, Write, Share! • Ask and Answer Questions • Collaborate to Use Digital Tools • Use Visuals

Children will do research to find out more about mechanical engineers. Encourage them to ask questions that begin with *who*, *what*, *where*, *when*, *why*, and *how*.

Collaboration

Small Groups Have children work in small groups to research mechanical engineers. Encourage group members to brainstorm and discuss questions. Have each group member research the answer to a particular question, and then have that group member share his or her findings.

Ask and Answer Questions • Collaborate to Use Digital Tools • Use Visuals Remind children that text and graphic features can help when asking and answering questions. Encourage children to work with others to write and publish their findings. They should add drawings or other visuals, such as charts or videos, to help clarify ideas.

Explore more online. ▶

Engineer It • Make Your Lunchbox Better

Children use the last three steps of the design process to improve the design of a lunchbox.

Read, Write, Share!

Find out more about mechanical engineers.

Ask questions, such as:

- What do they do?
- Where do they work?
- How do they work?

Do research to answer your questions.

Ask and Answer Questions • Collaborate to Use Digital Tools • Use Visuals
Go to the online handbook for tips.

✏️▷ Draw or write to record your answers.

Check children's work.

_____

_____

© Houghton Mifflin Harcourt • Image Credits: (t) ©Susana Gonzalez/Bloomberg Video RR/Getty Images

16

Explore online. ▶   Have children explore online to find out more about how ramps are used.

Lesson Check

Lesson Check   Name _____

Explore online. ▶

Can You Solve It?

✏️ How can a ramp solve a problem?

Be sure to

• Explain how a ramp helps move objects.

• Describe the steps of a design process.

Sample answer: A ramp can help solve the problem of how

to move people and objects up and down. The first step of a

design process is to define a problem. Next, you plan and build

a model. Then, you test, improve, and redesign the model. Last,

you communicate what you did.

Lesson 1 • Engineer It • What Is a Design Process?   17

Lesson Check

Can You Solve It?

Have children reread their answer to the Can You Solve It? prompt at the beginning of the lesson.

DCI **Defining and Delimiting Engineering Problems** . . . .

If children have difficulty responding to the question, have them carefully observe the pictures and think about how the different ramps are used to solve a problem. **Ask: How are the ramps alike?** They all help move people or objects up and down.

CCC **Structure and Function** . . . .

Ask: Why is the material the ramp is made of important to its purpose? It is important because a ramp will need to be hard and sturdy in order to move objects up and down.

Scoring Guidelines

• Children should explain how a ramp helps move objects.
• Children should describe the steps of a design process.

Collaboration

Cultivating New Questions As children complete this lesson and prepare for the next lesson, ask them to identify additional questions they have about what engineers do and the steps of the design process. **Ask: What are some other types of engineers? How do they apply the design process?** A robot engineer uses the steps of the design process to plan and build robots. As children continue to the next lesson, they will apply concepts related to the design process.

Lesson Check, continued

SUMMATIVE ASSESSMENT
Self Check

1. Children should choose B—The old plan is redesigned; and C—New redesigns are tested. If children choose A, discuss what it means if a design does not work. Discuss how redesigning the model or making a new model can improve it.

2. Children should state the following: It is important to test a design to see if it works as intended to solve the problem. If it does not work as intended or if it could work better, you improve the design. For children who answer incorrectly, refer them back to the section titled Step 3—Test and Improve.

Self Check
1. What happens during a design process when a tested design does not work? Choose all correct answers.

Ⓐ A design process ends.

🅑 The old plan is redesigned.

🅒 New redesigns are tested.

2. Why is it important to test and improve a design?

It is important to test a design to see if it works as intended to

solve the problem. If it does not work as intended or if it could

work better, you improve the design.

© Houghton Mifflin Harcourt

18

3. Which step of a design
   process is the girl doing?

   Ⓐ Define a Problem
   🅑 Plan and Build
   Ⓒ Test and Improve

4. Sam makes a ramp. He puts toy cars on it, but the
   ramp does not work well. What is Sam's next step?
   Ⓐ Plan and Build
   Ⓑ Test and Improve
   🅒 Redesign

5. Which step of a design
   process are the children
   doing?

   Ⓐ Define a Problem
   Ⓑ Plan and Build
   🅒 Test and Improve

3. Children should choose B—Plan and Build. If children choose
   A—Define a Problem, guide them to see that the girl has
   already defined a problem. She has a plan in her hand and
   appears to be building her model. If children choose C—Test
   and Improve, remind them that the test and improve step
   would involve testing a completed model. The model does not
   appear to be finished in this picture.

4. Children should choose C—Redesign. If children choose A—
   Plan and Build, remind them that Sam has defined his problem
   and built a ramp, but the ramp does not work well. The next
   step would be to redesign his ramp that is not working well. If
   children choose B—Test and Improve, remind them that Sam
   has already completed that step since he put toy cars on the
   ramp and found that it does not work well.

5. Children should choose C—Test and Improve. If children
   choose A—Define a Problem, remind them that these children
   have already defined a problem: they are trying to drop an
   egg without breaking it. If children choose B—Plan and Build,
   remind them that the children already have a model, which is
   what the boy is dropping in the picture.

Lesson 2 • Engineer It • How Can We Compare Design Solutions?

Building to the Performance Expectation

The learning experiences in this lesson prepare children for mastery of:

K-2-ETS1-3 Analyze data from tests of two objects designed to solve the same problem to compare the strengths and weaknesses of how each performs.

Trace Tool to the NGSS
Go online to view the complete coverage of these standards across this lesson, unit, and time.

 SEP ### Science & Engineering Practices

Analyzing and Interpreting Data
Analyze data from tests of an object or tool to determine if it works as intended.

 VIDEO SEPs: Analyzing and Interpreting Data/Using Mathematics and Computational Thinking

 DCI ### Disciplinary Core Ideas

ETS1.A: Defining and Delimiting Engineering Problems
- A situation that people want to change or create…solved through engineering.
- Asking questions, making observations…helpful in thinking about problems.
- Before beginning to design a solution…clearly understand the problem.

ETS1.B: Developing Possible Solutions
Designs can be conveyed through sketches, drawings, or physical models. These representations are useful in communicating ideas…to other people.

ETS1.C: Optimizing the Design Solution
Because there is always more than one possible solution to a problem, it is useful to compare and test designs.

 **CCC** ### Crosscutting Concepts

Structure and Function
The shape and stability of structures of natural and designed objects are related to their function(s).

▶ **VIDEO** CCC: Structure and Function

CONNECTIONS TO MATH

MP.2 Reason abstractly and quantitatively.

MP.4 Model with mathematics.

MP.5 Use appropriate tools strategically.

2.MD.D.10 Draw a picture graph and a bar graph (with single-unit scale) to represent a data set with up to four categories. Solve simple put-together, take-apart, and compare problems using information presented in a bar graph.

CONNECTIONS TO ENGLISH LANGUAGE ARTS

W.2.6 With guidance and support from adults, use a variety of digital tools to produce and publish writing, including in collaboration with peers.

W.2.8 Recall information from experiences or gather information from provided sources to answer a question.

Supporting All Students, All Standards

Integrating the Three Dimensions of Learning

This lesson focuses on comparing solutions to a problem. Children first analyze the strengths and weaknesses of a design (**SEP Analyzing and Interpreting Data**) for a stop sign. The engineering process is then modeled as a child identifies the straps on his backpack as a problem and builds, tests, and evaluates four solutions (**DCI Developing Possible Solutions, DCI Optimizing the Design Solution**) using materials with different characteristics (**CCC Structure and Function**). Then, children build and test designs for bridges and towers (**DCI Developing Possible Solutions, DCI Optimizing the Design Solution**), analyzing and comparing solutions (**SEP Analyzing and Interpreting Data**), relating the shape and stability of their structures to their functions (**CCC Structure and Function**), and using prior knowledge to improve their designs (**SEP Analyzing and Interpreting Data**).

 Professional Development Go online to view **Professional Development videos** with strategies to integrate CCCs and SEPs, including the ones used in this lesson.

Build on Prior Knowledge

Children should already know and be prepared to build on the following concepts:

- Data can be analyzed to see if a model works as intended. *(Grade 2, Unit 1, Lesson 1)*
- Engineers use math and science to solve problems. *(Grade 2, Unit 1, Lesson 1)*
- A design process is a set of steps that engineers follow to solve problems. *(Grade 2, Unit 1, Lesson 1)*
- A problem can have more than one solution. *(Grade 2, Unit 1, Lesson 1)*
- The structure of an object effects how the object can be used. *(Grade 2, Unit 1, Lesson 1)*

Differentiate Instruction

Lesson Vocabulary
- strengths
- weaknesses

Reinforcing Vocabulary Children may be familiar with the words *strength* and *weakness*, but not in regards to engineering and design. Discuss how these words are used in everyday language. Then model the process of identifying strengths and weaknesses in designs for children, and remind them to look for both strengths and weaknesses in their own designs. Discuss various designs in the classroom, and how they may have both strengths and weaknesses.

RTI/Extra Support Place children into small groups. Present a problem and two solutions. Have children discuss both solutions in their group. They should compare the two solutions and explain which solution best solves the problem.

Extension Have children define a problem in the classroom, such as untidy books in the class library or congestion in the coat closet. Have them work in pairs to design and test solutions to the problem. Children should identify weaknesses and strengths in their solutions in order to decide on the best design.

ELL Make use of labeled diagrams to clarify content in this lesson. This will reinforce the core idea that drawings and models are useful to convey designs and will also help children understand the content and develop vocabulary in context.

Lesson Problem

Build on Prior Lessons

In Lesson 1, children explored **how engineers use the design process to plan and build solutions to problems.** Lesson 2 builds on these concepts to explore the importance of **comparing and analyzing multiple solutions to a problem.**

Lesson Objective

Analyze and compare multiple design solutions.

About This Image

Ask: How is this bridge different from other bridges you have seen? It is very long, and it has cables. How is it the same as other bridges? It helps people get from one side to the other. Do you think the design is better or worse than bridges you have seen? Why? Accept all reasonable answers.

Encourage children to see that the problem of getting from one side of a body of water to another can be solved in different ways.

 **Analyzing and Interpreting Data**

Alternative Engage Strategy

| **So Many Shoes** | small groups |
| | 10–15 minutes |

Ask: What problem do shoes help us solve? Shoes help us keep our feet clean and safe. Show children a variety of shoes, for example, a sandal, a sneaker, a rain boot, a work boot, and a dress shoe. Point out that all of the shoes help to solve this problem in a different way. Have children work in small groups for about 5 minutes to compare and contrast two of the shoes. Then, for another 5 to 10 minutes, discuss some of the differences children determined as a class. Encourage children to see that these very different shoe designs all solve the same problem.

Lesson 2 **Engineer It • How Can We Compare Design Solutions?**

Different solutions can solve the same problem.

By the End of This Lesson

I will be able to compare the strengths and weaknesses of different design solutions.

20

© Houghton Mifflin Harcourt • Image Credits: ©Sean Pavone/iStock/Getty Images Plus/Getty Images

How We Use a Design Process Every Day

Look at the picture to explore the stop sign design.

Explore online. ▶

The stop sign is made of strong metal, but its solid design twists in the wind. What are the weaknesses in its design? What changes to its structure could make the stop sign design stronger?

Can You Solve It?

▭▭▷ Identify strengths and weaknesses in the stop sign's design. What are two ways to make it better?

Accept all reasonable answers.

_____

Can You Solve It?

How We Use a Design Process Every Day Design processes have been used to help make many of the objects we use every day, such as traffic lights and stop signs. The video shows how a stop sign is falling over in the wind. If the video is not available, have children look at the picture.

Ask children to record their initial thoughts about the strengths and the weaknesses of the stop sign's design and to suggest how the design could be improved. At the end of this lesson, children will revisit this question in the Lesson Check. At this point, children should be able to identify strengths and weaknesses in the design as well as ways to make it better.

Collaboration

Build on Prior Knowledge You may want children to view and discuss the video or picture as a whole-class activity. In this way, you can assess their prior knowledge about strengths and weaknesses of designs.

Have children think about what they saw in the video or picture. Then have them work with a classmate to fold a piece of paper in half and list the strengths they identified in the stop sign on one half of the paper and the weaknesses they identified on the other half. They should use details from the video or picture to support the information in their lists.

Support for Unit Project and Performance Task

The **Unit Project** Runaway Wagon and **Unit Performance Task** Engineer It • Build a Water Bottle Holder supports content in this lesson.

One Problem, Many Solutions

3D Learning Objective

Children explore how there are many solutions to a problem. They **design two solutions to a backpack problem**, **test their solutions**, **and analyze the results**.

DCI Developing Possible Solutions. . . . .

Ask: Why do you think Diego developed four solutions to his backpack problem? He developed four solutions to see if some of the solutions worked better than others. **How can testing several solutions help him find the best solution?** He can compare how well each model worked to see which one best solves the problem.

Collaboration

Think, Pair, Share Have children pick their favorite solution to Diego's problem and explain why to a classmate. Then have each pair share with the class. Have children use this information to make their own bar graph of the class's favorite solution to Diego's backpack problem.

 FORMATIVE ASSESSMENT

Remind children of the steps in the design process. Provide them with craft materials to help them build their solutions.

Scoring Guidelines
• designs two original solutions to Diego's backpack problem
• tests both solutions
• determines which solution is better

Analyzing and Interpreting Data Children will use data from their tests to decide which solution is better.

One Problem, Many Solutions

Look at the pictures to explore how Diego plans and builds solutions to improve his backpack.

Explore online. ▶

Most problems have many solutions. Diego has defined a problem with his backpack. Its thin straps hurt his shoulders. Diego comes up with several solutions.

One solution uses bandages. A second uses bubble wrap. A third uses a pool noodle, and the fourth uses a paper towel roll. Diego tests all to see which one works best.

Apply What You Know

 Work with a partner to design two more solutions to Diego's backpack problem. Test your solutions. Record the results. Then compare the results to decide which solution is better.

Analyzing and Interpreting Data Go to the online handbook for tips.

22

Do the Math!

Diego's classmates tested his backpack solutions. Then they took a class poll to find out which solution each child thought worked the best.

💡 **Make a Bar Graph**
Go to the online handbook for tips.

Explore online. ▶

Which solution was most comfortable?

• Six children liked the bandages best.
• Ten children liked the bubble wrap best.
• Four children liked the pool noodle best.
• One child liked the paper towel roll best.

✏️ **Use this data to draw bars in the graph.**

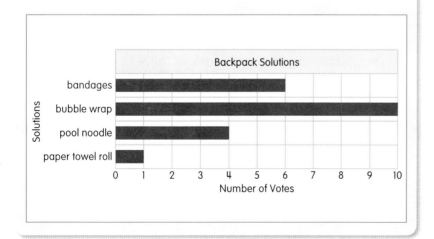

© Houghton Mifflin Harcourt

Do the Math! • Make a Bar Graph

Children should complete a bar graph to display the results from the poll that Diego's classmates took. They should draw four bars, one for each solution. The length of each bar should correspond to the number of children who voted for that solution. **Ask: What conclusions can you draw from your graph?** Bubble wrap was the most popular solution. The paper towel roll was the least popular solution. **How did the graph help you draw those conclusions?** The bars were different lengths, so I could see which solution got the most votes and which got the fewest.

💡 **Make a Bar Graph • Reason Abstractly and Quantitatively • Model with Mathematics • Use Appropriate Tools** Children use the given data to draw bars in the graph. For each solution, they should start at 0 and use the numbers on the horizontal scale to determine where the bar for that solution ends.

Differentiate Instruction

ELL Provide bandages, bubble wrap, a pool noodle, and a paper towel roll for children to handle. Discuss the characteristics of each object with children, highlighting key words to help build vocabulary related to each solution.

Connection to Physical Science

Structure and Properties of Matter Have children work in small groups and choose one of the materials that Diego and his classmates tested as backpack solutions. Make sure that each material is chosen by at least one group. Have each group make a list or a chart to describe these properties of the material: color, shape, hardness, texture, and flexibility. Then have children share their descriptions with other groups. As a class, discuss how a material's properties relate to its function.

Build and Test a Solution

3D Learning Objective

Children **analyze a paper bridge to determine why it does not work as intended.** They use their analysis to **plan, build, and test a new design** that **improves the stability of the bridge.**

SEP Analyzing and Interpreting Data . . . .

Help children understand that a design that does not function as intended is not a failure, but an opportunity to find out how to make it better. **Ask: What information can the children gain from this design?** They can think about why it did not work and what they can do differently to make it work. **Do you think the children's second solution will be better? Why?** Yes, because they will make it stronger now that they know that one flat piece of paper will not hold up a pencil.

DCI Optimizing the Design Solution . . . .

Ask: Why is it important to come up with several solutions? To compare the strengths and weaknesses of the solutions.

CCC Structure and Function . . . .

Ask: How do you think the structure of the bridge affects the way it works? The structure needs to be strong enough to hold more than one pencil.

 FORMATIVE ASSESSMENT

Provide children with the materials they will need to complete their models. Remind children to think about the strengths and weaknesses in their new designs.

Scoring Guidelines
- redesigns and builds a stronger paper bridge
- tests their bridge
- shares their results with the class

Build and Test a Solution

Explore online. ▶

Look at the pictures to explore how children use books and paper to build a bridge design.

The children test a bridge design. They observe the flat paper is too weak and thin to hold the pencil.

Engineers plan and build many possible solutions. They test each one to see how well it works and to find ways to improve it. Engineers identify **strengths**, or good features, and **weaknesses**, or flawed features, in each solution. A solution may not work at all.

✏️▷ Underline the sentence that tells why the children's bridge design does not work.

Apply What You Know

As a group, redesign the children's bridge to make it stronger. Test your design. Share your results with your class.

24

Compare Design Solutions

Compare Design Solutions

Explore online. ▶

Look at the pictures to explore how children improve their bridge design.

The first bridge design did not work because the structure of the flat paper is too weak and too thin to support the pencil. The children fold the paper like a fan and test their new design to see if it works better. They observe the folded paper is stronger and does not bend easily. This new design can support many pencils.

Why does the folded paper design work better? Choose all correct answers.

Ⓐ It is taller

🅱 It is stronger.

🅲 It does not bend easily.

Lesson 2 • Engineer It • How Can We Compare Design Solutions?

25

3D Learning Objective

Children **analyze** and compare different solutions to a problem. They explore how structure and function are related.

DCI **Defining and Delimiting Engineering Problems** . . . .

Guide children to see the benefits of understanding the problem before developing a solution. **Ask: How did knowing what the bridge was for help the children develop a solution?** They knew the bridge had to be strong enough to support several pencils.

DCI **Optimizing the Design Solution** . . . .

Ask: Why was it important to compare and test the bridge solutions? to understand that there is more than one solution to a problem

CCC **Structure and Function** . . . .

Draw children's attention to the difference in stability between the unfolded paper used in the previous section of this lesson and the folded paper used here. Invite children to share the redesigned bridge solutions they developed in the previous section. Some may have folded the paper as they did here, but others may have developed other solutions. **Ask: Was your paper bridge stronger than the original bridge? Was it stronger than the folded paper bridge?** My paper bridge was stronger than the original bridge, but not as strong as the folded paper bridge. **What were the strengths of your design?** Answers will vary.

Children should select B—It is stronger; and C—It does not bend easily. If children choose A, have them carefully observe the photos to see that there is no evidence to support this answer choice.

Differentiate Instruction

RTI/Extra Support Provide physical models of each tower for children to refer to, or allow children to build them before they analyze their strengths and weaknesses.

Extension Challenge children to use their tower designs in the Hands-On Activity and their bridge designs earlier in the lesson to build a new tower to support a marshmallow using only paper.

 FORMATIVE ASSESSMENT

Read, Write, Share! • Evidence Notebook

Children will work with a partner to compare pictures of two towers and to communicate the results of their comparisons. Children will identify the strengths and weaknesses that make one tower better able to hold a marshmallow. Children can communicate their results using words and diagrams. They should include evidence to support their conclusions based on their own experiences with building towers.

Scoring Guidelines

• identifies weaknesses in both towers
• identifies strengths in both towers
• uses evidence from the tests of their own towers in the Hands-On Activity to support their answers

💡 **Structure and Function • Recall Information • Collaborate To Use Digital Tools** Remind children that the shape and stability of human-made or natural objects are connected to how well the objects work. Children should use evidence from the Hands-On Activity to support their analysis of the two towers shown in the pictures on this page.

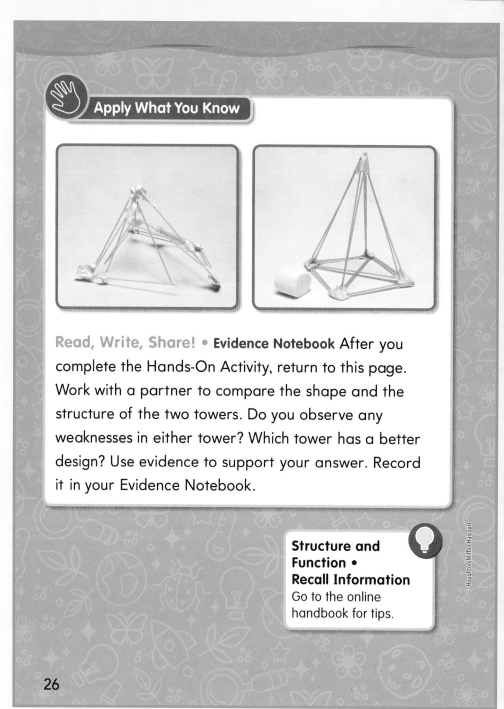

🖐 **Apply What You Know**

Read, Write, Share! • **Evidence Notebook** After you complete the Hands-On Activity, return to this page. Work with a partner to compare the shape and the structure of the two towers. Do you observe any weaknesses in either tower? Which tower has a better design? Use evidence to support your answer. Record it in your Evidence Notebook.

💡 **Structure and Function • Recall Information** Go to the online handbook for tips.

26

Name _____

Hands-On Activity

Engineer It • Compare Strengths and Weaknesses of Design Solutions

Materials

_____

_____

Ask a Question
Answers will vary. Sample answer: What can I find out about improving my designs by comparing design solutions?

Test and Record Data Explore online. ▶

Step 1

Plan two solutions to build towers that will each hold a marshmallow on top. Draw and label your solutions.

Drawings will vary but should show two possible solutions with labels.

Step 2
Use the materials. Follow your plan. Build your solutions.

Step 3
Test your design solutions. Place a marshmallow on the top of each one.

© Houghton Mifflin Harcourt

Hands-On Activity 👥 small groups 🕐 1 class period

Engineer It • Compare Strengths and Weaknesses of Design Solutions

3D Learning Objective

SEP Analyzing and Interpreting Data . . . .

Children will plan two solutions to a problem, and then compare the strengths and weaknesses of the solutions.

Suggested Materials uncooked spaghetti, marshmallows, masking tape, scissors, string. Alternative materials such as blocks, a small book, and a sheet of paper can be used.

Preparation
Preassemble materials bundles for each group of children. Include 20 pieces of spaghetti, 1 meter of kitchen string, 1 meter of masking tape, scissors, and 1 marshmallow.

Activity
As a class, view the video. Then, discuss the question that will need to be answered. Have children record the question.

DCI Developing Possible Solutions. . . . .

STEP 1 Ask: Why is it helpful to make a drawing of your tower design? It can help me remember how to build my tower. It can help me show others what my solution looks like.

Instead of using labels, some children may color code their drawings and provide a key. Point out that both are acceptable ways to communicate information about a design.

STEP 2 Encourage children to work together to build one tower at a time, following the drawing.

STEP 3 Tell children they will need to use the results of their tests as evidence later, and encourage them to take notes as they test each tower.

Hands-On Activity, continued

SEP Analyzing and Interpreting Data . . . .

CCC Structure and Function . . . .

STEP 4 Encourage children to think about why one tower design supports a marshmallow better than the other design. **Ask: What is it about the way the materials are put together that helps the tower support a marshmallow?** Sample answer: I used pieces of spaghetti going diagonally, as well as up and down.

STEP 5 Ask: How might your solution to this problem have been different if you had built only one tower? Why? It would not have been as stable. Because I built two towers, I could combine the best parts of both towers to make a really stable one.

Claims, Evidence, and Reasoning

Ask: How did you change your design after you tested your two solutions? One solution had more triangles in it, so it was more stable, but the other solution was taller. We built some extra triangles into the taller tower to make it more stable.

	Scoring Rubric for Hands-On Activity
3	States a claim supported with evidence about the benefits of testing and comparing more than one solution to a problem
2	States a claim somewhat supported with evidence about the benefits of testing and comparing more than one solution to a problem
1	States a claim that is not supported by evidence
0	Does not state a claim and does not provide evidence

Step 4

Compare your test results. Identify strengths and weaknesses of each design. Make changes to your designs to make the towers stronger and taller.

Strengths	Weaknesses
Check children's work.	Answers will vary.

Step 5

Communicate your results.

Make a claim that answers your question.

Answers should explain how comparing design solutions

helps children improve their designs.

What is your evidence?

Answers should cite evidence from children's comparisons

of design solutions.

28

Take It Further

People in Science & Engineering •
Gustave Eiffel

Children explore Gustave Eiffel's work as a structural engineer. He began his career by building bridges. Then he moved onto projects such as an observatory in Nice and even the Statue of Liberty in New York. During the construction of the Eiffel tower, he became interested in aerodynamics and even built a lab at its base, which was later moved to another part of Paris.

Remind children about the stop sign problem they observed at the beginning of the lesson. Explain that Gustave Eiffel solved a similar problem, but for a much larger structure.

DCI Defining and Delimiting Engineering Problems . . . .

Guide children to recognize that it is important to take the time to understand a problem in order to develop a more successful solution. **Ask: What questions do you think Eiffel asked to help him understand what his tower would need to do?** How strong are the winds in Paris? Are the winds stronger higher up? Will building holes into the tower make it resist winds better?

DCI Developing Possible Solutions. . . . .

Ask: Do you think Eiffel made many models before he built the Eiffel Tower? Why? Yes, because he needed to figure out which model would work best in order to resist the high winds the tower would encounter.

Take It Further

People in Science & Engineering •
Gustave Eiffel

Explore more online.
• Blast to the Past

Explore online.

Gustave Eiffel was a structural engineer. He designed bridges and other structures made of metal. He studied how air moved around things. He used what he found out to build structures that could stand up to strong winds.

© Houghton Mifflin Harcourt • Image Credits: (t) ©Bettmann/Getty Images; (b) ©Shutterstock

Eiffel designed the Eiffel Tower in Paris, France. The tower was built in 1889. It was 986 feet tall. For many years, it was the tallest building in the world. How could such a tall building resist high winds? Eiffel designed the tower to solve this problem.

Lesson 2 • Engineer It • How Can We Compare Design Solutions?   29

Take It Further, continued

DCI **Optimizing the Design Solution** . . . .

SEP **Analyzing and Interpreting Data** . . . .

Children will identify that Eiffel used all three techniques mentioned to build a tower that resists high winds. Have children observe the pictures and read the accompanying text. **Ask: How do you think Eiffel knew that these ideas would help his tower resist high winds?** He probably tested several models and used data from his tests to decide what worked well and what did not work well.

CCC **Structure and Function** . . . .

Discuss with children how the shape and stability of human-made objects are connected to how the objects work. As a whole-class activity, have children underline text on the page that explains how the shape of the frame, the structure of the base, and the materials used help with the stability of the tower. Then have children answer the question at the bottom of the page. Children should choose A, B, and C. If children do not choose all answer choices, have them observe the pictures again and review the text they underlined.

Explore more online. ▶

Blast to the Past

Children discover how designs have changed over time to enhance their functionality.

How did Eiffel design the tower to resist high winds? First, he used a special kind of iron to make the tower strong. Then, he built two kinds of bases to set it firmly in the ground.

Eiffel designed a curved frame so wind could move around it. Then he had workers heat the metal pins that held pieces together. When the pins cooled, they shrank to a tight fit. All these ideas made the tower strong.

How did Gustave Eiffel design the Eiffel Tower to resist high winds? Choose all correct answers.

Ⓐ He used a special, stronger kind of iron.

Ⓑ He included curves in the metal design.

Ⓒ He set the tower on two kinds of bases.

30

Explore online. ▶   Have children explore online to find out more about weaknesses in the design of the stop sign.

Lesson Check

Lesson Check   Name _____

Explore online. ▶

Can You Solve It?

✏️▷ Identify strengths and weaknesses in the stop sign's design. What are two ways to make it better? Be sure to

• Identify weaknesses in the stop sign's design.
• Describe two solutions that will make the design stronger.

Sample answer: Weaknesses include a solid sign that does

not let the air pass through and a base that is not firmly set

in the ground. Two solutions to make the design stronger

are a sign with holes in it that let air pass through and a base

that is buried deeper into the ground.

Lesson 2 • Engineer It • How Can We Compare Design Solutions?   31

Lesson Check

Can You Solve It?

Have children reread their answer to the Can You Solve It? prompt at the beginning of the lesson.

DCI **Optimizing the Design Solution** . . . .

Ask: Why is it important to come up with two solutions to the stop sign problem? It is important because there is usually more than one way to solve a problem.

CCC **Structure and Function** . . . .

Have children think about the purpose of the stop sign and its shape and stability. **Ask: Why does the stop sign fall over in the wind?** Sample answers: The stop sign does not let air pass through. The stop sign is not firmly set in the ground.

Scoring Guidelines
• Children should identify weaknesses in the design.
• Children should describe two ways to make the stop sign's design stronger by improving its ability to resist wind.

Collaboration

Cultivating New Questions As children complete this lesson and prepare for the next lesson, ask them to identify additional questions they have about comparing solutions to problems. **Ask: How do the materials used in a solution affect the quality of the design?** The type of material is important because some materials work better than others depending on what you are building. As children continue to the next unit, they will apply concepts related to the design process to matter and its properties.

Lesson Check, continued

Self Check

1. Children should choose A—Test and Improve. If children choose B or C, discuss with them the steps of a design procces, focusing on Steps 3 through 5: test and improve, redesign, and communicate. Guide children to see that the children in the photos are testing the models to see how well they work.

2. Children should choose A—make changes; and C—test new designs. If children choose B, refer them to the Build and Test a Solution section of the lesson. **Ask: What is the purpose of testing a design?** to find its strengths and weaknesses **What can you do once you know the weaknesses?** You can improve the design. **What would happen if engineers tried only one solution, then gave up?** They would miss out on inventing many useful things.

3. Children should choose B—data. If children choose A or C, ensure that they understand that the data is the information Alma gathers while testing her models. Refer children to the picture of the paper bridge in the Build and Test a Solution section of the lesson. **Ask: How did the children know that the first bridge built did not work very well?** It would not support even one pencil. Guide children to realize that it is the data from such tests that tell how well each model works.

Self Check

1. Which **best** describes the step in a design process that the children are doing?

Ⓐ Test and Improve
Ⓑ Redesign
Ⓒ Communicate

2. What does an engineer do when a design solution does not work? Choose all correct answers.
Ⓐ make changes
Ⓑ define a new problem
Ⓒ test new designs

3. Alma builds two bridge models. Then she tests them. What tells her how well each model works? Choose the **best** answer.
Ⓐ questions
Ⓑ data
Ⓒ designs

32

4. Tariq tested three paper airplane models.
   The bar graph shows how far each model
   flew. Which model worked **best**?

   Ⓐ Cobra

   Ⓑ Dart

   Ⓒ Shadow

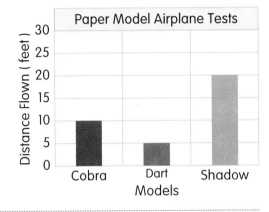

Paper Model Airplane Tests

5. This door will not stay closed. Why is it important
   to find more than one solution to this problem?

   Ⓐ The first solution never works,
      so other ideas are needed.

   Ⓑ Developing more than one
      solution helps to find the
      best one.

   Ⓒ Working on several designs
      gives time for the door to
      fix itself.

4. Children should choose C—Shadow. If children choose A or B,
   refer them to the Do the Math! section of the lesson to review
   bar graphs. Explain to children that they need to analyze the bar
   graph to see which model flew the farthest. This will help them
   figure out which model worked the best. **Ask: Look at the bar
   graph. Which plane flew the greatest distance?** Shadow **How
   do you know?** The bar for Shadow is the tallest.

5. Children should choose B—Developing more than one solution
   helps to find the best one. If children choose A, remind them
   about Diego's backpack problem in the One Problem, Many
   Solutions section of the lesson. Diego developed several
   solutions that worked, but some worked better than others.
   If children choose C, remind them that a problem will not fix
   itself and that a solution is required. Have children think back
   to the towers they built in the Hands-On Activity. **Ask: What
   advantages were there to developing more than one design
   for the tower?** By comparing different designs, I could find
   the best possible solution.

Unit 1 Performance Task

Engineer It • Build a Water Bottle Holder

👥 small groups 🕐 2 class periods

Objective
Children **define a problem to solve** and **develop possible solutions** that take into account the **structure and function** of their water bottle holder.

Suggested Materials
reusable water bottle, ribbon, fabric, string, straw, tape, rubber bands, scissors, chenille sticks, glue

Preparation
Review Lessons 1 and 2 to provide context for this Unit Performance Task. In advance of this activity, collect several plastic bottles of the same size and shape.

 Asking Questions and Defining Problems . . . .

Review the title of the activity. **Ask: What is the problem in this activity?** Sample answer: The problem is to build a water bottle holder. **Ask: What do you think a big challenge will be?** Sample answer: A big challenge will be to keep the water nearby so I can reach it.

STEPS

Step 1 • Define a Problem
Guide children in a discussion about the problem they will solve.

Step 2 • Plan and Build
Remind children that engineers think about different ways to solve a problem and analyze which may be the best solution. **Ask: What are two ways you could solve the problem of keeping a water bottle nearby without using your hands?** Sample answer: I could make something that I can hang on my body that holds the water bottle, or I could find a way to attach it to my desk.

🔍 Unit 1 Performance Task
Engineer It • Build a Water Bottle Holder

Materials
_____
_____

STEPS

Step 1

Define a Problem You want to build a water bottle holder that will keep your hands free but your water bottle nearby.

Step 2

Plan and Build Plan at least two solutions. Think about the materials you will need and then build your solutions.

Step 3

Test and Improve Test your designs. Which one works better? How can you improve that design?

34

© Houghton Mifflin Harcourt

Step 4

Redesign Change the materials, or change how you put the materials together to make the water bottle holder better.

Step 5

Communicate Share your solution. Explain which materials make up your water bottle holder and why you chose to use them. Use evidence to tell how your design solves the problem.

✔️ Check

_____ I built a water bottle holder that keeps my hands free but my water nearby.

_____ I tested my water bottle holder.

_____ I redesigned my water bottle holder to make it work better.

_____ I used evidence to show how my solution solved the problem.

_____ I shared my design with others.

© Houghton Mifflin Harcourt

Step 3 • Test and Improve

ccc Structure and Function . . . .

Children may have limited ideas for ways to build a bottle holder. Consider having groups critique each other's designs, and discuss ways to improve them.

Step 4 • Redesign

DCI Developing Possible Solutions . . . .

Prompt children to make one improvement discussed at Step 3. Children should retest their bottle holders in order to evaluate its ability to keep the bottle nearby with the improvement in place. **Ask: Did the improvement make the bottle holder work better? Did it change in the way that you thought it would?** Answers will vary.

Step 5 • Communicate

Children should communicate their results, including an explanation of each step of a design process they followed. Children should explain, based on their test results, which materials are best suited for use as a water bottle holder.

Scoring Rubric for Performance Task	
3	Builds, tests, and redesigns a water bottle holder, and then shares the solution and uses evidence to explain the design
2	Builds, tests, and redesigns a water bottle holder, but does not share the solution or use evidence to explain the design
1	Builds a water bottle holder, but does not test it, redesign it, or share a solution
0	Does not build, test, or redesign a water bottle holder

Unit 1 Review

SUMMATIVE ASSESSMENT

1. Children should choose A—They use science and math to solve problems; and C—They use a design process to solve problems. If children choose B, reinforce that engineers work to solve problems rather than cause problems. By completing What Engineers Do in Lesson 1, children explored the steps of a design process that an engineer follows and what an engineer uses (math and science) during a design process to help solve problems. Children who answer incorrectly should refer back to Lesson 1.

2. Children should choose B—data. If children choose A or C, refer them back to Step 3—Test and Improve in Lesson 1. Discuss what steps are involved once a test has been performed, and what information is useful during these steps. Children who answer incorrectly should refer back to Lesson 1.

3. Children should choose B—Car 2. If children choose A or C, reinforce how to read and analyze a bar graph. Guide children to observe that the car with the tallest bar is the car that traveled farthest.

Unit 1 Review   Name _____

1. Which is **true** about engineers? Choose all correct answers.
    - (A) They use science and math to solve problems.
    - (B) They design solutions that cause problems.
    - (C) They use a design process to solve problems.

2. Carlo tests model cars he built for a race. What helps him decide which car to choose for the race? Choose the **best** answer.
    - (A) color
    - (B) data
    - (C) questions

3. The bar graph shows results from the three cars Carlo tested. Which model car traveled farthest?

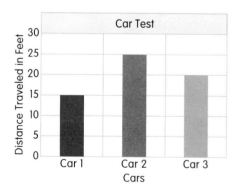

    - (A) Car 1
    - (B) Car 2
    - (C) Car 3

36

4. This boy is having trouble riding his bike. Which step of a design process does this picture show?

Ⓐ Define a Problem
Ⓑ Plan and Build
Ⓒ Test and Improve

5. Arum sees a boy with his pant leg caught on a bike chain. She plans and builds a design solution to solve this problem. What will she do next?
Ⓐ Redesign
Ⓑ Test and Improve
Ⓒ Communicate

6. Josie has redesigned and tested her model. The new model solves her problem. What should she do next?
Ⓐ communicate her results
Ⓑ find a new problem
Ⓒ redesign again

4. Children should choose A—Define a Problem. If children choose B or C, review what happens at each step of a design process. By completing What Engineers Do in Lesson 1, children explored the steps of a design process that an engineer follows. Children who answer incorrectly should refer back to Lesson 1.

5. Children should choose B—Test and Improve. If children choose A or C, reinforce that Test and Improve is the next step after Plan and Build. By completing What Engineers Do in Lesson 1, children explored the steps of a design process. Children who answer incorrectly should refer back to Lesson 1.

6. Children should choose A—communicate her results. If children choose B or C, reinforce that once a problem is solved, the results need to be communicated with others. By completing Step 5—Communicate, children explored the last step in a design process. Children who answer incorrectly should refer back to Lesson 1.

3D Item Analysis	1	2	3	4	5	6
SEP Asking Questions and Defining Problems				•		
SEP Analyzing and Interpreting Data		•	•			
SEP Developing and Using Models		•			•	
DCI Defining and Delimiting Engineering Problems	•			•		•
DCI Developing Possible Solutions	•				•	
DCI Optimizing the Design Solution		•	•			

7. Children should choose C—its bottom. If children choose A or B, review the vocabulary word *weakness* with them. By completing Build and Test a Solution in Lesson 2, children explored how designs can have strengths and weaknesses. Children should observe that the shopping bag's contents have broken through the bottom of the bag.

8. Children should choose A—sun hat. If children choose B or C, review the vocabulary word *strength* with them. By completing Build and Test a Solution in Lesson 2, children explored how designs can have strengths and weaknesses. Discuss how much sun the knit hat or narrow brim hat would keep off Yolanda's face as compared to the sun hat.

9. Children should choose A—test new designs, and C—make changes to improve the design. If children choose B, reinforce that a test will not change the design. There is no reason to keep testing unless your first test was not completed correctly.

10. Children should choose B—Test and Improve. If children choose A or C, reinforce that Test and Improve is the next step after Plan and Build. By completing What Engineers Do in Lesson 1, children explored the steps of a design process.

3D Item Analysis		7	8	9	10
SEP	Asking Questions and Defining Problems				
SEP	Developing and Using Models				•
DCI	Developing Possible Solutions			•	
DCI	Optimizing the Design Solution	•	•	•	
CCC	Structure and Function	•	•		•

7. What is the design weakness in this shopping bag?
   Ⓐ its sides
   Ⓑ its handles
   Ⓒ its bottom

8. Yolanda wants to keep the sun off her face. Which hat should she choose for its design strength?

   Ⓐ sun hat   Ⓑ knit hat   Ⓒ narrow brim hat

9. What should you do if your design solution does not work? Choose all correct answers.
   Ⓐ test new designs
   Ⓑ test the design until it works
   Ⓒ make changes to improve the design

10. Aaron built a launcher. Which step of a design process is he doing now?
    Ⓐ Redesign
    Ⓑ Test and Improve
    Ⓒ Plan and Build

Unit 2
Matter

Unit Project • Explore Melting
What is the fastest way to change ice to water? Investigate to find out.

Unit 2 • Matter   39

Unit 2 • Matter

Unit Overview

In this unit, children will . . .
- describe and classify materials by their observable properties.
- select and use materials based on these properties.
- use evidence to describe how heating and cooling cause changes to matter.
- use evidence to describe reversible and irreversible changes to matter.
- explore how an object can be taken apart and its pieces used to make another object.

About This Image

Guide children in a discussion about the picture on this page.
Ask: Have you ever seen icicles like this before? What change caused the icicles to form? Heat was taken away from the water, and the water froze. **Ask: What change causes the icicles in the picture to melt?** The sun adds heat to the icicles, which causes them to melt and return to their liquid state.

Unit Project • Explore Melting

Have children plan and conduct an investigation that identifies the fastest way to cause ice to change to water. The time for the ice to change to water will vary depending on the room temperature, the size of the ice cubes, and the starting temperature of the ice; however, 20 minutes is a good estimate. The temperature at which all the ice has melted will be 32 degrees Fahrenheit as this is the melting/freezing point of water.

To begin, share details about the melting/freezing point of water or challenge children to use online resources to identify it. More support for the Unit Project can be found on pp. 41K–41N.

Unit 2 At a Glance

The learning experiences in this unit prepare children for mastery of:

Performance Expectations

2-PS1-1. Plan and conduct an investigation to describe and classify different kinds of materials by their observable properties.

2-PS1-2. Analyze data obtained from testing different materials to determine which materials have the properties that are best suited for an intended purpose.

2-PS1-3. Make observations to construct an evidence-based account of how an object made of a small set of pieces can be disassembled and made into a new object.

2-PS1-4. Construct an argument with evidence that some changes caused by heating or cooling can be reversed and some cannot.

Explore online. ▶

In addition to the print resources, the following resources are available online to support this unit.

Unit Pretest
Lesson 1 Engineer It • What Are Properties of Matter?
- Interactive Online Student Edition
- Lesson Quiz
Lesson 2 How Are Objects Put Together?
- Interactive Online Student Edition
- Lesson Quiz
Lesson 3 How Do Heating and Cooling Change Matter?
- Interactive Online Student Edition
- Lesson Quiz
Lesson 4 How Does Matter Change?
- Interactive Online Student Edition
- Lesson Quiz
You Solve It Changes to Matter
Unit Performance Task
Unit Test

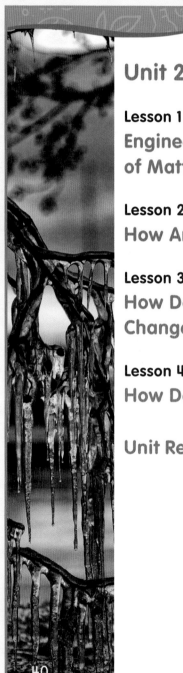

40

© Houghton Mifflin Harcourt • Image Credits: ©Preartiq/Shutterstock

Unit Vocabulary

matter anything that takes up space (p. 44)

property one part of what something is like (p. 45)

solid a state of matter that keeps its shape (p. 48)

liquid a state of matter that takes the shape of its container (p. 49)

melt a change when a solid becomes a liquid (p.74)

freeze a change when a liquid becomes a solid (p. 80)

reversible a change that can be undone (p. 90)

irreversible a change that cannot be undone (p. 93)

Vocabulary Game • **Make a Match**

Materials
- 1 set of word cards
- 1 set of definition cards

How to Play
1. Work with your partner to make word and definition cards.
2. Place the cards face up on a table.
3. Take turns picking a word card, reading the word, and matching it to a definition.
4. If you make a match, keep the cards.
5. If there is no match, put the cards back.

Unit Vocabulary

The Next Generation Science Standards emphasize explanation and demonstration of understanding versus rote memorization of science vocabulary words. Keep in mind that these vocabulary words are tools for clear communication. Use these words as a starting point, not an end goal, for children to build deeper understanding of science concepts.

Children can explore all vocabulary words in the **Online Glossary**.

Vocabulary Strategies

- Have children review the vocabulary words. Then have children work in pairs to share an example of each word and explain why they think it's an example. Have pairs record their examples to refer back to during the unit.
- Have children think about how each word relates to matter.
- Have children work in pairs and share their ideas with a partner.

Differentiate Instruction

RTI/Extra Support Pronounce each word and have children repeat it after you. Have children find each highlighted word within the unit content. Have children work in pairs and explain to a partner what they think each word means based on the surrounding context of imagery and text.

Extension Have children select two vocabulary words and work in small groups to illustrate and explain the words to a first-grade child.

Vocabulary Game • **Make a Match**

Preparation Assemble vocabulary game cards. Assign children to teams. Appoint one scorekeeper, and rotate children through the position during gameplay. Establish a winning score or set number of words per round.

Integrating the NGSS* Three Dimensions of Learning

Building to the Performance Expectations

The learning experiences in this unit prepare children for mastery of the following Performance Expectations:

Matter and its Interactions

2-PS1-1. Plan and conduct an investigation to describe and classify different kinds of materials by their observable properties.

2-PS1-2. Analyze data obtained from testing different materials to determine which materials have the properties that are best suited for an intended purpose.

2-PS1-3. Make observations to construct an evidence-based account of how an object made of a small set of pieces can be disassembled and made into a new object.

2-PS1-4. Construct an argument with evidence that some changes caused by heating and cooling can be reversed and some cannot.

Assessing Student Progress

After completing the lessons, the **Unit Project** Explore Melting provides children with opportunities to practice aspects of and to demonstrate their understanding of the Performance Expectations as they determine the fastest way to change solid ice to liquid water.

Additionally, children can further practice or be assessed on aspects of the Performance Expectations by completing the **Unit Performance Task** Engineer It • Build a Model Boat, in which children consider properties of matter and follow the steps of a design process to determine the best design and materials to use in building a model boat that will both float on water and move by wind.

Lesson 1
Engineer It • What Are Properties of Matter?

In Lesson 1, children explore properties of matter as they discover that matter can be described and classified by their properties (DCI Structure and Properties of Matter), and that these properties have patterns (CCC Patterns). Children plan and conduct an investigation to determine which materials are best suited to a purpose based on these properties (SEP Planning and Carrying Out Investigations) (SEP Analyzing and Interpreting Data) (CCC Cause and Effect.)

Lesson 2
How Are Objects Put Together?

In Lesson 2, children explore how objects can be put together from a small set of pieces (DCI Structure and Properties of Matter). They will deepen their understanding of matter by exploring how those pieces can be taken apart and reused to make another object (SEP Constructing Explanations and Designing Solutions) (CCC Energy and Matter).

Lesson 3
How Do Heating and Cooling Change Matter?

In Lesson 3, children explore how heating and cooling can cause changes to matter (DCI Chemical Reactions) (SEP Science Models, Laws, Mechanisms, and Theories Explain Natural Phenomena) and that those changes generate observable patterns (CCC Cause and Effect). Children use evidence to support their claim about matter (SEP Engaging in Argument from Evidence).

Lesson 4
How Does Matter Change?

In Lesson 4, children deepen their understanding of matter by exploring that some changes to matter are reversible and some are not (DCI Chemical Reactions). As they explore, children observe patterns in reversible and irreversible changes caused by heating and cooling (CCC Cause and Effect). Children use evidence in order to support their claim about matter (SEP Engaging in Argument from Evidence).

Standards Supported by This Unit

Explore online. Online only.

Next Generation Science Standards	Unit Project	Lesson 1	Lesson 2	Lesson 3	Lesson 4	Unit Performance Task	You Solve It
SEP Planning and Carrying Out Investigations	•	•				•	
SEP Analyzing and Interpreting Data		•				•	
SEP Constructing Explanations and Designing Solutions			•				
SEP Engaging in Argument from Evidence	•			•	•		•
SEP Science Models, Laws, Mechanisms, and Theories Explain Natural Phenomena				•	•		
DCI **PS1.A** Structure and Properties of Matter	•	•	•	•	•	•	
DCI **PS1.B** Chemical Reactions	•			•	•		•
CCC Patterns		•					
CCC Cause and Effect	•	•		•	•	•	•
CCC Energy and Matter			•				
CCC Influence of Engineering, Technology, and Science on Society and the Natural World		•					

NGSS* Across the Grades

Before	Grade 2	After
Coverage of the **Performance Expectations** within this unit originates in Grade 2.	**Matter and its Interactions** 2-PS1-1. 2-PS1-2. 2-PS1-3. 2-PS1-4.	**Matter and its Interactions** 5-PS1-1. Develop a model to describe that matter is made of particles too small to be seen. 5-PS1-2. Measure and graph quantities to provide evidence that regardless of the type of change that occurs when heating, cooling, or mixing substances, the total weight of matter is conserved. 5-PS1-3. Make observations and measurements to identify materials based on their properties. 5-PS1-4. Conduct an investigation to determine whether the mixing of two or more substances results in new substances.

Trace Tool to the NGSS™   Go online to view the complete coverage of these standards across this grade level and time.

3D Unit Planning

Lesson 1 Engineer It • What Are Properties of Matter? pp. 42–59

Overview

Objective Use evidence to describe and classify materials based on their observable properties.

SEP Planning and Carrying Out Investigations
SEP Analyzing and Interpreting Data
DCI **PS1.A** Structure and Properties of Matter
CCC Patterns
CCC Cause and Effect
CCC Influence of Engineering, Technology, and Science on Society and the Natural World

Math and **English Language Arts** standards and features are detailed on lesson planning pages.

	Print and Online **Student Editions**	Explore online. ▶
ENGAGE	**Lesson Problem** pp. 42–43 **Can You Explain It?** Materials Are Different	▶ **Can You Explain It?** Video
EXPLORE/ EXPLAIN	**Properties of Matter** **States of Matter—Solids** **States of Matter—Liquids** **Which Materials Are Best?** **Hands-On Activity** Engineer It • Explore Properties of Matter pp. 51–52	**Hands-On** Worksheet
ELABORATE	**Take It Further** pp. 55–56 People in Science & Engineering • Dr. Eugene Tssui	Take It Further Another Kind of Matter
EVALUATE	**Lesson Check** p. 57 **Self Check** pp. 58–59	Lesson Quiz

Hands-On Activity Planning

Engineer It • Explore Properties of Matter

Objective Children will plan and carry out tests on each of several different materials to determine their suitability as a pillow filler.

👥 small groups
🕐 1 class period

Suggested Materials
- cotton
- foam
- feathers
- tissues
- zippered pillowcase

Preparation/Tip

Pre-assemble material bundles for pairs or groups. Each group will need four different materials to test. You can also use alternative materials that are harder or less flexible in order to help children decide which is the better pillow filler.

Lesson 2 How Are Objects Put Together? pp. 60–71

Overview

Objective Use observations as evidence to explain how an object made of a small set of pieces can be taken apart and made into a new object.

SEP Constructing Explanations and Designing Solutions
DCI **PS1.A** Structure and Properties of Matter
CCC Energy and Matter

Math and **English Language Arts** standards and features are detailed on lesson planning pages.

	Print and Online **Student Editions**	Explore online.
ENGAGE	Lesson Phenomenon pp. 60–61 **Can You Explain It?** Taking Apart, Putting Together	▶ Can You Explain It? Photos
EXPLORE/ EXPLAIN	Build It Up, Break It Down **What Is the Same?** Hands-On Activity Build Objects from Smaller Pieces pp. 65–66	Hands-On Worksheet
ELABORATE	Take It Further pp. 67–68 Careers in Science & Engineering • Architect	Take It Further What's Old Is New Again
EVALUATE	Lesson Check p. 69 Self Check pp. 70–71	Lesson Quiz

Hands-On Activity Planning

Build Objects from Smaller Pieces

Objective Children will design and implement a plan to find out how many objects they can build from the same set of pieces. They will record the objects they build and analyze the results.

👥 individuals
🕐 1 class period

Suggested Materials
• set of small pieces

Preparation/Tip
Organize sets of small pieces for each child. Alternatively, children may do this activity at home or in small groups if limited materials are available.

3D Unit Planning, continued

Lesson 3 How Do Heating and Cooling Change Matter? pp. 72–87

Overview

Objective Use evidence to describe how heating and cooling matter may cause changes that can be observed.

SEP Engaging in Argument from Evidence
SEP Science Models, Laws, Mechanisms, and Theories Explain Natural Phenomena
DCI **PS1.A** Structure and Properties of Matter
DCI **PS1.B** Chemical Reactions
CCC Cause and Effect

Math and **English Language Arts** standards and features are detailed on lesson planning pages.

	Print and Online Student Editions	Explore online. ▶
ENGAGE	Lesson Phenomenon pp. 72–73 Can You Explain It? Matter Can Change	▶ Can You Explain It? Video
EXPLORE/ EXPLAIN	Melt It Cook It Burn It Cool It Down 🔍 Hands-On Activity Explore Cooling pp. 81–82	Hands-On Worksheet
ELABORATE	Take It Further pp. 83–84 Careers in Science & Engineering • Chefs at Work	Take It Further Changes All Around Take It Further Find a Recipe
EVALUATE	Lesson Check p. 85 Self Check pp. 86–87	Lesson Quiz

Hands-On Activity Planning

Explore Cooling

Objective Children explore how cooling causes changes to different materials, such as a flower, an ice-cube tray, and orange juice. Children identify patterns based on these events.

👥 small groups
🕐 1 class period

Suggested Materials
- a flower
- a container of orange juice
- an ice-cube tray
- a paper plate

Preparation/Tip
Pre-assemble materials bundles for pairs or groups. Arrange access to a freezer prior to the activity. Alternatively, children may do this activity at home.

Lesson 4 How Does Matter Change? pp. 88–101

Overview

Objective Construct an argument with evidence that some changes to matter can be reversed and some cannot.

SEP Engaging in Argument from Evidence
SEP Science Models, Laws, Mechanisms, and Theories Explain Natural Phenomena
DCI **PS1.A** Structure and Properties of Matter
DCI **PS1.B** Chemical Reactions
CCC Cause and Effect

Math and **English Language Arts** standards and features are detailed on lesson planning pages.

Print and Online Student Editions	Explore online. ▶
ENGAGE	Lesson Phenomenon pp. 88–89 Can You Explain It? Fire It Up	▶ Can You Explain It? Video
EXPLORE/ EXPLAIN	Reversible Changes Irreversible Changes Hands-On Activity Explore Changes to Matter pp. 95–96	Hands-On Worksheet You Solve It Changes to Matter
ELABORATE	Take It Further pp. 97–98 How Foods Change	Take It Further Dissolve It
EVALUATE	Lesson Check p. 99 Self Check pp. 100–101	Lesson Quiz

Hands-On Activity Planning

Explore Changes to Matter

Objective Children will make a claim about the reversibility or irreversibility of changes caused by cooking in a microwave. They will support their claim with evidence from their observations during the investigation.

👥 small groups
🕐 1 class period

Suggested Materials
- microwave
- microwave-safe container
- uncooked food such as popcorn kernels
- plastic measuring cup

Preparation/Tip
Pre-assemble materials bundles for groups. Arrange access to a microwave prior to the activity. Alternatively, children may do this activity at home or as a whole-class activity if limited materials are available.

3D Unit Planning, continued

 You Solve It   Go online for an additional interactive activity.

Changes to Matter

This interactive activity offers practice in support of **PE 2-PS1-4.**

SEP Engaging in Argument from Evidence
DCI PS1.B Chemical Reactions
CCC Cause and Effect

3D Learning Objectives
- Children use evidence to support a claim that some changes to matter caused by heating or cooling are reversible and others are irreversible.
- Children recognize observable patterns that are generated when matter is changed.

Activity Problem
You are in the kitchen exploring how matter can change when heat is added or removed. Are the changes reversible? Your task is to:
- move items from a refrigerator to a frying pan and back to the refrigerator
- determine if the change is reversible or not
- describe a pattern observed in the changes

Interaction Summary
- chooses items from a refrigerator to change
- fills in a chart with examples of reversible and irreversible changes
- states a claim supported by evidence of how each item changed and whether the change is reversible or irreversible
- provides an example of an observable pattern in the changes that occurred to the different kinds of matter

Assessment Planning

Preassessment
Assessment Guide, Unit Pretest
The Unit Pretest focuses on prerequisite knowledge and is composed of items that evaluate children's preparedness for the content covered within this unit.

Formative Assessment
Interactive Worktext, Apply What You Know, Lesson Check, and Self Check

Summative Assessment
Assessment Guide, Lesson Quiz
The Lesson Quiz provides a quick assessment of each lesson objective and of the portion of the Performance Expectation aligned to the lesson.

Interactive Worktext, Performance Task pp.102–103
The Performance Task presents the opportunity for children to collaborate with classmates in in order to complete the steps of each Performance Task. Each Performance Task provides a formal Scoring Rubric for evaluating children's work.

Interactive Worktext, Unit 2 Review, pp. 104–106
Assessment Guide, Unit Test
The Unit Test provides an in-depth assessment of the Performance Expectations aligned to the unit. This test evaluates children's ability to apply knowledge in order to explain phenomena and to solve problems. Within this test Constructed Response items apply a three-dimensional rubric for evaluating children's mastery on all three dimensions of the Next Generation Science Standards.

 **Assessment Online**   Go online to view the complete assessment items for this unit.

Teacher Notes

Differentiate Instruction

Leveled Readers

The Science & Engineering Leveled Readers provide additional nonfiction reading practice in this unit's subject area.

On Level • **What Can We Learn About Matter?**
This reader reinforces unit concepts and includes response activities for your children.

Extra Support • **What Can We Learn About Matter?**
This reader shares title, illustrations, vocabulary, and concepts with the On-Level Reader; however, the text is linguistically accommodated to provide simplified sentence structures and comprehension aids. It also includes response activities.

Enrichment • **Making Coins**
This high-interest, nonfiction reader will extend and enrich unit concepts and vocabulary and includes response activities.

Teacher Guide
The accompanying Teacher Guide provides teaching strategies and support for using all the readers.

ELL

English Language Learner support resources include a glossary and Leveled Readers in Spanish and English. ELL teaching strategies appear throughout this unit:

pp. 42B, 44, 60B, 63, 72B, 75, 83, 88B, 94

RTI/Extra Support

Strategies for children who need extra support appear throughout this unit:

pp. 41, 41K, 42B, 46, 47, 55, 60B, 68, 72B, 78, 88B, 93, 98

Extension

Strategies for children who have mastered core content and are ready for additional challenges appear throughout this unit:

pp. 41, 41K, 42B, 46, 47, 55, 60B, 68, 72B, 78, 88B, 93, 98

Leveled Readers All readers are available online as well as in an innovative, engaging format for use with touchscreen mobile devices. Contact your HMH Sales Representative for more information.

Connecting with NGSS

Connections to Community

Use these opportunities for informal science learning to provide local context and to extend and enhance unit concepts.

At Home

Classify Objects Have children work with a family member to identify and classify objects in their home by shape, mass, temperature, texture, and flexibility. Children should record their observations in a chart. Have children share their findings with the class and explain why they added objects to the chart the way they did.
Use with Lesson 1.

In the Community

Guest Speaker Invite an architect, a contractor, or a structural engineer to speak to the class about how a building is constructed from start to finish. Have children prepare questions for him or her to answer. Encourage children to ask a mix of appropriate science and engineering questions.
Use with Lesson 2.

What's Cooking? Plan a class field trip to a local restaurant or grocery store where food is prepared in the store. Have children bring the list of questions they prepared for Lesson 3 Careers in Science & Engineering Ask a Chef. Have children record the answers to their questions. Guide children to identify reversible and irreversible changes they observe.
Use with Lesson 3 or 4.

Culture

Visual Arts Take children on a virtual tour of a museum with a decorative arts collection. Have them compare baskets or other storage vessels from various cultures or countries. Children should make observations to identify properties of matter for each basket. As a group, discuss why the materials were suited for use for each basket.
Use with Lesson 1.

Home Letters Go online to view the Home Letters for this unit.

Collaboration

Collaboration opportunities in this unit:

Build on Prior Knowledge
pp. 43, 59, 61, 73, 89

Think, Draw, Pair, Share
p. 62

Small Groups
pp. 79, 97

Cultivating New Questions
pp. 57, 69, 85, 99

Think, Pair, Share
pp. 56, 84, 90

Connections to Science

Connections to Science opportunities in this unit:

Connection to Engineering Design
Developing Possible Solutions Lesson 1, p. 45
Connection to Life Science
Structure and Function Lesson 2, p. 67
Connection to Life Science
Cause and Effect Lesson 3, p. 77
Connection to Earth and Space Sciences
Patterns Lesson 4, p. 91

Unit Project

👥 small groups 🕙 1 class period

Explore Melting

There are many ways to complete this Unit Project. The steps and Suggested Materials indicate one way to complete the investigation. Encourage children to come up with their own ideas of how to melt ice the fastest. Be sure to review each group's plans before children begin. This Unit Project supports content in Lessons 1, 3, and 4.

3D Learning Objective

SEP Engaging in Argument from Evidence
Explore the fastest way to cause ice to change to water by planning and conducting an investigation.
Collect data to use as evidence to answer a question.
Construct an argument using evidence to support a claim.

Skills and Standards Focus

This project supports building children's mastery of **Perfomance Expectation 2-PS1-4.**	**SEP** Engaging in Argument from Evidence
	SEP Planning and Carrying Out Investigations
	DCI **PS1.A** Structure and Properties of Matter
	DCI **PS1.B** Chemical Reactions
	CCC Cause and Effect

Suggested Materials

- 2 same-sized ice cubes
- 2 bowls
- tin can
- clock with second hand or stopwatch

Preparation

Have enough ice cubes prepared in advance for each pair or group of children. The time for the ice to change to water will vary depending on the room temperature, the size of the ice cubes, and the starting temperature of the ice. However, 20 minutes is a good estimate. The temperature at which all the ice has melted will be 32 degrees Fahrenheit as this is the melting/freezing point of water. Before beginning the project, share details about the melting/freezing point of water or challenge children to use online resources to identify it.

Unit 2
Matter

Unit Project • Explore Melting
What is the fastest way to change ice to water? Investigate to find out.

Unit 2 • Matter

39

Differentiate Instruction

RTI/Extra Support Children can be provided with 2–4 different already-determined ways to melt the ice. They can then choose their method to investigate.

Extension Provide children with constraints before allowing them to investigate. An example of a constraint could be you can not use your hands to melt the ice.

Unit 2 Project
Explore Melting

Name _____

What's the fastest way to change ice to water? Can you think of two different ways to test this? Write your ideas on the lines below. Then choose one. Plan and conduct an investigation to find out.

Children should write two ideas they have for investigating how ice

can be changed to water.

Materials
Draw and label the materials you will need.

Children should draw and label materials. The following are possible materials children can use for this investigation: ice cubes, bowls, tin cans, a clock.

Unit 2 Project • Page 1 of 3

Unit 2 Project

Explore Melting

 Planning and Carrying Out Investigations . . . .

Pose the unit project question to children. Encourage them to think of two ways to demonstrate the fastest way to cause ice to change to water. Discuss all of the ideas as a class. Some alternative ideas to melting the ice cube could be setting it near a sunny window, placing it outside, or placing it under a heat source. Have children choose one to investigate.

In the sample investigation shown, children compare the melting time of an ice cube with the melting time of an ice cube that has been broken into smaller pieces.

Children will place one ice cube in a bowl. They will place the other ice cube in the tin can and shake it long enough to break up the ice cube into smaller pieces. The smaller pieces should then be placed in the second bowl. **Ask: Which ice cube do you think will melt the fastest? Why?** I think the broken pieces of ice will melt faster because they are smaller than the ice cube.

ESSENTIAL QUESTIONS Prepare children for their project by asking the following questions.

- What ways can you change a solid to a liquid?
- What evidence can be collected to show a change has occurred?
- What cause and effect relationship will occur when you melt the ice?

Ask: What happens to matter inside a freezer? What changes do you expect to be caused when the solid and the liquid are placed in the freezer? Material is cooled in a freezer. I think the solid will be colder but will still be solid. I think the liquid will become a solid.

Steps

Discuss with children the importance of listing out steps in their investigation. If children need help, brainstorm the steps as a class.

DCI **Structure and Properties of Matter** . . . .

Before beginning the investigation, have children observe the properties of one of the ice cubes.

Ask: How would you describe the ice? The ice is hard and cold. Challenge children to identify its state of matter. **Ask: What state of matter is the ice in?** The ice is in a solid form. Refer children to Lesson 1 Engineer It • What Are Properties of Matter? Have them record their observations using words and pictures.

Have children observe both bowls every 10 minutes until all of the ice has completely melted. At the end of the investigation, children will need to be able to tell which bowl of ice melted the fastest based on the amount of time it took each one to completely melt. Children should record their observations using words and pictures.

Data

Remind children to make observations as they investigate and use them as data to determine the outcome of the investigation.

DCI **Chemical Reactions** . . . .

Ask: What happened to the ice cube? What happened to the broken ice? Children should describe how the solid ice melted to become liquid water.

CCC **Cause and Effect** . . . .

Remind children that a cause is why something happens and an effect is what actually happens. **Ask: What do you think caused the ice to melt?** The temperature of the air in the room is warmer than the ice. The temperature of the air in the room caused the ice to heat up and melt. Refer children to Lesson 3 How Do Heating and Cooling Change Matter?

Steps Write the steps you will do.

Answers may vary but should reflect a logical order of

steps in the investigation. Sample steps listed:

1. Put one ice cube in a bowl.

2. Place the other ice cube in the tin can.

3. Shake the can until the ice cube is broken into smaller pieces.

4. Place the small pieces of ice in the other bowl.

5. Observe and record how each bowl of ice changes every

10 minutes until all of the ice has completely melted.

Data
Record your data.

Answers and drawings may vary but should reflect that the broken pieces of ice melted faster than the ice cube.

_____ mins   _____ mins   _____ mins

© Houghton Mifflin Harcourt Publishing Company

Analyze Your Results

Look for patterns in your data.

Restate Your Question

Write the question you investigated.

Answers should identify the question children initially chose at the

beginning of the investigation.

Claims, Evidence, and Reasoning

Make a claim that answers your question.

Answer should identify the method that caused ice to melt the fastest.

Review the data. What evidence from the investigation supports your claim?

Answer should cite evidence from the investigation to support which

method melted the ice the fastest.

Compare your results as a class to find out which way was the fastest.

Analyze Your Results

Have children analyze their data. Elicit from them any patterns they noticed. Encourage them to share their data with the other groups in order to compare test results. **Ask: Which bowl of ice melted faster?** the bowl with the broken ice

Claims, Evidence, and Reasoning

Children should understand that the bowl with the broken pieces of ice melted faster than the bowl with the ice cube.

SEP **Engaging in Argument from Evidence** . . . .

Review with children what it means to make a claim. Guide them to understand that the data they collected will be used as evidence to support their claim. **Ask: What can you use as evidence from your investigation?** The data collected, such as the drawings, writings, and recorded times.

Ask: What claim can you make? The bowl of broken ice melted faster than the ice cube. **Ask: How does your evidence support your claim?** My evidence supports this because it took less time for the broken pieces of ice to melt than the ice cube. Encourage children to discuss their reasoning. Have the groups compare their results to find out which method was the fastest.

Scoring Rubric for Unit Project	
3	States a claim supported with evidence that smaller pieces of ice melt faster than one solid piece of ice
2	States a claim somewhat supported with evidence that smaller pieces of ice melt faster than one solid piece of ice
1	States a claim that is not supported by evidence
0	Does not state a claim and does not provide evidence

Engineer It • What Are Properties of Matter?

Building to the Performance Expectations

The learning experiences in this lesson prepare children for mastery of:

2-PS1-1 Plan and conduct an investigation to describe and classify different kinds of materials by their observable properties.

2-PS1-2 Analyze data obtained from testing different materials to determine which materials have the properties that are best suited for an intended purpose.

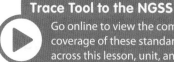
Trace Tool to the NGSS
Go online to view the complete coverage of these standards across this lesson, unit, and time.

 **Science & Engineering Practices**

Planning and Carrying Out Investigations
Plan and conduct an investigation collaboratively to produce data . . . for evidence to answer a question.

 **VIDEO** SEP: Planning and Carrying Out Investigations

Analyzing and Interpreting Data
Analyze data from tests of an object or tool to determine if it works as intended.

 **VIDEO** SEPs: Analyzing and Interpreting Data / Using Mathematics and Computational Thinking

 Disciplinary Core Ideas

PS1.A: Structure and Properties of Matter
- Different kinds of matter exist and many of them can be either solid or liquid, depending on temperature. Matter can be described and classified by its observable properties.
- Different properties are suited to different purposes.

 **Crosscutting Concepts**

Patterns
Patterns in the natural and human designed world can be observed.

Cause and Effect
Simple tests can be designed to gather evidence to support or refute student ideas about causes.

Influence of Engineering, Technology, and Science on Society and the Natural World
Every human-made product is designed by applying some knowledge of the natural world and is built using materials derived from the natural world.

CONNECTIONS TO MATH

MP.4 Model with mathematics.

2.MD.D.10 Draw a picture graph and a bar graph . . . with up to four categories. Solve simple put-together, take-apart, and compare problems using . . . a bar graph.

CONNECTION TO ENGLISH LANGUAGE ARTS

W.2.8 Recall information from experiences or gather information from provided sources to answer a question.

Supporting All Students, All Standards

Integrating the Three Dimensions of Learning

This lesson focuses on observable properties of matter and identifying properties that make materials best suited to their purposes **(DCI Structure and Properties of Matter)**. The lesson begins with children exploring various properties, including states of matter. Children will build on prior knowledge by identifying patterns in the properties of liquids and solids **(CCC Patterns)**. Children will also build on prior knowledge by planning and conducting an investigation. Within this investigation, they will identify which material is best suited for use as a filler for a pillow **(SEP Planning and Carrying Out Investigations, CCC Cause and Effect)**. Then they will analyze and look for patterns in the data about the different materials they tested as pillow fillers **(SEP Analyzing and Interpreting Data)**. Finally, children will connect buildings to the natural forms on which they are based **(CCC Influence of Engineering, Technology, and Science on Society and the Natural World)**.

Professional Development

Go online to view **Professional Development videos** with strategies to integrate CCCs and SEPs, including the ones used in this lesson.

Build on Prior Knowledge

Children should already know and be prepared to build on the following concepts:

- Planning and conducting an investigation can produce results, which can be used as data. *(Grade 1, Unit 2, Lesson 1)*
- Objects have different shapes, colors, and materials.
- Patterns repeat over and over. *(Grade K, Unit 3, Lesson 1)*
- Patterns can be observed in nature. *(Grade K, Unit 3, Lesson 1)*
- Patterns can be observed in human-made objects. *(Grade K, Unit 3, Lesson 1)*

Differentiate Instruction

Lesson Vocabulary

- matter
- property
- solid
- liquid

Reinforcing Vocabulary Have children share their understanding of the vocabulary words. Be aware that children may suggest alternate meanings for *matter* and *property*. Discuss the alternate meanings and explain why they do not apply in the context of this lesson. Ask children to provide examples of solids and liquids. Point out that the first time they see each word it will be highlighted in yellow.

RTI/Extra Support As a class, brainstorm a list of words that are associated with different properties of matter, such as *shape, color, size,* and *texture*. List children's suggestions under each property. Allow children to use the list as a resource as they proceed through the lesson.

Extension Children who want to find out more can do research on properties of matter. Have children collect a variety of materials that can be categorized by their properties. Children can make a poster or slide show to share what they found out with the class.

ELL Be sure to point out all labels, pictures, captions, and headings throughout the lesson to assist children with strategies to summarize chunks of content. Discuss with children real-life connections to content and provide hands-on examples of materials when possible to best support the needs of these learners.

Lesson Problem

Build on Prior Lessons

In Unit 1, children defined problems and designed solutions. They asked questions, made observations, and gathered evidence. Children chose materials based on their structure in order to plan, build, test, and improve models. This lesson builds on these concepts to explore structure and properties of matter.

Lesson Objective

Use evidence to describe and classify materials based on their observable properties.

About This Image

Direct children's attention to the different balls on this page. **Ask:** What properties does each ball have? Are the balls alike or different? Most of the balls are round and have the same shape. They are all different colors and sizes. Lead children in a discussion about their observations.

DCI Structure and Properties of Matter

Alternative Engage Strategy

Play Ball!	 whole class 🕑 20–30 minutes

Gather a collection of balls with a variety of sizes, colors, and textures. Take children to an appropriate play area such as the gymnasium or playground. Have children play with the balls in small groups. Every few minutes, call out a property and have children hold up a ball if it has that property. Ask children holding up the balls to explain why they held up the ball.

Lesson 1   Engineer It • What Are Properties of Matter?

These balls have different properties.

By the End of This Lesson

I will describe and classify materials by their properties. I will choose the best materials to fit my purpose.

42

Can You Explain It?

Materials Are Different The videos show how bicycle tires are used. If the videos are not available, direct children's attention to the picture. Have children discuss why bike tires are made of rubber and what makes rubber different from other materials.

Ask children to record their initial thoughts about another use for rubber. At the end of this lesson, children will revisit this question in the Lesson Check. At that point, children should be able to use what they have explored to describe the properties of rubber and name another use for rubber.

Collaboration

Build on Prior Knowledge Invite children to tell about their experiences riding a bicycle on different surfaces. Have children draw a picture that shows them riding a bicycle on a paved road, a sidewalk, or a bike trail. Ask children to share their pictures and to describe how the rubber tires help them on each surface.

Support for Unit Project and Performance Task

The **Unit Project** Explore Melting and **Unit Performance Task** Engineer It • Build a Model Boat supports content in this lesson.

Materials Are Different

Think about how bike tires are used. Why are bike tires made of rubber? What makes this material different from other materials?

Explore online. ▶

Can You Explain It?

✏ What is another use for rubber?

Accept all reasonable answers.

_____

_____

_____

Lesson 1 • Engineer It • What Are Properties of Matter?   43

Properties of Matter

3D Learning Objective

Children observe the **pattern** that matter takes up space and has properties. They will make observations about different materials and **describe their properties**.

DCI Structure and Properties of Matter . . . .

Have children look at the properties on these two pages and name them. Discuss with children how properties can be used to classify objects. **Ask: What words are used to describe the property of color?** green and red **Ask: What words are used to describe the property of shape?** cone and rectangular prism **Ask: What words are used to describe the property of hardness?** hard and soft **Ask: What words are used to describe the property of texture?** rough and smooth **Ask: What words are used to describe the property of flexibility?** flexible and stiff

Discuss with children that you use your senses to observe properties. **Ask: What senses do you use to observe?** senses of sight, smell, sound, taste, and touch **Ask: What properties can you observe with sight?** color, size, and shape with sight

---

Differentiate Instruction

ELL Provide additional visual examples of the adjectives used to describe each property. Have children use the sentence frame "The _____ is _____." for each example. Ask children to provide examples from their own experiences.

Properties of Matter

Matter is anything that takes up space. Look at the pictures to explore some properties of matter.

color

Color is a property you can see. One leaf is green. The other leaf is red.

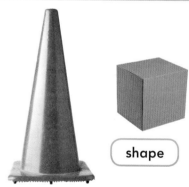

shape

Shape is the form a material has. It is a property you can see. The safety object is shaped like a cone. The box is shaped like a rectangular prism.

hardness

Hardness is how easy it is to change the shape of a material. It is a property you can feel. A marble is hard. A cotton ball is soft.

44

© Houghton Mifflin Harcourt • Image Credits: (bl) ©David Selman/Corbis; (br) ©Carlos Santa Maria/Shutterstock; (tr) ©Nguyen Thai/Shutterstock; (tl) ©George Diebold/Getty Images; (cl) ©Photodisc/Getty Images; (cr) ©Carlos Santa Maria/Shutterstock

texture

Texture is what a material feels like. It is a property you can feel. The light brown rock is rough. The dark brown rock is smooth.

flexibility

Flexibility is how much a material can bend. It is easy to bend the chenille sticks. They are flexible. It is not easy to bend the craft sticks. They are stiff.

Matter has properties. A **property** is one part of what something is like. You can observe properties of matter with all your senses.

Color, shape, hardness, and flexibility are some properties of matter. These properties can be used over and over to describe matter. This forms a pattern.

Patterns
Go to the online handbook for tips.

© Houghton Mifflin Harcourt • Image Credits: (tl) ©Valentina Razumova/Shutterstock; ((br) ©Freedom_Studio/Shutterstock; (tr) ©ovidguten/Shutterstock

Lesson 1 • Engineer It • What Are Properties of Matter?

45

DCI Structure and Properties of Matter . . . .

Have children read aloud the sections on hardness and texture. **Ask: What properties can you observe with touch?** hardness and texture **Ask: What other properties not shown on these pages can you observe with touch?** I can observe temperature with touch. I can observe how wet or dry something is with touch.

CCC Patterns . . . .

Discuss other examples of matter that are flexible, such as a beach noodle and an elastic band. Have children identify objects in the classroom that are flexible. **Ask: How can you find out if an object is flexible?** I can check to see if it is easy to bend. Point out that this is a pattern because it is a thing or an event that repeats. If something is easy to bend, then it is flexible. Discuss observable patterns with the other properties.

CCC Patterns . . . .

Ask: How is all matter alike? All matter takes up space and has properties. Point out that this is a pattern because it is something that is repeated. If something takes up space, it is matter. **Ask: What are some examples of matter?** chairs, people, pencils, etc.

💡 **Patterns** When looking for patterns, you look for things or events that repeat. Remind children to think about things that are true of all matter.

Connection to Engineering Design

Developing Possible Solutions Provide children with various crafts materials. Have them work in pairs to design name tags to be used in the classroom. Then have them share their designs with the class and describe these properties of the object: color, shape, hardness, texture, and flexibility.

DCI Structure and Properties of Matter . . . .

Have children read aloud the directions. Invite them to look at the two objects and name them. Walk through the layout of the chart with children by describing the rows and columns and what each contains. **Ask: What properties are you going to be describing for each object?** color, shape, texture, hardness, and flexibility

Differentiate Instruction

RTI/Extra Support Divide a tabletop or magnetic board into two sections. Label the sections *Matter* and *Property*. Display cards with an example of matter or an example of a property written on them. Ask children to place each card in the correct section. **Ask: What do you notice about the examples of matter?** They take up space. They have properties. **What do you notice about the examples of properties?** They describe things.

Extension Have children work in small groups. Provide each group with an assortment of classroom objects and a different property by which to sort their objects. For example, one group could sort by size, another by color, and another by texture. Allow 5 minutes to complete the activity. Children can present their sorting to the other groups.

✎➤ Write words in the chart below to identify the properties of each object.

color: green	green	
shape: round		round
texture: rough	rough	
hardness: hard		hard
flexibility: bends	bends	

46

Apply What You Know

Evidence Notebook • Can something have more than one property? Work with a partner to find out. Use all your senses to observe this box. Then, make a list to identify all properties of the box. Use evidence to support your answer. Record your answer in your Evidence Notebook.

© Houghton Mifflin Harcourt

Differentiate Instruction

RTI/Extra Support Provide children with a box that is as similar as possible to the box in the photo. This may help children identify properties that are not observable by sight.

Extension Have each group present their lists of properties. Make a classroom list that includes all of the properties suggested by the groups. Guide children to identify additional properties by drawing their attention to a particular part or feature of the box.

 FORMATIVE ASSESSMENT

Evidence Notebook
Encourage children to make an organized list of properties by adding headings that name the senses. Children may need guidance to list properties that cannot be observed using sight. Have children think about holding the box and how the box would feel.

Scoring Guidelines
- accurately identifies the properties of the box (rectangular, blue, hard, smooth)
- uses evidence to support their answer
- concludes that something can have more than one property

Explore online. ▶   Have children explore online to find out more about solids.

States of Matter—Solids

3D Learning Objective

Children will observe the pattern that a solid is a state of matter that keeps it shape.

DCI Structure and Properties of Matter . . . .

Have children work in small groups. Provide each group with blocks or other building materials. Allow 5 minutes for children to build with the blocks. **Ask: What happens to the shape of a block when you move it?** The shape stays the same. **Ask: What happens to the shape of a block when you stack another block on top of it?** The shape stays the same. Solids can be used to make other things because they do not change their shape when you move them.

CCC Patterns . . . .

Provide children with a variety of small, solid objects. Have children investigate by pushing the objects around their desks. **Ask: What happens if you move a solid?** It keeps its shape. This is a pattern because it is something that is repeated. If something does not change its shape when you move it, it is a solid.

  FORMATIVE ASSESSMENT

Evidence Notebook

Children observe properties of solid objects as they identify examples of soft solids. Remind children to use evidence to support their answers.

Scoring Guidelines

- accurately identifies examples of soft solids
- provides evidence to support examples

States of Matter—Solids

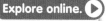

Look at the pictures to explore some solids.

A **solid** is a state of matter that keeps its shape. It will not change unless you do something to it, such as cut, bend, or break. A solid keeps its shape even when you move it. These properties can be used over and over to describe solids. This forms a pattern. Buildings, trucks, and chairs are all solids. ▭▭▶ Draw a line under the words that tell what a solid is like.

Credits: (tl) ©Houghton Mifflin Harcourt • Image Credits: (tl) ©Zhu Difeng/Shutterstock; (tr) ©Hero Images/Getty Images

✋ Apply What You Know

Evidence Notebook • Not all solids are hard. Solids can be soft like a cotton ball. What are some examples of soft solids? Discuss as a class. Use evidence to support your examples and record them in your Evidence Notebook.

48

States of Matter—Liquids

States of Matter—Liquids

Look at the pictures to explore some liquids.

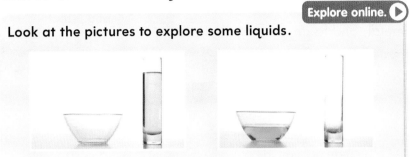

Explore online. ▶

A **liquid** is a state of matter that (does not have its own shape. It flows to take the shape of its container.) The liquid in the tall glass has the same shape as the glass. If the liquid is poured into a wide bowl, the liquid takes the bowl's shape. These properties can be used over and over to describe liquids. This forms a pattern.

✏️➤ Circle the words that tell what a liquid is like.

✋ Apply What You Know

Work in a small group to investigate what happens when you shake a clear jar of water. Compare changes to the water and the jar. Identify patterns.

💡 **Planning and Carrying Out Investigations**
Go to the online handbook for tips.

States of Matter— Liquids

3D Learning Objective

Children will observe the **pattern** that a **liquid does not have its own shape.** They will **plan and conduct an investigation** to compare a solid and a liquid.

DCI **Structure and Properties of Matter . . . .**

Ask: What happens to the liquid when it is poured into the tall glass? It takes the shape of the glass. What happens when the liquid is poured into the bowl? It takes the shape of the bowl.

CCC **Patterns . . . .**

Ask: How are all liquids alike? All liquids flow to take the shape of their container. Point out that this is a pattern.

SEP **Planning and Carrying Out Investigations . . . .**

Discuss with children how to plan and conduct an investigation.
Ask: Why is it important to plan an investigation before you begin? Sample answer: So you know the steps to follow and what materials you need.

✋ FORMATIVE ASSESSMENT

Children investigate what happens when they shake a clear jar of water. Guide children to focus on the shape of the materials before, during, and after the investigation.

Scoring Guidelines
• compares changes to the water and the jar
• identifies patterns

 Planning and Carrying Out Investigations Doing an investigation is a way to study something carefully. Children should make a plan before doing the investigation.

Which Materials Are Best?

3D Learning Objective

Children will determine which **materials are best suited for a purpose based on their properties of matter**. They will identify what properties **cause** each material to be a good choice for each bike part.

ccc Cause and Effect . . . .

For each part of the bicycle, have children identify the property that caused the material to be a good choice. **Ask: Why was foam chosen for the seat?**   because it is soft and firm   **Why was metal chosen for the frame?**   because metal is strong and hard   **Why was rubber chosen for the tires?**   because it is strong and flexible

💡 **Cause and Effect** Properties of matter cause particular materials to be suited to particular tasks. The properties are the causes. The suitability is the effect.

DCI Structure and Properties of Matter . . . .

Discuss the picture of the bicycle. Help children connect properties of materials with their purposes by discussing the effect of using other, less suitable materials.   **Ask: How would the seat feel if it were made of wood?**   It would be uncomfortable to sit on.   **What would happen if the frame were made of string?**   It would collapse.   **What would happen if the tires were made of balloons?**   They might pop when they ride over something rough or sharp.

Which Materials Are Best?

A bike has parts made from rubber, metal, and foam. Why were these materials picked for the bike?

> **Cause and Effect**
> Go to the online handbook for tips.

Explore online. ▶

foam seat
The seat is foam. Foam is soft, but firm enough to hold the weight of a rider. These properties of foam make the seat comfortable.

rubber tires
These tires are rubber. Rubber is strong and flexible. These properties of rubber give bike tires a smooth ride.

metal frame
The frame is metal. Metal is strong and hard. These properties of metal help the bike keep its shape.

50

Name _____

Hands-On Activity

Engineer It • Explore Properties of Matter

Materials _____

_____

Ask a Question

Which material makes the best filler for a pillow? _____

Test and Record Data   Explore online. ▶

Step 1

Observe the properties of each material. Compare the shape, texture, hardness, and flexibility of each one. Record your observations.

Check children's work.

Material 1	Material 2	Material 3	Material 4

© Houghton Mifflin Harcourt

Lesson 1 • Engineer It • What Are Properties of Matter?   51

Hands-On Activity 👥 small groups ⏱ 1 class period

Engineer It • Explore Properties of Matter

3D Learning Objective

SEP Planning and Carrying Out Investigations . . . .

SEP Analyzing and Interpreting Data . . . .

Children will plan and carry out tests on each of several different materials to determine their suitability as a pillow filler.

Suggested Materials cotton, foam, feathers, tissues, zippered pillowcase. You may choose to use alternative materials that are harder or less flexible in order to help children decide which is the better pillow filler. Alternatively, as a class brainstorm a list of materials that children would like to test.

Preparation

Pre-assemble materials bundles for pairs or groups. Each group will need four different materials to test.

Activity

As a class, view the video. Then discuss the question that will need to be answered. Have children record the question.

STEP 1 Remind children to use more than one sense when observing the properties of each material. Guide children to look at and touch each material before they record their observations.

DCI Structure and Properties of Matter . . . .

Ask: What properties make a material a good choice for a pillow filler? Sample answer: soft, flexible, smooth **How can you observe those properties?** Sample answer: I can use my senses to observe them. **What test can you perform to check if a material has each of those properties?** Answers will vary but should describe the plan children have to test each material.

Hands-On Activity, continued

STEP 2 To help children make their plan, refer them back to the question they want to answer.

DCI **Structure and Properties of Matter** . . . .

STEP 3 **Ask:** Why is it important to record the results of each material you tested? I can use data to help me identify which pillow filler worked best.

SEP **Analyzing and Interpreting Data** . . . .

STEP 4 Guide children in analyzing their data from each test of the materials. **Ask: Which material worked best and why?** Sample answer: The cotton worked best because it was soft.

Claims, Evidence, and Reasoning

Children should make a claim that identifies one of the materials as a good filler for a pillow. They should cite evidence to support their claim. **Ask: What properties should a pillow filler have?** Sample answer: A pillow filler should be soft so it is comfortable, but it should be firm enough to support my head.

Scoring Rubric for Hands-On Activity	
3	States a claim supported with evidence that one of the materials is a good filler for a pillow
2	States a claim somewhat supported with evidence that one of the materials is a good filler for a pillow
1	States a claim that is not supported by evidence
0	Does not state a claim and does not provide evidence

Step ②
Make a plan to test each material to find out if it is a good pillow filler.

Step ③
Follow the steps of your plan to test each one. Record and compare the results of each material tested.

Data Recording Chart

Material 1	Material 2	Material 3	Material 4

Check children's work. Results will vary.

Step ④
Analyze your results. Look for patterns.

Make a claim that answers your question.

Answer should identify one of the materials as a good filler

for a pillow.

What is your evidence?

Answer should cite evidence from the test to support the choice

of material for a good filler for a pillow.

52

© Houghton Mifflin Harcourt

Do the Math! • Which material made the better pillow filler? Make a bar graph to show the number of properties that each material had. Which one was liked best? Use the graph to answer the question.

Display Data Go to the online handbook for tips.

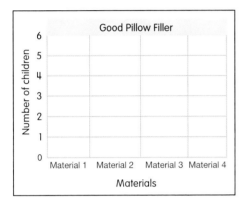

Which material did your class like best? Use data from your bar graph as evidence.

Answer should cite evidence from the graph to support the choice

of material for a good filler for a pillow.

Evidence Notebook • Think of other questions you have about the properties of materials. Record your work in your Evidence Notebook.

© Houghton Mifflin Harcourt

Do the Math! • Display Data

Guide children to the "Good Pillow Filler" bar graph. They should analyze the data in the bar graph to help them answer the question.

Ask: How many children liked each material best? How does the graph help you answer these questions? Sample answer: Six children liked the cotton the best; one child liked the sponges the best. The tallest bar shows the material most children liked, and the shortest bar shows the material that the least number of children liked. **Ask:** Why do you think children liked the cotton the best? The cotton was soft and thick enough to fill the pillow.

Display Data • Model with Mathematics To complete a bar graph, children draw bars to show how many in each category. Then they can read the graph to answer the questions. Children should look for the tallest bar to find the category with the "most," and the shortest bar to find the category with the "least."

Evidence Notebook

Pair children and have them discuss other questions they have about the properties of materials. As children move through the other lessons in this unit, have them return to the questions they wrote in their Evidence Notebook. Discuss as a class how their questions can be answered now that they have found out more about materials and their properties.

Differentiate Instruction

ELL As a class, brainstorm a list of words that could be used to complete each blank in the sentence frames. Children can use this list as a resource as they complete their riddles. If children have difficulty completing their riddles, have them return to the Properties of Matter section of the lesson.

 FORMATIVE ASSESSMENT

Read, Write, Share! • Recall Information

Children will use their understanding of properties of matter as they write specific properties to complete a riddle that describes an object.

Scoring Guidelines

• chooses properties that match the chosen object

💡 **Recall Information** As children listen to their partner's riddle, they should think about the information the riddle is giving. Then they can use that information, along with their own knowledge of objects, to complete the riddle.

 Apply What You Know

Read, Write, Share! • How can you describe an object's properties? Choose an object at home or in your classroom. Then write words to complete the riddle.

Recall Information
Go to the online handbook for tips.

This object is _____ and_____.
                          [color]   [shape]
It has a _____ surface that is _____.
                  [texture]   [hardness]
It is also _____.
         [another property]
What is it? _____

Read your riddle to a partner. Can your partner answer the riddle?
Riddles should include properties that match the chosen objects.

© Houghton Mifflin Harcourt

54

Explore online. ▶ Guide children to the Interactive Online Student Edition where they can choose from and explore both paths.

Take It Further

People in Science & Engineering •
Dr. Eugene Tssui

Explore more online.
• Another Kind of Matter

Explore online. ▶

Meet Dr. Eugene Tssui. Dr. Tssui is an architect. An architect designs homes and other buildings.

When Dr. Tssui designs homes and buildings, he studies forms in nature, such as fish fins. He bases many designs on what he finds out. Look for the fish fin in the design of the house.

Dr. Eugene Tssui

This is the inside of the house.

What does the design of this house look like?

Take It Further

People in Science & Engineering •
Dr. Eugene Tssui

Introduce children to Dr. Eugene Tssui, an architect. An architect designs homes and other buildings. When Dr. Tssui designs homes and buildings, he studies forms in nature. He bases many of his designs on what he finds out from nature. Dr. Tssui says that nature is our greatest teacher.

 Influence of Engineering, Technology, and Science on Society and the Natural World. . . .

Dr. Tssui bases his designs on forms in nature. **Ask: What properties of the fish fin did Dr. Tssui use in his design?** The house has a shape like a fish fin, and its texture looks scaly.

Differentiate Instruction

RTI/Extra Support Have children tell what Dr. Tssui designs and how he gets his ideas.

Extension Challenge children to think of a plant or animal whose properties might influence a designer. **Ask: What properties does the plant or animal have that would be useful in an object? For what object would those properties be useful?** Sample answer: A penguin has feathers to keep it warm and dry. Those properties would be useful for making clothes for swimming, diving, and other water sports.

Take It Further, continued

Dr. Tssui's Designs

 **Patterns** . . . .

Guide children to observe and describe each building on this page. As children observe Dr. Tssui's designs, remind them to look for patterns. **Ask: What ideas from nature were used in making this building?** A fish and a dragonfly are some things from nature that helped in the design of this building.

Patterns Dr. Tssui uses shapes and patterns found in nature when designing buildings.

Collaboration

Think, Pair, Share You may want to have children complete this activity in pairs. Guide children in a discussion about the properties of each natural form and the properties of each building. Children should be able to identify the properties of the natural form that make it a good choice for the building.

 Explore more online.

Another Kind of Matter

Children investigate gases, another state of matter.

Dr. Tssui's Designs

Draw a line to match each building to the natural form on which it is based.

Patterns
Go to the online handbook for tips.

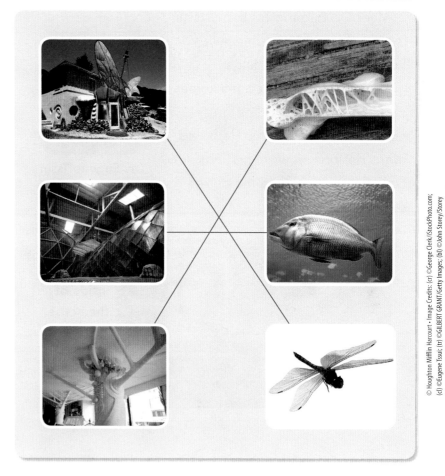

© Houghton Mifflin Harcourt • Image Credits: (cr) ©George Clerk/iStockPhoto.com; (cl) ©Eugene Tssui; (tr) ©GILBERT GRANT/Getty Images; (bl) ©John Storey/Storey Photography; (br) ©Brand X Pictures/Jupiterimages/Getty Images; (tl) ©Eugene Tssui

56

Lesson Check

Lesson Check   Name _____

Explore online. ▶

Can You Explain It?

✏️ What is another use for rubber?

Be sure to

• Describe the properties of rubber.

• Name the object you would make using rubber.

• Explain why these properties make rubber good to use for your object.

Sample answer: Rubber is strong and flexible. I would use

rubber for a car's tires. A car's tires need to be strong

because they are used a lot on hard roads. They should be

flexible so they can be molded into a tire shape and give the

car a smooth ride.

Lesson 1 • Engineer It • What Are Properties of Matter?   57

© Houghton Mifflin Harcourt • Image Credits: ©Vetta/Getty Images

Can You Explain It?

Have children reread their answers to the Can You Explain It? prompt at the beginning of the lesson.

DCI **Structure and Properties of Matter** . . . .

If children have difficulty responding to the Can You Explain It? question, have them look at the picture of the bicycle and think about the properties of rubber. **Ask: What makes rubber a unique material?** Rubber is strong and can be molded to make different shapes. It can also stretch and get bigger like a balloon.

CCC **Cause and Effect** . . . .

Children should implicitly or explicitly refer to the cause-and-effect relationship between the properties of rubber and the reasons why rubber is an appropriate material for the object described.

Scoring Guidelines

• Children should describe the properties of rubber.

• Children should choose an object to make using rubber.

• Children should explain why the properties make rubber a good material for their chosen object.

Collaboration

Cultivating New Questions As children complete this lesson and prepare for the next lesson, ask them to identify additional questions they have about properties of matter. **Ask: Are there any other properties of matter you can observe?** size, odor, taste, ability to sink or float As children continue to the next lesson, they will apply concepts related to properties of matter.

Lesson Check, continued

SUMMATIVE ASSESSMENT
Self Check

1. Children should choose A—soft; and D—round. If children choose either B or C, have them review the Properties of Matter section of the lesson. Ask children to think about what they would see and feel when they observe a cotton ball.

2. Children should choose B—A liquid takes the shape of its container. If children choose A or C, ask them to observe the containers in the pictures. Point out that the liquid from the tall container was poured into the short container. Then have children read the answer choices again and choose the pattern they see.

3. Children should write *red; round; smooth; does not bend* for the red vase; and *white; round bottom, cylinder top; bumpy; does not bend* for the white vase. If children do not correctly describe the properties of each vase, have them revisit the Properties of Matter section of the lesson. Remind children that there can be more than one property to describe each vase, and the vases may have some of the same properties.

Self Check

1. Which properties describe a cotton ball? Choose all correct answers.
   - Ⓐ soft
   - Ⓑ rough
   - Ⓒ stiff
   - Ⓓ round

2. Look at the pictures. What pattern do you see?
   - Ⓐ A liquid keeps its shape.
   - Ⓑ A liquid takes the shape of its container.
   - Ⓒ A liquid spreads out to fill its container.

3. What are the properties of each vase? The vases may share some of the same properties.

	color	shape	texture	flexibility
	red	round	smooth	does not bend
	white	round bottom, cylinder top	bumpy	does not bend

58

4. Which pictures show a liquid? Circle each one.

5. What is a solid? What is a liquid? Write **solid** or **liquid** to make each sentence true.

Matter that keeps its shape is called a ___solid___.
Matter that flows to take the shape of its container is called a ___liquid___.

6. Answer this riddle. This object is yellow and crescent-shaped. It has smooth skin that you can peel off. Its insides are soft and sweet to eat. What is it?

Ⓐ a lemon
Ⓑ the moon
Ⓒ a banana

4. Children should circle the acorn and pinecone and buttons. If children circle either the drink or the shampoo, review the definition of a solid. Then work through each answer choice to discuss whether it is a solid. Ask questions such as, "Is an acorn a solid? How do you know?"

5. Children should complete the first sentence with *solid* and the second sentence with *liquid*. If children complete the sentences incorrectly, have them revisit the States of Matter—Solids and States of Matter—Liquids sections of the lesson. To help children respond with the correct answers, rephrase each statement as a question: "What do we call matter that keeps its shape? What do we call matter that flows to take the shape of its container?"

6. Children should choose C—a banana. If children choose A or B, have them compare the properties of a lemon, a banana, and the moon. Ask guiding questions such as, "Is a lemon yellow and crescent-shaped?" Some children may benefit from making a list or chart to identify the color, shape, texture, hardness, and flexibility of each object.

Lesson 2 — How Are Objects Put Together?

Building to the Performance Expectation

The learning experiences in this lesson prepare children for mastery of:

2-PS1-3 Make observations to construct an evidence-based account of how an object made of a small set of pieces can be disassembled and made into a new object.

Trace Tool to the NGSS
Go online to view the complete coverage of these standards across the lesson, unit, and time.

SEP — Science & Engineering Practices

Constructing Explanations and Designing Solutions
Make observations (firsthand or from media) to construct an evidence-based account for natural phenomena.

 VIDEO SEPs: Constructing Explanations and Designing Solutions/Engaging in Argument from Evidence

DCI — Disciplinary Core Ideas

PS1.A: Structure and Properties of Matter
A great variety of objects can be built up from a small set of pieces.

CCC — Crosscutting Concepts

Energy and Matter
Objects may break into smaller pieces and be put together into larger pieces, or change shapes.

 VIDEO CCC: Energy

VIDEO CCC: Matter

CONNECTION TO MATH

2.G.A.2 Partition a rectangle into rows and columns of same-size squares and count to find the total number of them.

CONNECTION TO ENGLISH LANGUAGE ARTS

W.2.8 Recall information from experiences or gather information from provided sources to answer a question.

Supporting All Students, All Standards

Integrating the Three Dimensions of Learning

The lesson begins with children exploring how objects can be built up from smaller pieces (**DCI Structure and Properties of Matter**). Children will explore how different objects can be built from the same pieces. As they explore, they will observe how the shapes of the objects can change and how an object's smaller pieces can be put together into larger pieces (**DCI Structure and Properties of Matter**) (**CCC Energy and Matter**). Finally, children will build on prior knowledge by using their observations as evidence to explain how an object can be taken apart and its component pieces put together to make a new object (**SEP Constructing Explanations and Designing Solutions**).

Professional Development Go online to view **Professional Development videos** with strategies to integrate CCCs and SEPs, including the ones used in this lesson.

Build on Prior Knowledge

Children should already know and be prepared to build on the following concepts:

- Use observations as evidence to construct explanations for phenomena in nature. *(Grade 1, Unit 3, Lesson 1)*
- Matter is anything that takes up space. *(Grade 2, Unit 2, Lesson 1)*
- Color, shape, flexibility, and hardness are properties of matter. *(Grade 2, Unit 2, Lesson 1)*
- Matter can be a solid. A solid keeps its shape. It will not change its shape unless you do something such as cut, bend, or break it. *(Grade 2, Unit 2, Lesson 1)*

Differentiate Instruction

RTI/Extra Support Allow children to explore building objects from smaller pieces, taking the object apart, and building a different object with the same pieces. Provide children with a variety of building materials, such as interlocking blocks, connecting cubes, wood blocks, and other toys.

Extension Children who want to find out more can do research on other careers that involve building objects from smaller pieces or taking objects apart. Children can use print and online resources or talk to adults with relevant careers. Children can share what they find out with the class by making a poster.

ELL Be sure to point out all labels, pictures, captions, and headings throughout the lesson to assist children with strategies to summarize chunks of content. Discuss with children real-life connections to content and provide hands-on examples of materials when possible to best support the needs of these learners.

Lesson Phenomenon

Build on Prior Lessons

In Lesson 1, children explored properties and states of matter. They planned an investigation and used observations to determine patterns in properties of objects. Lesson 2 builds on these concepts to explore how a variety of objects can be built from smaller pieces.

Lesson Objective

Use observations as evidence to explain how an object made of a small set of pieces can be taken apart and made into a new object.

About This Image

Guide children to look at and discuss the picture of the marble run. Discuss how the marble run was built. **Ask: Have you ever put together a marble run or similar object? How did you build it?** I put small pieces together. **Do you have to put the marble run together the same way every time?** No, I can build it differently by putting the pieces in a different order.

 SEP **Constructing Explanations and Designing Solutions**
Alternative Engage Strategy

Scavenger Hunt	👥 whole class 🕐 20–30 minutes

Take the class on a walk through the school or around school grounds. Explain to children that they should search for objects that are made up of or built from smaller pieces. After returning to the classroom, have children draw a picture of one of the objects found on the walk. Guide children to label or circle the different pieces that make up the object.

Lesson 2   How Are Objects Put Together?

Many objects are made up of smaller pieces.

By the End of This Lesson

I will be able to explain how an object made up of smaller pieces can be taken apart and put together to make a different object.

60

Taking Apart, Putting Together

What pieces do you see in the first object?
You can take this object apart. You can put the same pieces together to make a different object.

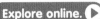
Explore online. ▶

Can You Explain It?

✏ How did the first object become a different one?

Accept all reasonable answers.

_____

_____

_____

_____

_____

Lesson 2 • How Are Objects Put Together?   61

Can You Explain It?

Taking Apart, Putting Together Objects can be taken apart and their pieces put together in different ways. Have children go online to look at the pictures. If they are unable to go online, have children look at the pictures on the page.

Ask children to record their initial thoughts about how the first object became the second one. At the end of this lesson, children will revisit the pictures as part of the Lesson Check. At this point, children should be able to use evidence to tell how objects are made of smaller pieces that can be taken apart and put back together to make different objects.

Collaboration

Build on Prior Knowledge You may want children to view and discuss the pictures as a whole-class activity. In this way, you can assess their prior knowledge of how objects are put together.

In small groups, have children discuss how the first object was taken apart and built into the second object. Children should compare and contrast the two objects and tell whether other objects could be built using the same pieces. Children can use evidence from the pictures or from their own experiences to support their answers.

Support for Unit Performance Task

The **Unit Performance Task** Engineer It • Build a Model Boat supports content in this lesson.

Build It Up, Break It Down

3D Learning Objective

Children will **make observations and use evidence** to describe how **objects can be built up from smaller pieces.** Children will observe that many **different objects can be built from the same set of pieces.**

DCI **Structure and Properties of Matter** . . . .

Guide children to make observations about the materials on the page. Have children discuss the characteristics of all the materials. **Ask:** How do you think these different materials will come together to make a house? Sample answer: The objects are all rectangles and can be stacked easily to make a house.

SEP **Constructing Explanations and Designing Solutions** . . . .

Guide children to think about their drawing. Have the class discuss why they think the houses look different. **Ask: What claim can you make about building objects from a set of pieces?** Sample answer: Different objects can be built from the same set of pieces **What is your evidence?** We used the same pieces to build different houses.

Collaboration

Think, Draw, Pair, Share Have children exchange their drawings with a partner. The partner can verify that all the pieces in the box were used in the house. Then children can compare their drawing with their partner's and discuss the similarities and differences. Pairs can share their drawings with the group and discuss the comparisons.

Build It Up, Break It Down

Look at these materials.

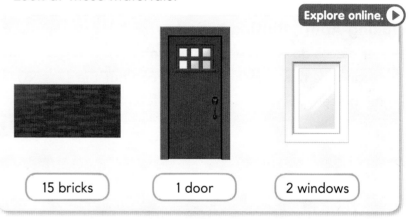

Explore online. ▶

| 15 bricks | 1 door | 2 windows |

You can make new objects from smaller pieces. Use the materials to make a house. Then compare your house to the houses your classmates made. How are your houses alike? How are they different?

✏️▷ Draw your house. Show the materials.

Drawings should include bricks, a door, and two windows.

© Houghton Mifflin Harcourt

62

Which smaller pieces make up this chair? Choose all correct answers.

Ⓐ legs

Ⓑ seat

Ⓒ arms

Ⓓ back

Ⓔ top

Apply What You Know

Evidence Notebook • How can different objects be made from the same set of pieces? Work with a partner to discuss what makes up different objects, such as your homes. Use evidence to support your answer. Record your answer in your Evidence Notebook.

 Constructing Explanations • Energy and Matter Go to the online handbook for tips.

Lesson 2 • How Are Objects Put Together?   63

---

ccc Energy and Matter . . . .

Have children share their answers to the question. Discuss with children that they should have selected legs, seat, and back. **Ask: How would the shape of the chair change if it had no back?** Sample answer: The shape would be like a stool instead of a chair.

Differentiate Instruction

ELL If children have difficulty naming the parts of the chair, help them connect each part to its use or appearance. For example, the legs of the chair help the chair stand, just like a person's legs help a person stand. When a person sits in a chair, their legs are near the legs of the chair. The back of the chair supports a person's back. The seat of the chair is where a person sits.

FORMATIVE ASSESSMENT

Evidence Notebook

Children explain how different objects can be made from the same set of pieces. They will work with a partner to discuss what makes up different objects. Make sure that children use evidence to support their answers.

Scoring Guidelines

• explains how different objects can be made from the same set of pieces
• provides sufficient evidence to support their answers

💡 **Constructing Explanations** Remind children that their observations can be used as evidence when making a claim.

💡 **Energy and Matter** Remind children that the characteristics of matter affect how parts can be put together to make new objects.

Lesson 2 • How Are Objects Put Together?   **63**

What Is the Same?

3D Learning Objective

Children will **make observations and use evidence** to describe how **objects can be built up from smaller pieces** and that those **pieces can be taken apart to build objects**.

 SEP **Constructing Explanations and Designing Solutions** . . . .

Have children make observations about the two different structures. **Ask: How are the buildings alike? The buildings both use the same pieces. How are the buildings different? The buildings have two different shapes.**

 FORMATIVE ASSESSMENT

Read, Write, Share! • Evidence Notebook

Children will work with the class to discuss what smaller pieces make up a wooden bench and how those pieces could be used to make something else. Make sure children use evidence to support the discussion.

Scoring Guidelines

- describes the smaller pieces that make up the bench
- describes something they can build with the same pieces
- provides sufficient evidence to support their answers

Constructing Explanations Remind children to base their explanations about events on their observations.

Energy and Matter Support children in their understanding of what pieces make up a bench. Provide a picture or model for extra support.

Gather Information Children can look for answers in books, encyclopedias, magazines, newspapers, digital audio, and the Internet. Children can ask questions about an object to gather information about it.

What Is the Same?

Observe the two toy buildings. How are they the same? Choose the best answer.

Ⓐ They are the same size.

Ⓑ They are the same shape.

Ⓒ They are made from the same set of pieces.

 Apply What You Know

Read, Write, Share! • Evidence Notebook • Work with your class. Discuss the smaller pieces that make up a wooden bench. What else could you build with the same set of pieces? Use evidence to support your discussion. Record your answers in your Evidence Notebook.

Constructing Explanations • Energy and Matter • Gather Information Go to the online handbook for tips.

64

© Houghton Mifflin Harcourt

Hands-On Activity 👥 individuals ⏱ 1 class period

Build Objects from Smaller Pieces

Name _____

Hands-On Activity

Build Objects from Smaller Pieces

Materials
_____

Ask a Question

How many objects can be built from the same set of pieces?

Test and Record Data   Explore online. ▶

Step 1

Make a plan to find out how many objects you can build from the same set of smaller pieces.

Plans will vary. Check children's work.

_____

_____

Step 2

Make observations as you follow your plan. Draw to record each object you build.

Check children's work.

Hands-On Activity 👥 individuals ⏱ 1 class period

Build Objects from Smaller Pieces

3D Learning Objective

SEP **Constructing Explanations and Designing Solutions** . . . .

Children will design and implement a plan to find out how many objects they can build from the same set of pieces. They will record the objects they build and analyze the results.

Suggested Materials set of small pieces

Preparation

Organize sets of small pieces for each child. Alternatively, children may do this activity at home or in small groups if limited materials are available.

Activity

As a class, view the video. Then discuss the question that will need to be answered. Have children record the question.

STEP 1 Remind children to make observations of the small pieces. Have children discuss the characteristics of the small objects and how they affect the objects' ability to be put together.

DCI **Structure and Properties of Matter** . . . .

Ask: **What characteristics allow the pieces to be put together easily?** Answers will vary depending on the objects used.   **What characteristics make it difficult for the pieces to be put together?** Answers will vary depending on the objects used.

STEP 2 Children can make quick sketches of each object, instead of a detailed drawing. Provide additional drawing paper if needed. If children are stuck and unable to build any more objects, allow them to quickly walk around and observe other groups to get ideas.

Hands-On Activity, continued

STEP 3 Children can count the number of objects at the end of the investigation or keep a tally as they work. **Ask: How were you able to use the same set of pieces to build more than one object?** Sample answer: I took each object apart after I recorded a description of it.

SEP **Constructing Explanations and Designing Solutions** . . . .

Have children discuss how building the objects would have been easier or more difficult if they had different smaller pieces. Guide children in brainstorming other smaller pieces they could use.

STEP 4 Have children share their results with a partner. **Ask: How does the number of objects you made compare to the number of objects made by your partner?** Answers may vary depending on their results.

Claims, Evidence, and Reasoning

Children should make a claim that states the number of objects they made. They should cite evidence from their plans and objects built to support their results. **Ask: Why did some classmates make more or fewer objects than you did?** Answers may vary depending on their results.

Scoring Rubric for Hands-On Activity	
3	States a claim supported with evidence about the number of objects that can be built from the same set of pieces
2	States a claim somewhat supported with evidence about the number of objects that can be built from the same set of pieces
1	States a claim that is not supported by evidence
0	Does not state a claim and does not provide evidence

Step 3

Record the number of objects you build.

Answers will vary.
_____

_____

Step 4

Analyze your results.

Make a claim that answers your question.

Answers should reflect children's solutions for how

many objects can be built from the same set of pieces.

_____

_____

What is your evidence?

Answers should cite evidence from children's plans

and objects built.

_____

_____

66

Explore online. ▶ Guide children to the Interactive Online Student Edition where they can choose from and explore both paths.

Take It Further

Careers in Science & Engineering •
Architect

Children investigate how architects design buildings so they can be put together by other people. Architects use math, science, and art to plan and design buildings that are strong, safe, and useful. When architects plan buildings, they think about the pieces that will be used to build the structure. Sometimes they build models of the buildings to help them plan the pieces that will make up their buildings. Architects may also plan and design changes to existing buildings. Such changes can make the buildings safer and stronger.

DCI **Structure and Properties of Matter** . . . .

Have children brainstorm what type of materials architects might use when they design structures. Discuss with children how these types of materials are important when building something using smaller pieces. **Ask: How does the type of material used for the smaller pieces affect the structures?** Sample answer: Using metal to make the smaller pieces makes the structure stronger.

> ## Connection to Life Science
>
> Structure and Function When architects plan and draw designs, they have to take into consideration the shape and stability of the materials used. They get inspiration from the natural world, such as from how a tree trunk is flexible but also strong enough to withstand high winds. They use these ideas in their design to ensure the structure is sound.

Take It Further

Careers in Science & Engineering •
Architect

Explore more online.
• What's Old Is New Again

Explore online. ▶

Architects plan and draw design ideas. They make models to show how their structures will look.

Architects work with others to improve their designs. They think of ways to make structures that are safe and strong.

Architects use sets of smaller pieces to build different models. They plan and design many types of structures, including houses, schools, and workplaces. Architects use art, math, and science in their work.

© Houghton Mifflin Harcourt • Image Credits: (t) ©Lou-foto/Alamy; (b) ©Creatas Video/Getty Images

Take It Further, continued

Design It!

Children will draw a design of a building they would like to build. Have children share their drawing with classmates and explain how they used smaller pieces to make up their structure.

Do the Math! • Partition Shapes

Children should choose B. If children chose A, they may have counted the number of blocks in a single row. If they chose C, they may have counted the total number of bricks needed to build the base, including the red blocks. Guide children to read the question carefully.

 Partition Shapes Remind children they can partition a rectangle into same-size squares and count to find the total number of them.

Differentiate Instruction

RTI/Extra Support Allow children to model the situation with concrete manipulatives. Provide children with square blocks in two different colors.

Extension Challenge children to draw as many different bases as they can using the same number of bricks as Kayla.

Explore more online. ▶

What's Old Is New Again

Children view images of sustainable art and sustainable architecture.

Design It!

Now it is your turn to be an architect.

✏️➤ Think of a structure you would like to build. Draw your design.

Check children's drawings.

Do the Math! • Kayla is building a model of her structure. Its base is a layer of square blocks that are all the same size. This drawing shows the red blocks Kayla is using. She wants to use blue blocks to fill the rest of the base.

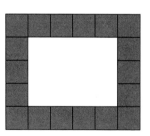

How many blue blocks does Kayla need to finish the base?

Ⓐ 4

🅑 12

Ⓒ 30

68

💡 **Partition Shapes**
Go to the online handbook for tips.

© Houghton Mifflin Harcourt

Lesson Check

Name _____

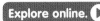

Explore online. ▶

Can You Explain It?

✏️▷ How did the first object become a different one?
Be sure to

• Explain how the first object is made up of a small set of pieces that can be taken apart.

• Explain how the same pieces can be put back together to make the new object.

• Use evidence to support your answer.

Sample answer: The first object is built from many

small pieces. You can take the object apart to separate

all the pieces. Then you can put the small pieces together in a

different way to make a new object. The new object has the

same wheels, rods, and fan blades.

Lesson Check

Can You Explain It?

Have children reread their answer to the Can You Explain It? prompt at the beginning of the lesson.

DCI **Structure and Properties of Matter** . . . .

Ask: What are the different pieces that make up the object in the first picture? What pieces are shown in the set in the second picture? What are the different pieces that make up the object in the third picture? Descriptions about how the pieces are used in each picture may vary, but all should refer to wheels, rods, and fan blades.

SEP **Constructing Explanations and Designing Solutions** . . . .

Remind children to use evidence as they formulate their answers.
Ask: What is the first object made of? many small pieces How do you know? I can see the different pieces in the picture.

Scoring Guidelines

• Children should effectively explain how the first object is made up of a small set of pieces that can be taken apart.

• Children should effectively explain how the same pieces can be put back together to make the new object.

• Children should provide evidence to support their answers.

Collaboration

Cultivating New Questions As children complete this lesson and prepare for the next lesson, ask them to identify additional questions they have about objects that can be built up from smaller sets of pieces. **Ask: What other objects can be built using smaller pieces?** tables, bikes, playground equipment As children continue to the next lesson, they will apply concepts related to matter changing shape.

Lesson Check, continued

SUMMATIVE ASSESSMENT
Self Check

1. Children should choose A—the tree house, and C—bookcase. If children do not choose both A and C, have them read the question carefully and choose all of the correct answers. If children choose B, discuss with children that the bridge is made of metal, not lumber.

2. Children should choose B—desk, and D—table. If children do not choose both B and D, have them read the question carefully and select all of the correct answers. If children choose C, have them draw a picture of a chair and label its parts. Guide children to recognize that a chair has four legs, a seat, and a back.

3. Children should choose A—Take the house apart to get the blocks. If children choose B, have them read the question carefully and draw their attention to the phrase *use the blocks to build something else*. Explain to children that this means the same blocks would be used. If children choose C, have them revisit the Taking Apart, Putting Together section of the lesson. Guide children to understand that the first house must be taken apart into smaller pieces before the pieces can be put together in a new way.

Self Check
1. What could be built from these materials? Circle all correct answers.

2. An object is made up of four legs and a flat top. What could it be? Choose all correct answers.
   - (A) rug
   - (A) desk
   - (C) lamp
   - (D) table

3. You built a house with blocks. Now you want to use the blocks to build something else. What is the first step you take?
   - (A) Take the house apart to get the blocks.
   - (B) Add blocks to your house.
   - (C) Put the blocks together in a new way.

70

4. How can you build this object? Number the pictures **1**, **2**, and **3** to show the correct order.

<u>   3   </u>   <u>   1   </u>   <u>   2   </u>

5. You take apart a bicycle. Which are part of the small set of pieces that make it up? Choose all correct answers.

Ⓐ seat

Ⓑ tires

Ⓒ engine

Ⓓ wipers

Ⓔ pedals

4. Children should label the first picture with 3, the second picture with 1, and the third picture with 2. If children do not label the pictures in the correct order, have them read the question carefully. Refer them to the Build It Up, Break It Down section. Remind children that they are supposed to show the order in which to build the structure from beginning to end.

5. Children should choose A—seat, B—tires, and E—pedals. If children do not choose all of the correct answers, have them read the question carefully. If children choose C and/or D, show children a picture of a bicycle and have them name the parts they see.

Lesson 3 — How Do Heating and Cooling Change Matter?

Building to the Performance Expectation

The learning experiences in this lesson prepare children for mastery of:

2-PS1-4 Construct an argument with evidence that some changes caused by heating and cooling can be reversed and some cannot.

Trace Tool to the NGSS
Go online to view the complete coverage of these standards across the lesson, unit, and time.

Science & Engineering Practices

Engaging in Argument from Evidence
Construct an argument with evidence to support a claim.

▶ **VIDEO:** SEPs: Constructing Explanations and Designing Solutions/Engaging in Argument from Evidence

Science Models, Laws, Mechanisms, and Theories Explain Natural Phenomena
Scientists search for cause and effect relationships to explain natural events.

Disciplinary Core Ideas

PS1.A: Structure and Properties of Matter
Different kinds of matter exist and many of them can be either solid or liquid, depending on temperature. Matter can be described and classified by its observable properties.

PS1.B: Chemical Reactions
Heating or cooling a substance may cause changes that can be observed. Sometimes these changes are reversible, and sometimes they are not.

Crosscutting Concepts

Cause and Effect
Events have causes that generate observable patterns.

CONNECTION TO MATH

2.NBT.A.4 Compare two three-digit numbers based on meanings of the hundreds, tens, and ones digits, using >, =, and < symbols to record the results of comparisons.

CONNECTION TO ENGLISH LANGUAGE ARTS

RI.2.1 Ask and answer such questions as *who, what, where, when, why,* and *how* to demonstrate understanding of key details in a text.

Supporting All Students, All Standards

Integrating the Three Dimensions of Learning

This lesson focuses on how heating and cooling change matter (**DCI Structure and Properties of Matter and DCI Chemical Reactions**). The lesson begins with children exploring how heat by melting, cooking, and burning causes changes to various materials (**SEP Science Models, Laws, Mechanisms, and Theories Explain Natural Phenomena**) and continues with children exploring how cooling causes changes to various materials. Through these explorations, children will observe patterns in changes caused by heating and cooling (**CCC Cause and Effect**). Finally, children will construct an argument using evidence from the lesson to support their claim of how heating and cooling cause changes to matter (**SEP Engaging in Argument from Evidence**).

Professional Development

Go online to view **Professional Development videos** with strategies to integrate CCCs and SEPs, including the ones used in this lesson.

Build on Prior Knowledge

Children should already know and be prepared to build on the following concepts:

- Observations and data can be used as evidence to construct an argument. *(Grade K, Unit 3, Lesson 4)*
- A state of matter is an observable property. *(Grade 2, Unit 2, Lesson 1)*
- Matter can be a solid. A solid keeps its shape. It will not change its shape unless you do something such as cut, bend, or break it. *(Grade 2, Unit 2, Lesson 1)*
- Matter can be a liquid. A liquid does not have its own shape. A liquid takes the shape of its container. *(Grade 2, Unit 2, Lesson 1)*
- Cause and effect relationships can generate patterns. *(Grade K, Unit 4, Lesson 1)*

Differentiate Instruction

Lesson Vocabulary

- melt
- freeze

Reinforcing Vocabulary To help children remember each vocabulary word, have them draw an illustration of each word. Then have them write the word beneath the illustration, define it, and use it in a sentence. Remind children to look for these highlighted words as they proceed through the lesson.

RTI/Extra Support Supply children with additional pictures of examples of solids and liquids and how these materials change from solid to liquid or from liquid to solid. Provide children with context of how these changes take place. For example, provide the context of a solid ice pop melting into a puddle on a sunny day or a pond freezing to ice in the winter.

Extension Children who want to find out more can do research on gases and on how heating can change liquids to gases. Children should use their data to make a poster that illustrates the three states of matter of one material (e.g., water) and how it changes states.

ELL Be sure to point out all labels, pictures, captions, and headings throughout the lesson to assist children with strategies to summarize chunks of content. Discuss with children real-life connections to content and provide hands-on examples of materials when possible to best support the needs of these learners.

Lesson Phenomenon

Build on Prior Lessons

In Lesson 2, children explored how a variety of objects can be built from a small set of pieces. They used observations as evidence to explain how objects can change shapes. Lesson 3 builds on these concepts to explore changes in objects caused by heating and cooling.

Lesson Objective

Use evidence to describe how heating and cooling matter may cause changes that can be observed.

About This Image

Ask: What happened to this waterfall? Have you ever seen anything like this before? I think the water froze into large icicles. I haven't see anything like this because I live in an area where it is very warm most of the time. As you explore, you'll find out how removing heat turned this once-liquid waterfall to ice.

 Structure and Properties of Matter

Alternative Engage Strategy

States of Food	👥 small groups ⏱ 15–25 minutes

Begin with a discussion about solids and liquids. List properties of each solid and liquid that children identify. Allow 5 minutes for children to brainstorm and discuss.

Then have children work in small groups to list all the foods and beverages they consumed the previous day and categorize them as a solid or a liquid. Have groups share their lists. Lead children in a discussion to clarify any misconceptions. Allow 10–20 minutes for children to brainstorm and discuss.

Lesson **3** How Do Heating and Cooling Change Matter?

Matter can change in some interesting ways.

By the End of This Lesson

I will be able to tell how heating and cooling cause matter to change.

72

Matter Can Change

Look at the crayons. You use crayons to draw.
How are these crayons being used differently?

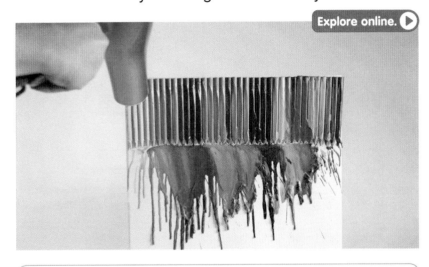

Explore online. ▶

Can You Explain It?

✏️▷ What caused the crayons to change?

Accept all reasonable answers.

© Houghton Mifflin Harcourt

Lesson 3 • How Do Heating and Cooling Change Matter?   73

Can You Explain It?

Matter Can Change Matter can change in some interesting ways. The video shows how to make crayon art. If the video is not available, direct children's attention to the picture.

Ask children to record their initial thoughts about what happened and how the crayons changed. At the end of this lesson, children will revisit this question in the Lesson Check. At that point, children should be able to use what they have explored to explain that heat by melting caused the crayons to change.

Collaboration

Build on Prior Knowledge You may want children to view and discuss the video or picture as a whole-class activity. In this way, you can assess their prior knowledge on changes in matter.

Have children think about what they saw in the video or picture. Remind them that they use crayons to draw in the classroom. Then have them discuss how what happened to the crayons was different and what caused the crayons to change. They should use details from the video or picture, and evidence, or facts, to support their answer.

Support for Unit Project

The **Unit Project** Explore Melting supports content in this lesson.

Melt It

3D Learning Objective

Children observe **changes caused by heating a substance by melting**. They identify **cause and effect relationships** and **patterns in the human-designed world**.

DCI Chemical Reactions ....

Ask: What happens when a material melts? Melting causes the material to change states from a solid to a liquid. Melting also causes the material to change shape. **How are solids different from liquids?** Solids keep their own shape and liquids do not.

SEP Science Models, Laws, Mechanisms, and Theories Explain Natural Phenomena ....

Ask children to identify each cause and effect referred to in the text. Guide children to summarize the cause and effect relationship between heat by melting and solid materials. **Ask: What are some examples of this cause and effect relationship in nature?** Examples include snow melting on a sunny day, frost melting when the sun comes up, warmer temperatures causing icebergs to melt, etc.

CCC Cause and Effect ....

Have children describe the *before* and *after* pictures. **Ask: What do the *before* pictures have in common? What do the *after* pictures have in common?** The before pictures are solids; the after pictures are liquids. **What is the pattern you observe?** The materials start as solids. Adding heat causes the materials to melt and become liquids.

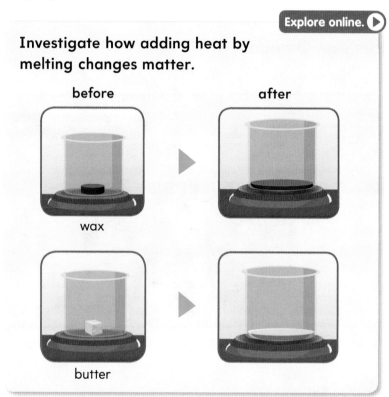

Melt It

Explore online. ▶

Investigate how adding heat by melting changes matter.

before   after

wax

butter

Heating can cause materials to change. Adding heat causes matter to melt, cook, and burn.

Adding heat to butter and wax will cause them to melt. When something **melts**, it changes from solid to liquid. Melting changes the state of matter. This is a pattern that happens when heat is added and something melts.

74

© Houghton Mifflin Harcourt

Think about the wax and butter.
What happened to the butter and
the wax when heat was added?

Ⓐ They changed from solid to liquid.

Ⓑ They changed from liquid to solid.

Ⓒ They changed color.

Apply What You Know

Evidence Notebook • Work with a partner to identify three examples of changes to materials caused by melting. How did adding heat change the material? Use evidence to tell how you know. Record your answer in your Evidence Notebook.

Engaging in Argument from Evidence
Go to the online handbook for tips.

©Houghton Mifflin Harcourt

SEP Engaging in Argument from Evidence . . . .

Children should choose A—They changed from solid to liquid. If children choose B, they may be mixing up the words *solid* and *liquid*. If they choose C, they may be misinterpreting what happened with the crayons. Point out that while some of the wax mixed together once it melted, it did not change color when it melted.

Differentiate Instruction

ELL Use pictures to illustrate the concept of states of matter. Show a picture of an ice cube and say *solid*. Show a picture of liquid water and say *liquid*. Then show the pictures again, and have children repeat each word aloud with you as you say it.

FORMATIVE ASSESSMENT

Evidence Notebook
Children identify examples of the cause and effect relationship between melting and solid materials.

Scoring Guidelines
• provides three examples
• describes how adding heat changed the materials
• uses evidence to support their answers

Engaging in Argument from Evidence Remind children that in science, a claim is an explanation of what you think is true. When you make an argument to support a claim, you want to use evidence, or proof, to show it is true.

Cook It

3D Learning Objective

Children observe **changes caused by heating a substance by cooking**. They identify **cause and effect relationships** and **patterns in the human-designed world**.

DCI Chemical Reactions . . . .

Ask: How is cooking like melting? How is cooking different from melting? They both cause change by adding heat. Cooking changes the properties of the matter, but melting only changes the state of the matter. **Can you reverse melting or cooking?** You can reverse melting, but you cannot reverse cooking.

SEP Science Models, Laws, Mechanisms, and Theories Explain Natural Phenomena . . . .

Discuss with children that some changes caused by heat cause the color and texture of the material to change. When heat is added to the pancake batter and the chicken, the food cooks. Both change color and become firmer. **Ask: What are some examples of changes to other materials by cooking?** A hamburger is soft and pink before it is heated; after it is heated, it is firm and brown.

CCC Cause and Effect . . . .

Ask children to describe changes they observe as pancake batter or chicken are heated by cooking. Elicit other examples of cooking food, and generate a list of these changes. **Ask: Look at the list of changes. How could you categorize the types of changes that occur when heat is added to food?** changes to color, changes to texture, changes to smell

---

Cook It

Explore online.

Look at the pictures to see how adding heat by cooking changes matter.

before | after

pancake batter → pancake batter

chicken → chicken

Think about what happens to foods when they are cooked. Heat from the skillet was added to the pancake batter and the chicken. Both times, heat caused the foods to change in the same ways. This is a pattern that happens when heat is added and something cooks.

76

© Houghton Mifflin Harcourt

Which properties of the batter and the chicken changed when they were heated? Choose all correct answers.

Ⓐ color

Ⓑ flexibility

Ⓒ texture

 Do you see any patterns in what happens when foods are cooked? If so, what are they? Record your answer.

When foods are cooked, their properties change.

 Apply What You Know

Evidence Notebook • Work with a partner to draw two examples of changes to materials by cooking. Be sure to show the material before and after heat was added. Do you see any patterns in how cooking changed the materials? Use evidence to support your answer. Record it in your Evidence Notebook.

 Cause and Effect
Go to the online handbook for tips.

© Houghton Mifflin Harcourt

ccc Cause and Effect ....

Children should choose A, B, and C. They should identify that the patterns in the changes to these physical properties are caused by adding heat to food. The pancake batter and the chicken both change color, flexibility, and texture. If children do not choose B or C, they may require additional support with the words *flexibility* and *texture*. Demonstrate the meanings of these two words by showing children a variety of materials that differ in flexibility and/or texture.

Connection to Life Science

Cause and Effect Cooking causes matter to change. This is an observable pattern that repeats over and over each time a food is cooked. Other events in the natural and human-made world have cause and effect relationships as well. Have children do research to find out what causes plants to grow and be healthful. They should summarize the information and identify the cause(s) and the effect.

FORMATIVE ASSESSMENT

Evidence Notebook
Children will work with a partner to illustrate examples of changes to materials caused by adding heat by cooking.

Scoring Guidelines
• draws two examples, each showing the material before and after heat was added
• uses evidence in support of patterns observed

💡 **Cause and Effect** Remind children that a cause is why something happens, and an effect is the result. A cause may result in a pattern, which is something that repeats again and again.

Burn It

3D Learning Objective

Children observe changes caused by heating a substance by burning. They identify cause and effect relationships and patterns in the human-designed world.

DCI Chemical Reactions . . . .

Ask: Have you ever seen a material changed by burning? How did the matter change? I saw wood burning in a fireplace. It started solid and light brown and ended black and crumbly.

SEP Science Models, Laws, Mechanisms, and Theories Explain Natural Phenomena . . . .

Burning can change matter in the natural world. As an example, discuss forest fires with children. **Ask: How can forest fires start? What damage can forest fires cause?** Forest fires can start from lightning or campfires. They can kill plants, trees, and animals. **How do forest fires change nature?** Forest fires add heat by burning, causing the wood and other materials to turn to ash.

CCC Cause and Effect . . . .

Ask: What patterns do you see in what happens when a material is heated by burning? Burning changes the properties of the material and makes it into a new kind of matter.
Children should select A—They turned black and changed to ash.

Differentiate Instruction

RTI/Extra Support Have children work in pairs to describe what properties of the wood changed when heat was added by burning.

Extension Challenge children to write a short paragraph to describe the difference between how burning and melting cause changes to matter.

Burn It

Explore online. ▶

Look at the pictures to see how adding heat by burning changes matter.

before   after

Heat from the flame is added to the wood and the leaf. This causes the materials to burn. Burning can also happen when you cook something too much. When something burns, heat changes its properties and makes it into another type of matter. This is a pattern that happens when heat is added and something burns.

What happened to the wood and the leaf when they were heated?

Ⓐ They turned black and changed to ash.

Ⓑ They changed from solids to liquids.

Ⓒ They did not change.

78

© Houghton Mifflin Harcourt

Apply What You Know

Work with a small group to compare and contrast changes caused by melting, cooking, and burning in order to summarize what you know about how heat changes matter. Do you see any patterns in these changes?

Cause and Effect • Patterns
Go to the online handbook for tips.

▭▭▷ Record your answer.

Answers will vary. Check children's work.

© Houghton Mifflin Harcourt

Collaboration

Small Groups You may choose to arrange children in small groups for this activity. Encourage children to ask each other questions. Remind children to use evidence to back up their arguments and to agree with or refute a claim.

 FORMATIVE ASSESSMENT

Evidence Notebook

Children will compare the concepts discussed so far in this lesson. They will identify patterns in changes caused by adding heat to matter by melting, cooking, and burning. Allow children to record their answers in paragraphs or in chart form. Children should provide evidence from the lesson or from personal experience to support the patterns they observe.

Scoring Guidelines

- compares and contrasts changes caused by melting, cooking, and burning
- identifies patterns in the changes

💡 **Cause and Effect • Patterns** Remind children that a cause is why something happens, and an effect is the result. A cause may result in a pattern, which is something that repeats again and again.

Cool It Down

3D Learning Objective

Children observe **changes caused by cooling a substance**. They identify **cause and effect relationships** and **patterns in the human-designed world**.

 Chemical Reactions ·

Ask: **What happens when something freezes?** It turns from a liquid into a solid. **How is solid water different from liquid water?** Solid water keeps its shape and is cooler than liquid water.

SEP **Science Models, Laws, Mechanisms, and Theories Explain Natural Phenomena** · · · · · · ·

Ask: **What causes water to change from liquid to solid in nature?** If the air is cold enough, it takes heat away from the water and causes it to freeze. Children may think that when cold is added, water can freeze. To address this misconception, discuss how water freezes when enough heat is taken away.

Do the Math! • Use Symbols

Guide children to use the symbols <, >, or = to compare numbers.

 FORMATIVE ASSESSMENT

Evidence Notebook
Children identify two materials to cool by freezing overnight and identify patterns in any changes they observe.

Scoring Guidelines
- identifies two materials to cool by freezing overnight
- identifies obesrvable patterns in the changes
- uses evidence to support their answer

💡 **Cause and Effect** A cause is why something happens. An effect is the result. A cause may result in a pattern.

Cool It Down

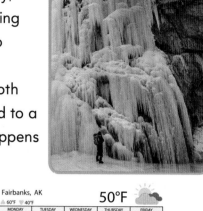

Explore online. ▶

What happened to the water in this waterfall? Heat was taken away, and the water froze. When something **freezes**, it changes from a liquid to a solid.

Liquids such as milk, tea, and broth will freeze and change from a liquid to a solid. Freezing is a pattern that happens when enough heat is taken away.

Do the Math! • Compare the temperatures for Fairbanks, Alaska, and Miami, Florida. Write <, >, or = to compare the temperatures.
Fairbanks $\underline{<}$ Miami

Fairbanks, AK   50°F
❄ 60°F ▾ 40°F

MONDAY	TUESDAY	WEDNESDAY	THURSDAY	FRIDAY
45°F	50°F	50°F	50°F	50°F

Miami, FL   90°F
❄ 90°F ▾ 75°F

MONDAY	TUESDAY	WEDNESDAY	THURSDAY	FRIDAY
85°F	90°F	90°F	87°F	88°F

 Apply What You Know

Evidence Notebook • Identify two materials to cool by freezing overnight. What patterns in how cooling changed these materials do you see? Use evidence to tell how you know, and record it in your Evidence Notebook.

💡 **Cause and Effect** Go to the online handbook for tips.

80

Hands-On Activity 👥 small groups 🕐 1 class period

Explore Cooling

3D Learning Objective

SEP **Science Models, Laws, Mechanisms, and Theories Explain Natural Phenomena** . . . .

Children explore how cooling causes changes to different materials, such as a flower, an ice-cube tray, and orange juice. Children identify patterns based on these events.

Suggested Materials a flower, a container of orange juice, an ice cube tray, a paper plate

Preparation

Pre-assemble materials bundles for pairs or groups. Arrange access to a freezer prior to the activity. Alternatively, children may do this activity at home.

Activity

As a class, view the video. Then discuss the question that will need to be answered. Have children record the question.

STEP 1 As children work to record their observations, circulate and monitor their work. Guide them to include observations based on senses other than vision. For example, children could touch the materials to check temperature, texture, flexibility, etc. **Ask: How is the solid different from the liquid?** The solid is hard and holds it shape. The liquid takes the shape of its container.

STEP 2 Children may require assistance pouring the liquid into the ice-cube trays.

DCI **Chemical Reactions** . . . .

Ask: What happens to matter inside a freezer? What changes do you expect to be caused when the solid and the liquid are placed in the freezer? Material is cooled in a freezer. I think the solid will be colder but will still be solid. I think the liquid will freeze and will become a solid.

Name _____

🔍 Hands-On Activity
Explore Cooling

┌─────────────────────────────────────┐
│ Materials   │
│   _____ │
│   │
│ _____│
└─────────────────────────────────────┘

Ask a Question

What happens to different materials when they are cooled?

Test and Record Data  Explore online. ▶

Step 1

Observe the solid and the liquid.
Record your observations.

Solid	Liquid
Check children's drawings.	

Step 2

Pour the liquid into the ice-cube tray.
Put the solid and the liquid in the freezer.
Wait until the next day to take them out.

© Houghton Mifflin Harcourt

Hands-On Activity, continued

STEP 3 Ask: Why is it important to record your observations immediately? If you wait too long, the objects could absorb heat and melt back into a liquid.

CCC Cause and Effect . . . .

STEP 4 Have children share their results. **Ask:** What pattern did you observe? matter freezing when enough heat is taken away

SEP Engaging in Argument from Evidence . . . .

Ask: How does your evidence support your claim? My claim is that cooling a liquid will cause it to change to a solid, and cooling a solid will not change it. My evidence supports this because the liquid changed to a solid, but the solid stayed a solid.

Claims, Evidence, and Reasoning

Children should make a claim that identifies the changes cooling causes to different materials. They should cite evidence to support their claim, including citing the properties before and after cooling. **Ask: What properties did you observe before and after cooling?** Sample answer: The orange juice was a liquid before cooling. It became a solid after cooling.

Scoring Rubric for Hands-On Activity	
3	States a claim that clearly and directly answers the question and is supported with evidence
2	States a claim that clearly and directly answers the question and is somewhat supported with evidence
1	States a claim that clearly and directly answers the question but is not supported with evidence
0	Does not state a claim and does not provide evidence

Step 3

Take the solid and the liquid out of the freezer. Did cooling cause any changes to the solid or the liquid? Observe them both carefully. Record any effects you observe.

Solid	Liquid
Check children's work. Results will vary.	

Step 4

Analyze your results. Identify causes and effects. Look for patterns.

Make a claim that answers your question.

Answers will vary. Children should describe what happens to

materials when they are cooled.

_____

What is your evidence?

Answers will vary. Children should cite evidence

from the test to support their descriptions.

82

© Houghton Mifflin Harcourt

Take It Further

Careers in Science & Engineering •
Chefs at Work

Explore more online.
• Changes All Around
• Find a Recipe

Chefs use math and science every day in their work. Chefs measure ingredients when they prepare food. When chefs cook, they have to know the right temperature to use for each food.

Explore online. ▶

Chefs can add heat to change food. Adding heat can cause food to cook, to melt, or even to burn. The heat from the flame causes the sugar on top of the dessert to turn brown. It also causes the top to become hard.

© Houghton Mifflin Harcourt • Image Credits: (t) ©Jetta Productions/Iconica/Getty Images

Lesson 3 • How Do Heating and Cooling Change Matter?   83

Take It Further

Careers in Science & Engineering •
Chefs at Work

Children investigate how chefs use science and math to prepare food. Chefs use heat to cause changes to food by melting, cooking, or burning it. In restaurants, chefs are responsible for overseeing all the activity in the kitchen. Chefs order the ingredients they need to complete recipes, prepare the food to be cooked by cutting or slicing it, season the food while it is cooking, and put it on a plate or into a container for the customer.

DCI **Structure and Properties of Matter** . . . .

Ask: How do chefs use heat when preparing food? Chefs use heat when preparing food by using it to cook the food. Heat can change food's state of matter to make the food ready to be eaten.

CCC **Cause and Effect** . . . .

When heat is applied to food, it can cause the food to change its state or its properties. **Ask: What are some observable changes heat causes to food?** Food can change from a solid to a liquid and a liquid to a gas and can even turn brown because it burns.

Differentiate Instruction

ELL Have children prepare flash cards for each key word in this section. Each flash card should have the key word on one side and a picture or description in the child's native language on the other side.

Take It Further, continued

Read, Write, Share! • Ask and Answer Questions

Remind children when formulating questions to ask about important details or things that are unclear.

💡 **Ask and Answer Questions** Children should begin questions with *who, what, when, where, why,* or *how.* Getting answers to their questions will help them understand more about using heat when cooking.

Collaboration

Think, Pair, Share Have children work in small groups to practice formulating questions about cooking. In turn, each child will ask a question that begins with *who, what, when, where, why,* or *how.* The next child will ask a related question but with a different question word. For example, the first child may ask "Who is cooking dinner?" The next child could ask "What are you cooking for dinner?" and so on. After each question word has been used, another child will take a turn to formulate the initial question.

Explore more online. ▶

Changes All Around

Children investigate how heating and cooling can cause changes to water in an environment over time.

Find a Recipe

Children investigate how heating and cooling can cause materials to change within recipes.

Ask a Chef

Read, Write, Share!

What questions would you ask a chef about using heat?

> **Ask and Answer Questions**
> Go to the online handbook for tips.

✏️ Draw or write to record your questions.

Questions will vary. Check children's work

_____

_____

_____

Get answers to your questions by asking a chef. Or, you can ask a cafeteria worker or an adult who likes to cook. Write about what you learn.

84

© Houghton Mifflin Harcourt

Explore online. ▶ Have children explore online to find out more about how matter can change.

Lesson Check

Lesson Check   Name _____

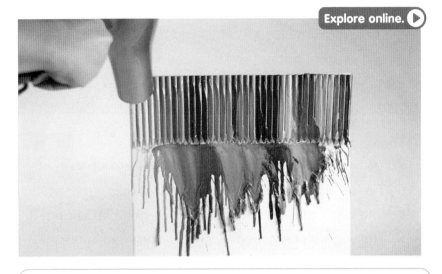

Explore online. ▶

Can You Explain It?

✎▷ What caused the crayons to change?

Be sure to:

• Tell whether the crayons were heated or cooled.

• Describe how the crayons changed.

• Explain what caused the crayons to change.

The blow dryer heated the crayons.
_____

This caused the crayons to melt.
_____

They changed from a solid to a liquid.
_____

_____

Lesson 3 • How Do Heating and Cooling Change Matter?   85

Lesson Check

Can You Explain It?

Have children reread their answer to the Can You Explain It? prompt at the beginning of the lesson.

DCI **Chemical Reactions** . . . .

If children have difficulty responding to the question, have them compare the crayons at the top of the picture with the crayons at the bottom. **Ask: How are these crayons different?** The crayons at the top are solid; the crayons at the bottom are liquid.

CCC **Cause and Effect** . . . .

Ask: What caused the change? The hot air from the hair dryer. **What was the effect?** The crayons melted. **What would happen if hot air from a hair dryer was pointed at butter?** Heat from a hair dryer can cause butter to melt.

Scoring Guidelines

• Children should indicate whether the crayons were heated or cooled and explain how their state of matter changed.

• Children should explain the cause and effect of the change to the crayons.

Collaboration

Cultivating New Questions As children complete this lesson and prepare for the next lesson, ask them to identify additional questions they have about how heating and cooling can change matter. **Ask: How does water change when heat is added to it? Can water go back to what it was once heat has been added?** When heat is added to water, it changes from a liquid to a gas. It can go back to being liquid if enough heat is removed. As children continue to the next lesson, they will apply concepts related to changes in matter.

Lesson Check, continued

SUMMATIVE ASSESSMENT
Self Check

1. Children should choose C—milk in a glass. If children choose A or B, reinforce that freezing is a change from a liquid state to a solid state. Ask children to identify the state of each material before it is cooled, and then discuss whether it will change states when it is cooled.

2. Children should choose B—The color and the texture of the vegetables changed. If children choose A, review the difference between cooking and freezing. If children choose C, review the difference between cooking and burning. Have children revisit the Cook It, Cool It Down, and Burn It sections of this lesson. Ask guiding questions as children read to ensure understanding.

3. Children should choose B—The materials changed from solid to liquid. If children choose A or C, have them reread the Melt It section of the lesson. Ask guiding questions as children read to ensure understanding. Some children may need to review the words *solid* and *liquid* in the lesson Engineer It • What Are Properties of Matter?

Self Check
1. Which material will freeze when you cool it?
   Ⓐ a plastic milk carton
   Ⓑ a glass milk bottle
   Ⓒ milk in a glass

2. Hector cooked some vegetables on a stove.
   The vegetables became soft and brown.
   What was the effect of cooking on the vegetables?
   Ⓐ The vegetables turned from liquid to solid.
   Ⓑ The color and the texture of the vegetables changed.
   Ⓒ The vegetables turned black and changed into ashes.

3. Look at the snow and wax. What patterns do you see?

   Ⓐ The materials changed from liquid to solid.
   Ⓑ The materials changed from solid to liquid.
   Ⓒ The materials turned black and changed into ashes.

4. Elizabeth places juice in a freezer. The next day she observes that the juice is frozen. What evidence does Elizabeth have to make the argument that the juice froze?

Ⓐ The juice changed from liquid to solid.

Ⓑ The juice changed from solid to liquid.

Ⓒ The juice changed in color only.

5. What happens when heat is added to wax? Choose all true statements.

Ⓐ It melts.

Ⓑ It changes from solid to liquid.

Ⓒ It changes to ashes.

6. What does burning cause wood to turn into?

Ⓐ black ashes

Ⓑ a liquid

Ⓒ ice

7. What would happen to a plastic bag if you put it into the freezer?

Ⓐ The bag would change to ashes.

Ⓑ The bag would change to a liquid.

Ⓒ The bag would stay solid.

© Houghton Mifflin Harcourt

Lesson 3 • How Do Heating and Cooling Change Matter?   87

4. Children should choose A—The juice changed from liquid to solid. If children choose B or C, direct them to review the Cool It Down section of the lesson. Some children may require additional review of the words *solid* and *liquid* in the lesson Engineer It • What Are Properties of Matter?

5. Children should choose A—It melts; and B—It changes from solid to liquid. If children choose either A or B, but not both, remind them to read the question carefully. Some children may benefit from a visual aid to help them answer this question. Have them look at the images of the candle in Item 3.

6. Children should choose A—black ashes. If children choose B or C, review the differences between melting, burning, and freezing. Have children revisit the Melt It, Burn It, and Cool It Down sections of the lesson.

7. Children should choose C—The bag would stay solid. If children choose A or B, direct them to review the Cool It Down section of the lesson. Point out to children that the plastic bag would get colder, but its state of matter would not change.

Lesson 3 • How Do Heating and Cooling Change Matter?   87

Building to the Performance Expectation

The learning experiences in this lesson prepare children for mastery of:

2-PS1-4 Construct an argument with evidence that some changes caused by heating or cooling can be reversed and some cannot.

Trace Tool to the NGSS
Go online to view the complete coverage of these standards across the lesson, unit, and time.

 Science & Engineering Practices

Engaging in Argument from Evidence
Construct an argument with evidence to support a claim.

▶ **VIDEO** SEPs: Constructing Explanations and Designing Solutions/Engaging in Argument from Evidence

Science Models, Laws, Mechanisms, and Theories Explain Natural Phenomena
Scientists search for cause and effect relationships to explain natural events.

 Disciplinary Core Ideas

PS1.A: Structure and Properties of Matter
Different kinds of matter exist and many of them can be either solid or liquid, depending on temperature. Matter can be described and classified by its observable properties.

PS1.B: Chemical Reactions
Heating or cooling a substance may cause changes that can be observed. Sometimes these changes are reversible, and sometimes they are not.

 Crosscutting Concepts

Cause and Effect
Events have causes that generate observable patterns.

CONNECTION TO MATH

2.OA.A.1 Use addition and subtraction within 100 to solve one- and two-step word problems involving situations of adding to, taking from, putting together, taking apart, and comparing, with unknowns in all positions, e.g., by using drawings and equations with a symbol for the unknown number to represent the problem.

CONNECTION TO ENGLISH LANGUAGE ARTS

RI.2.8 Describe how reasons support specific points the author makes in a text.

Supporting All Students, All Standards

Integrating the Three Dimensions of Learning

This lesson focuses on how heating and cooling cause reversible and irreversible changes to matter (**DCI Structure and Properties of Matter; DCI Chemical Reactions**). The lesson begins with children exploring how heating and cooling can cause reversible changes to matter and continues with children exploring irreversible changes (**SEP Science Models, Laws, Mechanisms, and Theories Explain Natural Phenomena**). As they explore, children will observe patterns in reversible and irreversible changes caused by heating and cooling (**CCC Cause and Effect**). Finally, children will construct an argument using evidence from the lesson to support their claim of whether observed changes are reversible or irreversible (**SEP Engaging in Argument from Evidence**).

Professional Development Go online to view **Professional Development videos** with strategies to integrate CCCs and SEPs, including the ones used in this lesson.

Build on Prior Knowledge

Children should already know and be prepared to build on the following concepts:

- Observations and data can be used as evidence to construct an argument. *(Grade 2, Unit 2, Lesson 3)*
- Melting changes matter from solid to liquid. *(Grade 2, Unit 2, Lesson 3)*
- Cooking changes matter's properties of color, texture, and flexibility. *(Grade 2, Unit 2, Lesson 3)*
- Burning changes matter into another type of matter. *(Grade 2, Unit 2, Lesson 3)*
- Freezing changes matter from liquid to solid. *(Grade 2, Unit 2, Lesson 3)*
- Cause and effect relationships can generate patterns. *(Grade 2, Unit 2, Lesson 3)*

Differentiate Instruction

Lesson Vocabulary
- reversible
- irreversible

Reinforcing Vocabulary To help children remember each vocabulary word, help them form real-life connections. Discuss with children the connection between the word *reversible* and the word *reverse*. Demonstrate the meaning of *reversible* by turning a sweater, jacket, or shirt inside out. Ask children to provide additional examples of reversible clothing, as well as examples of irreversible clothing (e.g,. shoes). Remind children to look for the highlighted words as they proceed through the lesson.

RTI/Extra Support Provide additional opportunity for hands-on discovery. Allow children to explore freezing, melting, and cooking, if equipment is available. Otherwise, show videos of cooking to demonstrate irreversible changes and videos of making ice pops to demonstrate reversible changes.

Extension Children who want to find out more can research other types of reversible and irreversible changes that are not caused by heating or cooling. Children can share what they find out with the class by making a poster or other display, or with a demonstration of the materials and process that are safe for the classroom.

ELL Be sure to point out all labels, pictures, captions, and headings throughout the lesson to assist children with strategies to summarize chunks of content. Discuss with children real-life connections to content and provide hands-on examples of materials when possible to best support the needs of these learners.

Lesson Phenomenon

Build on Prior Lessons

In Lesson 3, children explored how heating and cooling caused changes to matter. They used evidence to make a claim that matter can change when heat is added or removed. Properties and states of matter can change when it is either heated or cooled. Lesson 4 builds on these concepts to explore reversible and irreversible changes to matter.

Lesson Objective

Construct an argument with evidence that some changes to matter can be reversed and some cannot.

About This Image

Have children look at the pottery. Explain that the mugs, pitcher, and vase are made from clay that has been fired in a special oven called a kiln. **Ask: Have you ever worked with clay? Think about what the clay feels like when you touch it. What are some properties of clay?** Clay is soft and flexible. **What are some properties of the mugs?** The mugs are hard; they do not bend. Lead children in a discussion about the differences between pottery and the clay that is used to make it.

SEP **Science Models, Laws, Mechanisms, and Theories Explain Natural Phenomena**
Alternative Engage Strategy

Changes in Nature	 small groups 20–30 minutes

Have children work in small groups to draw a scene from nature. Discuss children's pictures and the season depicted in their work. Then discuss how nature changes as the seasons change. Have children work in their groups to depict the same scene during a different season. Then have them share their drawings and discuss how the scenes are different.

Lesson **4** How Does Matter Change?

Matter can change in ways that cannot be undone.

By the End of This Lesson
I will be able to explain that some changes to matter can be undone, but other changes cannot.

88

Fire It Up

Look at the pictures to explore what heat does to matter. What happens to wood when you burn it?

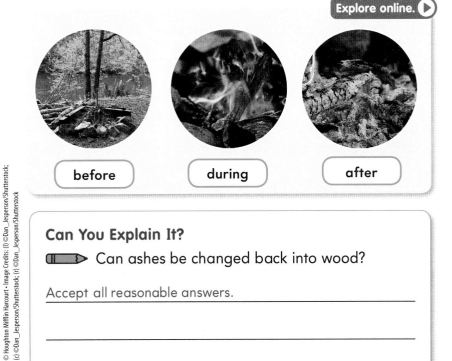

Explore online. ▶

before | during | after

Can You Explain It?

✏️ Can ashes be changed back into wood?

Accept all reasonable answers.
_____
_____
_____
_____

Lesson 4 • How Does Matter Change?   89

Can You Explain It?

Fire It Up Adding heat to matter can cause its properties and state to change. The video shows how burning changes wood. If the video is not available, guide children to observe the pictures.

Ask children to record their initial thoughts about whether ashes can be changed back into wood. At the end of this lesson, children will revisit this question as part of the Lesson Check. At that point, they should be able to use what they have observed to explain why ashes cannot be changed back into wood.

Collaboration

Build on Prior Knowledge You may want children to view and discuss the pictures as a whole-class activity. In this way, you can assess their prior knowledge of how matter changes.

In small groups, have children discuss the changes they observe in the wood and whether they think the ashes can be changed back into wood. Children can use evidence from the pictures or from their own experiences to support their answers.

Support for Unit Project

The **Unit Project** Explore Melting supports content in this lesson.

Reversible Changes

3D Learning Objective

Children will observe the pattern that freezing and melting cause reversible changes to matter. Children use their observations to identify cause and effect relationships.

DCI Structure and Properties of Matter . . . .

Discuss the three pictures with children. **Ask: What happens to lemonade if you put it in the freezer?** It changes from liquid to solid. **What happens when you take the lemonade out of the freezer and leave it at room temperature?** It melts and changes back from a solid to a liquid. **Does freezing or melting the lemonade change it to a different material?** No, it is still lemonade whether or not it is a liquid or a solid.

Collaboration

Think, Pair, Share Review with children the meanings of the words *melt* and *freeze*. Then have them work with a partner to brainstorm examples from their own experiences of materials melting and freezing. Have them share their examples with the class. Guide them to recognize the pattern that adding heat to some solids will cause the solids to change to liquids, and cooling some liquids will cause the liquids to change to solids.

Reversible Changes

What happens to lemonade if you put it in the freezer overnight? How does it change? How does it stay the same? Let's find out.

Explore online. ▶

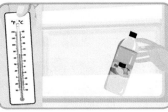

kitchen temperature 70°F

The boy has lemonade in a bottle. It is a liquid at room temperature. He puts the lemonade in the freezer overnight.

freezer temperature 1°F

The next morning the lemonade is a solid. The cold caused it to freeze. What will happen to the frozen lemonade if the boy leaves it out on the counter?

kitchen temperature 70°F

The next morning the change was undone. The lemonade had become liquid again. A change that can be undone, or reversed, is a **reversible** change. Freezing and melting can be reversible changes.

90

© Houghton Mifflin Harcourt

✏️ How does the lemonade change in each picture? Write to describe what happens.

Explore online. ▶

Sample answer: The lemonade is a liquid because it is at room temperature, or 70 °F.

Sample answer: The lemonade freezes and changes from a liquid to a solid.

Sample answer: The frozen lemonade melts and changes back to a liquid from a solid.

© Houghton Mifflin Harcourt

Lesson 4 • How Does Matter Change?   91

SEP Engaging in Argument from Evidence . . . .

Be sure that children provide evidence to support their claim about how lemonade changes in each picture. **Ask: How do you know that the lemonade in the first picture is a liquid?** It is at room temperature, and it takes the shape of the container. **How do you know that the lemonade in the second picture is a solid?** It is frozen, and freezing changes liquid lemonade to solid lemonade.

SEP Science Models, Laws, Mechanisms, and Theories Explain Natural Phenomena . . . .

CCC Cause and Effect . . . .

Remind children that events have causes and effects, and if the same effect occurs again and again, it is a pattern. **Ask: What pattern do you observe when liquid is cooled in a freezer?** It changes from liquid to solid. **What pattern do you observe when heat is added back to the lemonade?** It changes back to a liquid.

DCI Chemical Reactions . . . .

Discuss with children the meaning of *reversible* change. **Ask: What happens as the lemonade is frozen and then heated again?** It changes from liquid to solid and then back to liquid. **Is freezing lemonade a reversible change?** yes **How do you know?** The change can be undone, or reversed, by warming the lemonade back to room temperature.

Connection to Earth and Space Sciences

Patterns Freezing and melting can be reversible changes, as children observed when lemonade was put in the freezer and then left on the counter. Provide children with a list of changes in nature, such as a melting snowperson and a frozen puddle in winter. Have them tell if the change is reversible, and explain why or why not. Children may collaborate or do research, as needed.

Do the Math! • Solve Word Problems

Have children look at the pictures of the thermometers. Make sure they understand that a thermometer measures temperature in units called *degrees*. Provide assistance to those children who have trouble reading the temperature shown on each thermometer.

Children should choose C. If children choose A, they may not be reading the freezer temperature correctly. If they choose B, they are using the incorrect operation to solve the problem. Point out that the phrase *How much warmer* tells them that they are comparing two quantities, so they need to find the difference between the numbers.

 Solve Word Problems Remind children to read word problems carefully to help them choose the correct operation to solve the problem.

Do the Math! • A thermometer measures temperature in units called degrees. How much warmer is the room temperature than the freezer temperature? Which number sentence could you use to answer the question?

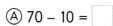

(A) 70 – 10 = ☐

(B) 1 + 70 = ☐

(C) 70 – 1 = ☐

room temperature   freezer temperature

Solve Word Problems
Go to the online handbook for tips.

 Apply What You Know

Read, Write, Share! • **Evidence Notebook** • Talk with a partner. What do you think would happen to milk if you put it in a freezer overnight? Use facts from the text as evidence to tell how you know. Record your answer in your Evidence Notebook.

Describe How Reasons Support a Text
Go to the online handbook for tips.

92

FORMATIVE ASSESSMENT

Read, Write, Share! • Evidence Notebook
Children will work with a partner as they discuss what would happen to milk if it were left in a freezer overnight, and they will provide evidence to support their prediction.

Scoring Guidelines
• states the outcome of leaving milk in a freezer overnight
• provides sufficient evidence to support the prediction

Describe How Reasons Support a Text An author may state a fact or an opinion. When children read a fact, guide them to ask, "What information does the author give to support this fact?"

Irreversible Changes

Irreversible Changes

Explore online. ▶

What happens to different materials when you cook, burn, or freeze them?

cooking

The raw vegetables are firm and dry. During cooking, they get softer, wet, and begin to turn brown. The cooked vegetables cannot change back into raw ones.

burning

The paper is white and in one piece. As the paper burns, it crumbles into powdery, gray ashes. The ashes cannot change back into a white piece of paper.

freezing

When the flower is frozen, its petals are cold and hard. Freezing the flower causes its shape to change. This change cannot be undone.

Some materials can be changed forever. A change that cannot be reversed, or undone, is an **irreversible** change.

Lesson 4 • How Does Matter Change?

93

3D Learning Objective

Children will observe the pattern that cooking, burning, and sometimes freezing, cause irreversible changes to matter. Children use their observations to identify cause and effect relationships.

DCI Chemical Reactions . . . .

Ask: What happens when the vegetables are cooked? They get softer and wet, and turn brown. **What happens when a piece of paper is burned?** It turns into powdery ash. **What happens when a flower is frozen?** It becomes cold and hard. **Can any of these materials go back to how they were before?** no **Are these changes irreversible?** yes **How do you know?** The changes cannot be reversed, or undone.

Differentiate Instruction

RTI/Extra Support Some children may have difficulty with the concept that freezing can cause both reversible change and irreversible change. Describe how freezing causes each type of change. Freezing can change the state of a material, which is a reversible change. Freezing can also change the properties of a material and change the type of matter, which is an irreversible change.

Extension Have children make a list of materials that undergo reversible change when frozen and materials that undergo irreversible change when frozen. Children can use books or the Internet for research as well as draw on personal experience. Challenge children to identify patterns in the types of materials in each category.

© Houghton Mifflin Harcourt

SEP **Science Models, Laws, Mechanisms, and Theories Explain Natural Phenomena** . . . .

 CCC **Cause and Effect** . . . .

Have children look at the pictures. Explain that a pattern occurs when a cause results in the same effect again and again. **Ask: What is the cause?** cooking or burning **What is the effect?** The properties of the material change. **What is the pattern?** Cooking or burning causes irreversible changes to matter, such as changing the color or turning it into ash.

Differentiate Instruction

ELL Review the words *heat, cook,* and *burn*. Provide pictures or videos of each word. Have children describe their own experiences with heating, cooking, and burning material. Children can make pictures or posters showing each word.

 FORMATIVE ASSESSMENT

Evidence Notebook
Children will work in small groups to provide additional examples of materials that can be changed by cooking or burning. They will describe the properties of the materials before and after cooking or burning and identify patterns.

Scoring Guidelines
- accurately describes the materials before and after they are cooked or burned
- identifies patterns in how cooking or burning changed the materials
- provides sufficient evidence to support their claims

Cause and Effect • Patterns A cause is why something happens. An effect is the result. A cause may result in a pattern, which is something that repeats again and again.

 Apply What You Know

Evidence Notebook • You have found out about irreversible changes to matter. Work with a small group to think about other materials you could change by cooking or burning. Describe the materials before they are cooked or burned. Then, describe them after being cooked or burned. Identify patterns in how cooking or burning changed all these materials. Use evidence to support your answer. Record your answer in your Evidence Notebook.

Cause and Effect • Patterns
Go to the online handbook for tips.

cook

burn

© Houghton Mifflin Harcourt

94

Name _____

Hands-On Activity
Explore Changes to Matter

Materials
_____
_____

Ask a Question

What changes happen when you cook food in a microwave? _____

Test and Record Data

Step 1

Observe the uncooked food.
Record your observations.

	Check children's work.
	Observations will vary.
	_____
	_____

Step 2

Put the food in a container.

Lesson 4 • How Does Matter Change?   95

Hands-On Activity   👥 small groups   🕐 1 class period
Explore Changes to Matter

3D Learning Objective

SEP **Engaging in Argument from Evidence** . . . .

Children will make a claim about the reversibility or irreversibility of changes caused by cooking in a microwave. They will support their claim with evidence from their observations during the investigation.

Suggested Materials microwave, microwave-safe container, uncooked food such as popcorn kernels, plastic measuring cup

Preparation

Pre-assemble materials bundles for groups. Arrange access to a microwave prior to the activity. Alternatively, children may do this activity at home or as a whole-class activity if limited materials are available.

Activity

As a class, view the video. Then discuss the question that will need to be answered. Have children record the question.

STEP 1 To guide children in making observations, remind them to use their senses of sight, touch, and smell. Children should record as many properties of the food as they can. Remind children to not eat any of the uncooked or cooked food during the investigation.

STEP 2 Guide children to choose a container that is appropriate for their food. For example, children could use a paper bag for popcorn.

© Houghton Mifflin Harcourt

Hands-On Activity, continued

 Chemical Reactions . . . .

STEP 3 Ask: What changes do you expect to be caused when the food is placed in the microwave? Do you think the changes will be reversible or irreversible? Material is cooked in a microwave, so I think the properties of the food will change. I think these changes will be irreversible.

STEP 4 Ask: What properties did you observe before cooking? How did these properties change? Sample answer: The kernels popped open.

 Science Models, Laws, Mechanisms, and Theories Explain Natural Phenomena . . . .

STEP 5 Ask: What was the cause? The cause was cooking the food in the microwave. **What was the effect?** The effect was changing the properties of the material.

Claims, Evidence, and Reasoning

Children should make a claim that tells what happens when food is cooked in a microwave. They should use evidence to support the claim. **Ask: How did the food change? Can this change be reversed?** Sample answer: The popcorn kernels popped open. This change cannot be reversed.

Scoring Rubric for Hands-On Activity	
3	States a claim supported with evidence about the effect of cooking food in a microwave
2	States a claim somewhat supported with evidence about the effect of cooking food in a microwave
1	States a claim that is not supported by evidence
0	Does not state a claim and does not provide evidence

Step 3
Place the food in the microwave. Turn it on when an adult tells you to do so.

Step 4
Take the food out of the microwave. Observe the cooked food. Record your observations.

	Sample answer: The popcorn kernels popped open.

Step 5
Analyze your results. Identify causes and effects.

Make a claim that answers your question.

Sample answer: When you cook food in the microwave, its changes are irreversible. The food cannot be changed back to the way it was before.

What is your evidence?

Sample answer: The popcorn kernels popped open.

96

Take It Further
How Foods Change

Explore more online.

• Dissolve It

What changes happen to apples, avocados, and bananas after you cut them and leave them out on the counter?

Explore online. ▶

© Houghton Mifflin Harcourt

Take It Further

How Foods Change

Children investigate what happens to apples, avocados, and bananas if they are cut up and left out on the counter. Children should observe that over time the fruits begin to change color and go from a white or light green color on the inside to brown.

DCI **Chemical Reactions** . . . .

Discuss with children how the properties of the fruits have changed. **Ask: What properties of the food have changed?** color and texture **What properties of the food have remained the same?** size and shape

Collaboration

Small Groups You may choose to have children complete the first part of this activity in small groups. Discuss the pairs of pictures and the changes children observe. Encourage children to draw on personal experiences as they attempt to explain the observed changes.

Take It Further, continued

How Did the Foods Change?

Children will tell whether the change is reversible and explain how they know. They will use evidence to support their answers. **Ask: How have the foods changed?** The foods have turned brown. **Is this change reversible?** no **How do you know?** The fruit cannot be changed back to its original color.

 Cause and Effect Remind children that events in nature have causes and effects. The reason something happens is the cause. What happens is the effect.

Differentiate Instruction

RTI/Extra Support Because the irreversible changes discussed previously in this lesson were caused by cooking or burning, children might have difficulty with the idea that simply air can cause an irreversible change. Reinforce the idea by having children draw on their personal experiences with fruit turning brown or other foods "going bad" when they are left out.

Extension Challenge children to find out more about the chemical reaction that causes the changes observed in the fruit. If time and resources permit, allow children to investigate ways to prevent fruit from turning brown.

Explore more online. ▶

Dissolve It

Children investigate whether solids will dissolve when mixed with water.

How Did the Foods Change?

How has the fruit changed? Is this change reversible? How do you know? Use evidence from the picture to support your answer.

Cause and Effect
Go to the online handbook for tips.

Sample answer: The fruit has turned brown. This change is

irreversible because the fruit cannot go back to what it looked like

before.

98

© Houghton Mifflin Harcourt

Explore online. ▶ **Have children explore online to find out more about how burning can cause changes to matter.**

Lesson Check   Name _____

Explore online. ▶

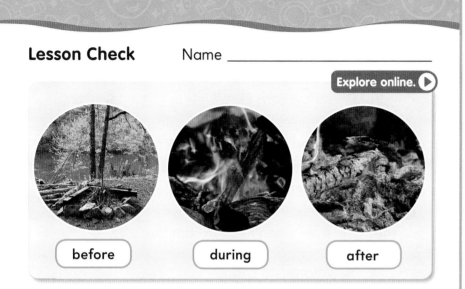

before   during   after

Can You Explain It?

✏️ ▷ Can ashes be changed back into wood?

Be sure to:

• Describe how the wood changed.

• Tell what caused the wood to change.

• Explain whether this change is reversible or irreversible.

Sample answer: The wood changed from solid and brown to

dusty gray ashes. The fire burned the wood, causing it to change

into a different material. This change is irreversible because the

ashes cannot be changed back into wood.

Lesson 4 • How Does Matter Change?   99

Lesson Check

Can You Explain It?

Have children reread their answer to the Can You Explain It? prompt at the beginning of the lesson.

SEP **Science Models, Laws, Mechanisms, and Theories Explain Natural Phenomena** . . . .

CCC **Cause and Effect** . . . .

Ask: What caused the wood to change to ashes? Burning the wood with fire caused it to change. **What was the effect of the fire?** The wood changed to ashes.

SEP **Engaging in Argument from Evidence** . . . .

Ask: Is this change reversible or irreversible? How do you know? irreversible; Ashes cannot be changed back into wood.

Scoring Guidelines

• Children should describe how the wood changed.
• Children should identify what caused the wood to change.
• Children should effectively explain whether the change is reversible or irreversible.

Collaboration

Cultivating New Questions As children complete this lesson and prepare for the next unit, ask them to identify additional questions they have about reversible and irreversible changes. **Ask:** What happens to other objects, such as metal or cloth, when heat is added? Is the change reversible or irreversible? A lot of heat would need to be added in order to melt metal. I think that change is reversible. Cloth would burn and turn to ash. I think that change would be irreversible. As children continue to the next unit, they will apply concepts related to matter and its properties in helping to understand that plants can be described by their properties.

Lesson 4 • How Does Matter Change?   99

Lesson Check, continued

SUMMATIVE ASSESSMENT
Self Check

1. Children should choose C—The material in the juice pop stays the same even when its form changes. If children choose A or B, have them revisit the Reversible Changes section of the lesson. Guide them to compare the pictures of the juice pop to the pictures of the lemonade and look for patterns. **Ask: How are the two pictures similar?** They both show juice pops. **How are the two pictures different?** In one, the juice pop is frozen, and in the other, it is melted. **Does the material change when the juice pop is frozen or melted?** no **What kind of change is this?** reversible

2. Children should write *burning* in the first blank, *cooking* in the second blank, and *melting* in the third blank. If children complete the blanks incorrectly, ask them guiding questions. For example, to help children correctly label the picture that shows melting, ask, "Which picture shows matter changing from a solid to a liquid? That picture shows melting."

3. Children should choose A—a fire burning in a fireplace; and C—muffins baking in the oven. If children choose B and/or D, have them revisit the Irreversible Changes section of the lesson. Guide children to think about whether melted ice cream can be refrozen in the freezer and whether a frozen lake will melt in the spring.

Self Check

1. What evidence do the pictures give to show that this change is reversible?

   (A) Freezing changes the juice pop into a different kind of material.

   (B) Adding heat to the juice pop makes it turn brown and melt.

   (C) The material in the juice pop stays the same even when its form changes.

2. What causes matter to change in each photo? Use a word from the box to identify each change.

   cooking
   burning
   melting

   burning   cooking   melting

3. Which are irreversible changes? Choose all that apply.

   (A) a fire burning in a fireplace

   (B) a melting ice-cream cone

   (C) muffins baking in the oven

   (D) a frozen lake in the winter

100

4. How do you know if a change is irreversible?
   Choose all that apply.

   (A) The material changes from a solid to a liquid.

   (B) The material becomes a different type of material.

   (C) The material can never go back to the way it was before the change.

   (D) The material stays the same type of material.

5. Read each cause and effect in the chart. Which changes are reversible? Which changes are irreversible? Write **reversible** or **irreversible** to identify each change.

Cause	Effect	Change
Fire burns wood.	Wood turns to ashes.	irreversible
Freezer freezes lemonade.	Lemonade turns to solid.	reversible
Heat cooks vegetables.	Vegetables shrink, soften, and turn brown.	irreversible
Heat cooks popcorn kernels.	Kernels turn white and fluffy.	irreversible

© Houghton Mifflin Harcourt

4. Children should choose B—The material becomes a different type of material; and C—The material can never go back to the way it was before the change. If children choose A or D, have them reread the question stem and underline the word *irreversible*. Remind children that irreversible changes cannot be undone, or reversed.

5. Children should write *reversible* for Freezer freezes lemonade. Children should write *irreversible* for Fire burns wood; Heat cooks vegetables; and Heat cooks popcorn kernels. If children complete the chart incorrectly, review the words *reversible* and *irreversible* with them. Some children may need to revisit the Reversible Changes and Irreversible Changes sections of the lesson.

Unit 2 Performance Task

Engineer It • Build a Model Boat

👥 small groups ⏱ 2 class periods

Objective

Children **design tests** and **analyze data to determine** which materials have **properties best suited** to their model boat.

Suggested Materials

plastic bottle, fabric, clay, straw, tape, scissors

Preparation

Review Lessons 1 and 2 to provide context for this Unit Performance Task. Collect several plastic bottles of the same size and shape in advance of this activity. Bring in a large plastic tub and arrange for sink access.

SEP **Planning and Carrying Out Investigations . . . .**

Ask: Which materials do you think will cause the boat to float? Which materials will cause the boat to move by wind? Sample answer: The plastic bottle will cause the boat to float. The fabric and straw made into a sail will cause the boat to move by catching wind.

STEPS

Step 1 • Define a Problem
Guide children in a discussion about the problem they will solve.

Step 2 • Plan and Build
Remind children that engineers think about what could go wrong with a design, and then they build in ways to prevent problems from happening. **Ask: What are three problems that your boat may have?** Sample answer: The fabric is too heavy or light to make a sail; the straw is not sturdy enough; and the straw is too short or too long.

Unit 2 Performance Task
Engineer It • Build a Model Boat

Materials

_____

_____

STEPS

Step 1

Define a Problem You want to build a model boat that will float on water and will move by wind.

Step 2

Plan and Build You will need to think about materials, come up with ideas, and then build a boat.

Step 3

Test and Improve Test your design. Does your boat float and move? How can you improve your design?

© Houghton Mifflin Harcourt

102

Step 4

Redesign Make changes to the materials to make the boat better.

Step 5

Communicate Explain which materials make up your boat and why you chose them. Describe how putting the materials together made them do things that each one could not do by itself.

✔ Check

_____ I built a boat that floats and moves by wind.

_____ I tested my model boat design.

_____ I redesigned my model boat to make it work better.

_____ I shared my design with others.

Step 3 • Test and Improve

SEP Analyzing and Interpreting Data . . . .

Children may have limited ideas for improvements. Consider having the groups critique each other's designs and reasoning. Use sentence frames to guide their discussions:

- I don't understand why you chose _____.
- How will _____ work with _____?
- Why did you choose _____ instead of _____?

Step 4 • Redesign

CCC Cause and Effect . . . .

Prompt children to implement one improvement discussed at Step 3. Children should retest their boat in order to evaluate the boat's performance with the improvement in place. **Ask: How did the improvement cause your boat to change? Did your boat change in the way that you thought it would?** Answers will vary.

Step 5 • Communicate

Children should communicate their results and include an explanation for each step of a design process that they followed. Children should explain, based on their test results, which materials are best suited for use in a model boat.

	Scoring Rubric for Performance Task	
3	Builds, tests, and redesigns a model boat that can float and move by wind, and communicates the results
2	Builds and tests a model boat, but does not redesign it or communicate results
1	Builds a model boat, but does not test it, redesign it, or communicate results
0	Does not build, test, or redesign a model boat

Unit 2 Review

SUMMATIVE ASSESSMENT

1. Children should choose C—It changes to a solid. If children choose A or B, reinforce that freezing is a change from a liquid to a solid. By completing Cool It Down in Lesson 3, children explored how water changes when heat is removed from it. Children who answer incorrectly should refer back to Lesson 3.

2. Children should choose B—It changes from a solid to a liquid. If children choose A or C, reinforce that melting is a change from a solid to a liquid. By completing Melt It in Lesson 3, children explored how matter changes by melting when heat is added to it. Children who answer incorrectly should refer back to Lesson 3.

3. Children should choose A—Heat caused the wax to melt; and B—Heat caused the muffin batter to cook. If children choose C, reinforce that cooking changes the properties of food. It can change the color, flexibility, and texture. By completing Cook It in Lesson 3, children explored how matter changes by cooking when heat is added to it. Children who answer incorrectly should refer back to Lesson 3.

Unit 2 Review Name _____

1. What happens to water when it freezes?
   Ⓐ It only changes color.
   Ⓑ It changes to a liquid.
   Ⓒ It changes to a solid.

---

2. How does matter change when it melts?
   Ⓐ It changes from a liquid to ashes.
   Ⓑ It changes from a solid to a liquid.
   Ⓒ It changes from a liquid to a solid.

---

3. Look at the wax and the muffin batter. Which statements are true? Choose all correct answers.

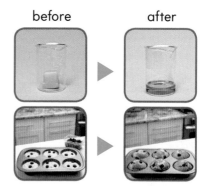

before   after

   Ⓐ Heat caused the wax to melt.
   Ⓑ Heat caused the muffin batter to cook.
   Ⓒ Heat caused the wax and muffin batter to burn and turn to ashes.

104

4. How will each container change when placed in a freezer? Choose all the containers that will not freeze.

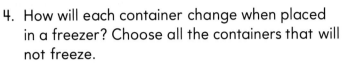

5. Which objects are solids? Choose all correct answers.

6. Which are properties of the pencil? Choose all correct answers.
   Ⓐ flexible
   🅑 hard
   Ⓒ yellow

7. Which change is irreversible?
   🅐 candle burning
   Ⓑ butter melting
   Ⓒ water freezing

4. Children should choose A—plastic milk bottle; B—plastic water bottle; and C—plastic sports drink bottle. If children do not choose all three containers, reinforce that solids do not freeze and change from a liquid to a solid. By completing Cool It Down in Lesson 3, children explored that freezing changes matter from a liquid to a solid. Children who answer incorrectly should refer back to Lesson 3.

5. Children should choose A—sneaker; and C—ceramic bowl. If children choose B, reinforce that a solid is a state of matter that keeps its shape. By completing States of Matter—Solids in Lesson 1, children explored characteristics of a solid. Children who answer incorrectly should refer back to Lesson 1.

6. Children should choose B—hard; and C—yellow. If children choose A, reinforce that a flexible object bends easily. By completing Properties of Matter in Lesson 1, children explored that color, shape, hardness, texture, and flexibility are properties of matter. Children who answer incorrectly should refer back to Lesson 1.

7. Children should choose A—candle burning. If children choose B or C, reinforce that when something burns, it changes into a different substance. It cannot change back to the way it was before burning. By completing Irreversible Changes in Lesson 4, children explored that an irreversible change cannot be reversed, or undone. Burning is an irreversible change. Children who answer incorrectly should refer back to Lesson 4.

8. Children should choose B—a finished cube built with toothpicks and clay balls. If children choose A or C, reinforce that the pictures show a sequence of building an object from small pieces. By completing Build It Up, Break It Down in Lesson 2, children explored how an object can be made of smaller pieces. Children who answer incorrectly should refer back to Lesson 2.

9. Children should choose A—wooden table; and B—wooden toy. If children choose C, reinforce that a glass vase cannot be built from wood. Glass and wood are different materials with different properties. By completing Which Materials Are Best? in Lesson 1, children explored that materials have different properties that are suited to different purposes. Children who answer incorrectly should refer back to Lesson 1.

10. Children should choose B—green; and C—round. If children choose A, reinforce that the soccer ball is green in color and round in shape. It is not flexible, so it does not bend. By completing Properties of Matter in Lesson 1, children explored that color, shape, hardness, texture, and flexibility are properties of matter. Children who answer incorrectly should refer back to Lesson 1.

3D Item Analysis	1	2	3	4	5	6	7	8	9	10
SEP Science Models, Laws, Mechanisms, and Theories Explain Natural Phenomena	•	•	•	•						
DCI Structure and Properties of Matter		•			•	•	•	•	•	•
DCI Chemical Reactions	•	•	•	•			•			
CCC Cause and Effect	•	•	•	•						
CCC Energy and Matter								•		

8. You are building a cube from toothpicks and clay balls. Which picture shows the finished cube?

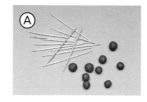 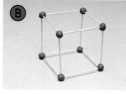 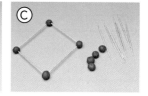

9. What could be built from these materials? Choose all correct answers.

10. Which are properties of the ball? Choose all correct answers.
Ⓐ bends
Ⓑ green
Ⓒ round

Unit 3

Environments for Living Things

Unit Project • Explore Habitats

Why do plants and animals live where they do? Investigate to find out.

Unit 3 • Environments for Living Things

Unit Overview

In this unit, children will…

- investigate what plants and animals need to live and grow.
- develop models to show how plants depend on animals.
- explore environments to identify observable patterns.
- observe plants and animals to compare diversity of life in water habitats.
- observe plants and animals to compare diversity of life in land habitats.

About This Image

Guide children in a discussion about the picture on this page. **Ask: Have you ever seen a bird that looks like this before? Where do you think it lives?** Sample answer: Parrots live in trees. Most parrots live in tropical or subtropical areas such as South America, Central America, and Australia. **Ask: What do you think this bird is doing?** It looks like it is eating a nut. Guide children to understand that, like other animals, a parrot needs food, air, water, and shelter to live and grow.

Unit Project • **Explore Habitats**

Have children plan and conduct an investigation to find out how plants and animals get what they need in their habitat. Plants and animals need slightly different things. Both need air, water, and food (nutrients). However, animals need shelter and plants need sunlight and room to grow.

To begin, share details about what most living things need or challenge children to use online resources to find out. More support for the Unit Project can be found on pp. 109K–109N.

Unit 3 At a Glance

The learning experiences in this unit prepare children for mastery of:

Performance Expectations

2-LS2-1. Plan and conduct an investigation to determine if plants need sunlight and water to grow.

2-LS2-2. Develop a simple model that mimics the function of an animal in dispersing seeds or pollinating plants.

2-LS4-1. Make observations of plants and animals to compare the diversity of life in different habitats.

Explore online. ▶

In addition to the print resources, the following resources are available online to support this unit.

Unit Pretest
Lesson 1 What Do Plants Need?
- Interactive Online Student Edition
- Lesson Quiz
Lesson 2 Engineer It • How Do Plants Depend on Animals?
- Interactive Online Student Edition
- Lesson Quiz
Lesson 3 What Plants and Animals Live in Water Habitats?
- Interactive Online Student Edition
- Lesson Quiz
Lesson 4 What Plants and Animals Live in Land Habitats?
- Interactive Online Student Edition
- Lesson Quiz
You Solve It City Habitats
Unit Performance Task
Unit Test

Unit 3 At a Glance

© Houghton Mifflin Harcourt • Image Credits: ©Jeff Mauritzen/Getty Images

Unit Vocabulary

nutrient anything that living things, such as plants, need as food (p. 112)

pollen a sticky powder that flowers need to make seeds (p. 132)

habitat a place where living things get the food, water, air, and shelter needed to live (pp. 142, 158)

Vocabulary Game • Show the Word!

Materials
- 1 set of word cards
- paper
- pencils or other drawing tools

How to Play
1. Work with your partner to make word cards.
2. Place the cards face down on the table.
3. Pick a card, but do not show the word.
4. Draw or act out the word for your partner to guess.
5. When the word is guessed correctly, your partner picks a card to draw or act out.

Unit Vocabulary

The Next Generation Science Standards emphasize explanation and demonstration of understanding versus rote memorization of science vocabulary words. Keep in mind that these vocabulary words are tools for clear communication. Use these words as a starting point, not an end goal, for children to build deeper understanding of science concepts.

Children can explore all vocabulary words in the **Online Glossary**.

Vocabulary Strategies

- Have children review the vocabulary words. Then have children work in pairs to share an example of each word and explain why they think it's an example. Have pairs record their examples to refer back to during the unit.
- Have children think about how each word relates to plants or animals. Have children work in pairs and share their ideas with a partner.

Differentiate Instruction

RTI/Extra Support Pronounce each word, and have children repeat it after you. Have children find each highlighted word within the unit content. Have children work in pairs and explain to a partner what they think each word means based on the surrounding context of imagery and text.

Extension Have children select two vocabulary words and work in small groups to illustrate and explain the words to a first-grade child.

Vocabulary Game • Show the Word!

Preparation Assemble vocabulary game cards. Assign partners for children. Provide instructions for how to play the game by drawing or acting out each word. Allow children to rotate through all three cards during gameplay.

© Houghton Mifflin Harcourt

Integrating the NGSS* Three Dimensions of Learning

Building to the Performance Expectations

The learning experiences in this unit prepare children for mastery of the following Performance Expectations:

Ecosystems: Interactions, Energy, and Dynamics

2-LS2-1. Plan and conduct an investigation to determine if plants need sunlight and water to grow.

2-LS2-2. Develop a simple model that mimics the function of an animal in dispersing seeds or pollinating plants.

Biological Evolution: Unity and Diversity

2-LS4-1. Make observations of plants and animals to compare the diversity of life in different habitats.

Assessing Student Progress

After completing the lessons, the **Unit Project Explore Habitats** provides children with opportunities to practice aspects of and to demonstrate their understanding of the Performance Expectations as they plan and conduct an investigation to find out why plants and animals live where they do.

Additionally, children can further practice or be assessed on aspects of the Performance Expectations by completing the **Unit Performance Task Observe an Ant Farm,** in which they carry out an investigation to observe ants and compare their lives within the ant farm habitat and to identify how its shape and stability relate to its function.

Lesson 1
What Do Plants Need?

In Lesson 1, children focus on what plants need to be healthy and grow (DCI Interdependent Relationships in Ecosystems). Children explore the things of a plant needs (water, sunlight, air, nutrients, and space) and why plants need these elements (CCC Cause and Effect). Finally, children investigate how a plant uses water to get what it needs (SEP Planning and Carrying Out Investigations).

Lesson 2
Engineer It • How Do Plants Depend on Animals?

In Lesson 2, children focus on how plants depend on animals for pollination and seed dispersal from one location to another (DCI Interdependent Relationships in Ecosystems). The lesson begins with children exploring ways that animals move plant seeds based on their shape and structure (CCC Structure and Function). As they explore, children plan and build a model tool to move seeds, too (SEP Developing and Using Models) (DCI Developing Possible Solutions). Finally, children explore how animals move pollen so new plants may grow (DCI Interdependent Relationships in Ecosystems).

Lesson 3
What Plants and Animals Live in Water Habitats?

In Lesson 3, children focus on living things found in the habitats within a pond, a river delta, and a tide pool (DCI Biodiversity and Humans). Children explore why specific plants and animals live in each habitat. Children find out how plants and animals can get the things they need in each habitat (SEP Scientific Knowledge is Based on Empirical Evidence) (CCC Patterns). Children compare the diversity of life found within different habitats (SEP Planning and Carrying Out Investigations).

Lesson 4
What Plants and Animals Live in Land Habitats?

In Lesson 4, children explore living things found in land habitats within a rain forest, a forest, and a savanna (DCI Biodiversity and Humans). Children use prior knowledge to explore the relationships and characteristics of plants and animals that live in each habitat (SEP Scientific Knowledge is Based on Empirical Evidence) (CCC Patterns). Finally, children will compare plants and animals across the habitats (SEP Planning and Carrying Out Investigations).

Standards Supported by This Unit

 Explore online. Online only.

Next Generation Science Standards	Unit Project	Lesson 1	Lesson 2	Lesson 3	Lesson 4	Unit Performance Task	You Solve It
SEP Developing and Using Models			•				
SEP Planning and Carrying Out Investigations	•	•		•	•	•	•
SEP Scientific Knowledge Is Based on Empirical Evidence				•	•		•
DCI LS2.A Interdependent Relationships in Ecosystems	•	•	•			•	
DCI LS4.D Biodiversity and Humans				•	•		•
DCI ETS1.B Developing Possible Solutions			•				
CCC Patterns				•	•		•
CCC Cause and Effect	•	•					
CCC Structure and Function			•			•	

NGSS* Across the Grades

Before
Interdependent Relationships in Ecosystems: Animals, Plants and Their Environment

K-LS1-1 Use observations to describe patterns in what plants and animals (including humans) need to survive.

Grade 2
Ecosystems: Interactions, Energy, and Dynamics
2-LS2-1
2-LS2-2
Biological Evolution: Unity and Diversity
2-LS4-1

After
Interdependent Relationships in Ecosystems

3-LS4-3 Construct an argument with evidence that in a particular habitat some organisms can survive well, some survive less well, and some cannot survive at all.

3-LS4-4 Make a claim about the merit of a solution to a problem caused when the environment changes and the types of plants and animals that live there may change.

 **Trace Tool to the NGSS™** Go online to view the complete coverage of these standards across this grade level and time.

3D Unit Planning

Lesson 1 What Do Plants Need? pp. 110–123

Overview

Objective Construct an argument with evidence that plants are living things that need certain things to grow and to stay healthy.

SEP Planning and Carrying Out Investigations
DCI **LS2.A** Interdependent Relationships in Ecosystems
CCC Cause and Effect

Math and **English Language Arts** standards and features are detailed on lesson planning pages.

	Print and Online Student Editions	Explore online.
ENGAGE	Lesson Phenomenon pp. 110–111 Can You Explain It? Plants Are Living Things	▶ Can You Explain It? Video
EXPLORE/ EXPLAIN	**What Plants Need** **Taking It In** **Hands-On Activity** Explore What a Plant Needs pp. 117–118	**Hands-On** Worksheet
ELABORATE	Take It Further pp. 119–120 Where Plants Grow	Take It Further Growing Plants Without Soil
EVALUATE	Lesson Check p. 121 Self Check pp. 122–123	Lesson Quiz

Hands-On Activity Planning

Explore What a Plant Needs

Objective Children plan and conduct an investigation to see how water moves through plants. They will use data to serve as evidence to answer their question.

👥 small groups
🕑 2 class periods

Suggested Materials
- 2 large clear plastic containers
- measuring cup
- water
- red food coloring
- 2 celery stalks with leaves
- red crayons

Preparation/Tip
Preassemble materials bundles for small groups. Use the lightest inner stalks of celery because they will provide the best results. Trim the bottom of the celery stalks with scissors or shears before the activity.

Lesson 2 Engineer It • How Do Plants Depend on Animals? pp. 124–139

Overview

Objective Develop a simple model to show how plants depend on animals within their environment.

SEP Developing and Using Models
DCI LS2.A Interdependent Relationships in Ecosystems
DCI ETS1.B Developing Possible Solutions
CCC Structure and Function

Math and **English Language Arts** standards and features are detailed on lesson planning pages.

	Print and Online **Student Editions**	Explore online. ▶
ENGAGE	**Lesson Problem** pp. 124–125 **Can You Solve It?** How Animals Help Plants	▶ Can You Solve It? Video
EXPLORE/ EXPLAIN	**Animals Help Spread Seeds** **How Animals Spread Pollen** **Hands-On Activity Engineer It •** Plan and Build a Model Tool pp. 129–131	**Hands-On** Worksheet
ELABORATE	**Take It Further** pp. 135–136 Careers in Science & Engineering • Horticulturalist	Take It Further Other Ways Seeds Travel
EVALUATE	**Lesson Check** p. 137 **Self Check** pp. 138–139	Lesson Quiz

🔍 Hands-On Activity Planning

Engineer It • Plan and Build a Model Tool

Objective Children build a model of a tool with a structure that supports its ability to pick up and move seeds similar to how animals move seeds in nature.

👥 small groups
🕐 1 class period

Suggested Materials
- three kinds of seeds
- drinking straws
- toothpicks
- craft sticks
- masking tape
- string

Preparation/Tip
Pre-assemble materials bundles for groups. Alternatively, children may do this activity at home or as a whole-class activity if limited materials are available.

3D Unit Planning, continued

Lesson 3 What Plants and Animals Live in Water Habitats? pp. 140–155

Overview

Objective Make observations of plants and animals to compare the diversity of life in water habitats.

SEP Planning and Carrying Out Investigations
SEP Scientific Knowledge is Based on Empirical Evidence
DCI **LS4.D** Biodiversity and Humans
CCC Patterns

Math and **English Language Arts** standards and features are detailed on lesson planning pages.

	Print and Online Student Editions	Explore online. ▶
ENGAGE	Lesson Phenomenon pp. 140–141 Can You Explain It? Water Habitats	▶ Can You Explain It? Video
EXPLORE/ EXPLAIN	Ponds River Deltas Tide Pools Hands-On Activity Make Model Habitats pp. 149–150	Hands-On Worksheet
ELABORATE	Take It Further pp. 151–152 Careers in Science & Engineering • Marine Biologist	Take It Further Coral Reefs
EVALUATE	Lesson Check p. 153 Self Check pp. 154–155	Lesson Quiz

🔍 Hands-On Activity Planning

Make Model Habitats

Objective Children plan and build models of habitats found in a tide pool. Children observe their habitats and identify patterns in their observations.

👥 small groups
🕐 1 class period

Suggested Materials
- empty, transparent plastic container
- various rocks
- markers
- various rubber sea creatures
- water

Preparation/Tip
Preassemble material bundles for groups. Have paper towels ready to clean up any spills.

Lesson 4 What Plants and Animals Live in Land Habitats? pp. 156–177

Overview

Objective Make observations of plants and animals to compare the diversity of life in land habitats.

SEP Planning and Carrying Out Investigations
SEP Scientific Knowledge is Based on Empirical Evidence
DCI **LS4.D** Biodiversity and Humans
CCC Patterns

Math and **English Language Arts** standards and features are detailed on lesson planning pages.

	Print and Online **Student Editions**	Explore online. ▶
ENGAGE	Lesson Phenomenon pp. 156–157 **Can You Explain It?** Land Habitats	▶ Can You Explain It? Video
EXPLORE/ EXPLAIN	**Rain Forest Habitats** **Forest Habitats** **Savanna Habitats** **Hands-On Activity** Make a Habitat Exhibit pp. 171–172	**Hands-On** Worksheet **You Solve It** City Habitats
ELABORATE	**Take It Further** pp. 173–174 People in Science & Engineering • Dr. Emilio Bruna	Take It Further Stepping on Habitats
EVALUATE	**Lesson Check** p. 175 **Self Check** pp. 176–177	Lesson Quiz

🔍 Hands-On Activity Planning

Make a Habitat Exhibit

Objective Children make a plan to research and compare plants and animals that live in a habitat found in the savanna and then display their results in an exhibit.

👥 small groups
🕐 1 class period

Suggested Materials
- books and fact cards about animals
- pencils
- posterboard or white construction paper
- markers

Preparation/Tip
Preassemble materials bundles for pairs or groups.

3D Unit Planning, continued

 You Solve It
Go online for an additional interactive activity.

City Habitats

This interactive activity offers practice in support of **PE.2-LS4-1.**

SEP Planning and Carrying Out Investigations

SEP Scientific Knowledge is Based on Empirical Evidence

DCI **LS4.D** Biodiversity and Humans

CCC Patterns

3D Learning Objectives

- Children identify and observe how plants and animals get what they need within a variety of habitats within a city.

Activity Problem

- Children find out what plants and animals live in different land and water habitats within a city.
- Children find out what these living things need in order to live and grow.

Interaction Summary

- Children use virtual tools to explore water and land habitats within a city and record their observations.
- Success should be measured by the number of plants and animals children discover and record, as well as by the detail of their observations.

Assessment

Preassessment

Assessment Guide, Unit Pretest

The Unit Pretest focuses on prerequisite knowledge and is composed of items that evaluate children's preparedness for the content covered within this unit.

Formative Assessment

Interactive Worktext, Apply What You Know, Lesson Check, and Self Check

Summative Assessment

Assessment Guide, Lesson Quiz

The Lesson Quiz provides a quick assessment of each lesson objective and of the portion of the Performance Expectation aligned to the lesson.

Interactive Worktext, Performance Task pp. 178–179

The Performance Task presents the opportunity for children to collaborate with classmates in order to complete the steps of each Performance Task. Each Performance Task provides a formal Scoring Rubric for evaluating children's work.

Interactive Worktext, Unit 3 Review, pp. 180–182
Assessment Guide, Unit Test

The Unit Test provides an in-depth assessment of the Performance Expectations aligned to the unit. This test evaluates children's ability to apply knowledge in order to explain phenomena and to solve problems. Within this test, Constructed Response items apply a three-dimensional rubric for evaluating children's mastery on all three dimensions of the Next Generation Science Standards.

 **Assessment Online**
Go online to view the complete assessment items for this unit.

Teacher Notes

Differentiate Instruction

Leveled Readers

The Science & Engineering Leveled Readers provide additional nonfiction reading practice in this unit's subject area.

On Level • How Do Living Things Survive in Their Environment?

This reader reinforces unit concepts and includes response activities for your children.

Extra Support • How Do Living Things Survive in Their Environment?

This reader shares title, illustrations, vocabulary, and concepts with the On-Level Reader; however, the text is linguistically accommodated to provide simplified sentence structures and comprehension aids. It also includes response activities.

Enrichment • Meet the Amazing Monarch Butterfly

This high-interest, nonfiction reader will extend and enrich unit concepts and vocabulary and includes response activities.

Teacher Guide

The accompanying Teacher Guide provides teaching strategies and support for using all the readers.

Leveled Readers

All readers are available online as well as in an innovative, engaging format for use with touchscreen mobile devices. Contact your HMH Sales Representative for more information.

ELL

English Language Learner support resources include a glossary and Leveled Readers in Spanish and English. ELL teaching strategies appear throughout this unit:

pp. 110B, 114, 124B, 128, 131, 140B, 146, 156B, 158, 166

RTI/Extra Support

Strategies for children who need extra support appear throughout this unit:

pp. 109, 109K, 110B, 115, 120, 124B, 133, 135, 140B, 145, 151, 156B, 159, 160, 161, 163, 174

Extension

Strategies for children who have mastered core content and are ready for additional challenges appear throughout this unit:

pp. 109, 109K, 110B, 115, 120, 124B, 133, 135, 140B, 145, 151, 156B, 159, 160, 161, 163, 174

Connecting with NGSS

Connections to Community

Use these opportunities for informal science learning to provide local context and to extend and enhance unit concepts.

At Home

What Grows Here? Have children work with a family member to identify the plants and animals that live near their homes. Children can record their observations and make claims about how the plants get what they need and how the plants depend on the animals to help with pollination and seed dispersal.
Use with Lesson 4.

In the Community

Guest Speaker Invite a gardener, nursery owner, or other plant enthusiast to speak to the class about what a plant needs and how plants get what they need. Have children prepare questions for him or her to answer.
Use with Lesson 1.

What Lives Here? Plan a class field trip to a local park, wooded area, tide pool, or other place. Help children identify the plants and animals they observe in habitats found in one of the places. After returning to the classroom, have children work together to make a mural of the plants and animals they observed in the habitat.
Use with Lesson 3 or 4.

Culture

Agriculture Explain to children that many Hispanic cultures come from countries that have warm, dry weather. Many chili peppers are grown there as part of their agricultural industry. Have children write to identify what they think the chili plant needs in terms of light and water. Have children do research to verify the accuracy of their ideas.
Use with Lesson 1

Home Letters Go online to view the Home Letters for this unit.

Collaboration

Collaboration opportunities in this unit:

Build on Prior Knowledge
pp. 111, 112, 125, 126, 141, 157, 164, 167

Think , Pair, Share
p. 119

Cultivating New Questions
pp. 121, 137, 153, 175

Whole Class
pp. 136, 173

Pairs
pp. 148, 152

Jigsaw
p. 142

Connections to Science

Connections to Science opportunities in this unit:

Connection to Earth and Space Sciences
Patterns Lesson 1, p. 115

Connection to Physical Science
Structure and Properties of Matter Lesson 2, p. 132

Connection to Engineering Design
Developing and Using Models Lesson 3, p. 144

Connection to Earth and Space Sciences
The History of Planet Earth Lesson 4, p. 162

Unit Project

👥 small groups 🕐 2 class periods

Explore Habitats

There are many ways to complete this Unit Project. The steps and Suggested Materials indicate one way to complete the investigation. Encourage children to come up with their own ideas of how to explore why plants and animal live where they do. If children decide to follow another process to complete their investigation, be sure to review each group's plans before the children begin. Provide guidance for groups that may have strayed off topic. This Unit Project supports content in Lessons 1, 3, and 4.

3D Learning Objective

SEP Planning and Carrying Out Investigations
Explore why livings things live where they do.
Make observations to collect data.
Use data to make comparisons.

Skills and Standards Focus

This project supports building children's mastery of **Performance Expectation 2-LS4-1.**

SEP Planning and Carrying Out Investigations
DCI **LS4.D** Biodiversity and Humans
CCC Patterns

Suggested Materials

- notebook
- hand lens (optional)
- camera (optional)
- markers
- colored pencils
- posterboard

Preparation

Before beginning the project, discuss what plants and animals need to live and grow in different habitats.

Unit 3
Environments for Living Things

Unit Project • Explore Habitats
Why do plants and animals live where they do? Investigate to find out.

Unit 3 • Environments for Living Things   107

Differentiate Instruction

RTI/Extra Support Have children practice making observations in the classroom. Relay the importance of taking good notes by using details in their writings or drawings.

Extension Have children research other environments, such as deserts and tundras. Have them identify habitats and living things found in the area.

Unit 3 Project

Explore Habitats

Name _____

Unit 3 Project

Explore Habitats

Why do plants and animals live where they do? Think about the living things around your school. Go outside. Explore and compare two habitats. Write your ideas on the lines below.

Children should write their ideas of why plants and animals live in

certain places.

_____

Materials

Draw and label the materials you will need.

Children should draw and label materials. The following are possible materials children can use for this investigation: notebook, hand lens, camera, markers, colored pencils, posterboard

© Houghton Mifflin Harcourt Publishing Company

Unit 3 Project • Page 1 of 3

SEP Planning and Carrying Out Investigations . . . .

Encourage children to think of various habitats that can be found around the school. Discuss all ideas as a class. Have children choose two habitats in order to compare the living things found in each.

In this sample investigation, children will identify two different habitats, such as a tree and the edges of a pond, and compare the living things found there.

With adult supervision, children will go outside and explore their school to find various habitats. They will collect data by making observations of each habitat. **Ask: What kinds of habitats can you observe at school?** trees, bushes, soil, flower beds

ESSENTIAL QUESTIONS Prepare children for their project by asking the following questions.

- What do plants and animals need to live and grow?
- How can I collect and compare data?
- What patterns can I observe?

Ask: Do you think there will be different kinds of plants and animals in the two habitats? Why or why not? I think that the two habitats will have different kinds of plants and animals because not all living things live in the same places.

Steps

Discuss with children the importance of listing out steps in their investigation. If children need help, brainstorm the steps as a class.

DCI Biodiversity and Humans . . . .

Before taking the class outside, discuss places where plants and animals live. **Ask: Where are some places plants live? Where are some places animals live? How are these places the same? How are they different?** Accept all reasonable answers.

SEP Planning and Carrying Out Investigations . . . .

Guide children to understand that observing is an important part of this investigation. Their observations will be the data used to compare living things and their habitats. Remind children to pay close attention when making observations. Their observations can be drawings, writings, or even pictures taken with a camera. Explain the need for taking good notes so that when they return to the classroom they have solid data. **Ask: Why is it important to make and record observations?** So I can remember what I have observed and be able to use that information to answer a question.

Data

Remind children that their data will be used to make comparisons and to answer their question.

CCC Patterns . . . .

Explain to children that a pattern is something that repeats over and over. Patterns can be observed in the natural world. **Ask: What patterns did you observe during the investigation?** I observed that some birds built nests in trees, while other birds, such as ducks, spent time near the edge of the pond.

Steps Write the steps you will do.

Answers may vary but should reflect a logical order of steps taken during the investigation.

Sample steps listed:

1. Find habitats around the school, such as a tree or an edge of a pond.

2. Record the living things found in a tree.

3. Record the living things found near the edge of a pond.

4. Compare your observations. Tell why the living things are found there.

5. Make a poster to share your results with the class.

Data

Record your data.

Answers and drawings may vary but should reflect children's observations of two habitats around their school, such as a tree and the edge of a pond. These observations should identify the plants and animals found there.

Analyze Your Results

Look for patterns in your data.

Restate Your Question

Write the question you investigated.

Answers should identify the question children initially chose at the

beginning of the investigation.

Claims, Evidence, and Reasoning

Make a claim that answers your question.

Answers should explain that plants and animals live in habitats where

they can get the things they need.

Review the data. What evidence from the investigation supports your claim?

Answer should cite evidence from the investigation to support their

claim.

Discuss your reasoning with a partner.

Unit 3 Project • Page 3 of 3

© Houghton Mifflin Harcourt Publishing Company

Analyze Your Results

Have children analyze their data and identify patterns. Encourage children to share their data with other groups and to compare their results. **Ask: Compare the living things in each habitat.** Different plants and animals lived in both the tree and the edge of the pond. **Ask: What patterns did you observe?** I observed that living things only live in places where they can get the things they need.

Claims, Evidence, and Reasoning

Children should understand that living things only live in places where they can get the things they need. They should cite evidence to support their claim by using their drawings, pictures, and written notations. **Ask: What claim can you make?** Plants and animals live in habitats where they can get the things they need. **Ask: How does your evidence support your claim?** My observations show different plants and animals living in different habitats. Encourage children to discuss their reasoning.

Scoring Rubric for Unit Project	
3	States a claim supported with evidence that plants and animals live in places where they can get the things they need
2	States a claim somewhat supported with evidence that plants and animals live in places where they can get the things they need
1	States a claim that is not supported by evidence
0	Does not state a claim and does not provide evidence

Building to the Performance Expectation

The learning experiences in this lesson prepare children for mastery of:

2-LS2-1 Plan and conduct an investigation to determine if plants need sunlight and water to grow.

Trace Tool to the NGSS
Go online to view the complete coverage of these standards across this lesson, unit, and time.

Science & Engineering Practices (SEP)

Planning and Carrying Out Investigations

Plan and conduct an investigation collaboratively to produce data to serve as the basis for evidence to answer a question.

 VIDEO SEP: Planning and Carrying Out Investigations

Disciplinary Core Ideas (DCI)

LS2.A: Interdependent Relationships in Ecosystems
Plants depend on water and light to grow.

Crosscutting Concepts (CCC)

Cause and Effect
Events have causes that generate observable patterns.

CONNECTIONS TO MATH

MP.2 Reason abstractly and quantitatively.

MP.4 Model with mathematics.

2.OA.C.4 Use addition to find the total number of objects arranged in rectangular arrays with up to 5 rows and up to 5 columns; write an equation to express the total as a sum of equal addends.

CONNECTIONS TO ENGLISH LANGUAGE ARTS

W.2.7 Participate in shared research and writing projects (e.g., read a number of books on a single topic to produce a report; record science observations).

W.2.8 Recall information from experiences or gather information from provided sources to answer a question.

Supporting All Students, All Standards

Integrating the Three Dimensions of Learning

This lesson focuses on what plants need to be healthy and grow (DCI Interdependent Relationships in Ecosystems). The lesson begins with children exploring the things a plant needs (water, sunlight, air, nutrients, and space) and why plants need these elements (CCC Cause and Effect). Finally, children investigate how a plant uses water to get what it needs (SEP Planning and Carrying Out Investigations).

Professional Development Go online to view **Professional Development videos** with strategies to integrate CCCs and SEPs, including the ones used in this lesson.

Build on Prior Knowledge

Children should already know and be prepared to build on the following concepts:
- Planning and conducting an investigation can produce results. *(Grade 2, Unit 2, Lesson 1)*
- Results of an investigation can be used as data. *(Grade 2, Unit 2, Lesson 1)*
- Plants are living things. *(Grade K, Unit 3, Lesson 1)*
- Plants have parts that help them live. *(Grade 1, Unit 4, Lesson 1)*
- Plants can live in different environments. *(Grade K, Unit 3, Lesson 3)*
- Plants respond to the environment where they live. *(Grade 1, Unit 4, Lesson 4)*
- Cause and effect relationships produce patterns that can be observed. *(Grade 2, Unit 2, Lesson 3)*

Differentiate Instruction

Lesson Vocabulary
- nutrient

Reinforcing Vocabulary To help children understand what a nutrient is, help them form real-life connections. Discuss with children the nutrients they need in order to be healthy and live. Remind children that plants are also living things, just like a person is a living thing and needs nutrients. Demonstrate the meaning of *nutrient* by making a list of things children eat and reminding children that the foods on this list contain nutrients. Remind children to look for the highlighted word as they proceed through the lesson.

RTI/Extra Support Provide an additional opportunity for hands-on discovery. Have children plant lettuce in soils that have different amounts of sand, humus, and clay. Be sure they receive the same amount of water and sunlight. Have children observe and record their observations every three days for two weeks.

Extension Children who want to find out more can do research on a variety of plants and their growth. Plants such as cacti, ferns, and sunflowers require different amounts of sunlight and water and different kinds of soil. Have children make a poster to share their findings with the class.

ELL Be sure to point out all labels, pictures, captions, and headings throughout the lesson to assist children with strategies to summarize chunks of content. Discuss with children real-life connections to content and provide hands-on examples of materials when possible to best support the needs of these learners.

Lesson Phenomenon

Build on Prior Lessons

In Unit 2, children explored **properties and changes to matter.** Lesson 1 builds on the concepts of properties to explore how properties and **parts of plants help them live and grow.**

Lesson Objective

Construct an argument with evidence that plants are living things that need certain things to grow and to stay healthy.

About This Image

Have children observe the flowers in the picture. Discuss that plants are living things that grow when they have the things they need. **Ask: What are some things plants need to grow?** Plants need water, sunlight, space, and soil. Lead children in a discussion about the ways a plant gets water, sunlight, space, and soil.

 Interdependent Relationships in Ecosystems

Alternative Engage Strategy

Plant Questions	👥 small groups ⏱ 15–20 minutes

Ask: What questions do you have about what plants need to help them grow and stay healthy? Sample questions: Do different plants need different amounts of sunlight? Do different plants need different amounts of water? Allow 5 minutes for children to brainstorm some questions. Record these for the class to see. Have children read through their list of questions to see how many they can answer before they begin the lesson. Post the list of questions in the classroom for children to refer back to and answer as they continue through the lesson.

Lesson 1 **What Do Plants Need?**

Plants need certain things to live and grow.

By the End of This Lesson

I will be able to tell what a plant needs to grow and be healthy.

110

© Houghton Mifflin Harcourt • Image Credits ©Takashi Rodriguez/EyeEm/Getty Images

Plants Are Living Things

Look at the pictures. What does a plant need?

Explore online. ▶

Can You Explain It?

✏️ What would happen if a plant does not get the things it needs?

Accept all reasonable answers.

_____

_____

_____

_____

_____

© Houghton Mifflin Harcourt

Lesson 1 • What Do Plants Need?

111

Can You Explain It?

Plants Are Living Things Plants grow and change over time when they get the things they need. Play the video to see what a plant needs to live and stay healthy. If the video is not available, have children review and discuss the two pictures of the same plant at different stages. Explain that the plants are the same plant, but shown at different stages of growth. **Ask: What causes this plant to change?** Plants are living things that grow when they have the things they need. **What are some of the things plants need to grow?** Plants need water, sunlight, space, and soil.

Ask children to record their initial thoughts about what would happen if a plant didn't get the things it needed. At the end of this lesson, children will revisit this question as part of the Lesson Check. At this point, children should be able to explain that plants that don't get the things they need will wilt and not grow.

Collaboration

Build on Prior Knowledge You may want children to view and discuss the pictures as a whole-class activity. In this way, you can assess their prior knowledge of how plants grow and what they need to stay healthy.

Have children think about what they saw in the pictures, or think about a plant they have at home. **Ask: What changes have you observed in the plant? What do you have to do to keep the plant growing? How does a plant stay healthy? Use evidence from the images or from your own experiences to support your answer.** Answers will vary.

Support for Unit Project

The **Unit Project** Explore Habitats supports content in this lesson.

What Plants Need

3D Learning Objective

Children explore **what a plant needs** to stay healthy and **the effects** when a plant does not get the things it needs.

DCI Interdependent Relationships
in Ecosystems . . . .

Have children observe and discuss each picture. **Ask: What do plants need to live?** Plants need water, air, nutrients, sunlight, and space to grow. **How do plants get water?** Plants get water from rain, or by people watering them. **Why does a plant need air and water?** Plants need air and water to make their own food. **What is a nutrient?** A nutrient is a substance that helps plants grow. **Where does a plant get the nutrients it needs?** Plants get nutrients from the soil. **How does a plant use sunlight?** Plants use sunlight to make their own food. **Why does a plant need space?** Plants need space so their roots and leaves have room to grow.

SEP Planning and Carrying Out Investigations . . . .

Ask: You want to know if different plants need different amounts of sunlight in order to grow. How can you answer your question? I can do an investigation. **Ask: What can you use as evidence?** I can use my observations as evidence.

Collaboration

Build on Prior Knowledge Review with children the image of the field with evenly spaced plants in a row. Have children brainstorm reasons why a farmer plants crops in rows like this. Guide children to recognize what would happen if farmers did not plant their crops this way. For example, if the plants were planted too close together they may not have enough space for their roots, stems, and leaves to grow properly.

What Plants Need

Explore online. ▶

Look at the pictures to explore what plants need to live and grow.

water
air
nutrients
sunlight
space to grow

Plants need water, air, sunlight, nutrients, and space to grow. Plants get water from rain. People can also water plants. Plants use air, water, and sunlight to make their own food. Many plants also get nutrients from the soil. A **nutrient** is anything that living things, such as plants, need as food. Plants also need space so their roots and leaves have room to grow.

112

© Houghton Mifflin Harcourt • Image Credits: (tl) ©Zoom Team/Shutterstock; (tc) ©Pawelk/Shutterstock; (tr) ©iStock/Getty Images Plus/Getty Images; (bl) ©iStock/Getty Images Plus/Getty Images; (br) ©Pichugin Dmitry/Shutterstock

✏️ Which plant is getting everything it needs to live and grow? Circle Plant 1 or Plant 2.

Plant 1

Plant 2

✋ Apply What You Know

Read, Write, Share! • Evidence Notebook • Look at the two pictures of the plants. Work in a small group to discuss what Plant 1 needs to look more like Plant 2. Identify patterns you observe. Use evidence to support your answer. Record it in your Evidence Notebook.

Cause and Effect • Gather Information
Go to the online handbook for tips.

Lesson 1 • What Do Plants Need?   113

DCI Interdependent Relationships in Ecosystems . . . .

Have children observe and describe each picture. **Ask: How can you tell that Plant 2 is getting what it needs to live and grow?** The leaves are not wilted or drooping and the flower is standing straight up.

CCC Cause and Effect . . . .

Remind children that a cause is why something happens and an effect is what happened. Cause-and-effect relationships can generate observable patterns. **Ask: A plant does not get the things it needs. What is the effect?** The plant will not grow. **Ask: A plant does get the things it needs. What is the effect?** The plant will grow. **Ask: What pattern can we observe?** Plants that get the things they need will grow, while plants that do not get the things they need will not grow.

✋ FORMATIVE ASSESSMENT

Read, Write, Share! • Evidence Notebook
Remind children what plants need to live and grow. Discuss how both healthful and unhealthful plants look.

Scoring Guidelines
- describes what Plant 1 needs to make it look more like Plant 2
- provides evidence to support their answer

💡 **Cause and Effect • Gather Information • Participate in a Writing Project** Remind children of the causes and effects of plants getting and not getting the things they need. These can produce patterns in which healthful plants get what they need, while unhealthful plants do not. Children can gather information from resources such as books, magazines, or the Internet. Encourage them to take notes in order to help them remember the information.

Taking It In

3D Learning Objective

Children explore **the effects and observe patterns** when a plant uses its parts to help it live and grow.

DCI **Interdependent Relationships in Ecosystems** . . . .

As a class, discuss the diagram and accompanying text. **Ask: What is this a diagram of and how does it help you?** The diagram shows the different parts of a plant. It helps me to see what each part looks like and where it is located. **Ask: How do roots help a plant grow?** Roots grow into the soil, which helps the plant stay in place. The roots take in water and nutrients from the soil that the plants uses to grow. **How does a stem help a plant grow?** The stem holds the plant up. Water and nutrients move up the stem to the other parts of the plant. **How do leaves help a plant grow?** Leaves use sunlight, air, and water to make food.

CCC **Cause and Effect** . . . .

Ask: Suppose one of the plant's parts got damaged. What do you think the effect would be on the plant? The plant might not be able to grow or survive if it could not use its parts to get the things it needs.

Remind children that they can observe patterns when an event repeats. **Ask: What pattern can you observe when roots, stems, and leaves help a plant?** Plants use these parts to get what they need to survive over and over again.

Differentiate Instruction

ELL Have children compare and contrast additional pictures of roots, stems, and leaves. Help them understand that even though these parts may look differently, they serve the same purpose.

Taking It In

Explore online. ▶

Look at the picture to explore the parts a plant has that help it get what it needs to live and grow.

Roots grow into the soil and hold a plant in place. The roots take in water and nutrients from the soil. Roots need space to grow.

A stem holds up a plant. A stem carries water and nutrients to other parts of a plant.

Leaves use sunlight, air, and water to make food for a plant. Leaves need space to grow so a plant can take in the air and sunlight it needs.

114

© Houghton Mifflin Harcourt

✏️ Complete the sentences to tell what parts of a plant do. Use the words from the word bank.

roots	leaves	stem

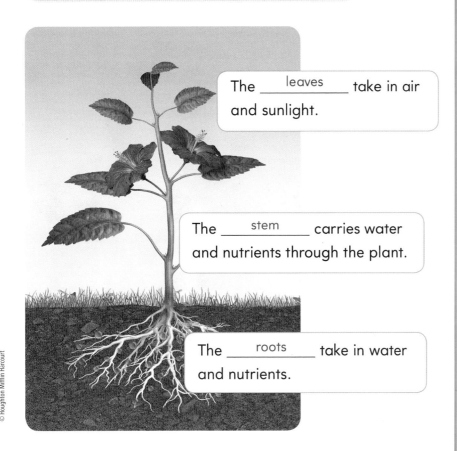

The ____leaves____ take in air and sunlight.

The ____stem____ carries water and nutrients through the plant.

The ____roots____ take in water and nutrients.

© Houghton Mifflin Harcourt

Lesson 1 • What Do Plants Need?   115

DCI **Interdependent Relationships in Ecosystems** . . . .

Before beginning this task, have children look back at the diagram and text on the previous page and underline how each plant part helps a plant to live and grow. Then have children observe this picture and read the words in the word bank. Children should write *leaves* in the first blank, *stem* in the second blank, and *roots* in the third blank. If children struggle to complete the sentences, refer them back to the statements they underlined on the previous page.

Differentiate Instruction

RTI/Extra Support Place an illustration of a labeled plant on a large chart or bulletin board. Use flash cards to describe the purpose of each plant part. Have children match the purpose to the part of the plant shown in the illustration.

Extension Challenge children to think about other parts a plant might have, such as seeds, flowers, and fruits. Have them use resources such as books or the Internet to identify other plant parts and what they do. Then have them present their findings to the class.

Connection to Earth and Space Sciences

Patterns Plants getting the things they need to live and grow is a pattern. Discuss other patterns in nature, such as certain bodies of water freezing and thawing depending on the temperature. Talk about which state the water is in during cold and warm weather. **Ask: What can happen to some ponds and lakes during very cold weather?** The water freezes and becomes a solid. **What can happen when warmer weather arrives?** The water thaws and becomes liquid again. **What pattern can we observe?** Water can change states depending on the temperature.

Do the Math! • Use Equal Groups

Ask: How many plants are there in each row? 5 How many rows of plants are there? 2 How can you use equal groups to find the total number of plants? I can add 5 and 5 to get the answer.

Children should write 10 on the blank to show the total number of plants Mr. Baker will have to water.

 Use Equal Groups • Reason Abstractly and Quantitatively • Model with Mathematics Draw a picture of 2 rows of 5 plants each to represent the problem visually. Children should recognize that equal groups were used to make the picture. Have children write the addition sentence 5 + 5 = _____. Finally, have them complete the addition sentence to find the total.

ccc Cause and Effect . . . .

Ask: What causes a plant to become dry and wilted? not getting enough water What is the effect of a plant getting too much water? The plant may droop and its leaves turn yellow. What pattern can we observe? Too much or too little water causes a plant to become unhealthy, while just the right amount of water helps the plant stay healthy.

FORMATIVE ASSESSMENT

Evidence Notebook

With a partner, have children observe and describe how each plant looks in the picture. Remind children to think about the things a plant needs and what could happen if a plant gets too much or too little of the things they need. Guide children to use evidence from the pictures to support their answers.

Scoring Guidelines

• identifies how much water each plant received
• accurately describes if each plant is healthy and explains why or why not
• provides sufficient evidence to support their claims

Do the Math! • Mr. Baker has 2 rows of plants in his garden. If he puts 5 plants in each row, how many plants will he have to water in all?

____10____ plants

Use Equal Groups
Go to the online handbook for tips.

Apply What You Know

Evidence Notebook • A plant that gets enough water is healthy. A plant that does not get enough water is dry and wilted. What happens if a plant gets too much water? It may droop, and its leaves may turn yellow.

Observe these plants. Work with a partner. Use evidence to support your answer. Record your answers in your Evidence Notebook.

116

© Houghton Mifflin Harcourt

Name _____

Hands-On Activity
Explore What a Plant Needs

Materials

_____

Ask a Question

What happens when a plant is placed in colored water?

Test and Record Data

Step 1

Pour water into each cup. Add red food coloring to one of the cups and stir. Place one plant in each cup. Leave the plants in the cups until the next day.

Step 2

Observe the plants.
Record your observations.

	Check children's observations.
	_____
	_____
	_____

© Houghton Mifflin Harcourt

Lesson 1 • What Do Plants Need?   117

Hands-On Activity 👥 small groups ⏱ 2 class periods

Explore What a Plant Needs

3D Learning Objective

SEP **Planning and Carrying Out Investigations . . . .**

Children plan and conduct an investigation to see how water moves through plants. They will use data to serve as evidence to answer their question.

Suggested Materials 2 large clear plastic containers, measuring cup, water, red food coloring, 2 celery stalks with leaves, and a red crayon per group

Preparation

Pre-assemble materials bundles for small groups. Use the lightest inner stalks of celery because they will provide the best results. Trim the bottom of the celery stalks with scissors or shears before the activity.

Activity

As a class, brainstorm questions that children have about the things plants need and parts of plants. **Ask: What is a question we could do an investigation on?** What happens when a plant is placed in colored water?

STEP 1 Children may need assistance pouring the water. Be sure that the same amount of water is in both cups. Remind children that part of their data should include how much water they used.

STEP 2 **Ask: What do our celery stalks look like now?** The celery is green and looks healthy.

Hands-On Activity, continued

STEP 3 Guide children to observe the plants in each cup and record any effects they see. **Ask: What has happened to each of the celery stalks?** The celery stalk in the cup with red food coloring is beginning to turn red. The celery stalk in the plain cup of water is still green. **What has happened to the water in your container?** The water level has gone down in both containers.

(ccc) **Cause and Effect** . . . .

STEP 4 Children should analyze the results of their investigation and look for patterns. **Ask: Why did the celery stalk turn red in color?** The stem of the celery stalk moves water to all parts of the plant. Parts of the celery stalk started to turn red when the stem moved the water through the plant.

Claims, Evidence, and Reasoning

Children should make a claim that identifies what happens to a plant when it is placed in colored water. They should cite evidence to support their claim. **Ask: How can we tell that water moves up the stem?** We can see the red coloring in the celery placed in the red colored water.

Scoring Rubric for Hands-On Activity	
3	States a claim supported with evidence about the movement of water within each celery stalk
2	States a claim somewhat supported with evidence about the movement of water within each celery stalk
1	States a claim not supported by evidence
0	Does not state a claim and does not provide evidence

Step ③

Observe the plants in each cup.
Record any effects you observe.

Plant 1	Plant 2
Check children's observations.	

Step ④

Analyze your results. Identify causes and effects.
Look for patterns.

Make a claim that answers your question.

Answers should reflect children's ideas about what

happens to a plant when it is placed in colored water.

What is your evidence?

Answers should cite evidence from the plant activity.

118

Explore online. ▶ Guide children to the Interactive Online Student Edition where they can choose from and explore both paths.

Take It Further
Where Plants Grow

Explore more online.
- Growing Plants Without Soil

North America has many climates, or patterns of weather. Tundras, deserts, and wetlands all have different climates and plants.

Explore online. ▶

A tundra has short, cool summers and long, cold winters. Most plants grow close together and low to the ground to protect against the cold and the wind.

tundra

desert

Alaska (U.S.)

Canada

United States

Mexico

A desert is dry. In some deserts, temperatures can go from hot to cold within one day. Many plants have thick stems or waxy leaves that store water for times when it is dry.

wetlands

Wetlands are hot and humid with a lot of rain. Plants here grow well in very wet soil or water.

Take It Further

Where Plants Grow

Lead a discussion about the climates shown in the pictures. Tundra can be divided up into Arctic and Alpine. Both are cold, with the Arctic being the coldest. Very few trees grow in the Alpine, while none are found in the Arctic. Liverworts and reindeer moss are found in the Arctic tundra. Dwarf trees and tussock grasses are found in the Alpine.

Deserts can be hot and dry or cold. The Sahara is the largest hot desert in the world. The Gobi desert in Asia is one of the few cold deserts. Plants that live in dry deserts grow long roots in order to reach deep water.

Marshes, swamps, and bogs are a few types of wetlands. Cypress trees and eelgrasses are some kinds of plants that can be found there.

DCI **Interdependent Relationships in Ecosystems** . . . .

Ask: **What are some of the differences you see in the different climates?** Some are warm while others may be cold and snowy. Temperatures can change, the amount of water can change, and the soil may be different. Remind children that plants need certain things to live and grow. **How are plants able to live and grow in the desert?** Even though deserts are dry, desert plants still get the amount of sunlight and water they need. **Would a plant living in wetlands be able to live in a desert? Why or why not?** No, because plants that live in wetlands need lots of water and deserts are very dry.

Collaboration

Think, Pair, Share Partner children and have them think about plants that grow in the area or experiences they have had with planting a garden. Have partners share with the class why these plants grow well in their area.

Take It Further, continued

Children use their observations of where plants live to write the name of the place under the picture that shows a plant living in that area. **Ask: What place do you see in the top left picture?** wetlands **What place do you see in the top right picture?** tundra **What place do you see in the bottom picture?** desert

DCI **Interdependent Relationships in Ecosystems** . . . .

Ask: How can you tell that the top left picture shows a plant in wetlands? The plant is growing in water. **How can you tell that the top right picture shows plants in a tundra?** The plants are growing close together and low to the ground. **How can you tell that the bottom picture shows a plant in the desert?** The leaves are waxy-looking.

Differentiate Instruction

RTI/Extra Support Guide children to describe the plants shown in the pictures. Encourage children to identify the parts of the plant and what makes them able to survive in the place where they live. As needed, have children refer back to the pictures and text on the previous page.

Extension Challenge children to research two plants that could live in each climate. Provide resources, such as books or the Internet, to help children gather information. Have them draw a picture and label the name of each plant and which climate it lives in.

Explore more online. ▶

Growing Plants Without Soil

Children explore what kind of plants can grow without soil.

✏▶ Where does each plant live? Label the pictures using the words in the box.

| desert | tundra | wetlands |

wetlands

tundra

desert

120

Explore online. ▶   Have children explore online to find out more about what causes a plant to grow and be healthy.

Lesson Check

Name _____

Explore online. ▶

Can You Explain It?

✏️ What would happen if a plant does not get the things it needs?

Be sure to
- Describe how the plant might look.
- Explain what could happen if the plant continues to not get the things it needs.

Sample answer: A plant that does not get air, water,

sunlight, nutrients, and space to grow would look wilted and

droopy. It would not grow or be able to survive if it continued

to not get the things it needs.

Lesson Check

Can You Explain It?

Have children reread their answers to the Can You Explain It? prompt at the beginning of the lesson.

🔵 **Interdependent Relationships in**
DCI **Ecosystems** . . . .

Review both pictures and discuss how the plant has changed over time. **Ask: What do plants need to grow and be healthy?** Sunlight, water, air, nutrients, and space are the things that plants need in order to live, grow, and stay healthy. **How does a plant's parts help it survive?** The roots take in water and nutrients. The stem helps hold up the plant and moves water and nutrients to other parts of the plant. The leaves use air, water, and sunlight to make food.

Scoring Guidelines
- Children should describe how the plant might look.
- Children should effectively explain what would happen to the plant if it continued to not get the things it needs.

Collaboration

Cultivating New Questions As children complete this lesson and prepare for the next lesson, ask them to identify additional questions they have about what plants need or plant parts. **Ask: How do flowers help a plant? How do fruits help a plant?** Flowers make seeds and fruits hold and protect the seeds. As children continue to the next lesson, they will apply concepts related to plants and how they grow.

Lesson Check, continued

SUMMATIVE ASSESSMENT
Self Check

1. Children should circle the first and third pictures. Plants need water and sunlight to grow. If children circle the middle picture, guide them to What Plants Need and have them compare the pictures on both pages to look for patterns.

2. Children should circle the middle plant. If children circle the first or third picture, guide them to the Apply What You Know from What Plants Need. Review what happens when plants receive too little water.

3. Children should choose B—sunlight; and C—air. If children do not choose B or C, or they choose A instead, guide them to Taking It In. Discuss what plants need to make food.

Self Check

1. What do plants need to grow? Circle all correct answers.

2. Tyler and his family go away for two weeks. No one waters the plants while they are gone. What will the plants look like when they get home?

3. What do plants need to make food? Choose all correct answers.
   Ⓐ shelter
   🅑 sunlight
   🅒 air

122

4. What does each plant part do? Draw a line to match the picture of the plant part to the label that tells what it does.

| moves water through the plant | takes in sunlight and air to make food | takes in water and nutrients from the soil |

5. Why did the celery in the picture turn red?

Ⓐ The celery plant was kept in the dark.

🅑 The water moved up the stem into the leaves.

Ⓒ The celery plant did not get enough nutrients.

4. Children should complete the following matches:

Picture 1: leaves is matched with the middle label—takes in sunlight and air to make food

Picture 2: roots is matched with the last label—takes in water and nutrients from the soil

Picture 3: stem is matched with the first label—moves water through the plant

If children incorrectly match the pictures with the labels, guide them to Taking It In and review what each part of a plant does to help the plant grow and stay healthy.

5. Children should choose B—The water moved up the stem into the leaves. If children choose A or C, briefly review the Hands-On Activity and discuss what happened to the celery placed in red food coloring.

Engineer It • How Do Plants Depend on Animals?

Building to the Performance Expectation

The learning experiences in this lesson prepare children for mastery of:

2-LS2-2 Develop a simple model that mimics the function of an animal in dispersing seeds or pollinating plants.

Trace Tool to the NGSS
Go online to view the complete coverage of these standards across this lesson, unit, and time.

 **Science & Engineering Practices**

Developing and Using Models
Develop a simple model based on evidence to represent a proposed object or tool.

 VIDEO SEP: Developing and Using Models

(DCI) Disciplinary Core Ideas

LS2.A: Interdependent Relationships in Ecosystems
Plants depend on animals for pollination or to move their seeds around.

ETS1.B: Developing Possible Solutions
Designs can be conveyed through sketches, drawings, or physical models. These representations are useful in communicating ideas for a problem's solutions to other people.

(CCC) Crosscutting Concepts

Structure and Function
The shape and stability of structures of natural and designed objects are related to their function(s).

 VIDEO CCC: Structure and Function

CONNECTIONS TO MATH

MP.4 Model with mathematics.

2.MD.D.10 Draw a picture graph and a bar graph (with single-unit scale) to represent a data set with up to four categories. Solve simple put-together, take-apart, and compare problems using information presented in a bar graph.

CONNECTION TO ENGLISH LANGUAGE ARTS

SL.2.5 Create audio recordings of stories or poems; add drawings or other visual displays to stories or recounts of experiences when appropriate to clarify ideas, thoughts, and feelings.

Supporting All Students, All Standards

Integrating the Three Dimensions of Learning

This lesson focuses on how plants depend on animals for pollination and seed dispersal (**DCI Interdependent Relationships in Ecosystems**). The lesson begins with children exploring how animals help plants by moving their seeds. Seeds are dispersed by animals in different ways depending on the shape and structure of the seeds (**CCC Structure and Function**). As they explore, children will make a plan to build a model tool to move seeds around like animals do (**SEP Developing and Using Models**) (**DCI Developing Possible Solutions**). Finally, children will explore how animals help plants by moving pollen from flower to flower so that new plants may grow in different places (**DCI Interdependent Relationships in Ecosystems**).

Professional Development Go online to view **Professional Development videos** with strategies to integrate CCCs and SEPs, including the ones used in this lesson.

Build on Prior Knowledge

Children should already know and be prepared to build on the following concepts:

- Evidence can be used to help develop models. *(Grade 2, Unit 1, Lesson 1)*
- Sketches and drawings influence the development of models. *(Grade 2, Unit 1, Lesson 1)*
- Plants and animals need certain things to live and grow. *(Grade K, Unit 3, Lessons 1 and 2)*
- Animals eat plants, animals, or both in order to survive. *(Grade K, Unit 3, Lesson 2)*
- Living things have external parts that help them survive. *(Grade 1, Unit 4, Lessons 1-3)*
- The shape and structure of an object is related to its function. *(Grade 2, Unit 1, Lesson 1)*

Differentiate Instruction

Lesson Vocabulary
- pollen

Reinforcing Vocabulary To help children remember the vocabulary word, help them form real-life connections. Discuss with children the connection between the word *pollen* and the word *flowers*. Show them some pictures of pollen. Have them brainstorm how pollen helps make new seeds and how it can be moved from flower to flower.

RTI/Extra Support Provide children with additional pictures and videos of pollen in flowers and animals transporting it.

Extension Children who want to find out more can do research on pollen and how it is needed for plants to make new seeds. Children can share their findings with the class by making a poster or other display.

ELL Be sure to point out all labels, pictures, captions, and headings throughout the lesson to assist children with strategies to summarize chunks of content. Discuss with children real-life connections to content and provide hands-on examples of materials when possible to best support the needs of these learners.

Lesson Problem

Build on Prior Lessons

In Lesson 1, children explored **what plants need and parts of plants**. They **investigated** how **plants getting what they need affects how they grow**. Lesson 2 builds on these concepts to **model** how **plants depend on animals to help them make or move seeds**.

Lesson Objective

Develop a simple model to show how plants depend on animals within their environment.

About This Image

Remind children that pollen is a powdery substance that plants need to make seeds. Have children observe the picture of the bee landing on the flower. Explain that the bees are actually helping the flower. **Ask: Have you ever seen a bee or another insect land on a flower or other type of plant?** Accept all reasonable responses. **What do you think the bee is doing?** drinking the nectar **How could the insects be helping the plants?** They are helping them by spreading the pollen around. Lead children in a discussion about how animals and plants can help each other.

 DCI **Interdependent Relationships in Ecosystems**

Alternative Engage Strategy

Animal Helpers	👥 small groups 🕐 20 minutes

Have children work in small groups to draw a picture of an animal helping a plant. Discuss the animals and plants in their pictures. Then, discuss how the animals are helping the plants. Have children work in their small groups to brainstorm more ways that animals can help plants.

Lesson 2 **Engineer It • How Do Plants Depend on Animals?**

Plants depend on animals in many ways.

By the End of This Lesson
I will be able to explain how plants depend on animals to help move seeds and pollen.

124

How Animals Help Plants

Look at the bee on the flower. The flower is providing the bee with nectar. How is the bee helping the plant?

Explore online. ▶

Can You Solve It?

✏️ You want to add more flowers to your garden. How can bees help solve this problem?

Accept all reasonable answers.

_____

_____

_____

Lesson 2 • Engineer It • How Do Plants Depend on Animals?   125

Can You Solve It?

How Animals Help Plants Animals can help plants in some interesting ways. The video shows how bees can help flowers by moving pollen. If the video is not available, have children observe the picture on the page.

Ask children to record their initial thoughts about how a bee can help solve the problem of adding more flowers to a garden. At the end of this lesson, children will revisit this question in the Lesson Check. At that point, children should be able to explain how bees are able to help plants by moving pollen so new plants can grow in different places.

Collaboration

Build on Prior Knowledge You may want children to view and discuss the video or picture as a whole-class activity. In this way, you can assess their prior knowledge of how animals help plants.

Have children think about what they saw in the video or picture, or think about animals they have seen interacting with plants. Then have them discuss how the bee or other animals helped the plants. Children should use evidence from the video or picture, or from their own experiences to support their answer.

Animals Help Spread Seeds

3D Learning Objective

Children explore **how animals help plants by dispersing their seeds to new places.** They observe how a **seed's movement is dependent upon its shape and structure.**

DCI **Interdependent Relationships in Ecosystems** . . . .

Discuss the three pictures with children. **Ask: How do you think animals spreading seeds helps plants?** It helps plants by getting their seeds to different areas where they can grow into new plants. This way plants grow in many different areas instead of just one location. **Ask: Name three ways that animals help spread seeds?** Seeds stick to animal fur and then fall off in a different place. Birds drop seeds as they fly. Squirrels bury seeds in new places. **Ask: What happens to the seeds after they have been left in a new place by an animal?** Some seeds will grow into new plants. **Ask: Do you think all seeds that are moved by animals grow into new plants? Why or why not?** No, they may not all grow if they are placed in a location where they are not able to get all of the things they need.

Collaboration

Build on Prior Knowledge Review with children the meanings of the word *spread*. Have children brainstorm examples from their own experiences of items being spread out. Guide children to recognize that the seeds may not have been able to grow if they had not been placed in a new location with enough space.

Animals Help Spread Seeds

Explore online. ▶

Look at the pictures to explore how animals can help some plants spread their seeds.

Some plants have seeds covered in hooks and spines called burrs. These burrs hook onto an animal's fur. Over time, the burrs fall off. New plants may grow from the seeds.

Birds eat seeds and fruits that have seeds in them. They fly away with seeds in their beaks. Some seeds drop to the ground. New plants grow from the seeds.

Squirrels gather and hide acorns to eat later. Sometimes they do not come back for the acorns they have buried. Now trees can grow from these seeds.

126

© Houghton Mifflin Harcourt • Image Credits: (t) ©Serguei Liachenko/Getty Images; (c) ©Franz Leitner/age fotostock; (b) ©bkpix/Glow Images

✏️➡️ **Draw a line to match each animal with the way it can move seeds.**

💡 **Structure and Function** Go to the online handbook for tips.

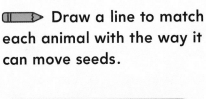

Seeds are buried in the ground.

Seeds fall from its fur.

Seeds drop from its mouth or beak.

Lesson 2 • Engineer It • How Do Plants Depend on Animals?   127

DCI **Interdependent Relationships in Ecosystems** . . . .

Children should draw a line matching the picture of the sheep to *Seeds fall from its fur.*; from the picture of the bird to *Seeds drop from its mouth or beak.*; and from the picture of the chipmunk to *Seeds are buried in the ground*. If children do not correctly match the animal with the way it moves seeds, have them review the pictures and text on the previous page.

Ask: What happens after seeds have been moved from one place to another? The seeds might grow into new plants.

CCC **Structure and Function** . . . .

Ask: How does the structure of the seeds help them stick to the sheep? The seeds are covered in hooks and spines called burrs that help them stick to the sheep. **Ask:** If the structure of the seeds were different would they be able to travel the same way? No; the seeds would not move with the animal if they did not stick to its fur.

💡 **Structure and Function** Have children think of things in nature or things that people make. The shape and stability of such things are connected to how they work.

SEP **Developing and Using Models** . . . .

DCI **Developing Possible Solutions** . . . .

Ask: You have a problem. You need to move seeds from one place to another. How can looking at the picture of the bird help you? I can observe the shape of the bird's beak. Then I could use materials to make a model that is similar in shape to help me move seeds.

**Interdependent Relationships
in Ecosystems** . . . .

Ask: How can people help plants move seeds? Just like with an animal's fur, seeds can get stuck to a person's clothing. As the person is traveling along, seeds can fall off and new plants can grow.

Differentiate Instruction

ELL Have children discuss this topic in small groups before writing or drawing to have them become more familiar with the concept. Talk about different ways they may have moved seeds in the past. Allow them to share their experiences together in the group to help generate ideas for writing.

 FORMATIVE ASSESSMENT

Read, Write, Share! • Use Visuals
Remind children how seeds can be moved by animals. Have them think about the different seeds they have encountered as well as their shape and size. The structure of a seed can influence how it is moved.

Scoring Guidelines
• describes a time they moved seeds or how they might move seeds
• writes, draws, or uses pictures to support their ideas

💡 **Use Visuals** Remind children that pictures help support facts. They can add more detailed information. Children can draw pictures or look for pictures in magazines or online.

 Apply What You Know

Read, Write, Share! • Have you ever walked through the woods and found burrs stuck to your socks? If so, you have moved seeds. Think about a time you moved seeds or how you might move seeds. Use drawings or other pictures to support your ideas.

✏️ Draw or write about your ideas.

Use Visuals
Go to the online handbook for tips.

Check children's work.
_____

_____

_____

_____

128

Hands-On Activity 👥 small groups ⏱ 1 class period

Engineer It • Plan and Build a Model Tool

3D Learning Objective

SEP Developing and Using Models . . . .

DCI Interdependent Relationships in Ecosystems . . . .

Children build a model of a tool with a structure that supports its ability to pick up and disperse seeds from one place to another similar to how animals disperse seeds in nature.

Suggested Materials three kinds of seeds and classroom materials, such as drinking straws, toothpicks, craft sticks, masking tape, and string

Preparation

Pre-assemble materials bundles for groups. Alternatively, children may do this activity at home or as a whole-class activity if limited materials are available.

Activity

As a class, view the video. Then, discuss the question that will need to be answered. Have children record the question.

DCI Developing Possible Solutions. . . . .

STEP 1 To guide children in making a plan, remind them to look at all the materials available to them and to think of other uses for each material.

STEP 2 Guide children to choose materials that are appropriate for making their model. Allow children time to build their tool. Be sure that children have several of each of the three types of seeds. Provide children with guidelines for how to move the seeds. Allow children time to test their tool and to find out which types of seeds it can move and which seeds it cannot move.

Name _____

🔍 **Hands-On Activity**

Engineer It • Plan and Build a Model Tool

> Materials
>
> _____

Ask a Question

How can you make a model tool to pick up and move seeds?

Test and Record Data Explore online. ▶

Step 1

Make a plan to build a tool that will pick up and move different seeds. Record your plan.

> Plans will vary. Check children's work.

Step 2

Select your materials. Draw to design a model of your tool. Then build your model.

Lesson 2 • Engineer It • How Do Plants Depend on Animals?   129

Hands-On Activity, continued

SEP Developing and Using Models . . . .

STEP 3 Ask: What happens to seeds when they are carried by a bird? Do you think your tool will work in the same way as a bird's beak? When a bird carries seeds, it sometimes drops some of the seeds. I think the tool will work in the same way because it would be hard to carry all of the seeds at once.

CCC Structure and Function . . . .

STEP 4 Ask: Which seeds were hard to move? Which seeds were easy to move? How did the shape and the structure of your tool help you pick up the seeds? How did the shape and structure of your tool make it more difficult to pick up the seeds? Answers will vary based on children's designs.

Claims, Evidence, and Reasoning

Children should make a claim that identifies the structure and function of their tool and if they were able to move the seeds using their tool. They should cite evidence from their proposed solutions. **Ask:** Did your tool work in the way that you thought it would? What is your evidence? My tool worked for the larger seeds, but not for the smaller ones. My evidence that my tool worked is that I was able to move the larger seeds from one place to another.

Scoring Rubric for Hands-On Activity	
3	States a claim supported with evidence about the tool that was designed
2	States a claim somewhat supported with evidence about the tool that was designed
1	States a claim that is not supported by evidence
0	Does not state a claim and does not provide evidence

Step 3

Test your tool to find out which seeds it can move. Record your data.

	Data will vary.
	Check children's work.

Step 4

Analyze your results. Identify how the shape and structure of your tool affected how it worked.

Make a claim that answers your question.

Answers should reflect children's solutions for how

to build a model tool to pick up and move seeds.

What is your evidence?

Answers should cite evidence from children's

proposed solutions.

130

© Houghton Mifflin Harcourt

Do the Math! • Make a Bar Graph

Children complete a bar graph to show the results of testing the tool they built. Children should draw a bar for each type of seed they were able to move with their tool. They should write the name of each seed on the line below the bar.

Make a Bar Graph • Model with Mathematics

Remind children to use the data they collected from the Hands-On activity to complete their bar graph. For each type of seed, they should start at 0 and use the numbers on the vertical scale to determine where the bar for that type of seed ends.

Differentiate Instruction

ELL Review the words *graph* and *results*. Provide images of different types of bar graphs and review what the title and labels on each part of the graph mean before children get started completing the given graph. Remind children that *results* are the information, or data, they collected.

Children should compare the heights of the bars in the graph to answer the questions *Which seeds were easy to move?* and *Which seeds were hard to move?* The taller the bar, the easier it was to move the seed.

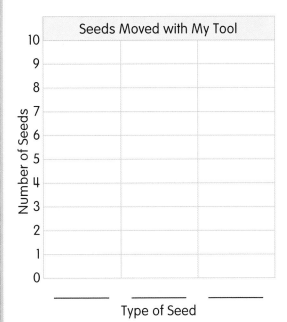

Do the Math! • How many of each seed were you able to move with your tool? Graph your results.

Graphs will vary. Check children's work.

Make a Bar Graph Go to the online handbook for tips.

Seeds Moved with My Tool

Number of Seeds

Type of Seed

Look at your graph. Answers will vary.

Which seeds were easy to move? _____

Which seeds were hard to move? _____

© Houghton Mifflin Harcourt

How Animals Spread Pollen

3D Learning Objective

Children explore **how plants depend on animals to spread pollen** and help them survive. They observe **the structure of pollen** and how it is moved from plant to plant.

(CCC) Structure and Function . . . .

Ask: Do you think all flowers have pollen that is too heavy for the wind to move? No, the wind can move some pollen. **Ask:** How does the structure of pollen help it to be moved? Pollen is sticky. When the bat sips nectar, the pollen sticks to it, allowing it to be moved to a new place. **Ask:** Why does moving the pollen from one flower to another help the plant? The plant needs the pollen to be moved so it can make new seeds.

(DCI) Interdependent Relationships in Ecosystems . . . .

Discuss with children the meaning of the vocabulary word *pollen*. **Ask:** Why do you think the bat is sipping the nectar from the flower? It drinks the nectar. Would the pollen in this flower be able to move without the animals? no How do you know? The pollen is too heavy for the wind to carry. It needs help from animals to move.

Connection to Physical Science

Structure and Properties of Matter Discuss how objects have properties that can be observed and described. Share pictures of pollen up close so children can see its structure. Have small groups describe these properties of pollen: color, shape, hardness, texture, and flexibility. Provide children with resources, such as books or the Internet. Have them share their findings with the class.

How Animals Spread Pollen

Explore online. ▶

Look at the pictures to explore how animals, such as insects and bats, can help move pollen.

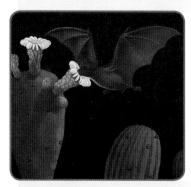

This tall cactus has large flowers. Its pollen is too heavy for the wind to move. Bats and other animals must help move this pollen. A bat pokes its nose into a flower to sip nectar. Pollen sticks to its head and neck.

The bat flies to another flower to sip nectar. It carries pollen with it. Some pollen from the first flower falls off the bat. New seeds can form. Without knowing it, the bat helps the cactus move pollen to make seeds.

Pollen is a sticky powder that flowers need to make seeds. Pollen must move from one flower to another for new seeds to form.

132

© Houghton Mifflin Harcourt

✏️➤ How does the bat help seeds form? Number each picture 1, 2, or 3 to show the correct order.

New flowers can grow.

_____ 3 _____

A bat gets pollen from the flower.

_____ 1 _____

The bat spreads pollen to other plants and new seeds form.

_____ 2 _____

© Houghton Mifflin Harcourt

Children should label the top picture 3, the middle picture 1, and the bottom picture 2. If children do not put the pictures in the correct order, refer them back to the previous page on *How Animals Spread Pollen*. Encourage children to underline text in the captions that might help them to put the pictures in the correct order.

DCI **Interdependent Relationships in Ecosystems** . . . .

Ask: What do you think would happen if the bat only drank the nectar from one flower? Would this still help new plants grow? **no** How do you know? Pollen must move from one flower to another for new seeds to form.

Differentiate Instruction

RTI/Extra Support Some children may have difficulty with the concept that the bat is actually doing a job. Explain to them that without knowing it, the bat is carrying pollen from one flower to the next and helping new plants grow. Show several examples of this process so that children will understand the order in which these events occur.

Extension Have children make a list of other animals they think help plants. Have children choose one animal from the list and write the steps, in order, telling how this animal helps plants. They can research these ideas online or in books, and then share their findings with the class.

Interdependent Relationships in Ecosystems . . . .

Discuss with children the different ways they have observed animals helping plants. **Ask: What are some ways that animals help plants?** They move seeds and spread pollen. **Could the plants you have observed survive without the help of the animals?** Yes, but they could not make new plants. **How do you know?** The plants need animals to spread seeds and move pollen in order to make new plants.

 FORMATIVE ASSESSMENT ━━━

Evidence Notebook

Have small groups go back through the lesson and find ways that different animals have helped plants. Discuss the kinds of animals that might help the sunflower. Remind children to provide evidence to support their answers.

Scoring Guidelines

- accurately describes two ways that an animal could help the sunflower
- provides sufficient evidence to support their ideas

 Apply What You Know

Evidence Notebook • Work with a small group. Look at this sunflower. Tell how animals might help this flower. Give two examples as evidence to support your ideas. Record your answers in your Evidence Notebook. Share your group's ideas with your class.

134

Explore online. ▶   Guide children to the Interactive Online Student Edition where they can choose from and explore both paths.

Take It Further

Careers in Science & Engineering • Horticulturalist

Explore online. ▶

Horticulturalists teach others how to care for plants. Some work with farmers. Others work at garden centers.

Explore more online.

• Other Ways Seeds Travel

Horticulturalists are scientists who study plants and how they grow. These scientists find out what plants need to stay healthy. They study ways for plants to grow more fruit or vegetables. They help move pollen so plants can make seeds.

Lesson 2 • Engineer It • How Do Plants Depend on Animals?   135

Take It Further

Careers in Science & Engineering • Horticulturalist

Horticulturalists are scientists who specialize in growing plants. However, there is a wide array of jobs that horticulturalists perform. They do research in gardening and pollinating plants. They also work to reduce erosion and may design parks or botanical gardens. Some work on exploring new plant varieties or can even inspect fruits and vegetables to ensure they are being grown properly.

DCI **Interdependent Relationships in Ecosystems** . . . .

Ask: How do you think horticulturalists work with farmers? They may bring bees to a farm to help pollinate the plants. What kinds of things might horticulturalists do at a garden center? They explain to others how the plants at a garden center grow and how to care for them.

Differentiate Instruction

RTI/Extra Support Because many children may not be familiar with horticulture as a career, provide them with more information about horticulturalists. Show pictures of different ways a horticulturalist works. Have children discuss the pictures in small groups.

Extension Challenge children to learn more about horticulturalists online. Have children write a paragraph summarizing the information they find. They can share their paragraphs in small groups or with the whole class.

Take It Further, continued

Horticulturalist

What Else Would you Like to Know?

Children will draw or write to record three questions they would like to ask a horticulturalist. Remind children when formulating questions to ask about important details or things that are unclear. If possible, invite a horticulturalist to speak to the class. Beforehand, have small groups pick 2-3 questions they would like to ask.

Have children observe the picture of the horticulturalist at a botanical garden. **Ask: What is the horticulturalist doing?** She is watering the plants. **How does this help the plants?** Plants need water in order to grow. **What are other things the horticulturalist can do to help the plants?** She can help move pollen in order to make new seeds. She can tell visitors to the garden how to help care for plants.

Collaboration

Whole Class You may choose to have children complete the first part of this activity as a whole class. Discuss the types of questions that could be asked and what the children want to know more about. Encourage children to think about things that they are curious about after watching the video and reading the provided information in the Interactive Online Student Edition.

Explore more online. ▶

Other Ways Seeds Travel

Have children go online to explore other ways seeds travel.

Horticulturalist

What Else Would You Like to Know?

Think of three questions you would like to ask a horticulturalist.

✏️ Draw or write to record your questions.

Check children's questions.

_____

_____

_____

Get answers to your questions by asking a horticulturalist. Or talk to someone who works at a garden center. Write about what you find out.

136

Lesson Check

Name _____

Explore online. ▶

Can You Solve It?

✏️▷ You want to add more flowers to your garden. How can bees help solve this problem? Be sure to

• Tell what happens when a bee sips nectar.

• Describe what happens when the bee moves to a new flower.

• Explain how moving pollen helps plants.

Sample answer: When a bee sips nectar, pollen from the flower sticks to its body. When the bee flies to another flower, some of the pollen falls off. When the bee moves the pollen from flower to flower, the plant can make seeds. This adds flowers to a garden.

© Houghton Mifflin Harcourt • Image Credits: ©Semjonow Juri/Shutterstock

Lesson Check

Can You Solve It?

Have children revisit their answer to the Can You Solve It? prompt at the beginning of the lesson.

DCI **Interdependent Relationships in Ecosystems** . . . .

Have children observe the picture. Point out the powdery substance on the bee and ask children what it is. If children struggle, remind them of how a bat can help plants spread pollen. **Ask: What is the bee sipping on the flower?** nectar **What happens while the bee is sipping nectar?** Pollen from the flower sticks to the bee's body. **What happens when the bee flies to another flower?** The pollen falls off. **How does this help plants?** New seeds form, and then new plants can grow.

Scoring Guidelines
• Children should describe what happens when a bee sips nectar.
• Children should describe how bees move pollen.
• Children should identify how pollen helps make new flowers.

Collaboration

Cultivating New Questions As children complete this lesson and prepare for the next lesson, ask them to identify additional questions they have about how plants depend on animals. **Ask: What might happen if animals stopped moving seeds?** Plants would only grow in one location instead of in many places. As children continue to the next lesson, they will apply concepts related to interdependence in describing how plants and animals found in various habitats get what they need to live and grow.

Lesson Check, continued

SUMMATIVE ASSESSMENT
Self Check

1. Children should choose B—It sticks to an animal's fur. If children choose A or C, guide them to the Animals Help Spread Seeds section of the lesson. Have them observe the pictures and reread the different ways animals help spread seeds.

2. Children should choose B—the shape of the seed; and C—the structure of the seed. If children choose A, the size of the seed, remind them that a real seed can be larger or smaller than a model of the seed.

3. Children should draw lines connecting the squirrel to the acorns, the toucan to the wild nutmeg seed, and the dog to the burr. If children draw lines from an animal to the incorrect seed, have them revisit the Animals Help Spread Seeds section of the lesson. Guide children to think about how each animal can move the seeds from one place to another.

Self Check

1. What is the most likely way this seed is moved?

   Ⓐ A bird carries it in its mouth.
   Ⓑ It sticks to an animal's fur.
   Ⓒ A chipmunk buries it.

---

2. What can you find out from a model of a seed? Choose all correct answers.

   Ⓐ the size of the seed
   Ⓑ the shape of the seed
   Ⓒ the structure of the seed

---

3. Which type of seed does each animal move? Draw a line to match each animal with the type of seed it moves.

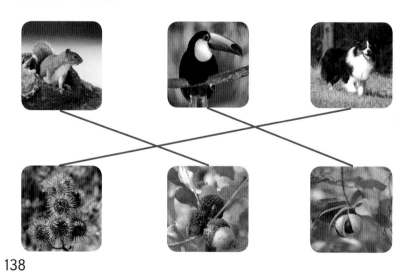

138

4. What causes a bee to move pollen?
   Choose the **best** answer.
   Ⓐ The pollen is light and sticky.
   Ⓑ The pollen has structures like wings.
   Ⓒ The pollen has hooks that catch onto the bee.

5. A farmer sees that his strawberry crop is not as large
   as it was last year. He reads in the newspaper that
   there are fewer bees in the area. What conclusion
   can you draw about why his crop is smaller?
   Ⓐ The crop grows better if bees do not move pollen.
   Ⓑ The crop grows better if many bees move pollen.
   Ⓒ The number of bees does not affect the crop.

4. Children should choose A—The pollen is light and sticky. If
   children choose B or C, have them revisit the How Animals
   Spread Pollen section of the lesson. Be sure children understand
   that pollen does not have wing-like structures or hooks.

5. Children should choose B—The crop grows better if many
   bees move pollen. If children choose A or C, have them reread
   the question stem and underline the text *crop is not as large*
   and *fewer bees in the area*. Then have them revisit the How
   Animals Spread Pollen section of the lesson.

Building to the Performance Expectation

The learning experiences in this lesson prepare children for mastery of:

2-LS4-1 Make observations of plants and animals to compare the diversity of life in different habitats.

Trace Tool to the NGSS
Go online to view the complete coverage of these standards across this lesson, unit, and time.

SEP Science & Engineering Practices

Planning and Carrying Out Investigations
Make observations (firsthand or from media) to collect data which can be used to make comparisons.

 VIDEO SEP: Planning and Carrying Out Investigations

Scientific Knowledge is Based on Empirical Evidence
Scientists look for patterns and order when making observations about the world.

DCI Disciplinary Core Ideas

LS4.D: Biodiversity and Humans
There are many different kinds of living things in any area, and they exist in different places on land and in water.

CCC Crosscutting Concepts

Patterns
Patterns in the natural and human designed world can be observed.

CONNECTIONS TO MATH

MP.2 Reason abstractly and quantitatively.

MP.4 Model with mathematics.

2.MD.D.10 Draw a picture graph and a bar graph (with single-unit scale) to represent a data set with up to four categories. Solve simple put-together, take-apart, and compare problems using information presented in a bar graph.

CONNECTIONS TO ENGLISH LANGUAGE ARTS

W.2.7 Participate in shared research and writing projects (e.g., read a number of books on a single topic to produce a report; record science observations).

W.2.8 Recall information from experiences or gather information from provided sources to answer a question.

Supporting All Students, All Standards

Integrating the Three Dimensions of Learning

This lesson focuses on living things found within three different water environments--a pond, a river delta, and a tide pool--and the many habitats within each one (**DCI Biodiversity and Humans**). Children begin the lesson by exploring why the specific plants and animals in each habitat live there. Children find out more about how the plants and animals live in each habitat because they can get the things they need there (**SEP Scientific Knowledge is Based on Empirical Evidence**) (**CCC Patterns**). Children use their observations to compare the diversity of life found within and across different habitats (**SEP Planning and Carrying Out Investigations**).

Professional Development

Go online to view **Professional Development videos** with strategies to integrate CCCs and SEPs, including the ones used in this lesson.

Build on Prior Knowledge

Children should already know and be prepared to build on the following concepts:

- Observations can be used to make comparisons and to identify patterns. *(Grade 1, Unit 6, Lessons 1 and 2)*
- Plants and animals need certain things to live and grow. *(Grade K, Unit 3, Lessons 1 and 2)*
- Plants have parts that help them survive. *(Grade 1, Unit 4, Lesson 1)*
- Animals have parts that help them stay safe and get the things they need. *(Grade 1, Unit 4, Lessons 2 and 3)*
- Patterns can be observed in nature and in the human-made world. *(Grade 2, Unit 2, Lesson 1)*

Differentiate Instruction

Lesson Vocabulary
- habitat

Reinforcing Vocabulary To help children remember the vocabulary word, have them draw a picture of a habitat. Then have them write the word and its definition below their drawings. Remind children to look for this highlighted word as they proceed through the lesson.

RTI/Extra Support Make a chart to compare the pond, river delta, and tide pool that are discussed in this lesson. Work with children to list the features of each place as well as the plants and animals in each one.

Extension Children who want to find out more can research another water habitat, such as the sea floor, shallow seas, or salt marshes. Children should make a visual display, such as a poster, slide show, or diorama, to share the information.

ELL Be sure to point out all labels, pictures, captions, and headings throughout the lesson to assist children with strategies to summarize chunks of content. Discuss with children real-life connections to content and provide hands-on examples of materials when possible to best support their needs.

Lesson Phenomenon

Build on Prior Lessons

In Lesson 2, children explored how **plants depend on animals to move seeds or for pollination.** They **developed models to help move seeds** based on structure and function. Lesson 3 builds on these concepts to explore and compare how living things get what they need from various water habitats.

Lesson Objective

Make observations of plants and animals to compare the diversity of life in water habitats.

About This Image

Guide children to observe the picture and to identify the body of water as a pond. Explain to children that a pond is usually a still body of fresh water. **Ask: What do you see in this picture?** Pink flowers and leaves floating on a pond. **What else do you think might live in this pond?** different types of fish and insects **What other bodies of water do plants and animals live in?** They also live in lakes, rivers, and oceans. Remind children that as they explore, they will find out more about different water habitats.

 **Biodiversity and Humans**

Alternative Engage Strategy

Visit a Pond	👥 whole class 🕐 15–25 minutes

Take the class to visit a nearby pond or other water environment. After returning to the classroom, have children draw a picture and then share their observations with others. **Ask: What do you see on the surface of the water? What do you think lives below the surface? What else do you see around the pond?** Accept all reasonable answers.

Lesson 3 What Plants and Animals Live in Water Habitats?

Many plants and animals live in a pond.

By the End of This Lesson
I will be able to compare plants and animals in different water habitats.

140

Can You Explain It?

Water Habitats A variety of living things can be found in various habitats. Play the video to find out more about water habitats. If the video is not available, review and compare the three pictures on the page. **Ask: How are these habitats similar?** They all contain water and probably have fish in them. **How are they different?** They are different shapes and sizes and have different plants. **Why might plants and animals live in each of these habitats?** Plants and animals live where they can get the things they need.

Ask children to record their initial thoughts about how the habitats are alike and different. At the end of the lesson, children will revisit these pictures as part of the Lesson Check. At this point, children should be able to explain that plants and animals live in habitats where they can get the things they need.

Water Habitats

Look at the pictures to explore some water habitats that plants and animals live in.
How are they alike? How are they different?

pond

river delta

Explore online. ▶

tide pool

Can You Explain It?

✏️ Why do some plants and animals only live in ponds, in river deltas, or in tide pools?

Accept all reasonable answers.

_____

_____

_____

Collaboration

Build on Prior Knowledge Have children work in pairs or small groups. Assign each group to make a poster about plants or animals. Each poster should show the things plants or animals need on it as well as the parts each one uses to get the things it needs. Then, pair plant groups with animal groups and have children share their information.

Support for Unit Project and Performance Task

The **Unit Project** Explore Habitats and **Unit Performance Task** Observe an Ant Farm supports content in this lesson.

Ponds

3D Learning Objective

Children **make observations** of plants and animals to compare the **diversity of life in pond habitats**. They **observe patterns** in the things that plants and animals need that live in ponds.

DCI **Biodiversity and Humans** . . . .

Discuss the plants and animals in the picture. **Ask: Where do plants and animals live in a pond?** They live on the water and under the water. **Ask: How does a crayfish get what it needs in a pond?** The crayfish eats the plants and animals in the pond and lives in its water.

SEP **Planning and Carrying Out Investigations** . . . .

Guide children to compare the plants and animals in the pond. **Ask: How are the iris and the duckweed alike?** Both are plants whose leaves are above the water to get sunlight. **Ask: How are they different?** An iris has roots in the bottom of the pond. Duckweed has no roots and floats on the surface.

Collaboration

Jigsaw Have children form six groups. Assign each group one of the plants or animals shown in the pond. Have each child in the group draw and label a picture of the plant or animal assigned to the group. Then form new groups of six children, so that each plant or animal is represented in each group. Have children work together and use their drawings to complete a poster of the pond.

Ponds

Explore online. ▶

● Most duckweed plants have no roots. They float on the water to get the sunlight they need.

● An iris's roots dig into the pond's bottom. Its leaves are above water to get sunlight.

● A dragonfly starts its life in the water, but lives on land as an adult. It eats flying insects.

● A crayfish uses gills to take in oxygen. It eats plants and animals.

● A sunfish lives in shallow water. It has gills and eats small animals.

● A tadpole is one stage in a frog's life. It has gills and eats plants and insects.

Most ponds are not very deep. They have fresh water, which is not salty. These are patterns. A pond can have many habitats. A **habitat** is a place where living things get the food, water, air, and shelter they need to live. Above water and below water are two kinds of habitats in a pond.

142

Circle the animals that live above the water. Put an X on the animals that live under the water.

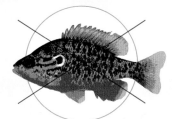 

 Apply What You Know

Evidence Notebook • With a partner, discuss what makes a pond a good place to live. Identify patterns. Use evidence to support your ideas. Record your answers in your Evidence Notebook.

Patterns
Go to the online handbook for tips.

Lesson 3 • What Plants and Animals Live in Water Habitats?

143

DCI **Biodiversity and Humans** . . . .

Remind children that ponds are made up of habitats, such as areas above the water and under the water. Children should circle the dragonfly. Children should put an X on the sunfish, the tadpole, and the crayfish. **Ask: Why do the sunfish, the tadpole, and the crayfish live under the water?** They live under the water so they can take in oxygen through their gills. **Why does the dragonfly live above the water?** The dragonfly is above the water to get insects to eat and to be able to fly.

 SEP **Scientific Knowledge is Based on Empirical Evidence** . . . .
 CCC **Patterns** . . . .

Ask: Which body part do a sunfish, a tadpole, and a crayfish all have? gills **How do gills help these animals get what they need?** Gills let them take in oxygen so they can breathe under water. **What pattern do you notice with living things that live under the water?** They have gills to help them breathe.

 FORMATIVE ASSESSMENT

Evidence Notebook
Children work with a partner to discuss why a pond is a good place to live for some living things. Make sure that children use evidence to support their answers.

Scoring Guidelines
• explains why a pond is a good place for some living things
• provides evidence to support their answer

💡 **Patterns** Remind children that patterns exist in nature. When observing something in nature, children should look for how it connects to other things. They should look for something that repeats. This is a pattern.

© Houghton Mifflin Harcourt

River Deltas

3D Learning Objective

Children **make observations** of plants and animals to compare the **diversity of life in river delta habitats**. They **observe patterns** in the things that plants and animals need that live in river deltas.

DCI Biodiversity and Humans . . . .

Discuss the plants and animals in the picture. **Ask: Where do plants and animals live in a river delta?** They live on the water, under the water, and on the surrounding land. **How does the river delta help an oyster get the things it needs?** The water in a river delta is salty, moving water that holds food for the oyster to eat.

SEP Planning and Carrying Out Investigations . . . .

Have children observe and compare this picture with the picture on ponds from the previous section. **Ask: How is the duckweed in the pond and the thalia plant in the river delta alike? How are they different?** Both are plants with parts that float on the water to get sunlight. Duckweed plants have no roots and float on the surface. A thalia plant has roots that dig into the river bottom. **How do the differences between the two places explain the differences in the plants?** Pond water is still, but the water in a river delta is moving. Duckweed plants can float with no roots on a calm pond, but the thalia plant needs roots to hold it in place in the moving water in the river delta.

Connection to Engineering Design

Developing and Using Models Have children think about how hurricanes and flooding could change a river delta. They can use print and online resources to help them gather information. Then have them make a model showing the river delta before and after a fast change.

River Deltas

- A cypress tree's roots grow under and above the water. Water helps spread its seeds.

- A thalia's stems and leaves float on the water. Its roots dig into the river bottom to hold it in place.

Explore online. ▶

- An alligator lives mostly in fresh water. Its lungs take in air. It hunts other animals.

- A catfish lives in fresh water. It feeds mostly at night and uses its whiskers to find food on the river bottom.

- An oyster lives in moving water that is salty or a mix of fresh and salty. The moving water helps bring it food.

- This crab lives in a mix of fresh and salty water. It uses its gills to take in oxygen from the water.

    A river delta forms when a river meets another body of water. In a river delta, there may be fresh water or a mix of fresh water and salty water. These are patterns. One type of habitat found in a river delta is above the water and the land around it. Another type is below the water.

144

© Houghton Mifflin Harcourt

Think about the type of water each animal needs in its habitat. Circle all animals that can live in water that is salty.

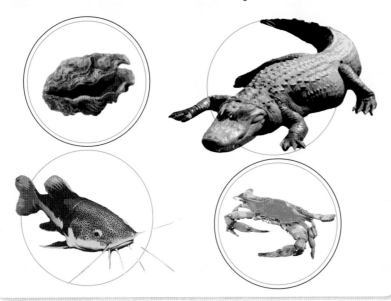

© Houghton Mifflin Harcourt

Apply What You Know

Evidence Notebook • With a partner, discuss why a river delta is a good place for some plants and animals to live. Record your answer in your Evidence Notebook.

Patterns
Go to the online handbook for tips.

Lesson 3 • What Plants and Animals Live in Water Habitats?   145

DCI Biodiversity and Humans . . . .

Children should circle the oyster and the crab. **Ask:** What type of water do the catfish and alligator live in? fresh water **Ask:** Why is a river delta a good place for all of these animals? A river delta has fresh water and salty water.

Differentiate Instruction

RTI/Extra Support Have children circle the name of each plant and animal in the river delta picture on the previous page and underline its features.

Extension Children can use print or online resources to find out more about one of the plants or animals in the river delta picture. Have children make a visual display, such as a model or poster, to share their findings with the class.

FORMATIVE ASSESSMENT

Evidence Notebook

Children work with a partner to discuss why a river delta is a good place for some plants and animals to live. Make sure that children use evidence to support their answer.

Scoring Guidelines

• explains why a river delta is a good place for some plants and animals to live
• provides evidence to support their answer

Patterns Remind children that patterns exist in nature, such as animals living in places where they can get the things they need. It is important to observe and to use those observations to look for things that repeat. This is a pattern.

Tide Pools

3D Learning Objective

Children **make observations** of plants and animals to compare the **diversity of life in tide pool habitats**. Children **observe patterns** in the things that plants and animals need that live in tide pools.

(CCC) Patterns . . . .

Discuss the pattern caused by rising and falling tides.
Ask: What happens at high tide? The water rises and covers the shore. **Ask: What happens at low tide?** The ocean falls back. **Ask: What pattern do the tides cause?** They cause the water to cover the shore and then fall back twice a day.

(SEP) Planning and Carrying Out Investigations . . . .

Have children compare the three zones. **Ask: When is each zone covered with water?** The high tide zone is only covered at high tide. The middle tide zone is covered at high tide but not at low tide. The low tide zone is covered by water most of the time.
Ask: What types of animals live in each zone? Why do you think those animals live there? Animals in the high tide zone have hard bodies because there is not much water. Animals in the middle tide zone can live on land or on water because there is usually some of both. Animals in the low tide zone have gills because they are always under water.

Differentiate Instruction

ELL To help children understand and remember the words introduced on this page, have them draw and label pictures to represent *ocean, shore, high tide,* and *low tide.*

Tide Pools

Tide pools have three parts called zones. Each zone is a habitat.

Explore online. ▶

The high tide zone is covered with water only at high tide. At low tide, there is little or no water. The animals that live in this zone usually have hard bodies or can hold onto rocks.

The middle tide zone is covered with water at high tide but not at low tide. This zone is home to many animals. That is why animals from other zones come here to find food.

The low tide zone is covered by water most of the time. Many animals that live in this zone use gills to take in oxygen from the water.

Twice a day, every day, the salty water at the ocean's shore rises and falls. At high tide, the water rises and covers the shore. At low tide, it falls back. It leaves pools of water between the rocks that are called tide pools. This is a pattern.

146

© Houghton Mifflin Harcourt · Image Credits: (t) ©Craig Tuttle/Corbis Documentary/Getty Images; (c) ©Craig Tuttle/Getty Images; (b) ©deebrowning/iStock/Getty Images

Very few plants live in the salty waters of a tide pool. Look at the picture to explore the many animals in the different tide zones.

Explore online. ▶

● As this crab moves, the anemone on its shell finds food and uses its stingers to protect the crab.

● Coral often grow in groups and stay in one place. They collect food as it floats by.

● A sea urchin has sharp spines to protect it. It uses its spines to move and to catch food.

● A zebra blenny can jump from pool to pool to escape danger. It eats plant-like algae.

● This shrimp eats tiny living things that grow on fish. When it is hungry, it dances to let the passing fish know.

● This worm has gills that look like feathers. It uses its gills to take in oxygen from the water and trap food.

Lesson 3 • What Plants and Animals Live in Water Habitats?   147

DCI Biodiversity and Humans . . . .

Review with children how a tide pool is made up of different habitats, such as the high tide, middle tide, and low tide zones. Habitats provide living things with the food, water, air, and shelter they need to live and grow. Tell children that all the animals in the picture have different ways to find and eat food. **Ask: How do these animals get food?** The worm traps food with its gills. The coral collects food as it passes by. The sea urchin uses its spines to catch food. The anemone finds food as the crab moves. The shrimp eats food that grows on fish.

CCC Patterns . . . .

Have children draw on prior knowledge to draw conclusions about patterns regarding the tide pool. **Ask: What do plants need?** Plants need sunlight, air, and fresh water. **Ask: Could a plant get what it needs? How?** The plant could have leaves on the surface of the tide pool to get air and sunlight. **Ask: Which of these needs would it be difficult to meet in a tide pool?** It would be difficult to get fresh water from a salty tide pool.

DCI Biodiversity and Humans . . . .

Ask: Why do you think the middle tide zone is a good place for many animals to get what they need? The middle tide zone has some water where animals with gills can live, but some land where animals can breathe. There are animals for other animals to eat. There might also be enough sunlight for some plants to grow and become food for animals.

Biodiversity and Humans . . . .

Children should match the picture of the crab with the high tide zone label; the picture of the sea urchin with the middle tide zone label; and the picture of the zebra blenny with the low tide zone label. **Ask: How did you decide which zone the crab lives in?** The hermit crab has a hard shell, so it lives in the high tide zone. **Ask: How did you decide which zone the zebra blenny lives in?** The fish has gills, so it lives in the low tide zone.

Collaboration

Pairs You may choose to have children complete this activity in pairs. Encourage children to ask each other questions to help them identify patterns and to use evidence to support their answers.

 FORMATIVE ASSESSMENT

Read, Write, Share! • Participate in a Research Project • Patterns

Provide access to a variety of print and online resources for children to use to research plants and animals in a water habitat close to where they live. Make sure that children identify patterns based on their research. Children should provide evidence to support the patterns they observe.

Scoring Guidelines
- identifies a water habitat close to where he or she lives
- identifies patterns in plants and animals that live in the water habitat
- makes a poster of these plants and animals

💡 **Participate in a Research Project • Gather Information • Patterns** Children should identify questions to answer with research and use their research to make and support claims. Remind children to look for patterns in nature.

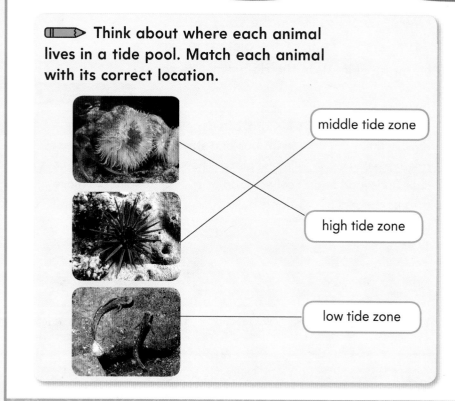

✏️ **Think about where each animal lives in a tide pool. Match each animal with its correct location.**

middle tide zone

high tide zone

low tide zone

🖐 **Apply What You Know**

Read, Write, Share! • Research the plants and animals that live in a water habitat close to you. Identify patterns. Make a poster of these plants and animals.

💡 **Participate in a Research Project • Patterns** Go to the online handbook for tips.

148

Name _____

 Hands-On Activity
Make Model Habitats

> ### Materials
> _____

Ask a Question

How can you build a model to show tide pool habitats? _____

Test and Record Data **Explore online.** ▶

Step 1

Make a plan to build your model habitats. Identify plants and animals that live in the habitat. Record your plan.

Plans will vary. Check children's work. _____

_____

_____

Step 2

Set up your habitats by filling your container with rocks, plants, and animals.

Lesson 3 • What Plants and Animals Live in Water Habitats?   149

Hands-On Activity 👥 small groups 🕐 1 class period
Make Model Habitats

3D Learning Objective

SEP **Scientific Knowledge is Based on Empirical Evidence** . . . .

Children plan and build a model of a habitat found in a tide pool. Children observe their habitat and identify patterns in their observations.

Suggested Materials empty, transparent plastic container; various rocks; markers; various rubber sea creatures; water

Preparation

Pre-assemble materials bundles for pairs or groups. Have paper towels handy to clean up any spills.

Activity

Read the title and ask children to develop a question based on the information they have gathered from the lesson, such as "How can you build a model to show tide pool habitats?"

STEP 1 Monitor children as they make a plan for their model habitats. **Ask: What parts of the habitats are you including in your model? What materials can you use for each part?** Accept all reasonable answers.

DCI **Biodiversity and Humans** . . . .

Ask: What type of water is in your habitats? What plants and animals live in your habitats? How can you show that the plants and animals are getting what they need in the habitats? The low tide zone of a tide pool has salt water. There are not many plants. The animals have gills because they are always under water. I am showing the food in the water that the animals grab.

STEP 2 Allow children time to build their model using the suggested materials. Remind children to follow their plan. **Ask: Is there anything in your plan that you decided not to include in your model? Did you forget to include anything in your plan?** Accept all reasonable answers.

© Houghton Mifflin Harcourt

Hands-On Activity, continued

STEP 3 Children may use words and drawings to record their observations.

STEP 4 Allow children time to analyze their results. Children should compare their models to share what they know about tide pools.

SEP Planning and Carrying Out Investigations . . . .

Ask: How is your model similar to habitats found in a tide pool? I used animals that are found in a low tide zone. **How is your model different?** The tide does not rise and fall.

Claims, Evidence, and Reasoning

Children should explain how to model habitats found in a tide pool and cite evidence to support their model choice. **Ask: Does your model behave like an actual habitat found in a tide pool? What would you change if you were to remake it?** The fish float like they would in a tide pool. If I remade it, I would make the tide rise and fall. I would use salt water.

Scoring Rubric for Hands-On Activity	
3	States a claim supported with evidence of how their model is an example of habitats found in a tide pool
2	States a claim somewhat supported with evidence of how their model is an example of habitats found in a tide pool
1	States a claim that is not supported by evidence
0	Does not state a claim and does not provide evidence

Step 3
Add water to your model. Observe your tide pool. Record your observations.

Check children's work.	
	_____
	_____
	_____

Step 4
Analyze your results. Make comparisons. Identify patterns.

Make a claim that answers your question.

Answers should reflect children's solutions for how to model

habitats.

_____

What is your evidence?

Answers should cite evidence from children's proposed solutions.

_____

_____

150

© Houghton Mifflin Harcourt

Take It Further

Careers in Science & Engineering •
Marine Biologist

Explore more online.
• Coral Reefs

Marine biologists are scientists. <u>They study living things in oceans and other bodies of salt water.</u>

Explore online.

These marine biologists study animals in a tide pool. <u>They keep track of the animals they see. They look for reasons that the numbers of some animals are low.</u>

Marine biologists care about the environment. They want people to care, too. <u>They teach people about plants and animals that live in different marine habitats.</u>

✏️➤ Draw a line under the sentences that tell what a marine biologist does.

Lesson 3 • What Plants and Animals Live in Water Habitats?   151

Take It Further

Careers in Science and Engineering •
Marine Biologist

Children explore how a marine biologist studies living things in the ocean and how they interact within their different habitats.

SEP **Planning and Carrying Out Investigations . . . .**

Have children describe and compare what is happening in the pictures. **Ask: What does a marine biologist study?** A marine biologist studies living things in oceans and other bodies of salt water. **What are some observations a marine biologist might make?** A marine biologist might observe the types of plants and animals in a habitat, the numbers of each type, and how the plants and animals meet their needs.

CCC **Patterns . . . .**

Ask: Why is it important for marine biologists to understand patterns in the numbers of animals? If the marine biologists understand the patterns, they will know when something changes or something is wrong.

Differentiate Instruction

RTI/Extra Support As a class, list things that children already know about a marine biologist. Then make a list of questions children have. Have children use the text to help answer the questions. If necessary, provide print or online resources to help answer any remaining questions.

Extension If children want to find out more about marine biologists, help them contact a local aquarium or university to speak with a marine biologist or someone in a related field. Help children make a list of questions to ask. Children can share what they find out with the class.

Take It Further, continued

Do the Math! • Make a Picture Graph

Review with children how to read a tally chart. Discuss how to take the information from the tally chart and transfer it into the picture graph. Children should draw six ovals for clam, five ovals for coral, four ovals for crab, and three ovals for sea star. Then they should add all of the pictures to get a total of 18 animals.

 Make a Picture Graph • Reason Abstractly and Quantitatively • Model with Mathematics Remind children that the title of the picture graph goes at the top, and the groups, or categories, on the left. Each picture in the graph stands for 1 thing. Children should draw pictures to show how many in each category.

SEP Planning and Carrying Out Investigations . . . .

Have children describe and compare the data in the tally chart and in the picture graph. **Ask: What does each tally mark in the tally chart stand for?** 1 animal **What does each picture in the graph stand for?** 1 animal **How can you find how many animals the marine biologist counted in all?** I can count the total number of pictures in the graph.

Collaboration

Pairs You may choose to have children work in pairs to ask and answer questions about the data in the picture graph. Encourage children to ask their partner put-together, take-apart, and compare problems. For example, How many more clams than crabs were there? How many sea stars and coral were there altogether?

Explore more online. ▶

Coral Reefs

Children watch a video about the coral reef habitat.

Do the Math! • A marine biologist counted the number of animals in a tide pool. Use the data in the tally chart to complete the picture graph.

Make a Picture Graph Go to the online handbook for tips.

Tide Pool Animals	
Animal	Tally
clam	ⵏⵏⵏ I
coral	ⵏⵏⵏ
crab	IIII
sea star	III

Tide Pool Animals						
clam	⬭	⬭	⬭	⬭	⬭	⬭
coral	⬭	⬭	⬭	⬭	⬭	
crab	⬭	⬭	⬭			
sea star	⬭	⬭	⬭			

Key: Each ⬭ stands for 1 animal.

How many animals did the marine biologist count in all? _____18_____ animals

152

© Houghton Mifflin Harcourt

Explore online. ▶ Have children explore online to find out more about water habitats.

Lesson Check

Name _____

pond

river delta

tide pool

Explore online. ▶

Can You Explain It?

✏️▷ Why do some plants and animals only live in ponds, in river deltas, or in tide pools?

Be sure to

• Describe where plants and animals live.

• Describe how they get what they need.

• Compare one plant or one animal from habitats found in ponds, river deltas, and tide pools.

Sample answer: Different plants and animals live in the water habitats where they can find the food, water, and shelter they need. For example, both a sunfish and a catfish live under fresh water, but a sunfish lives in a pond where it can eat animals, and a catfish lives in a river delta and looks for food on the river bottom. A zebra blenny is also a fish, but it lives under the salty water of a tide pool and eats algae.

Lesson 3 • What Plants and Animals Live in Water Habitats?   153

Lesson Check

Can You Explain It?

Have children reread their answers to the Can You Explain It? prompt at the beginning of the lesson.

DCI **Biodiversity and Humans** . . . .

Ask: What plants and animals live in ponds? What plants and animals live in river deltas? What plants and animals live in tide pools? Crayfish, sunfish, dragonflies, tadpoles, iris, and duckweed live in ponds. Alligators, crabs, oysters, catfish, cypress trees, and thalias live in river deltas. Worms, coral, sea urchins, crabs, zebra blenny, and shrimp live in tide pools.

SEP **Planning and Carrying Out Investigations** . . . .

Ask: How are the habitats in ponds, river deltas, and tide pools alike? Ponds, river deltas, and tide pools all have different water habitats. They are home to plants and animals. **How are they different?** Ponds have fresh water, tide pools have salt water, and river deltas have both fresh and salt water.

Scoring Guidelines

• Children should describe where the plants and animals live in each habitat and how they get what they need.

• Children should compare one plant or one animal from each habitat.

Collaboration

Cultivating New Questions As children complete this lesson and prepare for the next lesson, ask them to identify additional questions they have about water habitats. **Ask: What are some other kinds of water habitats?** above and below a lake or river As children continue to the next lesson, they will apply concepts related to diversity of life in water habitats to diversity of life in land habitats.

Lesson Check, continued

SUMMATIVE ASSESSMENT
Self Check

1. In the first row, from left to right, children should write tide pool, pond, and river delta. In the second row, from left to right, children should write pond, river delta, and tide pool. If children have difficulty identifying the correct place for each plant or animal, guide them to review the sections on ponds, river deltas, and tide pools.

2. Children should choose C—Some tide pool animals move to different zones.; and D—The amount of water in a tide pool can change. If children choose A, guide them to review the What Lives in a Tide Pool? section of the lesson. If children choose B, review the difference between fresh water and salt water, and discuss the type of water that is found in each of the different water habitats explored in this lesson.

Self Check

1. Where does each plant or animal live?
Write the correct name for each place.

| pond | river delta | tide pool |

| tide pool | pond | river delta |

| pond | river delta | tide pool |

2. Which are **true** about tide pools? Choose all correct answers.

  Ⓐ A tide pool has many plants.

  Ⓑ Many freshwater animals live in a tide pool.

  Ⓒ Some tide pool animals move to different zones.

  Ⓓ The amount of water in a tide pool can change.

154

3. How are a cypress tree and duckweed alike
   and different? Choose all correct answers.
   Ⓐ Both plants have large roots.
   🅑 Only one of these plants floats on the
      water's surface.
   🅒 Both plants live in habitats that provide
      everything they need to live.
   🅓 Only one of these plants digs its roots
      into the muddy bottom of its habitat.

4. What makes a river delta a good place
   for an oyster to live? Choose all correct answers.
   Ⓐ It can only survive deep underwater.
   🅑 It needs moving water to bring food to it.
   🅒 It can live in salty water or a mix of fresh
      and salty water.

5. Which are true about plants and animals that
   live in a pond?
   🅐 The animals living in water have gills.
   🅑 The plants and animals can live in fresh water.
   🅒 The plants and animals get what they need
      to live and grow.

3. Children should choose B—Only one of these plants floats on
   the water's surface.; C—Both plants live in habitats that provide
   everything they need to live.; and D—Only one of these plants
   digs its roots into the muddy bottom of its habitat. If children
   choose only one correct answer, remind them to read the
   question carefully. If children choose A, guide them to read
   about the duckweed plants in the Ponds section of the lesson.
   Challenge children to identify the plant referred to in answer
   choice D.

4. Children should choose B—It needs moving water to bring food
   to it.; and C—It can live in salty water or a mix of fresh and salty
   water. If children choose only one correct answer, remind them
   to read the question carefully. If children choose A, guide them
   to review the River Deltas section of the lesson.

5. Children should choose all three answer choices. If children
   choose only one or two of the correct answers, remind them
   to read the question carefully. Guide them to review the Ponds
   section of the lesson.

Lesson 4 — What Plants and Animals Live in Land Habitats?

Building to the Performance Expectation

The learning experiences in this lesson prepare children for mastery of:

2-LS4-1 Make observations of plants and animals to compare the diversity of life in different habitats.

Trace Tool to the NGSS
Go online to view the complete coverage of these standards across this lesson, unit, and time.

SEP — Science & Engineering Practices

Planning and Carrying Out Investigations
Make observations (firsthand or from media) to collect data which can be used to make comparisons.

 VIDEO SEP: Planning and Carrying Out Investigations

Scientific Knowledge is Based on Empirical Evidence
Scientists look for patterns and order when making observations about the world.

DCI — Disciplinary Core Ideas

LS4.D: Biodiversity and Humans
There are many different kinds of living things in any area, and they exist in different places on land and in water.

CCC — Crosscutting Concepts

Patterns
Patterns in the natural and human designed world can be observed.

CONNECTIONS TO MATH

MP.2 Reason abstractly and quantitatively

MP.4 Model with mathematics.

2.MD.D.10 Draw a picture graph and a bar graph (with single-unit scale) to represent a data set with up to four categories. Solve simple put-together, take-apart, and compare problems using information presented in a bar graph.

CONNECTIONS TO ENGLISH LANGUAGE ARTS

W.2.7 Participate in shared research and writing projects (e.g., read a number of books on a single topic to produce a report; record science observations).

W.2.8 Recall information from experiences or gather information from provided sources to answer a question.

Supporting All Students, All Standards

Integrating the Three Dimensions of Learning

This lesson focuses on living things found within three different land environments--a rain forest, a forest, and a savanna--and the many habitats within each one **(DCI Biodiversity and Humans)**. Children begin the lesson by exploring the specific plants and animals in each habitat. Children use prior knowledge to explain how living things live in places where they can get the things they need. **(SEP Scientific Knowledge is Based on Empirical Evidence) (CCC Patterns)**. Children use their observations to compare the diversity of life found within each habitat and across different habitats **(SEP Planning and Carrying Out Investigations)**.

Professional Development

Go online to view **Professional Development videos** with strategies to integrate CCCs and SEPs, including the ones used in this lesson.

Build on Prior Knowledge

Children should already know and be prepared to build on the following concepts:

- Observations can be used to make comparisons and to identify patterns. *(Grade 2, Unit 3, Lesson 3)*
- Plants and animals are living things. *(Grade K, Unit 3, Lesson 1)*
- Plants and animals live in different habitats. *(Grade 2, Unit 3, Lesson 3)*
- Plants and animals get the things they need from their habitat. *(Grade 2, Unit 3, Lesson 3)*
- Patterns can be observed in nature and in the human-made world. *(Grade 2, Unit 3, Lesson 3)*

Differentiate Instruction

Lesson Vocabulary
- habitat

Reinforcing Vocabulary To help children remember the vocabulary word, help them make real-life connections. Discuss with children that the home where they live is similar to a habitat, because they get things they need there, such as food and shelter. Remind children to look for the highlighted vocabulary word as they proceed through the lesson.

RTI/Extra Support Explore additional habitats by having children identify animals that live in different places. For example, a fish could live in an aquarium or a turtle could live in a terrarium. Keep a chart of how many different habitats children can locate.

Extension Have children make a list of habitats they see in their neighborhood. Discuss how the plants and animals get what they need. Children can make a poster to share what they have observed.

ELL Be sure to point out all labels, pictures, captions, and headings throughout the lesson to assist children with strategies to summarize chunks of content. Discuss with children real-life connections to content and provide hands-on examples of materials when possible to best support the needs of these learners.

Lesson Phenomenon

Build on Prior Lessons

In Lesson 3, children explored and **compared how living things get what they need from various water habitats.** They **made observations** and **looked for patterns in how plants and animals survived in their habitats.** Lesson 4 builds on these concepts to explore and **compare how living things get what they need from various land habitats.**

Lesson Objective

Make observations of plants and animals to compare the diversity of life in land habitats.

About This Image

Guide children to observe the picture and inform them that this is an environment called a rain forest that contains many habitats within it. **Ask: What kinds of plants and animals would live here?** Sample answer: Birds and trees can be found in a rain forest. There may be insects, snakes, and other animals, too.

 Biodiversity and Humans

Alternative Engage Strategy

Zoo Animals	👥 small groups
	⏱ 15–25 minutes

Ask: What kind of animals live in a zoo? Sample answer: birds, monkeys, turtles, elephants Allow 5 minutes for children to brainstorm how many animals they can think of that would live in a zoo. Record these ideas for the class to see. Have children work in small groups to categorize the list of animals and try to identify the habitats where each one lives. Allow each group to share one of their categories with the class.

Lesson 4 **What Plants and Animals Live in Land Habitats?**

Different kinds of plants and animals live in a rain forest.

By the End of This Lesson

I will be able to compare plants and animals in different land habitats.

156

Land Habitats

How are these places alike and how are they different?

rain forest

forest

Explore online. ▶

savanna

Can You Explain It?

✏️ Why do certain plants and animals only live in certain land habitats?

Accept all reasonable answers.

_____

_____

_____

_____

Lesson 4 • What Plants and Animals Live in Land Habitats?   157

Can You Explain It?

Land Habitats The video shows three land enviroments that contain many habitats. If the video is not available, review and compare the three pictures on the page. **Ask: What are some similarities you observe in these three environments?** Sample answer: All three environments have plants and animals living in them. **What are some differences you observe in these three environments?** Sample answer: The plants and animals in each environment are different. The environments have different names.

Have children record their initial thoughts about why certain plants and animals live in different areas. At the end of this lesson, children will revisit this question as part of the Lesson Check. At this point, children should be able to explain how plants and animals live in habitats that help them get the things they need.

Collaboration

Build on Prior Knowledge You may want children to view and discuss the video or pictures as a whole-class activity. In that way, you can assess their prior knowledge about land habitats.

Have children think about what they saw in the video or the pictures, or think about plants and animals they have seen in other places. Then have them discuss why they think certain plants and animals live in certain habitats. Children should use evidence from the video or pictures, or from their own experiences to support their answer.

Support for Unit Project and Performance Task

The **Unit Project** Explore Habitats and **Unit Performance Task** Observe an Ant Farm supports content in this lesson.

Rain Forest Habitats

3D Learning Objective

Children will **make observations** of plants and animals to compare the **diversity of life in rain forest habitats**. Children will observe patterns in the things that plants and animals need to live in a rain forest.

DCI **Biodiversity and Humans** . . . .

Review and discuss the text and three pictures with children.
Ask: What are some plants you observe in these pictures? I see vines, palm trees, and other trees, too. **What are some animals that may live in the rain forest habitats?** Some animals that may live in rain forest habitats include animals that live in treetops, birds, lizards, snakes, small animals, and worms. **Which part of the rain forest gets the most sunlight?** The canopy gets the most sunlight. **Tree frogs live in a rain forest. What do you think they eat?** Tree frogs eat insects that live in the rain forest. **Why do you think tree frogs live in a rain forest?** The rain forest provides the things that tree frogs need to live.

Differentiate Instruction

ELL Children may be unfamiliar with the word *canopy* and may require additional support to understand how it is used in the context of a rain forest. Explain that in everyday conversation, the word *canopy* can mean a covering. For example, if you are sitting on the beach, you may put an umbrella over you to help block out the sun. This is a type of canopy. **Ask: What gives a rain forest its canopy?** A rain forest canopy is made by all the treetops.

Rain Forest Habitats

It is warm and wet all year long in a rain forest. Plants grow quickly. These are patterns. Look at the pictures to explore some habitats in a rain forest.

The canopy gets a lot of sunlight. Flowers and fruits fill the trees. Many animals that live here never leave the top of the trees.

The understory is shady. Plants that need little sun do well here. So do birds, small animals, and reptiles such as lizards and snakes.

The floor is dark and damp. There are many leaves, fallen fruits, and tree roots. Animals that eat insects live here.

A **habitat** is a place where a living thing gets the food, water, and shelter it needs.

 How are these rain forest habitats alike?

Sample answer: They are warm and wet all year long.

158

Look at the picture to explore plants and animals that live in the rain forest canopy.

Explore online. ▶

● The tamarin uses its legs and claws to climb and jump. It eats fruit, small birds, and insects.

● A liana vine grows up a tree to reach sunlight. It has large leaves to take in sunlight.

● The sloth gets water from leaves and fruits it eats. Its sharp claws let it climb and hang upside-down.

● This tree frog has feet that can cling to leaves. Its sticky tongue catches insects.

● This orchid does not grow in soil. It grows on a tree to be close to the sunlight it needs.

● A harpy eagle has wings that are wide. It swoops down to grab animals with its sharp claws.

© Houghton Mifflin Harcourt

Lesson 4 • What Plants and Animals Live in Land Habitats?

159

DCI Biodiversity and Humans . . . .

Guide children to observe the picture of a canopy habitat.
Ask: Which animals live in the rain forest canopy? Children should note that the tamarin, the sloth, the tree frog, and the harpy eagle all live in the rain forest canopy.

SEP Scientific Knowledge is Based on Emperical Evidence . . . .

Discuss the picture of a canopy habitat. **Ask: How do animals get what they need in the rain forest canopy?** Children should respond that some animals eat the fruits, small birds, and insects found in the canopy of a rain forest. **How do plants get what they need in the rain forest canopy?** Some plants grow tall enough to reach the canopy on their own, while other plants climb up the taller trees to reach sunlight.

Differentiate Instruction

RTI/Extra Support Provide children with pictures of different rain forest animals and plants. Have children make a diorama of a rain forest making sure to place the animals that can be found in the canopy at the top of the diorama.

Extension Children may want to find out more about plants or animals that live in the rain forest. Allow children to gather more information about one of the plants or animals shown in the picture, or to research other plants or animals that may live in a rain forest canopy.

DCI Biodiversity and Humans . . . .

Have children observe the picture of an understory habitat. **Ask: Which animals live in the rain forest understory?** Children should note that butterflies, snakes, and ants all live in the rain forest understory.

CCC Patterns . . . .

Discuss the picture of an understory habitat. **Ask: How do animals get what they need in the rain forest understory?** Children should respond that some animals eat birds, plants, and insects found in the understory of a rain forest. **How do plants get what they need in the rain forest understory?** Sample answers: Some plants use their vines to take in sunlight. Some plants have leaves that collect rain. Some plants take in nutrients and moisture through their leaves.

Differentiate Instruction

RTI/Extra Support   Provide children with pictures of different plants and animals that live in the rain forest understory. Have children add them to their rain forest diorama, making sure to add them to the understory in the middle of the diorama.

Extension   Children may want to find out more about plants or animals that live in the rain forest understory. Allow children to gather more information about one of the plants or animals shown in the picture, or to research another plant or animal that may live in a rain forest understory.

Look at the picture to explore plants and animals that live in the rain forest understory.

● This butterfly's bad taste keeps birds away. The bad taste is from the leaves it ate as a caterpillar.

● This plant can start life in a tree. Its roots grow down for support. Its vines grow up to take in sunlight.

Explore online. ▶

● The boa blends in with the leaves. It lays on a branch and waits for a bird or lizard to pass by.

● These ants have sharp jaws to cut leaves. They use the leaves to make food in their nests.

● A bromeliad grows on other plants. Its leaves collect rain. Insects, snails, and tiny frogs live in the bromeliad.

● The zebra plant can grow in soil or on a tree. It takes in nutrients and moisture through its leaves.

© Houghton Mifflin Harcourt

160

These animals live on the rain forest floor. Identify which patterns explain why they live there. Choose all correct answers.

Ⓐ They blend in well with this habitat.

Ⓑ They have claws for climbing trees.

Ⓒ They do well in a warm, wet habitat.

Ⓓ They find the food they need in this habitat.

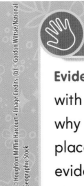

Apply What You Know

Evidence Notebook • Work with a partner. Explain why a rain forest is a good place for this iguana. Use evidence to support your ideas. Identify patterns. Record your answer in your Evidence Notebook.

Patterns Go to the online handbook for tips.

Lesson 4 • What Plants and Animals Live in Land Habitats?   161

CCC Patterns . . . .

Children should choose A—They blend in well with this habitat.; C—They do well in a warm, wet habitat.; and D—They find the food they need in this habitat. If children choose B or they don't choose all correct answer choices, discuss how the tortoise and the anteater get what they need in this habitat.

Differentiate Instruction

RTI/Extra Support Provide children with pictures of different plants and animals that live on the rain forest floor. Have children add them to their rain forest diorama, making sure to place them at the bottom of the diorama.

Extension Have children gather more information about one of the plants or animals shown on the rain forest floor in the picture. Alternatively, they may research another plant or animal that may live on the rain forest floor.

FORMATIVE ASSESSMENT

Evidence Notebook

Children work in pairs as they explore why a rain forest is a good place for the iguana, and provide evidence to support their ideas. Allow time for children to discuss their ideas, and guide them to record their answers in their Evidence Notebook.

Scoring Guidelines
- identifies why the rain forest is a good place for the iguana
- makes connections between the iguana and other living things in the rain forest
- provides sufficient evidence to support how the iguana lives in the rain forest

Patterns Guide children to look for information that shows how the iguana reacts to its surroundings. Children should look for a pattern, or things that repeat.

Forest Habitats

3D Learning Objective

Children will **make observations** of plants and animals to compare the **diversity of life in forest habitats**. Children will **observe patterns** in the things that plants and animals need to live in a forest.

DCI **Biodiversity and Humans** . . . .

Guide children in a discussion about the pictures. **Ask: What are some plants you observe?** I observe trees, bushes, wildflowers and other plants. **What are some animals that may live in these habitats?** Sample answers: bears, deer, skunks, insects, birds **How are these pictures of forest habitats alike?** They all change with the seasons.

Connection to Earth and Space Sciences

The History of Planet Earth Seasonal changes in weather can cause changes to Earth's surface. Have children think about how these changes can take place slowly over time and how they may impact a variety of habitats. Children can use print and online resources to help them gather information. Then they can make a visual display to support their findings and share them with the class.

Forest Habitats

In this forest, trees lose their leaves in the fall. They grow new ones in the spring. Many animals also change with the seasons. These are patterns. Look at the pictures to explore some habitats in a forest.

Explore online.

Sunlight comes through the trees to the forest floor. Bushes, wildflowers, and other plants can grow. Animals have food to eat and many places to take shelter.

The tree branches have many leaves, seeds, and nuts for animals to eat. In winter, the leaves fall. Animals may leave for warmer places. They may sleep for the winter or grow thick fur to stay warm.

How are these forest habitats alike?

Sample answer: They change with the seasons.

162

© Houghton Mifflin Harcourt • Image Credits: (t) ©Artbeats/Corbis; (c) ©Artbeats/Corbis; (b) ©Radius Images/Alamy; (c) ©Gabby Salazar/National Geographic/Getty Images

Look at the picture to explore plants and animals that live on the forest floor.

Explore online. ▶

● A deer's brown fur can change to gray. This helps it blend in with the changing forest. It eats plants.

● This fox eats fallen fruit and hunts animals. It can even find animals under the snow.

● A skunk hunts at night. It eats insects and small animals. In winter, it stays in an underground den.

● Ferns grow in moist, shady places. They have long leaves. Ferns lose their leaves in fall.

● Moss can grow on tree trunks and rocks. It takes in water from its stem and leaves.

● An aster can grow in the shade. Its flowers bloom in the fall and may attract butterflies.

© Houghton Mifflin Harcourt

Lesson 4 • What Plants and Animals Live in Land Habitats?

163

DCI Biodiversity and Humans . . . .

Discuss the picture of a forest floor habitat. **Ask: What types of plants and animals live on the forest floor?** Children should note that ferns, moss, and asters as well as deer, foxes, and skunks all live on the forest floor.

SEP Scientific Knowledge is Based on Emperical Evidence . . . .

CCC Patterns . . . .

Ask: What happens in winter months in a forest? Can you identify any patterns in these changes? In winter months when the temperatures are colder, many animals sleep, stay in dens, or grow thicker fur to help keep them warn. With the colder temperatures, the trees lose their leaves. Because the seasons repeat, these events are patterns that will happen year after year.

Differentiate Instruction

RTI/Extra Support Provide children with pictures of different animals and plants from a rain forest and a forest. Have children separate the animals into three groups; 1. rain forest habitats, 2. forest habitats, and 3. lives in both habitats.

Extension Children may want to find out more about plants or animals that live in a forest. Allow children to gather more information about one of the plants or animals shown in the picture, or to research another plant or animal that lives in a forest.

DCI Biodiversity and Humans . . . .

Discuss the picture of the forest tree habitat. **Ask: Which animals live in the branches of these trees?** Children should note that opossums, hawks, and bald eagles live in the tree branches.

CCC Patterns . . . .

Ask: Can you identify any patterns in how animals use tree habitats in a forest? Many animals build nests or homes in the branches and leaves of the trees. **Why do you think so many animals live in these trees?** The larger leaves of these trees help smaller animals keep themselves and their nest hidden from larger animals.

Collaboration

Build on Prior Knowledge Bring in several types of nuts or seeds from trees. Allow time for children to identify as many types of nuts or seeds as possible. (NOTE: If there are children with allergies in the class, use pictures of nuts and seeds instead.)

Look at the picture to explore plants and animals that live in the branches of trees.

An opossum's diet changes with the seasons. It nests in tree holes but sleeps underground in winter.

A hawk blends in with the trees. It builds a nest and stays in the forest all year. It hunts small animals.

Explore online. ▶

A hickory tree has bark that makes a good home for some animals. It has nuts with hard shells that split open.

A birch tree has smooth seeds that change from green to brown. The wind spins the seeds in the air.

A beech tree has leaves that make good hiding places for small animals. Its fruits split open with beechnuts.

Bald eagles hunt fish and small animals. They build nests near water. Eagles fly to warmer areas for the winter.

© Houghton Mifflin Harcourt

164

What are three patterns you observed in the forest?

Sample answer: Plants change with the seasons; animals

change with the seasons; animals blend in with the forest.

_____

_____

_____

Apply What You Know

Evidence Notebook • Choose all animals that might live in a forest. Use evidence to support your answer. Record it in your Evidence Notebook.

arctic fox	toucan	black bear

chipmunk	monkey	cardinal

CCC Patterns . . . .

Review patterns children observed in the various forest habitats. Children may include patterns related to plants or animals that live in the forest or may include patterns related to seasonal changes. **Ask: Can you identify any patterns between the habitats in the forest and the habitats in the rain forest? Both habitats have a great number of and variety of trees; both habitats have smaller plants that do not require a lot of sunlight that grow on the forest floor.**

FORMATIVE ASSESSMENT

Evidence Notebook

Have children work in pairs to research and discuss which animals live in a forest. Guide children to record their answers in their Evidence Notebook, and provide evidence to support their claims.

Scoring Guidelines

- identifies the black bear, chipmunk, and cardinal as animals that live in a forest habitat
- makes connections between the animal and its life in a forest
- cites evidence that explains why the animal lives in a forest

Savanna Habitats

3D Learning Objective

Children will **make observations** of plants and animals to compare the **diversity of life in savanna habitats.** Children will observe **patterns** in the things that plants and animals need to live in a savanna.

 Biodiversity and Humans . . . .

Discuss the text and pictures with children. **Ask: How would you describe the plants in a savanna?** The grasses are tall, and there are very few trees. The trees have short branches with very few leaves on them. **What are some characteristics of a savanna?** A savanna has rainy and dry seasons, and is warm all year long. They have a few trees that have flowers and fruit.

Differentiate Instruction

ELL Children may be unfamiliar with the word *savanna.* Explain that it means "grassland." Guide children to look at the pictures of savannas. **Ask: Why do you think this place is called a savanna?** Children should note that a savanna has a lot of grassland with just a few shrubs and trees.

Savanna Habitats

A savanna has tall grasses with a few shrubs and trees. It has a rainy season and a dry season. It is warm all year. These are patterns. Look at the pictures to explore some habitats in a savanna.

Explore online.

One savanna habitat is within the grasses. This is where small animals make their homes. These animals eat plants, insects, and seeds.

Each tree in the savanna is its own habitat. The trees have flowers and fruit. Some are a source of water for animals during the dry season.

 How are the savanna habitats alike?

Sample answer: They all have rainy and dry seasons.

166

Look at the picture to see plants and animals that live in the grasses of the savanna.

Explore online.

● Buffalo grass can grow to 3 feet. It grows well in the dry season. Its seeds grow at the top of the plant.

● A springhare lives in a burrow. It eats roots, grasses, stems, seeds, and leaves.

● A pangolin has scales to keep it safe. It hunts ants and termites. It gathers them with its sticky tongue.

● Stinking grass has a bad smell and grows in clumps. Animals like the taste of its new leaves.

● A mongoose eats ants and termites in the dry season. It eats beetles and grasshoppers in the rainy season.

● Guinea grass has stems that grow to 6 feet. When the stems bend and touch the ground, roots and new plants grow.

© Houghton Mifflin Harcourt

DCI Biodiversity and Humans . . . .

Point out that the word *savannah* means "grassland." Discuss the picture of the grassland habitat in a savanna. **Ask: What types of plants and animals live in the grassland habitat of a savanna?** Children should note that buffalo grass, stinking grass, and guinea grass, as well as springhares, pangolins, and mongooses all live in the grassland habitat of a savanna.

CCC Patterns . . . .

Ask: What patterns can you identify in the plants and animals that live in this habitat? Sample answer: Most of the grasses in this habitat are relatively short. Many of the animals that live there are smaller in size, too.

Collaboration

Build on Prior Knowledge Provide children with pictures of different animals and plants from habitats found in a rain forest, a forest, and a savanna. Have children group the pictures according to their habitat. Guide children to select one animal or plant and find one fact about that animal or plant to share with the class.

DCI   Biodiversity and Humans . . . .

Discuss the picture of the baobab tree. **Ask:** How do you know that the picture shows a baobab tree during the rainy season? It is full of leaves, flowers, and fruits. During the dry season, the baobab tree loses all of its leaves. Without its leaves, this tree's short branches look like tree roots sticking up in the air. For this reason, it is called an "upside-down" tree. **Ask:** How does the baobab tree get water during the dry season? During the rainy season, the tree stores up water in its trunk for use during the dry season.

CCC   Patterns . . . .

Ask: Can you identify any patterns in how animals get what they need in the baobab tree habitat? The smaller animals, such as the bush baby, the bat, and the parrot, as well as the larger animals, such as the elephant, all eat fruit from the baobab tree.

SEP   Scientific Knowledge is Based on Emperical Evidence . . . .

Remind children that scientists look for patterns when making observations. Have children discuss any patterns they observe about the animals that live in and around the baobab tree. **Ask:** How does the baobab tree support so many different animals? The baobab tree is huge and can provide shelter and food for many different animals.

Look at the picture to explore plants and animals that live in a baobab tree.

Explore online. ▶

● A bush baby makes its nest in the tree. It eats insects, fruit, and nectar. It licks water from the tree cracks.

● Bats visit the baobab tree at night. They sip nectar from the flowers and juice from the fruits.

● This parrot eats seeds, nuts, berries, fruit, and nectar. It eats seeds from the grasses during the dry season.

● A baobab tree loses its leaves in the dry season. It is full of leaves, flowers, and fruits in the rainy season. It stores water in its trunk.

● An elephant eats grasses, leaves, fruits, twigs, and bark. Its long trunk can pick a flower or rip a branch off a tree.

© Houghton Mifflin Harcourt

168

What things does the baobab tree provide for the animals? Choose all correct answers.

(A) It provides food.

(B) It provides shelter.

(C) It provides water.

Apply What You Know

Evidence Notebook • Elephants live in the savanna. Explain why the savanna is a good place for an elephant to live. Identify patterns and use evidence in your answer. Record it in your Evidence Notebook.

Lesson 4 • What Plants and Animals Live in Land Habitats?   169

(DCI) Biodiversity and Humans . . . .

Children should choose A—It provides food.; B—It provides shelter.; and C—It provides water. If children do not choose all the answers, tell them to look back at the picture of the baobab tree and look for patterns of what it provides to the animals. Remind children that a habitat is a place where living things get the food, water, air, and shelter needed to live.

FORMATIVE ASSESSMENT

Evidence Notebook

Children will work in small groups as they discuss information they have found out about savanna habitats. Allow time for children to discuss why a savanna is a good place for elephants to live. Guide children to record their answers in their Evidence Notebook, and to use evidence to support their claims.

Scoring Guidelines

• describes why the savanna is a good place for an elephant to live

• provides sufficient evidence to support how an elephant gets the things it needs in a savanna.

Do the Math! • Display Data

Children should draw bars on the graph to show 3 bats, 1 bush baby, 1 elephant, and 1 parrot.

💡 **Display Data • Reason Abstractly and Quantitatively • Model with Mathematics** Children should recognize this as a bar graph. There is a title at the top, the categories are listed in a row across the bottom, and numbers are listed on the scale at the left. Children will draw bars to show how many of each animal are in the given categories.

CCC Patterns . . . .

Ask: What category did you use to help you graph the animals?
Sample answer: I used the type of animal. Explain to children that there are many types of animals that are found in a savanna and that these animals can be grouped by their characteristics. These characteristics form a pattern, which provides a way to describe the similarities that the animals in the group share. Birds and mammals are two groups that are found in the picture. Almost all birds have wings, feathers, and fly. Almost all mammals have hair or fur. Discuss with children the two groups of animals seen in the picture. Have children work in pairs to identify each animal as either a bird or a mammal. Children may think the bat is a bird because it flies, but point out that it actually belongs in the mammal group.

SEP Scientific Knowledge is Based on Emperical Evidence . . . .

Ask: What are some other kinds of birds? What are some other kinds of mammals? Sample answer: Toucans and eagles are kinds of birds. Dogs and cats are kinds of mammals.

Do the Math! • Draw bars in the graph to show how many animals you see in the savanna.

💡 **Display Data**
Go to the online handbook for tips.

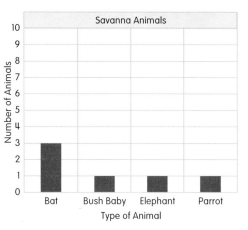

170

© Houghton Mifflin Harcourt

Hands-On Activity 👥 small groups ⏱ 1 class period

Make a Habitat Exhibit

3D Learning Objective

🔵SEP **Planning and Carrying Out Investigations . . . .**

Children make a plan to research and compare plants and animals that live in a habitat found in the savanna and then display their results in an exhibit.

Suggested Materials books and fact cards about animals, pencils, posterboard or white construction paper, and markers

Preparation
Pre-assemble materials bundles for pairs or groups.

Activity
As a class, view the video. Then discuss the question that will need to be answered. Have children record the question.

STEP 1 Ask: What should your group do first? Decide which habitat we will explore and make a plan for our group. Monitor groups as they discuss habitats they want to explore and begin planning. Be sure that children include all members of the group. Guide children to narrow down the plants and animals within the same habitat, and discuss what information they want to collect. Monitor groups to make sure there is a wide variety of habitats selected across the class as well as different plants and animals to use for the final comparison.

STEP 2 Guide children as they do research and record their observations. Allow each group time to make a poster about their selected plants and animals.

Name _____

🔍 Hands-On Activity
Make a Habitat Exhibit

Materials
_____

Ask a Question

How can you compare plants and animals that live in savanna habitats?

Test and Record Data Explore online. ▶

Step 1

Make a plan to research and compare plants and animals that live in a habitat found in the savanna. Identify the habitat and record your plan.

Children should record a plan to research and compare plants and

animals that live in a habitat found in the savanna.

Step 2

Research your plants and animals.
Record your observations. Make a poster.

Children should record their observations.

_____

_____

© Houghton Mifflin Harcourt

Hands-On Activity, continued

STEP 3 Guide children, as needed, in a review of all plants and animals in the class exhibit. **Ask: How are these animals alike? How are they different?** Answers will vary.

 **Patterns** . . . .

STEP 4 Children should analyze the results and look for patterns. **Ask: What patterns did you find?** Plants and animals live in a certain habitat because they get what they need there.

Claims, Evidence, and Reasoning

Children should explain how to compare plants and animals that live in a habitat and cite evidence to support their claim. **Ask: What similarities and differences did you find among the plants and animals?** Answers will vary.

	Scoring Rubric for Hands-On Activity
3	States a claim supported with evidence about the similarities and differences noted by the class exhibit
2	States a claim somewhat supported with evidence about the similarities and differences noted by the class exhibit
1	States a claim about the class exhibit that is not supported with evidence
0	Does not state a claim and does not provide evidence

Step 3

Set up your class exhibit. Compare the plants and animals in each habitat. Identify how they are alike and how they are different.

_____	Both	_____

Step 4

Analyze your results. Identify patterns.

Plants and animals live in certain habitats because they

get what they need there.

Make a claim that answers your question.

Answers should reflect children's solutions for making

a habitat exhibit.

What is your evidence?

Answers should cite evidence from children's proposed solutions.

_____

172

Explore online. ▶   Guide children to the Interactive Online Student Edition where they can choose from and explore both paths.

Take It Further

People in Science & Engineering •
Dr. Emilio Bruna

Explore more online.
• Stepping on Habitats

Dr. Emilio Bruna is an ecologist. He studies how plants, animals, and people interact in an environment.

Explore online. ▶

Dr. Bruna travels to Brazil to study the Amazon rain forest. He makes observations of how people cause changes to the rain forest. He wants to find out how these changes affect the plants and animals that live there.

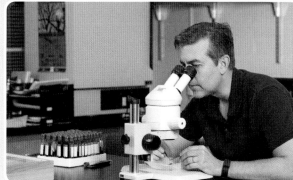

© Houghton Mifflin Harcourt

Take It Further

People in Science & Engineering •
Dr. Emilio Bruna

Children investigate the work of an ecologist, Dr. Emilio Bruna and produce a report to detail their findings. Dr. Bruna leads The Bruna Lab at the University of Florida in Gainesville, Florida. From there he conducts research on how changes to habitats impact the plants and animals who live there. Dr. Bruna focuses his research on the Amazon and the Cerrado—both in South America.

DCI **Biodiversity and Humans** . . . .

Discuss with children that an ecologist is a scientist that studies how plants, animals, and people interact in an environment.
Ask: What do you think Dr. Bruna is investigating in this picture?
Accept any reasonable answer, such as, Dr. Bruna wants to find out more information about this plant or animal.

Collaboration

Whole Class Guide children to list questions they may have about a career in ecology. Allow children to search for answers to any of the questions from the list and make a presentation about the information they found. Children can work independently or with a partner. Provide time for the class to share their discoveries.

Take It Further, continued

Read, Write, Share! • Participate in a Research and Writing Project

Children will do research to answer questions they have recorded about Dr. Bruna's work. Encourage children to think about some of the questions Dr. Bruna might have had, the discoveries he has made, or the dangers he faced while completing his research in the Amazon rain forest.

 Participate in a Research and Writing Project • Gather Information Children should use books, encyclopedias, magazines, newspapers, digital audio, and the Internet to do research. Remind children to take notes and record information that answers their questions.

Differentiate Instruction

RTI/Extra Support Guide children to think about the different rain forest habitats they explored. Encourage children to think of questions they had as they explored these habitats. Remind children of the information from the lesson as needed.

Extension Challenge children to find out more about a threat to the Amazon Rain Forest, such as deforestation, logging, litter or land pollution, or endangered plants or animals. Suggest children pick a topic that interests them and to think of a solution to decrease the threat.

Explore more online. ▶

Stepping on Habitats

Children explore how people can affect the plants and animals that live in various habitats.

Read, Write, Share! • What questions do you have about Dr. Bruna's work? Record your questions. Gather information from different sources to answer your questions. Record your answers.

Participate in a Research and Writing Project Go to the online handbook for tips.

✏ Write or draw to describe Dr. Bruna's studies.

Children should describe Dr. Bruna's work as an ecologist in the Amazon rain forest.

Accept all reasonable questions and answers about

Dr. Bruna's work.

174

© Houghton Mifflin Harcourt

Explore online. ▶   Have children explore online to find out more about land habitats.

Lesson Check

Lesson Check   Name _____

Explore online. ▶

| rain forest | forest | savanna |

Can You Explain It?

✏️ Why do certain plants and animals only live in certain land habitats?

Be sure to

- Compare two plants or animals from a habitat.
- Describe how each plant or animal gets the things it needs.
- Explain why the plants or animals only live in that habitat.

Plants live in a habitat where they can get the things they need.

Plants like mosses, ferns, and asters all live on the shady forest

floor because they need little light to grow.

_____

_____

Lesson 4 • What Plants and Animals Live in Land Habitats?   175

Can You Explain It?

Have children reread their answer to the Can You Explain It? prompt at the beginning of the lesson.

DCI **Biodiversity and Humans** . . . .

Review the three pictures and discuss why plants and animals live in habitats found in these areas. Ask probing questions to guide children as they explain why certain plants and animals live where they do. **Ask: How do these plants and animals get what they need where they live?** Accept answers that describe a habitat and how a plant or animal gets what it needs.

Scoring Guidelines

- Children should describe one habitat within a rain forest, forest, or savanna.
- Children should compare two plants or animals found within that habitat.
- Children should describe how each plant or animal gets what it needs.
- Children should explain why the plants or animals only live in that habitat.

Collaboration

Cultivating New Questions As children complete this lesson and prepare for the next unit, ask them to identify additional questions they have about land habitats. **Ask: What are some other kinds of land habitats?** caves in a forest, underground burrows in a desert

Lesson Check, continued

SUMMATIVE ASSESSMENT
Self Check

1. Children should choose B—in a rain forest. If children choose A or C, guide them to the Canopy Habitat section of the lesson. Have them review which environment includes the canopy habitat. Children can also look at the lesson opener page to observe macaws flying in a rain forest.

2. Children should choose A—in a forest. If children choose B or C, remind them that it is warm all year in a rain forest and in a savanna. This animal lives in the cold. Have children revisit the Forest Habitats and the On the Forest Floor sections of the lesson.

3. Children should write *rain forest* on the first line and *forest* on the second line. If children incorrectly complete the sentences, guide them to the Rain Forest Habitats and the Forest Habitats sections of the lesson.

Self Check

1. Answer this riddle. I am a colorful bird. My big beak helps me crack open nuts that grow in the canopy of tall trees. Where do I live?
   Ⓐ in a forest
   Ⓑ in a rain forest
   Ⓒ in a savanna

2. Answer this riddle. My fur is thick and black. It keeps me warm in the cold winter. Where do I live?
   Ⓐ in a forest
   Ⓑ in a rain forest
   Ⓒ in a savanna

3. What are features of rain forests and forests? Use the words **rain forest** and **forest** to complete the sentences below.

   Habitats in a rain forest and in a forest both have trees. Because it is warm and wet all year, these plants grow thicker and taller in a
   <u>rain forest</u>.

   During the fall, the leaves fall off the trees in a
   <u>forest</u>.

176

4. Where does each plant or animal live? Write the correct name for each place.

rain forest	forest	savanna

rain forest

forest

savanna

savanna

rain forest

forest

5. The zebra lives in the savanna. How does it get what it needs there?

(A) It can get water from the plants it eats.

(B) It can find the food it needs.

(C) It can take shelter in an underground burrow.

4. Children should label the pictures in the top row *rain forest, forest,* and *savanna.* They should label the pictures in the bottom row *savanna, rain forest,* and *forest.* If children incorrectly identify any of the places, guide them to review where each plant or animal lives from the appropriate section of the lesson.

5. Children should choose A—It can get water from the plants it eats; and B—It can find the food it needs. If children choose C, review the Savanna Habitats section of the lesson and discuss that small animals make their homes in the ground. Remind children that zebras are large animals that eat the grasses and move from place to place.

Unit 3 Performance Task

Observe an Ant Farm

 individuals ⏱ 1 class period plus 10 minutes 3 times a week for 2 weeks

Objective

Children **carry out an investigation** to **observe animals (ants)** in order to compare their lives within an ant farm habitat, and to identify how its **shape and stability relate to its function**.

Suggested Materials

ant farm kit, tunnel tool kit, ants, hand lens, dropper, plastic gloves, food crumbs, water

Preparation

Review Lessons 3 and 4 to provide context for this Unit Performance Task. Collect the suggested materials for children to build their ant farms. Determine where the ants will come from—if they came with the kits or if you have to purchase them.

SEP Planning and Carrying Out Investigations . . . .

Ask: What do you think you will find out from this investigation? Accept all reasonable answers.

STEPS

Step 1

Have children place the ant farms in different places around the room, making sure they are in a safe spot. **Ask: Do you think the location of the ant farm will affect how the ants act?** Sample answer: Ants are cold-blooded, so they slow down when they get cold. Ants placed in direct sunlight may get too hot.

Step 2

CCC Structure and Function . . . .

Remind children to feed their ants twice during the week, and place a few drops of water every other day. **Ask: What do the ants do when you place food in the ant farm?** Answers will vary.

 Unit 3 Performance Task
Observe an Ant Farm

Materials

_____

_____

STEPS

Step 1

Use the tool to begin making a few tunnels in the ant farm. Then place the ants inside.

Step 2

Feed the ants a couple of food crumbs twice a week. Use a dropper to place a few drops of water every other day.

© Houghton Mifflin Harcourt

Step 3

Use a hand lens to observe the ants three times a week for two weeks.

Step 4

What did the ants do with the food you left? How do they build tunnels? What do ants do when they meet each other in the tunnels? Draw and write to record your observations.

Step 5

Compare your ant farm with the ant farms of your classmates. What patterns do you see?

✔ Check

_____ I observed my ants to see how they make tunnels and find food.

_____ I recorded my observations.

_____ I compared my ant farm with others to look for patterns.

Step 3

 **Planning and Carrying Out Investigations . . . .**

Remind children to make observations of their ant farm at least three times a week for two weeks and record their observations. **Ask: What does the ant farm look like? Are the ants eating? Are the ants drinking? How do the ants seem to interact?** Answers will vary.

Step 4

DCI Interdependent Relationships in Ecosystems . . . .

Prompt children to investigate the questions noted in Step 4 on the Interactive Worktext page. Remind children to draw or write to record their observations.

Step 5

Children should communicate their results of their ant farm investigation with classmates. Have them discuss any patterns they can observe from these comparisons.

Scoring Rubric for Performance Task	
3	Plans investigation, records observations, communicates results, and identifies patterns about the ant farms
2	Plans investigation and records observations, but does not communicate results or identify patterns about the ant farms
1	Plans investigation, but does not record observations, communicate results, or identify patterns about the ant farms
0	Does not plan an investigation, record observations, communicate results, or identify patterns about the ant farms

Unit 3 Review

SUMMATIVE ASSESSMENT

1. Children should choose A—air; B—sunlight; and C—water. By completing What Plants Need in Lesson 1, children explored what plants need to live and grow.

2. Children should choose A—leaves. If children choose B or C, reinforce that the leaves use sunlight, air, and water to make food for a plant. By completing Taking It In in Lesson 1, children explored why a plant needs sunlight, and how sunlight helps the plant to live and grow.

3. Children should choose C—water. If children choose A or B, reinforce that when leaves wilt, the plant needs water. By completing What Plants Need in Lesson 1, children explored what a healthful plant looks like.

4. Children should choose B—They move seeds so new plants can grow; and C—They move pollen so plants can make seeds. If children choose A, remind them that some animals move pollen, and some animals spread seeds from plants. By completing Animals Help Spread Seeds and How Animals Spread Pollen in Lesson 2, children explored how new plants grow because of the relationship between plants and animals.

Unit 3 Review   Name _____

1. What do plants need to live and grow? Choose all correct answers.
   Ⓐ air
   Ⓑ sunlight
   Ⓒ water

2. Which plant part takes in sunlight to make food?
   Ⓐ leaves
   Ⓑ roots
   Ⓒ stem

3. Sadie's plant does not look well. What does it need?
   Ⓐ soil
   Ⓑ shelter
   Ⓒ water

4. How do plants depend on animals? Choose all correct answers.
   Ⓐ They move plants from place to place.
   Ⓑ They move seeds so new plants can grow.
   Ⓒ They move pollen so plants can make seeds.

180

5. What can an animal find in its habitat?
Choose all correct answers.
- Ⓐ food
- Ⓑ shelter
- Ⓒ water

6. What is **true** about a tide pool? Choose all correct answers.
- Ⓐ It has water that is salty.
- Ⓑ It has water that is fresh.
- Ⓒ It has water that rises and falls back.

7. Look at these pond plants. What patterns do you see?

- Ⓐ They both live underwater.
- Ⓑ The leaves of both plants are above the water.
- Ⓒ They both do not need sunlight.

5. Children should choose A—food; B—shelter; and C—water. If children do not choose all three answer choices, reinforce that a habitat is a place where living things get the food, water, air, and shelter they need to live. By completing Lesson 3 and Lesson 4, children explored different water and land habitats, and how plants and animals get what they need in each type of habitat.

6. Children should choose A—It has water that is salty; and C—It has water that rises and falls back. If children choose B, reinforce that tide pools are a result of the ocean's shore (which is salty water) rising and falling. By completing Tide Pools in Lesson 3, children explored characteristics of a tide pool.

7. Children should choose B—The leaves of both plants are above the water. If children choose A or C, reinforce that both plants are above the water. If children choose C, remind them that all plants need sunlight to make their own food. By completing Ponds in Lesson 3, children explored and identified patterns about ponds.

3D Item Analysis	1	2	3	4	5	6	7
SEP Planning and Carrying Out Investigations							•
SEP Scientific Knowledge is Based on Empirical Evidence						•	•
DCI Interdependent Relationships in Ecosystems	•	•	•	•			
DCI Biodiversity and Humans					•	•	•
CCC Cause and Effect	•	•	•				
CCC Structure and Function				•			
CCC Patterns						•	•

8. Children should choose B—rain forest. If children choose A or C, reinforce that the rain forest is a place that is warm and wet all year. By completing Rain Forest Habitats in Lesson 4, children explored characteristics of a rain forest.

9. Children should choose C—They both have different seasons. If children choose A, remind them that a savanna has only a few trees. If children choose B, remind them that elephants are probably too large to move around where there are lots of trees. By completing Forest Habitats and Savanna Habitats in Lesson 4, children explored the characteristics of these land habitats.

10. Children should make the following matches—top left picture to bottom right picture; middle left picture to middle right picture; and bottom left picture to top right picture. If children incorrectly match the animals with their habitat, have them review the land habitat patterns they observed in Lesson 4. By completing Rain Forest Habitats, Forest Habitats, and Savanna Habitats in Lesson 4, children explored the characteristics of these three land habitats.

3D Item Analysis	8	9	10
SEP Planning and Carrying Out Investigations		•	
SEP Scientific Knowledge is Based on Empirical Evidence	•	•	
DCI Biodiversity and Humans	•	•	•
CCC Patterns	•	•	•

8. Max reads about a plant that grows in a place that is warm and wet all year. Where does this plant most likely live?
   Ⓐ forest
   🅑 rain forest
   Ⓒ savanna

9. Which is true about **both** a forest and a savanna?
   Ⓐ They both have many trees.
   Ⓑ They are both homes for elephants.
   🅒 They both have different seasons.

10. Where does each animal live? Match each animal to where it lives.

182

Unit 4
Earth's Surface

Unit Project • Explore Ocean Water

Why does an ocean not freeze completely? Investigate to find out.

Unit 4 • Earth's Surface

Unit Overview

In this unit, children will...
- gather information to identify where water is located on Earth.
- develop maps to represent locations of land and water on Earth.

About This Image

Guide children in a discussion about the picture on this page. **Ask: Where is the water in this picture? Where do you think it comes from? Where do you think it is going? What is in the picture other than water?** Sample answer: We can see a river running through trees and grasslands. We can also see some mountains. The water is probably moving downhill. It could also be flowing down from the mountains.

Unit Project • Explore Ocean Water

Have children plan and conduct an investigation on why an ocean does not completely freeze. Lead children in a discussion about oceans. **Ask: Have you ever been close to an ocean before? What happens to the ocean when it gets cold?** Accept all reasonable answers. Remind children about the melting/freezing point of water and how large an ocean is. So, while the ocean water gets cooler, it takes a long time to cool down an entire ocean.

Once the class has brainstormed ideas on why the ocean does not freeze completely, challenge children to use resources to locate information that they may use as evidence to support their claim. More support for the Unit Project can be found on pp. 185I–185L.

Unit 4 At a Glance

The learning experiences in this unit prepare children for mastery of:

Performance Expectations

2-ESS2-2. Develop a model to represent the shapes and kinds of land and bodies of water in an area.

2-ESS2-3. Obtain information to identify where water is found on Earth and that it can be solid or liquid.

In addition to the print resources, the following resources are available online to support this unit.

Unit Pretest
Lesson 1 Where Is Water Found on Earth?
- Interactive Online Student Edition
- Lesson Quiz
Lesson 2 Engineer It • How Can We Map Land and Water?
- Interactive Online Student Edition
- Lesson Quiz
You Solve It Mapping Water
Unit Performance Task
Unit Test

184

Unit 4 At a Glance

© Houghton Mifflin Harcourt • Image Credits: ©iStock/Getty Images

Unit Vocabulary

map a drawing or model of a place (p. 204)

map title part of a map that tells what the map shows (p. 205)

map key part of a map that shows what the map colors and symbols mean (p. 205)

compass rose part of a map that shows the directions north, south, east, and west (p. 205)

Vocabulary Game • Guess the Word

Materials
• 1 set of word cards

How to Play
1. Work with a partner to make word cards.
2. Place the cards face down in a pile.
3. One player picks the top card, but does not show it.
4. The second player asks questions to guess the word.
5. When the word is guessed correctly, the second player takes a card. Then, the first player asks questions to guess the word.

Unit Vocabulary

The Next Generation Science Standards emphasize explanation and demonstration of understanding versus rote memorization of science vocabulary words. Keep in mind that these vocabulary words are tools for clear communication. Use these words as a starting point, not an end goal, for children to build deeper understanding of science concepts.

Children can explore all vocabulary words in the **Online Glossary**.

Vocabulary Strategies

- Have children review the vocabulary words. Then have children work in pairs to share an example of each word and explain why they think it's an example. Have pairs record their examples to refer back to during the unit.
- Have children think about how each word relates to learning about Earth's surface. Have children work in pairs and share their ideas with a partner.

Differentiate Instruction

RTI/Extra Support Pronounce each word, and have children repeat it after you. Have children find each highlighted word within the unit content. Have children work in pairs and explain to a partner what they think each word means based on the surrounding context of imagery and text.

Extension Have children select two vocabulary words and work in small groups to illustrate and explain the words to a first-grade child.

Vocabulary Game • Guess the Word

Preparation Assemble vocabulary game cards. Assign partners for children. Provide instructions for how to play the game. Allow children to rotate through all four cards during gameplay.

Integrating the NGSS* Three Dimensions of Learning

Building to the Performance Expectations

The learning experiences in this unit prepare children for mastery of the following Performance Expectations:

Earth's Systems

2-ESS2-2 Develop a model to represent the shapes and kinds of land and bodies of water in an area.

2-ESS2-3 Obtain information to identify where water is found on Earth and that it can be solid or liquid.

Assessing Student Progress

After completing the lessons, the **Unit Project** Explore Ocean Water provides children with opportunities to practice aspects of and to demonstrate their understanding of the Performance Expectations as they brainstorm ideas on why the ocean does not freeze completely and use resources to locate information that they may use as evidence in support of their claim.

Additionally, children can further practice or be assessed on aspects of the Performance Expectations by completing the **Unit Performance Task** Map an Island, in which children develop a model (map) to show where land and water are located and to represent patterns in the natural world.

Lesson 1
Where Is Water Found on Earth?

In Lesson 1, children begin exploring the concept that water can be found on Earth (DCI The Roles of Water in Earth's Surface Processes). The lesson begins with children exploring some of the different bodies of water (**SEP Obtaining, Evaluating, and Communicating Information**) (CCC Patterns). Then, children explore the concept that water exists in solid and liquid form (DCI The Roles of Water in Earth's Surface Processes) (CCC Patterns). Finally, children explore the topic of conserving and protecting Earth's water and observe bodies of water near where they live.

Lesson 2
Engineer It • How Can We Map Land and Water?

In Lesson 2, children explore maps as drawings or models that show where things are located (DCI Plate Tectonics and Large-Scale System Interactions). The lesson begins with children exploring how a map shows different types of land and bodies of water (DCI Plate Tectonics and Large-Scale System Interactions). Then, children explore the parts of a map, including the map title, map key, and compass rose, and use a map key to interpret a map of the United States (CCC Patterns). Finally, children extend their exploration in a hands-on activity in which they make a map of their school playground (**SEP Developing and Using Models**) (CCC Patterns).

Standards Supported by This Unit

Explore online.
Online only.

Next Generation Science Standards	Unit Project	Lesson 1	Lesson 2	Unit Performance Task	You Solve It
SEP Obtaining, Evaluating, and Communicating Information	•	•			•
SEP Developing and Using Models	•		•	•	
DCI **ESS2.B** Plate Tectonics and Large-Scale System Interactions			•	•	
DCI **ESS2.C** The Roles of Water in Earth's Surface Processes	•	•			•
CCC Patterns	•	•	•	•	•

NGSS* Across the Grades

Before

Coverage of the **Performance Expectations** within this unit originates in Grade 2.

Grade 2

Earth's Systems
2-ESS2-2
2-ESS2-3

After

Earth's Systems
4-ESS2-2 Analyze and interpret data from maps to describe patterns of Earth's features.

Trace Tool to the NGSS™

Go online to view the complete coverage of these standards across this grade level and time.

3D Unit Planning

Lesson 1 Where Is Water Found on Earth? pp. 186–201

Overview

Objective Gather information to identify that water is found in ponds, lakes, rivers, and oceans on Earth.

SEP Obtaining, Evaluating, and Communicating Information
DCI **ESS2.C** The Roles of Water in Earth's Surface Processes
CCC Patterns

Math and **English Language Arts** standards and features are detailed on lesson planning pages.

	Print and Online Student Editions	Explore online.
ENGAGE	**Lesson Phenomenon** pp. 186–187 **Can You Explain It?** Bodies of Water	▶ Can You Explain It? Video
EXPLORE/ EXPLAIN	**Lakes and Ponds** **Rivers and Oceans** **Liquid or Solid** 🔍 **Hands-On Activity** Locate Bodies of Water pp. 195–196	**Hands-On** Worksheet
ELABORATE	**Take It Further** pp. 197–198 People in Science & Engineering • John G. Ferris	Take It Further How Can We Conserve Earth's Water?
EVALUATE	**Lesson Check** p. 199 **Self Check** pp. 200–201	Lesson Quiz

🔍 Hands-On Activity Planning

Locate Bodies of Water

Objective Children will use a variety of resources to obtain information about bodies of water near where they live and will make posters to share this information with their classmates.

👥 small groups
🕐 1 class period

Suggested Materials
- print and online resources about an area where you live
- posterboard
- art materials

Preparation/Tip
Preassemble materials bundles for pairs or groups. Provide print and online resources.

Overview

Objective Develop a map to identify where land and water are located.

SEP Developing and Using Models
DCI **ESS2.B** Plate Tectonics and Large-Scale System Interactions
CCC Patterns

Math and **English Language Arts** standards and features are detailed on lesson planning pages.

	Print and Online Student Editions	Explore online.
ENGAGE	**Lesson Problem** pp. 202–203 **Can You Solve It?** Why We Use Maps	▶ Can You Solve It? Picture
EXPLORE/ EXPLAIN	**What Is a Map?** **Use a Map Key** **Hands-On Activity** Engineer It • Make a Map pp. 209–210	**Hands-On** Worksheet **You Solve It** Mapping Water
ELABORATE	**Take It Further** pp. 211–212 Careers in Science & Engineering • Mapmakers	Take It Further Use a Map Scale
EVALUATE	**Lesson Check** p. 213 **Self Check** pp. 214–215	Lesson Quiz

🔍 Hands-On Activity Planning

Engineer It • Make a Map

Objective Children make a map of their school playground, including a map title, a map key, and a compass rose. Children will compare their maps with their classmates' maps and look for patterns.

👥 small groups
🕒 1 class period

Suggested Materials
• posterboard
• art materials

Preparation/Tip

Preassemble materials bundles for pairs or groups. Plan to visit the playground during a time when it is not in use.

3D Unit Planning, continued

 You Solve It   Go online for an additional interactive activity.

Mapping Water

This interactive activity offers practice in support of **PE 2-ESS2-3.**

SEP Obtaining, Evaluating, and Communicating Information

DCI **ESS2.C** The Roles of Water in Earth's Surface Processes

CCC Patterns

3D Learning Objectives

- Identify where water is located on Earth.
- Identify and differentiate between bodies of water.
- Observe and identify patterns about the natural world.

Activity Problem

- Children use a map to find out about and identify different bodies of water found on Earth, such as rivers, lakes, and oceans.
- Children use a map to identify bodies of water that are fresh and bodies of water that are salty.
- Children will indicate the direction water flows, such as from high to low or from river to ocean.

Interaction Summary

- Look for patterns (rivers empty into other bodies of water, salt water doesn't freeze as easily as fresh water).
- Identify bodies of fresh water and salt water, and describe patterns.

Assessment

Preassessment

Assessment Guide, Unit Pretest

The Unit Pretest focuses on prerequisite knowledge and is composed of items that evaluate children's preparedness for the content covered within this unit.

Formative Assessment

Interactive Worktext, Apply What You Know, Lesson Check, and Self Check

Summative Assessment

Assessment Guide, Lesson Quiz

The Lesson Quiz provides a quick assessment of each lesson objective and of the portion of the Performance Expectation aligned to the lesson.

Interactive Worktext, Performance Task pp. 216–217

The Performance Task presents the opportunity for children to collaborate with classmates in order to complete the steps of each Performance Task. Each Performance Task provides a formal Scoring Rubric for evaluating children's work.

Interactive Worktext, Unit 4 Review, pp. 218–220

Assessment Guide, Unit Test

The Unit Test provides an in-depth assessment of the Performance Expectations aligned to the unit. This test evaluates children's ability to apply knowledge in order to explain phenomena and to solve problems. Within this test, Constructed Response items apply a three-dimensional rubric for evaluating children's mastery on all three dimensions of the Next Generation Science Standards.

 **Assessment Online**   Go online to view the complete assessment items for this unit.

Teacher Notes

_____

_____

_____

_____

_____

_____

_____

_____

_____

_____

_____

_____

Differentiate Instruction

Leveled Readers

The Science & Engineering Leveled Readers provide additional nonfiction reading practice in this unit's subject area.

On Level • Why Are Resources Important?
This reader reinforces unit concepts and includes response activities for your children.

Extra Support • Why Are Resources Important?
This reader shares title, illustrations, vocabulary, and concepts with the On-Level Reader; however, the text is linguistically accommodated to provide simplified sentence structures and comprehension aids. It also includes response activities.

Enrichment • All About Rocks
This high-interest, nonfiction reader will extend and enrich unit concepts and vocabulary and includes response activities.

Teacher Guide
The accompanying Teacher Guide provides teaching strategies and support for using all the readers.

ELL

English Language Learner support resources include a glossary and Leveled Readers in Spanish and English. ELL teaching strategies appear throughout this unit:

pp. 186B, 188, 202B, 206

RTI/Extra Support

Strategies for children who need extra support appear throughout this unit:

pp. 185, 185I, 186B, 191, 202B, 208, 212

Extension

Strategies for children who have mastered core content and are ready for additional challenges appear throughout this unit:

pp. 185, 185I, 186B, 191, 202B, 208, 212

Leveled Readers

All readers are available online as well as in an innovative, engaging format for use with touchscreen mobile devices. Contact your HMH Sales Representative for more information.

Connecting with NGSS

Connections to Community

Use these opportunities for informal science learning to provide local context and to extend and enhance unit concepts.

At Home

Map the Neighborhood Have children work with a family member to make a map of their neighborhood. Children should include a title, a key, and a compass rose. Have children share their maps with the class and identify any bodies of water on their maps.
Use with Lesson 2.

In the Community

Guest Speaker Invite a mapmaker to speak to the class about how maps are made and updated. Have children prepare questions for the mapmaker to answer. Encourage children to ask a mix of appropriate science and technology questions.
Use with Lesson 2.

Keeping Water Clean Plan a class field trip to a municipal water treatment plant. Before the field trip, work as a class to investigate how groundwater and surface water are made safe for drinking. Have children prepare a list of questions to ask of the employees at the water treatment plant.
Use with Lesson 1.

Culture

Resources Tell children that Aomori is a city on a harbor in Japan. Because the people there live on an island surrounded by the ocean, the people of Aomori eat seaweed, fish, and other seafood. Guide children to identify other bodies of water found in the surrounding area. Have children explain how the various communities use their water resources.
Use with Lesson 1

Home Letters Go online to view the Home Letters for this unit.

Collaboration

Collaboration opportunities in this unit:

Build on Prior Knowledge
pp. 187, 203

Cultivating New Questions
pp. 199, 213

Small Groups
p. 207

Jigsaw
p. 190

Connections to Science

Connections to Science opportunities in this unit:

Connection to Life Science
Patterns Lesson 1, p. 198

Connection to Life Science
Biodiversity and Humans Lesson 2, p. 207

Unit Project

👥 small groups 🕐 1 class period

Explore Ocean Water

There are many ways to complete this Unit Project. The steps and Suggested Materials indicate one way to complete the investigation. Encourage children to come up with their own ideas of why ocean water doesn't freeze completely and how to investigate their ideas. If children decide to follow another process to complete their investigation, be sure to review each group's plans before the children begin. This Unit Project supports content in Lessons 1 and 2.

3D Learning Objective

SEP Developing and Using Models

Explore why ocean water does not freeze completely by planning and conducting an investigation. Make models to represent ocean water (and to represent fresh water to make comparisons if desired). Construct an argument using evidence to support a claim.

Skills and Standards Focus

This project supports building children's mastery of **Performance Expectations 2-ESS2-2** and **2-ESS2-3.**

SEP Developing and Using Models
SEP Obtaining, Evaluating, and Communicating Information
DCI **ESS2.C** The Role of Water in Earth's Surface Processes
CCC Patterns

Suggested Materials

- small cup
- medium-sized bowl
- salt water and/or fresh water
- clock or stopwatch
- freezer

Preparation

Have a variety of containers available for each pair or group of children. If children choose to use salt water in different-sized containers, have them mix the salt water in the larger container and pour some into the smaller container. This will prevent the salt from affecting the freezing times. The time for the water to freeze will vary depending on the size of the containers, the starting temperature of the water, and the temperature of the freezer. However, 4–6 hours is a good estimate. The temperature at which the fresh water freezes will be around 32 degrees Fahrenheit (the melting/freezing point of fresh water.) Adding salt to the water will lower the freezing point. Before beginning the project, review the section Liquid or Solid in Lesson 1.

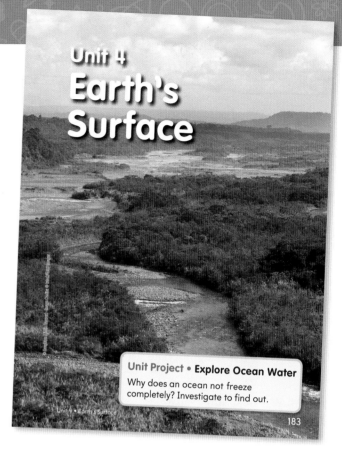

Unit 4
Earth's Surface

Unit Project • Explore Ocean Water
Why does an ocean not freeze completely? Investigate to find out.

Unit 4 • Earth's Surface
183

Differentiate Instruction

RTI/Extra Support Children can be provided with 2–4 different already-determined ways to investigate the freezing point of ocean water. They can then choose their method to investigate.

Extension Challenge children to investigate how moving water prevents oceans from freezing completely.

Name _____

Unit 4 Project
Explore Ocean Water

Why doesn't an ocean freeze completely? Write your ideas on the lines below. Then choose one idea to test. Plan and conduct an investigation to find out.

Children should write ideas they have for why an ocean doesn't freeze
_____
completely.
_____

_____

Materials
Draw and label the materials you will need.

> Children should draw and label materials. The following are possible materials children can use for this investigation: bowl, small cup, water, salt, freezer.

© Houghton Mifflin Harcourt Publishing Company

Unit 4 Project

Explore Ocean Water

SEP Developing and Using Models . . . .

Pose the unit project question to children. Encourage them to brainstorm reasons why an ocean doesn't freeze completely. Discuss all of the ideas as a class. Have children choose an idea to investigate and think of how they can make models to test that idea.

In the sample investigation shown, children compare the freezing time of a large container of salt water with the freezing time of a small container of salt water. **Ask: Which container of water do you think will freeze faster? Why?** I think the smaller container of water will freeze faster because there is less water.

ESSENTIAL QUESTIONS Prepare children for their project by asking the following questions.

- What happens when a liquid freezes?
- How are oceans different from other bodies of water?
- What cause-and-effect relationship will occur when you freeze the water?

Ask: What happens when a body of water freezes? Why do you think ponds freeze more easily than oceans? When a body of water freezes, it changes from liquid to solid. Ponds freeze more easily than oceans because ponds are much smaller and contain much less water.

Steps

Discuss with children why it is important to list the steps in their investigation. If children need support, brainstorm the steps together as a class.

SEP **Developing and Using Models** . . . .

Ask: Which container models the ocean? How do you know? The larger container models the ocean because oceans contain much more water than other bodies of water on Earth.

Have children observe containers of water every hour until all of the water has completely frozen. At the end of the investigation, children will need to be able to tell which container froze faster based on the amount of time it took each one to completely freeze. Children should record their observations using words and pictures.

DCI **The Role of Water in Earth's Surface Processes**

As children observe the water during the investigation, challenge them to identify the season in which they might find ocean water in that state. **Ask: In which seasons is ocean water completely liquid?** spring, summer, and fall **In which season might the surface of the ocean be frozen?** winter Refer children to Lesson 1 Where Is Water Found on Earth?

Data

Remind children to make observations as they investigate. Observations can be used as data to determine the outcome of the investigation.

Ask: Why is it important to record your data? so I can look at the data later and look for patterns **What did you expect would happen? Do your data agree with your prediction?** I thought the cup would freeze first. My data show that my prediction was correct.

Steps Write the steps you will do.

Answers may vary but should reflect a logical order of

steps in the investigation. Sample steps listed:

1. Fill the bowl with water. Add salt.

2. Fill the cup with water. Add salt.

3. Place the bowl and cup in the freezer.

4. Observe and record how the water in each container changes

every hour until both are frozen.

Data

Record your data.

Answers and drawings may vary but should reflect that the cup of water froze more quickly than the bowl of water.

_____ hours   _____ hours

bar

© Houghton Mifflin Harcourt Publishing Company

Unit 4 Project • Page 2 of 3

w

Analyze Your Results

Look for patterns in your data.

Restate Your Question

Write the question you investigated.

Answers should identify the question children initially chose at the

beginning of the investigation.

Claims, Evidence, and Reasoning

Make a claim that answers your question.

Answers should identify which container of water froze faster.

Review the data. What evidence from the investigation supports your claim?

Answer should cite evidence from the investigation to support which

container of water froze faster.

Discuss your reasoning with a partner.

Analyze Your Results

Have children analyze their data. Ask them to describe any patterns they noticed. Encourage them to share their data with the other groups.

 Patterns . . . .

Remind children that patterns exist in nature and can be used to explain observed phenomena. **Ask: What pattern exists in the way different bodies of water on Earth freeze?** Ponds, lakes, and rivers freeze faster than oceans. Smaller bodies of water freeze faster than larger bodies. **How do your data show that pattern?** The smaller container froze before the larger container.

Claims, Evidence, and Reasoning

Ask: What claim can you make? The cup of water froze faster than the bowl of water. **How does your evidence support your claim?** My evidence supports this because it took less time for the cup of water to freeze than it took for the bowl of water.

SEP **Obtaining, Evaluating, and Communicating Information** . . . .

Guide children to understand that they should evaluate their data and use the data as evidence to support their claim. **Ask: What can you use as evidence from your investigation?** the data collected, such as the drawings, writings, and recorded times

Scoring Rubric for Unit Project	
3	States a claim supported with evidence that the model of ocean water freezes more slowly
2	States a claim somewhat supported with evidence that the model of ocean water freezes more slowly
1	States a claim that is not supported by evidence
0	Does not state a claim and does not provide evidence

Lesson 1 # Where Is Water Found on Earth?

Building to the Performance Expectation

The learning experiences in this lesson prepare children for mastery of:

2-ESS2-3 Obtain information to identify where water is found on Earth and that it can be solid or liquid.

 Trace Tool to the NGSS
Go online to view the complete coverage of these standards across the lesson, unit, and time.

(SEP) Science & Engineering Practices

Obtaining, Evaluating, and Communicating Information
Obtain information using various texts, text features (e.g., headings, tables of contents, glossaries, electronic menus, icons), and other media that will be useful in answering a scientific question.

 VIDEO SEP: Obtaining, Evaluating, and Communicating Information

(DCI) Disciplinary Core Ideas

ESS2.C: The Roles of Water in Earth's Surface Processes
Water is found in the ocean, rivers, lakes, and ponds. Water exists as solid ice and in liquid form.

(CCC) Crosscutting Concepts

Patterns
Patterns in the natural world can be observed.

CONNECTIONS TO MATH

MP.2 Reason abstractly and quantitatively.

MP.4 Model with mathematics.

2.NBT.A.4 Compare two three-digit numbers based on meanings of the hundreds, tens, and ones digits, using >, =, and < symbols to record the results of comparisons.

2.MD.D.10 Draw a picture graph and a bar graph (with single-unit scale) to represent a data set with up to four categories. Solve simple put-together, take-apart, and compare problems using information presented in a bar graph.

CONNECTION TO ENGLISH LANGUAGE ARTS

W.2.8 Recall information from experiences, or gather information from provided sources to answer a question.

Integrating the Three Dimensions of Learning

This lesson introduces children to the concept that water can be found on Earth (**DCI The Roles of Water in Earth's Surface Processes**). The lesson begins with children exploring some of the different bodies of water (**SEP Obtaining, Evaluating, and Communicating Information**) (**CCC Patterns**). Then, children explore the concept that water exists in solid and liquid form (**DCI The Roles of Water in Earth's Surface Processes**) (**CCC Patterns**). Finally, children explore the topic of conserving and protecting Earth's water and observe bodies of water near where they live.

Professional Development Go online to view **Professional Development videos** with strategies to integrate CCCs and SEPs, including the ones used in this lesson.

Build on Prior Knowledge

Children should already know and be prepared to build on the following concepts:

- Information can be obtained from various sources. (*Grade 1, Unit 5, Lesson 3*)
- Matter exists in solid and liquid forms. (*Grade 2, Unit 2, Lesson 1*)
- Heating a solid can change it to a liquid. Cooling a liquid can change it to a solid. (*Grade 2, Unit 2, Lesson 3*)
- Patterns can be observed in the natural world. (*Grade 2, Unit 3, Lesson 3*)

Differentiate Instruction

RTI/Extra Support Make a chart to compare the bodies of water discussed in this lesson—ponds, lakes, rivers, and oceans. Work with children to list the features of each body of water, including size, surroundings, and type of water.

Extension Children who want to find out more can research a local body of water. They can share their findings with the class by drawing a map of the body of water. For example, children can research a local river to find out how it flows to the ocean and map and label the river and the other bodies of water into which it flows.

ELL Help children connect bodies of water to their own experiences by providing specific examples of ponds, lakes, rivers, and oceans with which they may be familiar. Be sure to point out all labels, pictures, captions, and headings throughout the lesson to assist children with strategies to summarize chunks of content.

Lesson Phenomenon

Build on Prior Lessons

In Unit 3, children **made observations** and **compared the diversity of life in water and land habitats to look for patterns in the natural world.** Lesson 1 builds on these concepts by exploring **places on Earth where water can be found** by obtaining information from various sources and looking for patterns in the natural world.

Lesson Objective

Gather information to identify that water is found in ponds, lakes, rivers, and oceans on Earth.

About This Image

Ask: **What do you see in this picture?** a wave **Where might you find a wave this size?** Sample answer: at the beach **Where else would you find water on Earth?** There are ponds and rivers in my neighborhood. Remind children that as they explore, they will find out more about different bodies of water on Earth.

 **The Roles of Water in Earth's Surface Processes**

Alternative Engage Strategy

Lists of Bodies of Water	👥 small groups 🕐 15–20 minutes

Have children form small groups. Guide each group to list the names of ponds, rivers, lakes, and oceans that they have visited or heard of. Allow 10 minutes for this portion of the activity. Then bring the children together to share their lists. Record the bodies of water in a single list under appropriate headings.

Lesson 1 Where Is Water Found on Earth?

Water is found in many places on Earth.

By the End of This Lesson

I will be able to identify where water is found on Earth. I will be able to describe characteristics of bodies of water.

186

Bodies of Water

Water can be found in many places on Earth. Look at the pictures to explore some bodies of water.

lakes

Explore online. ▶
river

ocean

pond

Can You Explain It?

✏️➤ Which body of water is closest to where you live? Describe what it is like.

Accept all reasonable answers.

_____

_____

Lesson 1 • Where Is Water Found on Earth?

187

Can You Explain It?

Bodies of Water Water can be found in different places on Earth. Allow children time to watch the video to find out more about bodies of water. If the video is not available, then review the four pictures showing lakes, a river, an ocean, and a pond. Ask children to share their observations about the bodies of water.

Have children record their initial thoughts about which body of water is closest to where they live and what it is like. Remind children not to be concerned if they are unsure of their answers. At the end of this lesson, children will revisit this question in the Lesson Check. At that point, they should be able to use details from the lesson to revise their answers, as needed.

Collaboration

Build on Prior Knowledge You may want children to view and discuss the pictures as a whole-class activity. In this way, you can assess their prior knowledge of bodies of water. **Ask: How are the pond and the lake similar? How is the river different from both the pond and the lake? Based on your experiences, how is an ocean different from ponds and lakes?** Answers will vary but should use details from the pictures as evidence to support the answers.

Support for Unit Project and Performance Task

The **Unit Project** Explore Ocean Water and **Unit Performance Task** Map an Island supports content in this lesson.

Lakes and Ponds

3D Learning Objective

Children **obtain information** to **identify patterns** in where **lakes and ponds** are found on Earth.

DCI **The Roles of Water in Earth's Surface Processes** . . . .

Have children compare and contrast lakes and ponds. **Ask: How are lakes and ponds alike?** They are both bodies of water that are surrounded by land. The water does not flow. The bottoms are covered with mud. The water is usually fresh water. **Ask: How are lakes and ponds different?** Lakes are usually bigger and deeper than ponds. Sometimes the water in a lake is salt water.

CCC **Patterns** . . . .

Ask: Suppose you find a body of water that is surrounded by land. What pattern would you look for to decide if it is a lake or a pond? Sample answer: I would look at the size of the body of water. Lakes are usually bigger and deeper than ponds. I would also look at the type of water. If the water is salty, it is a lake.

💡 **Patterns** Remind children to observe nature and look for a pattern, or something that repeats. They can use the pattern to describe what happens, or as proof of an idea.

Differentiate Instruction

ELL Some children may not know what fresh water is. Write *fresh* on the board. Explain that it can mean "not salty" or "new or recent" as in *fresh food*. Read aloud the sentence "Most lakes and all ponds have fresh water." Ask children to raise their hands when they hear the word "fresh." Discuss the meaning of this word as it relates to lakes and ponds.

Lakes and Ponds

Explore online. ▶

Look at the pictures to explore lakes and ponds.

lake

pond

Lakes are bigger and deeper than ponds, but lakes and ponds are alike in many ways.

Lakes and ponds are both surrounded by land. The water in both does not flow. The bottoms of lakes and ponds are covered with mud. Most lakes and all ponds have fresh water. These features are patterns because they show what lakes and ponds have in common.

💡 **Patterns**
Go to the online handbook for tips.

188

How are lakes and ponds alike?

Ⓐ They are both very deep.

Ⓑ They are both surrounded by land.

Ⓒ They are both made up of salt water.

Evaluating Information
Go to the online handbook for tips.

✋ **Apply What You Know**

Measure 1 gallon of water and 1 tablespoon of water. The gallon stands for all water on Earth. The tablespoon stands for all fresh water that people can drink. How does the total amount of water on Earth compare to the amount of water that people can drink?

The total amount of water on Earth is much greater

than the amount of water that people can drink.

© Houghton Mifflin Harcourt

SEP **Obtaining, Evaluating, and Communicating Information.** . . . .

Children should choose B—They are both surrounded by land. If children choose A or C, have them carefully observe the pictures of the lake and pond on the previous page. **Ask: How can you use these pictures to find out how lakes and ponds are alike?** Sample answer: I can see from the photos that both ponds and lakes are surrounded by land.

CCC **Patterns** . . . .

Discuss with children how they can use the patterns they found about lakes and ponds to find out how lakes and ponds are alike. **Ask: Which bodies of water are deep—ponds, lakes, or both?** lakes **Ask: Which bodies of water are surrounded by land—ponds, lakes, or both?** both **Ask: Which bodies of water can be made up of salt water—ponds, lakes, or both?** lakes, but only sometimes

 Evaluating Information Children can find out more about nature from reading and from pictures. They can also get information from headings, glossaries, and tables of contents. They can use what they find out to answer questions about nature and to tell why a fact is true.

✋ **FORMATIVE ASSESSMENT**

Children measure water to make a concrete model with which to compare the total amount of water on Earth to the amount of water that people can drink. Children may use words and pictures to answer the question.

Scoring Guidelines
- accurately compares the two amounts of water
- effectively communicates the comparison

Rivers and Oceans

3D Learning Objective

Children **obtain information** to **identify patterns** in where **rivers and oceans are found on Earth.**

(CCC) Patterns . . . .

Guide children to connect their personal experiences with the patterns described for rivers and oceans. **Ask: Have you ever seen a river in person or in a movie? What was the river like? How does it match the patterns about rivers?** Yes; the water in the river was fast; the water was not salty. **Ask: Have you ever seen an ocean in person or in a movie? What was the ocean like? How does it match the patterns about oceans?** Yes; the ocean was very big; the water was salty.

(DCI) The Roles of Water in Earth's Surface Processes . . . .

Children should write *rivers* in the first blank and *oceans* in the second blank. **Ask: Which word goes in the first blank? How do you know?** *Rivers* goes in the first blank because rivers are bodies of water that flow. **Ask: Which word goes in the second blank? How do you know?** *Oceans* goes in the second blank because rivers flow into other rivers, lakes, and oceans.

Collaboration

Jigsaw Have children form four groups. Assign each group a body of water—a pond, a lake, a river, or an ocean. Provide children with access to print and online resources. Challenge each group to identify two additional facts about their assigned body of water. Then reorganize children into groups of four with one child representing each body of water. Have children share their new patterns with the rest of their group.

Rivers and Oceans

Explore online. ▶

Look at the pictures to explore rivers and oceans.

river

ocean

Most rivers contain fresh water. Rivers may be wide or narrow. They all have land on two sides. Rivers begin on high ground. They flow downward into other rivers, lakes, and oceans. These features are patterns because they show what rivers have in common.

Oceans are the largest bodies of water on Earth. Ocean water is salty. Oceans cover most of Earth's surface and hold almost all its water. These features are patterns because they show what oceans have in common.

✏️ Write **oceans** or **rivers** to complete the following sentence:

There are different bodies of water.
___Rivers___ flow into ___oceans___.

190

Label each picture using the terms in the box.

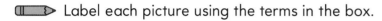

lake   ocean   pond   river

ocean

river

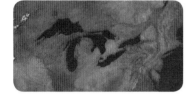

lake

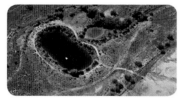

pond

Apply What You Know

Evidence Notebook • How does this map show that most water on Earth is salt water? Use evidence to support your answer. Record it in your Evidence Notebook. Compare your answer with a partner.

 **Communicating Information** Go to the online handbook for tips.

Lesson 1 • Where Is Water Found on Earth?   191

CCC Patterns

Ask: Which patterns about bodies of water did you use to label each picture? Sample answer: The picture on the top left shows a very big body of water, so I labeled it *ocean*. The top right shows flowing water with land on two sides, so I labeled it *river*. In the two bottom pictures, both bodies of water have land on all sides. The body of water on the left is bigger, so I labeled it *lake* and labeled the other one *pond*.

Differentiate Instruction

RTI/Extra Support Have children write features of bodies of water on index cards, one per card. Have children sort the index cards into *pond*, *lake*, *river*, and *ocean*. Remind children that some cards may go in more than one section.

Extension Children can work in pairs or small groups to make a game that teaches about bodies of water. Make sure children include facts about different bodies of water.

FORMATIVE ASSESSMENT

Evidence Notebook

Children explain how a world map shows that most water on Earth is salt water. They use evidence to support their answers and compare their answers with a partner.

Scoring Guidelines

• explains how the map shows that most water on Earth is salt water

• provides evidence to support their answer

Communicating Information Children can use drawings, writing, or both in order to communicate their answers. Remind children that it is important to share their information with others.

Liquid or Solid

3D Learning Objective

Children **obtain information** that water exists in solid and liquid forms on Earth and **identify patterns** in these forms.

ccc Patterns . . . .

Ask: Which type of water freezes at the higher temperature, salt water or fresh water? fresh water As the temperature gets colder and colder, which would you expect to freeze first, rivers or oceans? I would expect rivers to freeze first because they have fresh water and are smaller in size.

Do the Math! • Use Symbols

Children will use symbols to compare the temperature of a warm ocean, 71 °F, and the temperature of a cold ocean, 26 °F. Children should write the *greater than* symbol, >.

Use Symbols • Reason Abstractly and Quantitatively • Model with Mathematics Children can use symbols to represent the relationship between two quantities. To compare two-digit numbers, children can use place value. They start by looking at the digits in the greatest place value position, the tens. The number with more tens is the greater number. If the tens are the same, then children compare the ones.

DCI The Roles of Water in Earth's Surface Processes . . . .

Help children connect the temperatures with the effects on the oceans. **Ask:** Which ocean is warmer? How do you think it would feel to put your feet in that ocean? The 71 °F ocean is warmer. It might feel a bit cool to put my feet in. Which ocean is colder? How do you think it would feel to put your feet in that ocean? The 26 °F ocean is colder. It would feel very cold to put my feet in. Why did parts of the ocean in the picture on the right freeze? Parts of the ocean froze because the temperature dropped below 28 °F.

Liquid or Solid

Explore online. ▶

Look at the pictures to explore how bodies of water can be liquid or solid.

liquid at 71 °F

solid at 26 °F

In warm places, bodies of water are liquid. In cold places, ponds, rivers, and lakes may freeze if the temperature is low enough. Fresh water freezes at 32 degrees Fahrenheit (32 °F). Ocean water freezes at about 28 °F. An ocean will never freeze completely. It is too big and salty, and it moves too much. These features are patterns because they show what oceans have in common.

Do the Math! • You can use symbols to compare temperatures of a warm ocean and a cold ocean. Compare the numbers. Write >, <, or =.

71 °F (>) 26 °F

Use Symbols
Go to the online handbook for tips.

192

Look at the pictures to explore a lake in the summer and in the winter.

Explore online. ▶

summer

winter

Temperatures are warmer in summer and cooler in winter. This is a pattern. Sometimes it gets cold enough that water freezes.

Patterns • Evaluating Information Go to the online handbook for tips.

✏ Write **liquid** or **solid** to classify each body of water.

liquid   solid

liquid   solid

Lesson 1 • Where Is Water Found on Earth?   193

CCC Patterns . . . .

Discuss with children the patterns found in temperatures during the year. If temperatures in your area do not fluctuate very much, provide children with pictures of typical summer activities and clothing and pictures of typical winter activities and clothing.

Ask: How do temperatures change during the year? Sample answer: It is the warmest in summer and coolest in winter. Fall and spring are in the middle. **What can happen to ponds, rivers, and lakes if it gets cold enough?** They can freeze.

DCI The Roles of Water in Earth's Surface Processes . . . .

Children should write *liquid* next to the two pictures on the left and *solid* next to the two pictures on the right. **Ask: What happened to the bodies of water in the pictures on the right?** The temperature got cold, and the water froze. **What time of year do you think these pictures were most likely taken? How do you know?** in the winter, because temperatures are usually colder

💡 **Patterns** Remind children to observe nature and look for a pattern, or something that repeats. They can use the pattern to describe what happens or as proof of an idea.

💡 **Evaluating Information** Children can find out more about nature from reading and from pictures. They also get information from headings, glossaries, and tables of contents. Children can use what they find out to answer questions and to tell why a fact is true.

FORMATIVE ASSESSMENT

Children use a thermometer to measure the temperature at the same time each day for one school week and then use the data to make a bar graph. Children will discuss patterns in the data and determine if fresh water or salt water would freeze at the measured temperatures. Set aside time at the same time each day for one school week to allow children to measure the temperature.

Scoring Guidelines

• accurately measures temperature for one week
• uses the data to make a bar graph
• determines if fresh water or salt water would freeze at the measured temperatures
• discusses patterns with the class

💡 **Display Data • Reason Abstractly and Quantitatively • Model with Mathematics** Children can make a bar graph to display data. They can write the day of the week under each column. Then fill in each column based on what the temperature was each day. Once the bar graph is completed, children can analyze their data to look for patterns.

DCI The Roles of Water in Earth's Surface Processes . . . .

Ask: At what temperature will fresh water freeze? 32 °F **Ask:** At what temperature will salt water freeze? 28 °F **Ask:** Did you observe any temperatures below the freezing temperatures of fresh water and salt water? Answers will vary.

Apply What You Know

Does the temperature stay the same from day to day? Use a thermometer to measure temperature at the same time each day for one week. Use your data to complete the graph. Would fresh or salt water freeze at these temperatures? As a class, discuss patterns you see.

Display Data
Go to the online handbook for tips.

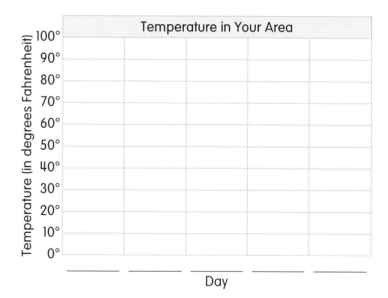

Accept reasonable answers. Check children's graphs.

194

Name _____

Hands-On Activity
Locate Bodies of Water

Materials
_____
_____

Ask a Question

What bodies of water are located near where I live?

Test and Record Data Explore online. ▶

Step 1
Make a plan to research bodies of water where you live.

Sample plan: I will look at a map of

my area to locate bodies of water.

Step 2
Record your data.

Bodies of Water	Characteristics
Check children's work.	

Lesson 1 • Where Is Water Found on Earth?   195

© Houghton Mifflin Harcourt

Hands-On Activity 👥 small groups 🕐 1 class period
Locate Bodies of Water

3D Learning Objective
SEP **Obtaining, Evaluating, and Communicating Information.** . . . .
Children will use a variety of resources to obtain information about bodies of water near where they live and will make posters to share this information with their classmates.

Suggested Materials print and online resources about an area where you live, posterboard, art materials

Preparation
Pre-assemble materials bundles for pairs or groups. Provide print and online resources.

Activity
As a class, view the video. Then discuss the question that will need to be answered. Have children record the question.

STEP 1 Guide children as they make a plan to research bodies of water where they live. **Ask: What types of resources would be helpful? What search words can you use**? Sample answer: A map of the local area and a computer would be helpful. I could use names from the map to help me search for information about the different bodies of water on the computer.

STEP 2 Allow children time to research and record their data. Remind children to use all of the resources they included in their plans. Encourage children to share with their group members as they identify a body of water.

CCC **Patterns** . . . .

Ask: What characteristics does the body of water have? Do these characteristics follow any patterns? Sample answer: I found a pond, a lake, and a river. Both the pond and the lake had fresh water and land surrounding it, but the lake was much bigger. The river had water on both sides of it and flowed into another river.

Hands-On Activity, continued

SEP **Obtaining, Evaluating, and Communicating Information. . . . .**

STEP 3 Ask: How can you organize your data? What titles and labels will you include? How can you show whether each body of water is a pond, lake, river, or ocean? Answers will vary.

STEP 4 Allow time for groups to share their posters with the class. Encourage children to ask their classmates questions during the presentations.

Claims, Evidence, and Reasoning

Children should make a claim about the bodies of water located near where they live. They should cite evidence based on the characteristics of the bodies of water.

Ask: How do you know if there is a lake nearby? Sample answer: The map shows a body of water that is surrounded by land and has a small river flowing into it.

	Scoring Rubric for Hands-On Activity
3	States a claim supported with evidence about the locations of bodies of water
2	States a claim somewhat supported with evidence about the locations of bodies of water
1	States a claim that is not supported with evidence
0	Does not state a claim and does not provide evidence

Step 3

Use your data to make a poster about bodies of water near where you live. Include a simple map that shows where the bodies of water are located.

Check children's posters.

Step 4

Share your poster with the class.

Make a claim that answers your question.

Answer should reflect the locations of local bodies of water.

_____

_____

_____

What is your evidence?

Answer should cite evidence from children's research.

_____

_____

_____

196

Explore online. ▶ Guide children to the Interactive Online Student Edition where they can choose from and explore both paths.

Take It Further

People in Science & Engineering •
John G. Ferris

Explore more online.
• How Can We Conserve Earth's Water?

Explore online. ▶

John G. Ferris was a scientist. He worked hard to take care of groundwater. Groundwater is water under Earth's surface between pieces of soil and rock. Groundwater is important. People drink it. People also use it to water crops. Ferris studied problems with groundwater, such as how to store it and how to keep it clean. He taught people how to care for groundwater.

© Houghton Mifflin Harcourt

Lesson 1 • Where Is Water Found on Earth?   197

Take It Further

People in Science & Engineering •
John G. Ferris

Children find out more about John G. Ferris, a scientist who studied groundwater. Groundwater is water under Earth's surface that acts as a source for drinking water and water for crops. John G. Ferris studied how to store, maintain, and care for groundwater.

DCI **The Roles of Water in Earth's Surface Processes . . . .**

Ask: Where do you think groundwater comes from? Sample answer: It comes from rain. **Why is groundwater important?** People use it to drink and to water crops. **What do you think it means to keep groundwater clean?** It means to keep dangerous things out of it. **Why should we try to keep groundwater clean?** If it isn't clean, it could make us sick from drinking it, or it could harm crops.

SEP **Obtaining, Evaluating, and Communicating Information. . . . .**

Discuss with children how they can find out more information about John G. Ferris and his work. **Ask: Where can you go to find out more about John G. Ferris and the importance of groundwater?** I can go to the library or lookup information on my computer. **Ask: What resources can help me?** non fiction books, encyclopedias, videos

Take It Further, continued

Exploring Groundwater

 SEP **Obtaining, Evaluating, and Communicating Information.** . . . .

Direct children to read the captions in the water cycle diagram, starting at the top left. **Ask: How many steps are in the water cycle?** 5 **Ask: What happens after water becomes surface water?** The cycle starts again. **Ask: Do you have to start at a particular place in the diagram? Explain why or why not.** No, it is a cycle, so you can start anywhere.

Connection to Life Science

Patterns The water cycle is a pattern that repeats over and over. Think about what plants need to live and grow. Have children work with a partner to write about the importance of the water cycle to plants.

Read, Write, Share! • Recall Information

Ask: What work did Dr. Ferris do with groundwater? He taught people why it is important and how to take care of it. **Ask: Why is groundwater important?** Sample answer: People drink groundwater and use it for crops. It is also part of the water cycle.

 Recall Information Remind children to read the question carefully. They should ask: "What information is this question asking about? Do I remember this information from something I've done or read?"

Explore more online.

How Can We Conserve Earth's Water?

Children explore pictures to find out more about water conservation.

Exploring Groundwater

Water on Earth moves from Earth into the air and back again. This movement is called the water cycle. This cycle includes groundwater.

Recall Information Go to the online handbook for tips.

The sun heats the water and turns it to a vapor. Water vapor rises into the sky and becomes water droplets.

Explore online.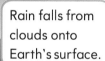

The water droplets form clouds. When the droplets become too heavy, it rains.

Rain falls from clouds onto Earth's surface.

The water flows into bodies of water and becomes surface water. The water cycle starts again.

Much of the rainwater seeps into the soil and becomes groundwater.

Read, Write, Share! • How has Dr. Ferris's work with groundwater helped make our lives better?

Sample answer: He taught people why groundwater

is important. People drink it and use it to water crops.

198

Explore online. ▶ Have children explore online to find out more about different bodies of water.

Lesson Check

Lesson Check   Name _____

Explore online. ▶

Can You Explain It?

✏️➤ Which body of water is closest to where you live? Describe what it is like.

Be sure to

• Name the body of water.
• Tell whether it is a pond, a lake, a river, or an ocean.
• Explain where it is located.

Check children's answers.

_____

_____

_____

Lesson 1 • Where Is Water Found on Earth?   199

Can You Explain It?

Have children reread their answers to the Can You Explain It? prompt at the beginning of the lesson.

DCI The Roles of Water in Earth's Surface Processes . . . .

Ask: Which of these pictures is most like the body of water closest to where you live? How can you identify the type of body of water? The picture of the river is most like the body of water where I live. I know it's a river because it has land on two sides and flows into another river.

CCC Patterns . . . .

Ask: Does the body of water change throughout the year? How? What does that tell you about the type of body of water? The river stays the same throughout the year because I live in a very warm area.

Scoring Guidelines

• Children should name the body of water that is closest to where they live.
• Children should tell whether the body of water is a pond, a lake, a river, or an ocean.
• Children should explain where the body of water is located.

Collaboration

Cultivating New Questions As children complete this lesson and prepare for the next lesson, ask them to identify additional questions they have about where water can be found. **Ask: What are some other bodies of water?** creeks, streams, seas, bays, estuaries, gulfs As children continue to the next lesson, they will apply concepts related to bodies of water in how to map water and land.

Lesson 1 • Where Is Water Found on Earth?   **199**

Lesson Check, continued

SUMMATIVE ASSESSMENT
Self Check

1. Children should choose C—They can be short or long. They can be narrow or wide. If children choose A, have them review the Rivers and Oceans section of the lesson. If children choose B, have them think about where a river starts.

2. Children should choose B—lake; and C—pond. If children choose only one correct answer, have them read the question carefully. If children choose A, have them review the Lakes and Ponds section of the lesson. You may want to have children look at the pictures of the four bodies of water on the Lesson Check page for additional support.

3. Children should choose A—river. If children choose B or C, remind them that lakes and ponds are surrounded by land. Then have them revisit the Lakes and Ponds section and the Rivers and Oceans section of the lesson.

Self Check

1. Which is true of rivers?
   - Ⓐ They are made up of salt water.
   - Ⓑ They flow from a low place to a high place.
   - **Ⓒ** They can be short or long. They can be narrow or wide.

2. Which has land all around it? Choose all correct answers.
   - Ⓐ ocean
   - **Ⓑ** lake
   - **Ⓒ** pond

3. Which flows into other bodies of water?
   - **Ⓐ** river
   - Ⓑ lake
   - Ⓒ pond

200

© Houghton Mifflin Harcourt

4. Which is true of oceans?
  Ⓐ They flow into rivers.
  Ⓑ They are smaller than lakes.
  Ⓒ They are made up of salt water.

5. Write **solid** or **liquid** to describe each body of water.

solid   liquid   liquid

6. What happens to a lake when it is very cold outside?
  Ⓐ Ice changes to liquid water.
  Ⓑ Liquid water changes to ice.
  Ⓒ Liquid water stays the same.

4. Children should choose C—They are made up of salt water. If children choose A or B, remind them that most of the water on Earth is salt water and oceans are the largest bodies of water. If possible, have children look at a world map and guide them to make the connection between the size of the oceans and the type of water that makes them up. Then have children review the Rivers and Oceans section of the lesson.

5. Children should label the first image as *solid* and each of the second and third images as *liquid*. If children answer incorrectly, review the differences between solids and liquids and have children provide examples of each from their personal experiences. Then have children revisit the Liquid or Solid section of the lesson.

6. Children should choose B—Liquid water changes to ice. If children choose A, remind them that ice is solid water and it changes to liquid when it is heated. If children choose C, have them read the question carefully. Point out that while water does not always freeze when it gets cold, the phrase "very cold outside" indicates that it is cold enough for the water to freeze. You may also direct their attention to the picture and ask whether the family is on solid water or liquid water.

Engineer It • How Can We Map Land and Water?

Building to the Performance Expectation

The learning experiences in this lesson prepare children for mastery of:

2-ESS2-2 Develop a model to represent the shapes and kinds of land and bodies of water in an area.

Trace Tool to the NGSS
Go online to view the complete coverage of these standards across the lesson, unit, and time.

 Science & Engineering Practices

Developing and Using Models
Develop a model to represent patterns in the natural world.

 VIDEO SEP: Developing and Using Models

 Disciplinary Core Ideas

ESS2.B: Plate Tectonics and Large-Scale System Interactions
Maps show where things are located. One can map the shapes and kinds of land and water in any area.

CCC Crosscutting Concepts

Patterns
Patterns in the natural world can be observed.

CONNECTIONS TO MATH

MP.2 Reason abstractly and quantitatively.

MP.4 Model with mathematics.

2.NBT.A.3 Read and write numbers to 1000 using base-ten numerals, number names, and expanded form.

2.MD.B.5 Use addition and subtraction within 100 to solve word problems involving lengths that are given in the same units, e.g., by using drawings (such as drawings of rulers) and equations with a symbol for the unknown number to represent the problem.

CONNECTION TO ENGLISH LANGUAGE ARTS

W.2.8 Recall information from experiences, or gather information from provided sources to answer a question.

Supporting All Students, All Standards

Integrating the Three Dimensions of Learning

This lesson introduces children to maps as drawings or models that show where things are located **(DCI Plate Tectonics and Large-Scale System Interactions)**. The lesson begins with children exploring how a map shows different types of land and bodies of water **(DCI Plate Tectonics and Large-Scale System Interactions)**. Then, children explore the parts of a map, including the map title, map key, and compass rose, and use a map key to interpret a map of the United States **(CCC Patterns)**. Finally, children extend their exploration in a hands-on activity in which they make a map of their school playground **(SEP Developing and Using Models)(CCC Patterns)**.

Professional Development Go online to view **Professional Development videos** with strategies to integrate CCCs and SEPs, including the ones used in this lesson.

Build on Prior Knowledge

Children should already know and be prepared to build on the following concepts:

- Models can be used to represent relationships in the natural world. (*Grade K, Unit 3, Lesson 3*)
- Water is found in ponds, lakes, rivers, and oceans. (*Grade 2, Unit 4, Lesson 1*)
- Patterns can be observed in the natural world. (*Grade 2, Unit 4, Lesson 1*)

Differentiate Instruction

Lesson Vocabulary

- map
- compass rose
- map title
- map key

Reinforcing Vocabulary To help children remember the vocabulary words, display a clearly labeled map in the classroom. Then have children define the words and use them in a sentence. Remind children to look for these highlighted words as they proceed through the lesson.

RTI/Extra Support Display a map of an area with which children are familiar. Help them connect the features of the map with the landforms and bodies of water they have seen before.

Extension   Children who want to find out more can investigate other types of maps that show land and water, such as topographical maps and 3D maps. Have children compare a topographical map or 3D map with a traditional physical map and share their observations with the class.

ELL Be sure to point out all labels, pictures, captions, and headings throughout the lesson to assist children with strategies to summarize chunks of content. Discuss with children real-life connections to content and provide hands-on examples of materials when possible to best support the needs of these learners.

Lesson Problem

Build on Prior Lessons

In Lesson 1, children used **various sources to obtain and evaluate information** about water on Earth in order to look for patterns. Lesson 2 builds on these concepts by exploring how **a map can be used to model** the shapes of both water and land in order to represent patterns in the natural world.

Lesson Objective

Develop a map to identify where land and water are located.

About This Image

Ask: What do you see in this picture? Sample answer: water and land This is a three-dimensional map. Why might a map like this be useful? Sample answer: It shows different types of landforms, such as mountains. Remind children that as they explore, they will find out more about how maps show different types of land and water.

 **Plate Tectonics and Large-Scale System Interactions**

Alternative Engage Strategy

Plan a Field Trip	small groups 15–20 minutes

Have children form small groups. Provide each group with a map of an amusement park, zoo, museum, or other destination. Have each group use their map to plan a field trip. Allow 10 minutes for this portion of the activity. Then have each group share their plan with the class. Make sure children explain how they used the map to help plan their visit.

Lesson 2

Engineer It • How Can We Map Land and Water?

This is a three-dimensional map.

By the End of This Lesson

I will be able to find locations using a map. I will be able to make a map.

202

Why We Use Maps

Look at this picture to explore a map.

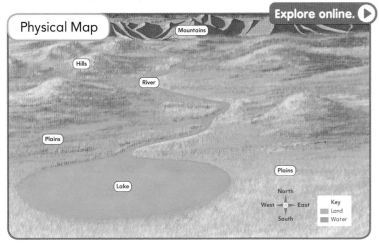

Physical Map

Explore online. ▶

Mountains

Hills

River

Plains

Plains

Lake

North
West ◆ East
South

Key
■ Land
■ Water

Can you find the land on this map? Can you find the water?

Can You Explain It?

✏️ What can you find out by exploring a map?

Accept all reasonable answers.

_____

_____

© Houghton Mifflin Harcourt

Can You Explain It?

Why We Use Maps Maps can help us find our way around or locate types of landforms and bodies of water. Have children look at the picture of the map on the page and describe what they see. **Ask: How do you know which parts of the map show land and which parts show water?** I can use the key in the corner of the map to tell me that the green parts are land and the blue parts are water.

Have children record their initial thoughts about some things they can find out by exploring a map. Remind children not to be concerned if they are unsure of their answers. At the end of this lesson, children will revisit this question in the Lesson Check. At that point, they should be able to identify types of land and bodies of water on the map. They should also be able to tell how to find directions.

Collaboration

Build on Prior Knowledge You may want children to view and discuss the map as a whole-class activity. Have children identify the various landforms and bodies of water shown on the map. Then ask them to compare and contrast different parts of the map (e.g., lakes and rivers, mountains and plains).

Support for Unit Project and Performance Task

The **Unit Project** Explore Ocean Water and **Unit Performance Task** Map an Island supports content in this lesson.

What Is a Map?

3D Learning Objective

Children explore maps that **model the natural world** and **show where things are located.** They will **identify patterns** in how maps represent **shapes and kinds of land and water.**

SEP **Developing and Using Models** . . . .

Remind children that a model is used to represent something. **Ask: What is the model?** the map **Ask: What does the map represent?** Sample answer: The map represents an area such as a country, a state, or a city.

DCI **Plate Tectonics and Large-Scale System Interactions** . . . .

Ask: What do these maps tell you about the United States, California, and Denver, Colorado? Sample answer: The maps all show the locations of different types of land and water.

Allow time for children to answer these questions and explain how they can use the map of the United States. **Ask: What does the map show?** It shows bodies of water and types of land. **What can you use the map to find?** You can find out where bodies of water and different types of land are, such as mountains, hills, plains, and deserts.

What Is a Map?

Look at these maps to explore the locations of different types of land and bodies of water.

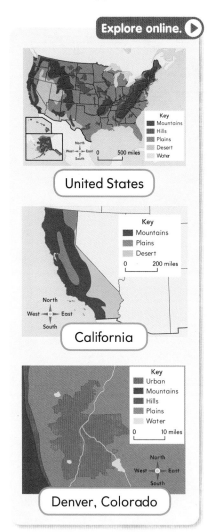

Explore online.

United States

Key
- Mountains
- Hills
- Plains
- Desert
- Water

North West East South   0   500 miles

California

Key
- Mountains
- Plains
- Desert

0   200 miles

North West East South

Denver, Colorado

Key
- Urban
- Mountains
- Hills
- Plains
- Water

0   10 miles

North West East South

A **map** is a drawing or a model of a place. It also shows the distance between two places. Some maps show the shapes of land and bodies of water in a location.

▭▶ **How can you use this map of the United States?**

You can use it to find

large bodies of water and

different types of land in

the United States.

_____

_____

204

© Houghton Mifflin Harcourt

✏️▷ Explore the parts of this map. Underline the sentence that tells what a map key shows. Circle the sentence that tells what a compass rose shows.

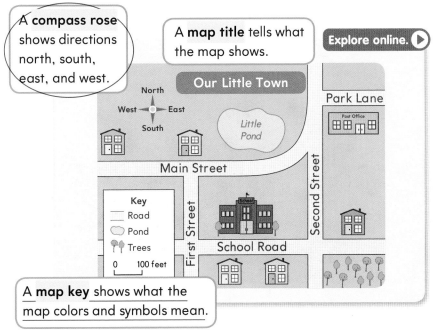

A **compass rose** shows directions north, south, east, and west.

A **map title** tells what the map shows.

Explore online. ▶

A **map key** shows what the map colors and symbols mean.

Our Little Town

Park Lane

Post Office

North
West — East
South

Little Pond

Main Street

First Street

Second Street

School

School Road

Key
— Road
⌒ Pond
🌳 Trees
0   100 feet

Apply What You Know

Evidence Notebook • With a small group, discuss why a map needs to have a compass rose. Use evidence to support your answer. Record it in your Evidence Notebook.

Patterns • Developing and Using Models
Go to the online handbook for tips.

© Houghton Mifflin Harcourt

SEP Developing and Using Models . . . .

Ask: How is this map like the maps on the previous page? It shows where different things are located. **How is it different?** It shows more details and things made by humans, such as roads and buildings, instead of just bodies of water and types of land.

CCC Patterns . . . .

Ask: What does the map key tell you? The map key tells you what the different symbols and colors on the map mean. **What does a compass rose tell you?** A compass rose tells you directions on a map. Guide children to see that these are patterns because a key and a compass rose are used again and again on different maps. Have children look at the compass rose on this page and the ones on the opposite page. **Ask: Do you see other patterns in the compass rose?** Sample answers: The compass rose shows north, south, east, and west. In these maps, the top is north, the bottom is south, the right side is east, and the left side is west.

 FORMATIVE ASSESSMENT

Evidence Notebook
Children should work in small groups to discuss why a map needs to have a compass rose. Make sure that children use evidence to support their answers.

Scoring Guidelines
- effectively communicates why a map needs to have a compass rose
- uses evidence to support their answer

💡 **Patterns** Children can observe nature and look for a pattern, or something that repeats. They can use the pattern to describe what happens or as proof of an idea.

💡 **Developing and Using Models** A model can show how something works. It can be a drawing or something you build. Children can use a model to show how things in nature are connected.

Use a Map Key

3D Learning Objective

Children use a map key to identify land and water features on a map and to observe patterns in the natural world. Children will construct a map to **represent patterns in the natural world.**

DCI **Plate Tectonics and Large-Scale System Interactions.** . . . .

Discuss the different types of land that are shown on the map. Have children describe or point to where each type of land is found on the map. **Ask: Where can you find mountains on the map? hills? plains? deserts?** Children should identify purple areas as mountains, green areas as hills, orange areas as plains, and yellow areas as deserts.

CCC **Patterns** . . . .

Tell children that some types of land are often found near each other. **Ask: What pattern do you notice in the locations of the mountains?** Sample answer: The mountains form long lines. **What pattern do you notice in the locations of the hills?** Sample answer: The hills are around mountains.

Differentiate Instruction

ELL Write the words *desert, hill, mountain,* and *plain* on the board. Have children read each word after you. Explain that these words tell about different types of land. Ask children to work in pairs to locate each land type label above or below the map. Then discuss how they can use the colors in the key to find these land types on the map.

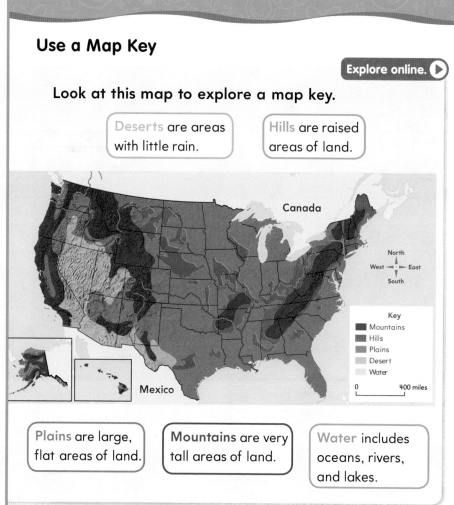

Use a Map Key

Explore online. ▶

Look at this map to explore a map key.

Deserts are areas with little rain.

Hills are raised areas of land.

Canada

North
West ✦ East
South

Key
■ Mountains
▨ Hills
▨ Plains
▨ Desert
▨ Water

0   400 miles

Mexico

Plains are large, flat areas of land.

Mountains are very tall areas of land.

Water includes oceans, rivers, and lakes.

© Houghton Mifflin Harcourt

Each color on a map key stands for a type of land. On the map, these colors show where each type of land is located. The map also shows where water can be found.

206

Which type of land covers most of the United States?

Ⓐ mountains

Ⓑ plains

Ⓒ deserts

✏️➤ Where is your state on the map of the United States? Locate it and record its name below.

Children should write the name of their state.

_____

✏️➤ What types of land and bodies of water are located in your state?

Children should identify all land types and bodies of water

in their state that are evident on the U.S. map.

_____

_____

_____

© Houghton Mifflin Harcourt

DCI Plate Tectonics and Large-Scale System Interactions . . . .

Children should select B—plains. If children answer incorrectly, review with children how to use the map key to identify the types of land on the map.

Ask: What types of land and bodies of water have you visited in our state or in neighboring states? Answers will vary. **Ask:** How can you use these types of land and bodies of water to help you find our state on the map? Sample answer: I know that we have mountains and we are near a desert, so I will look on the left side of the map.

Collaboration

Small Groups Allow children to work in pairs or small groups to locate your state on a map of the United States. Guide them to identify the types of land and bodies of water in your state. Monitor children as they work to ensure that they are collaborating and allowing each group member to contribute. Encourage children to explain their thinking and ask each other clarifying questions.

Connection to Life Science

Biodiversity and Humans Discuss with children how plants and animals live in different habitats on Earth. Point to the area showing a desert. Have children work in small groups to research the plants and animals that live in various habitats in a desert. Children should record their findings and share them with other groups.

FORMATIVE ASSESSMENT

Evidence Notebook

Children work with a partner to compare and contrast the Our Little Town map with a physical map of the United States. Make sure they use evidence to support their answers.

Scoring Guidelines

- effectively explains how the maps are alike and how they are different
- identifies patterns within and between the maps
- provides evidence to support their answers

Patterns Children observe nature and look for a pattern, or something that repeats. They can use the pattern to describe what happens or as proof of an idea.

Differentiate Instruction

RTI/Extra Support Have children work in pairs and make a list of the types of land shown on the physical map of the United States. Children should identify the color used for each type of land.

Extension Have children research online or in books to find a map of a city or state in the United States that shows mountains, hills, plains, desert, and/or water. Children should share their map with the rest of the class.

 Apply What You Know

Evidence Notebook • How are these maps alike? How are they different? What patterns do you see? Work with a partner to answer these questions. Use evidence to support your answers. Record them in your Evidence Notebook.

 Patterns Go to the online handbook for tips.

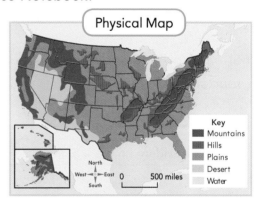

Physical Map

Key
Mountains
Hills
Plains
Desert
Water

North West—East South 0 500 miles

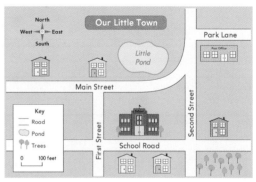

Our Little Town

North West—East South

Park Lane

Little Pond

Main Street

Key
— Road
Pond
Trees
0 100 feet

First Street
Second Street
School Road

208

Name _____

Hands-On Activity
Engineer It • Make a Map

Materials _____
_____

Ask a Question

How can I make a map of my school playground?

Test and Record Data Explore online. ▶

Step 1

Make a plan for your map. Record ideas and observations about your map's location.

Children's ideas should reflect the layout of the school playground.

_____

Step 2

Make your map. Be sure to include
• a title
• a key
• a compass rose

Children's maps should reflect the layout of the school playground and include a title, a key, and a compass rose.

Hands-On Activity 👥 small groups 🕐 1 class period

Engineer It • Make a Map

3D Learning Objective

SEP Developing and Using Models . . . .

Children make a map of their school playground, including a map title, a map key, and a compass rose. Children will compare their maps with their classmates' maps and look for patterns.

Suggested Materials posterboard, art materials

Preparation
Pre-assemble materials bundles for pairs or groups. Plan to visit the playground during a time when it is not in use.

Activity
As a class, view the video. Then discuss the question that will need to be answered. Have children record the question.

STEP 1 Guide children as they make a plan for their map. Take children to the playground, and have them record observations. Encourage children to stand on the highest safe surface available to get a bird's-eye view of the playground. Show children which direction is north, and have volunteers identify the other three directions. **Ask: Where is the entrance to the playground? What do you see when you first enter? How is the equipment arranged?** Answers will vary.

DCI Plate Tectonics and Large-Scale System Interactions . . . .
STEP 2 Distribute materials, and allow children time to make their maps. Remind children to use all of the parts they included in their plans. Encourage children to discuss with their group members as they decide on a key for their map.

Hands-On Activity, continued

STEP 3 Encourage children to use complete sentences to describe their map and their process for making it.

STEP 4 Have groups share and compare their maps. Alternatively, have groups present their maps to the class.

ccc Patterns . . . .

Have children discuss any patterns they observed in the maps. **Ask: What do all of your maps have in common?** Answers will vary depending on playground features. **Ask: Why is this a pattern?** It is a pattern because it happens again and again in our maps.

Claims, Evidence, and Reasoning

Children should write a claim about how they can make a map of the school playground. They should cite evidence to support the claim. **Ask: How did you decide where to place each item in the playground?** Sample answer: I thought about what other items it is near. **Ask: Why did you choose those colors for your key?** Sample answer: I chose green for grass because grass is green. I chose brown for the sandbox because the sand is light brown.

Scoring Rubric for Hands-On Activity	
3	States a claim supported with evidence about how to make a map of the playground
2	States a claim somewhat supported with evidence about how to make a map of the playground
1	States a claim that is not supported with evidence
0	Does not state a claim and does not provide evidence

Step 3

Describe your map and how you made it.

Check children's descriptions.

_____

_____

Step 4

Compare your map with the maps of your classmates. Identify patterns.

Make a claim that answers your question.

Answer should reflect items that appear on a school

playground (e.g., playground equipment, trees, water,

and other important features).

What is your evidence?

Answer should cite evidence from children's playground maps.

_____

_____

210

Explore online. ▶

Guide children to the Interactive Online Student Edition where they can choose from and explore both paths.

Take It Further

Careers in Science & Engineering •
Mapmakers

Explore more online.
• Use a Map Scale

Explore online. ▶

Mapmakers make maps and keep them up to date. They begin by collecting information about a location from other maps and from pictures taken from space. Then, mapmakers use tools such as computers, measurement tools, and the Global Positioning System (GPS) to make different maps.

Read, Write, Share! • **Find Out More About Mapmakers**

Do research to answer these questions.
• How do you become a mapmaker?
• What types of maps are made?
• What tools do mapmakers use?
• Would you like to be a mapmaker? Explain.

Gather Information
Go to the online handbook for tips.

Take It Further

Careers in Science & Engineering • Mapmakers

Children find out more about mapmakers and the process they follow to make and update maps. Mapmakers are also called cartographers. They use math, science, art, and technology to help them make maps.

DCI **Plate Tectonics and Large-Scale System Interactions** . . . .

SEP **Developing and Using Models** . . . .

Ask: Why do you think it is important for mapmakers to keep maps up to date? Sample answer: Places on the map could change, and the map needs to change to show what it looks like now. Do you think types of land or bodies of water are more likely to change? Why? Types of land are more likely to change because people might build something where there was a forest or field. How can mapmakers use technology such as computers, GPS, and pictures taken from space to improve their maps? Mapmakers can use technology to make sure the information is correct and to show types of land or water that they might not be able to see on their own, such as the tops of mountains or islands in the ocean.

Read, Write, Share! • **Find Out More About Mapmakers**

Provide children with access to print and online resources to conduct research about mapmakers.

💡 **Gather Information** When gathering information, children should listen carefully to the question to find out what information the question is asking about. Children can use the index and table of contents in books to find answers. They can also use the Internet to find answers.

Take It Further, continued

Do the Math! • Read Numbers

SEP Developing and Using Models . . . .

Discuss with children how a map scale shows how distances on the map relate to the actual distances. Guide children to see that this relationship is the same for all parts of the map. If objects on the map are the same size, they are the same size in real life. **Ask: Is a map the same size as the place it shows?** No, it is much smaller.

Children should write a 6 in each blank of the addition sentence. Be sure they understand that they are adding feet, not inches.

Read Numbers • Add Lengths • Reason Abstractly and Quantitatively • Model with Mathematics Children should read all of the numbers in a problem and think about what each number means. They should use a ruler to measure and write an addition sentence in order to solve the problem.

Differentiate Instruction

RTI/Extra Support Provide children with scale drawings of objects in the classroom. Use a scale of 1 inch = 1 foot for the drawings. Have children measure length in the drawings using a 12-inch ruler and the actual length using a ruler or yardstick. Guide children to understand the relationship between the sizes of objects in the drawing and in real life.

Extension Have children interpret the scale used in maps of your local area. Children can use the scale to find the actual distances between locations.

Explore more online. ▶

Use a Map Scale

Children explore how to use a map scale.

Do the Math! • Mapmakers must show distances on a map correctly. They must figure out a scale for each map. A map scale shows the relationship between the distance shown on a map and the actual distance it stands for.

Read Numbers
Go to the online handbook for tips.

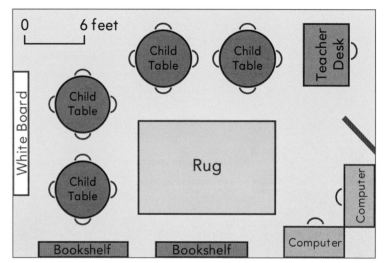

The scale on this classroom map is 1 inch = 6 feet.
The classroom is 36 feet long.
Use a 12-inch ruler to measure the map.
How long is the classroom on the map? _6_ inches.
Write an addition sentence to model how the map's measurement relates to the length of the room.

_6_ + _6_ + _6_ + _6_ + _6_ + _6_ = 36 feet

212

Explore online. ▶   Have children explore online to find out about the land and water shown on a physical map.

Lesson Check   Name _____

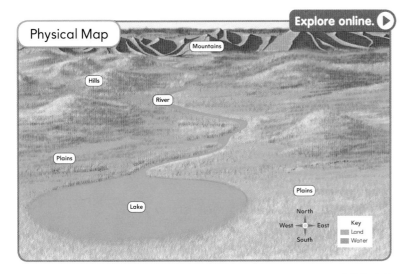

Physical Map

Explore online. ▶

Mountains

Hills

River

Plains

Plains

Lake

North

West ◆ East

South

Key
■ Land
■ Water

Can You Explain It?

✏️▷ What can you find out by exploring a map?

Be sure to

• Explain how to locate types of land and bodies of water on a map.

• Tell how to find directions.

Sample answer: This map shows the land and water in a location. You can use a map key to find out what types

of land and water are shown on the map and where they

are located. You can also find the directions north, south,

east, and west by looking at a compass rose.

Lesson 2 • Engineer It • How Can We Map Land and Water?   213

Lesson Check

Can You Explain It?

Have children reread their answers to the Can You Explain It? prompt at the beginning of the lesson.

DCI **Plate Tectonics and Large-Scale System Interactions** . . . .

If children have difficulty answering the question, have them look back at other maps in this lesson and review how the information was presented. **Ask: How do you know what the different colors show on the map?** I can look at the map key. **Ask: How do you know which direction the map is facing?** I can look at the compass rose.

SEP **Developing and Using Models** . . . .

Ask: How is this map like other maps you have seen in this lesson? How is it different? Sample answer: It is like other maps because it shows where the types of land and bodies of water are. It is different because it does not have a map scale and the key does not show the different types of landforms.

Scoring Guidelines

• Children should communicate how to locate types of land, bodies of water, and find directions on a map.

Collaboration

Cultivating New Questions As children complete this lesson and prepare for the next unit, ask them to identify additional questions they have about maps and what they show. **Ask: What are some other types of land that can be found on a map?** plateaus and valleys As children continue to the next unit, they will apply concepts related to types of land in order to explore how both fast and slow changes can affect Earth's surface.

Lesson Check, continued

SUMMATIVE ASSESSMENT
Self Check

1. Children should choose A—part of a map that tells direction. If children choose B or C, have them review the What Is a Map? section of the lesson. Guide children to name the parts of a map described in answer choice B (the title) and answer choice C (the key).

2. Children should choose C—the meaning of each color or symbol. If children choose A or B, have them review the What Is a Map? section of the lesson. Guide children to explain the purpose of the parts of a map described in answer choice A (to tell what the map shows) and answer choice B (to show the directions north, south, east, and west).

3. Children should choose A—a title; B—a compass rose; and C—a key with colors or symbols. If children choose only one correct answer, remind them to read the directions carefully and to choose all correct answers.

Self Check
1. What is a compass rose?
   Ⓐ part of a map that tells direction
   Ⓑ part of a map that tells what the map is about
   Ⓒ part of a map that tells what each color or symbol on the map means

2. What does the key on a map show you?
   Ⓐ the title
   Ⓑ the directions
   Ⓒ the meaning of each color or symbol

3. A teacher wants to make a map of her classroom. What should she include? Choose all correct answers.
   Ⓐ a title
   Ⓑ a compass rose
   Ⓒ a key with colors or symbols

214

© Houghton Mifflin Harcourt

4. Which parts of the map show mountains? Circle them.

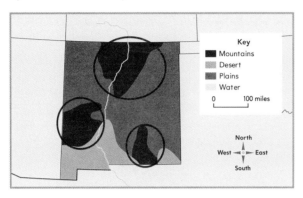

5. Which are shown on the map? Choose all correct answers.

Ⓐ desert
Ⓑ plains
Ⓒ water

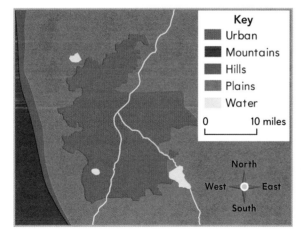

Lesson 2 • Engineer It • How Can We Map Land and Water?   215

4. Children should circle the three purple parts of the map. If children do not circle the correct parts of the map, have them revisit the Use a Map Key section of the lesson. Guide children to observe that mountains are shown on this map by the color purple.

5. Children should choose B—plains; and C—water. If children choose only one correct answer, remind them to reread the question carefully. If children choose A, have them look carefully at the key to identify the different types of land shown on the map.

Unit 4 Performance Task

Map an Island

 small groups ⏱ 1 class period

Objective

Children **develop a model (map)** to **show where land and water are located** and **to represent patterns in the natural world**.

Suggested Materials

paper, pencil, crayons or markers, examples of island maps

Preparation

Review Lessons 1 and 2 to provide context for this Unit Performance Task. Collect several maps showing islands in advance of this activity. Bring in an assortment of drawing tools, and have paper available for children to plan and design their map of an island.

SEP Developing and Using Models . . . .

Display the island maps for children to observe. **Ask: What do these different maps show?** Sample answer: The maps show all different kinds of islands.

STEPS

CCC Patterns . . . .

Step 1

Guide children in a discussion about the parts of a map and the structure of islands.

Step 2

Remind children what their maps need to include according to the directions in Step 2. **Ask: What are two different bodies of water you could include on your map?** Sample answer: We could include a river or a pond in addition to the ocean surrounding our island. **What are two types of land you could include on your map?** Sample answer: We could include plains and mountains.

 Unit 4 Performance Task
Map an Island

Materials

_____

_____

STEPS

Step 1

Look at maps of different islands. What pattern do you notice about islands? What does this tell you about the island you will draw?

Step 2

Make a plan for a map of your island and draw it. Include at least two different bodies of water and two different types of land. Look at other maps for ideas.

216

Step 3

Draw your map. Use colors and symbols to show the different bodies of water and land.

Step 4

Give your map a title. Add a compass rose and a map key to your map so others can read and understand it.

Step 5

Share your map with classmates, and describe your island. Compare maps, and look for patterns.

✔ Check

_____ I planned and drew a map of an island.
_____ I included two different bodies of water and two kinds of land.
_____ I included a title, a compass rose, and a map key.
_____ I compared my map to the maps of others.

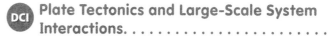

Plate Tectonics and Large-Scale System Interactions. . . . .

Step 3

Prompt children to draw a map of their island. **Ask: Where will you place water? How will someone else know it's water? What symbols will you use? What will those symbols mean or represent? How are colors helpful when you try to read a map?** Answers will vary.

Step 4

Guide children to add a map key and a compass rose to their map. **Ask: What information should you include in your map key? How does a compass rose help someone as they read your map?** The map key should identify bodies of water and types of land. The compass rose shows the directions north, south, east, and west.

Step 5

Children should share their maps with classmates. Guide children to compare maps and look for patterns.

Scoring Rubric for Performance Task	
3	Plans and designs a map of an island, includes a title, a compass rose, and a map key, and compares maps with other classmates to identify patterns
2	Plans and designs a map of an island, includes a title, a compass rose, and a map key, but does not compare maps with other classmates
1	Plans and designs a map of an island, but does not include a title, a compass rose, or a map key, and does not compare maps with other classmates
0	Does not plan, design, and share a map of an island

Unit 4 Review

SUMMATIVE ASSESSMENT

1. Children should choose C—a river. If children choose A or B, reinforce that rivers all have land on two sides. By completing Lakes and Ponds in Lesson 1, children explored water in lakes and ponds. By completing Rivers and Oceans in Lesson 1, children explored water in rivers and oceans.

2. Children should choose A—They are surrounded by land; and B—They contain fresh water. If children choose C, reinforce that ponds are smaller than lakes. By completing Lakes and Ponds in Lesson 1, children explored patterns in both lakes and ponds.

3. Children should choose A—The temperature fell below 32 °F. If children choose B or C, reinforce that fresh water will only freeze if the temperature falls to 32 °F or below. By completing Liquid or Solid in Lesson 1, children explored how temperature affects bodies of water.

4. Children should choose A—Most of Earth's water is salt water; and C—Most of Earth's water is in oceans. If children choose B, remind them of the map in the Apply What You Know activity in Lesson 1, in which they observed that most of Earth's surface is an ocean, as well as the Rivers and Oceans section in Lesson 1, in which they explored how ocean water is salty.

Unit 4 Review   Name _____

1. You see a body of water with land on two sides and flowing water. Which body of water is it?
   Ⓐ a lake
   Ⓑ a pond
   ● a river

2. Which are **true** of ponds? Choose all correct answers.
   Ⓐ They are surrounded by land.
   Ⓑ They contain fresh water.
   Ⓒ They are bigger than lakes.

3. Why did this pond freeze?
   Ⓐ The temperature fell below 32 °F.
   Ⓑ The temperature went above 32 °F.
   Ⓒ It is winter, and all ponds freeze in winter.

4. Which is **true** of Earth's water? Choose all correct answers.
   Ⓐ Most of Earth's water is salt water.
   Ⓑ Most of Earth's water is fresh water.
   ● Most of Earth's water is in oceans.

218

5. Why won't an ocean freeze completely?
   Choose all correct answers.
   (A) It is too big.
   (B) It is too salty.
   (C) It moves too much.

6. What are the different parts of a map? Draw a line to match each map part with the words that describe it.

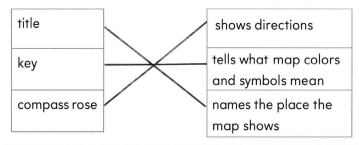

title	shows directions
key	tells what map colors and symbols mean
compass rose	names the place the map shows

7. Look at the map of New Mexico.
   What types of land does New Mexico have?
   Choose all correct answers.
   (A) desert
   (B) mountains
   (C) plains

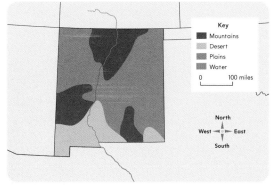

Key
■ Mountains
▨ Desert
▨ Plains
▨ Water
0   100 miles

North
West ◄─◆─► East
South

5. Children should choose all three answers: A—It is too big; B—It is too salty; C—It moves too much. Remind children of how large the ocean is and that it is filled with salt water that is constantly moving. By completing Liquid or Solid in Lesson 1, children explored why oceans do not freeze completely.

6. Children should make the following matches—*title* matched with *names the place the map shows*; *key* matched with *tells what map colors and symbols mean*; *compass rose* matched with *shows directions*. If children incorrectly match the map parts to their definitions, review the parts of the map. By completing What Is a Map? in Lesson 2, children explored the different parts of a map.

7. Children should choose all three answers: A—desert, B—mountains, and C—plains. Remind children that you can tell what information is found on a map by looking at the key. Children who answer incorrectly should refer back to Use a Map Key in Lesson 2.

8. Children should choose A—different types of land and water; and B—the distance between two places. If children choose C, have them think about their own experiences with using maps. By completing What Is a Map? in Lesson 2, children explored how maps can be used.

9. Children should choose A—10 + 10 = 20 miles. If children choose B or C, remind them that 1 inch on the map represents 10 miles. By completing Take It Further in Lesson 2, children explored using a map scale.

10. Children should choose B—south. If children choose A or C, review how to use the compass rose to locate direction. By completing What Is a Map? in Lesson 2, children explored how to use a compass rose.

3D Item Analysis	1	2	3	4	5	6	7	8	9	10
SEP Obtaining, Evaluating and Communicating Information							•			•
DCI The Roles of Water in Earth's Surface Processes	•	•	•	•	•					
DCI Plate Tectonics and Large-Scale System Interactions						•	•	•	•	•
CCC Patterns	•	•	•	•			•			•

8. What can a map show?
   Choose all correct answers.
   Ⓐ different types of land and water
   Ⓑ the distance between two places
   Ⓒ the time it takes to get to a place

9. Fay looks at a map that has a map scale with 1 inch = 10 miles. She measures 2 inches between her town and the next town. Which number sentence shows how many miles it is to the next town?
   Ⓐ 10 + 10 = 20 miles
   Ⓑ 10 + 2 = 12 miles
   Ⓒ 10 − 2 = 8 miles

10. Layla is at Little Pond. In what direction should she walk to get to the school?
   Ⓐ north
   Ⓑ south
   Ⓒ west

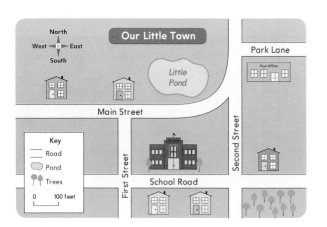

Unit 5
Changes to Earth's Surface

Unit Project • Make a Windbreak

How can you stop wind from changing the land? Investigate to find out.

Unit 5 • Changes to Earth's Surface   221

Unit 5 • Changes to Earth's Surface

Unit Overview

In this unit, children will…
- use evidence to explain that some changes to Earth happen slowly.
- use evidence to explain that some changes to Earth happen quickly.
- find solutions to prevent wind from changing the land.
- find solutions to prevent water from changing the land.

About This Image

Guide children in a discussion about the picture on this page. **Ask: What do you think is happening in this picture?** This is a dust storm caused by wind. **Ask: Why do you think this happens?** The wind picks up sand and pieces of dust or soil from Earth's surface and moves it to a new place.

Unit Project • **Make a Windbreak**

Have children plan and conduct an investigation to identify what a windbreak is and how to make a windbreak that will stop wind from changing the land. To begin, ask children if anyone knows what a windbreak is, or have children brainstorm ideas for what a windbreak may be. Discuss how a windbreak may stop wind from changing the land.

Ask children if they know other ways people have tried to stop wind from changing the land. Challenge them to use online resources to find information on the topic. More support for the Unit Project can be found on pp. 223I–223L.

Unit 5 At a Glance

The learning experiences in this unit prepare children for mastery of:

Performance Expectations

2-ESS1-1. Use information from several sources to provide evidence that Earth events can occur quickly or slowly.

2-ESS2-1. Compare multiple solutions designed to slow or prevent wind or water from changing the shape of the land.

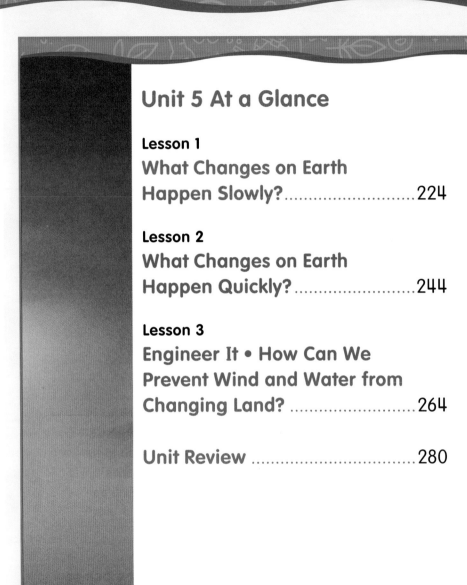

Unit 5 At a Glance

© Houghton Mifflin Harcourt • Image Credits: ©Henrik Johansson/Getty Images

Unit Vocabulary

weathering a process that breaks rock into smaller pieces (p. 226)

erosion the process of picking up and moving rocks, soil, and sand from one place to another (p. 232)

earthquake a sudden shaking of the ground (p. 246)

volcano an opening where lava erupts (p. 248)

landslide the sliding of soil down a slope (p. 250)

hurricane a storm with rain and strong winds (p. 253)

flood water that overflows or soaks an area (p. 255)

windbreak a row of trees used to block wind (p. 270)

dike a wall by a body of water (p.271)

Vocabulary Game • Make a Match

Materials
- 1 set of word cards
- 1 set of definition cards

How to Play
1. Make word and definition cards.
2. Place the cards face down on the table.
3. Pick a word card and a definition card.
4. If you make a match, keep the cards.
5. If not, put the cards back.

Unit Vocabulary

The Next Generation Science Standards emphasize explanation and demonstration of understanding versus rote memorization of science vocabulary words. Keep in mind that these vocabulary words are tools for clear communication. Use these words as a starting point, not an end goal, for children to build deeper understanding of science concepts.

Children can explore all vocabulary words in the **Online Glossary**.

Vocabulary Strategies

- Have children review the vocabulary words. Then have children work in pairs to share an example of each word and explain why they think it's an example. Have pairs record their examples to refer back to during the unit.
- Have children think about how each word relates to changes to Earth's surface. Have children work in pairs and share their ideas with a partner.

Differentiate Instruction

RTI/Extra Support Pronounce each word, and have children repeat it after you. Have children find each highlighted word within the unit content. Have children work in pairs and explain to a partner what they think each word means based on the surrounding context of imagery and text.

Extension Have children select two vocabulary words and work in small groups to illustrate and explain the words to a first-grade child.

Vocabulary Game • Make a Match

Preparation Assemble vocabulary and definition game cards. Assign partners or small groups for children to play the game. Provide instructions for how to play. Allow children to continue playing until all seven definition cards are used during gameplay.

Integrating the NGSS* Three Dimensions of Learning

Building to the Performance Expectations

The learning experiences in this unit prepare children for mastery of the following Performance Expectations:

Earth's Place in the Universe

2-ESS1-1 Use information from several sources to provide evidence that Earth events can occur quickly or slowly.

Earth's Systems

2-ESS2-1 Compare multiple solutions designed to slow or prevent wind or water from changing the shape of the land.

Assessing Student Progress

After completing the lessons, the **Unit Project** Make a Windbreak provides children with opportunities to practice aspects of and to demonstrate their understanding of the Performance Expectations as they plan and conduct an investigation to identify what a windbreak is and how to make a windbreak that will stop wind from changing the land.

Additionally, children can further practice or be assessed on aspects of the Performance Expectations by completing the **Unit Performance Task** Engineer It • Build an Earthquake-Proof Structure, in which children plan and design a solution to a problem in order to compare and test possible solutions for an earthquake-proof structure.

Lesson 1
What Changes on Earth Happen Slowly?

In Lesson 1, children observe how weathering by wind, water, ice, and plants causes Earth's surface to change slowly (**SEP Constructing Explanations and Designing Solutions**) (**DCI The History of Planet Earth**) (**CCC Stability and Change**). Then children observe how erosion by wind, water, and ice causes slow changes to Earth (**SEP Constructing Explanations and Designing Solutions**) (**DCI The History of Planet Earth**) (**CCC Stability and Change**). Finally, children extend their exploration in a hands-on activity in which they model erosion by water (**SEP Constructing Explanations and Designing Solutions**) (**DCI The History of Planet Earth**).

Lesson 2
What Changes on Earth Happen Quickly?

In Lesson 2, children explore how earthquakes, volcanoes, landslides, hurricanes, and floods cause Earth's surface to change quickly (**SEP Constructing Explanations and Designing Solutions**) (**DCI The History of the Planet Earth**) (**CCC Stability and Change**). Then, children will extend their exploration by modeling how a flood can cause Earth's surface to change quickly.

Lesson 3
Engineer It • How Can We Prevent Wind and Water from Changing Land?

In Lesson 3, children explore how wind and water cause the land to change over time (**DCI Earth Materials and Systems**) (**CCC Stability and Change**). Next, children explore ways to prevent changes to land through the use of different types of technology (**DCI Optimizing the Design Solution**) (**CCC Influence of Engineering, Technology, and Science on Society and the Natural World; CCC Science Addresses Questions About the Natural and Material World**). Finally, children will design, test, and compare possible solutions that will prevent water from changing the land (**SEP Constructing Explanations and Designing Solutions**).

Standards Supported by This Unit

Explore online.
Online only.

Next Generation Science Standards	Unit Project	Lesson 1	Lesson 2	Lesson 3	Unit Performance Task	You Solve It
SEP Constructing Explanations and Designing Solutions	•	•	•	•	•	•
DCI **ESS2.A** Earth Materials and Systems	•			•		•
DCI **ESS1.C** The History of Planet Earth		•	•			
DCI **ETS1.C** Optimizing the Design Solution	•			•	•	•
CCC Stability and Change		•	•	•	•	•
CCC Influence of Engineering, Technology, and Science on Society and the Natural World	•			•		
CCC Science Addresses Questions About the Natural and Material World				•		

NGSS* Across the Grades

Before

Coverage of the **Performance Expectations** within this unit originates in Grade 2.

Grade 2

Earth's Place in the Universe
2-ESS1-1
Earth's Systems
2-ESS2-1

After

Earth's Systems
4-ESS2-1 Make observations and/or measurements to provide evidence of the effects of weathering or the rate of erosion by water, ice, wind, or vegetation.

 **Trace Tool to the NGSS™** Go online to view the complete coverage of these standards across this grade level and time.

3D Unit Planning

Lesson 1 What Changes on Earth Happen Slowly? pp. 224–243

Overview

Objective Use information from several sources to provide evidence that some changes to Earth happen slowly over time.

SEP Constructing Explanations and Designing Solutions
DCI **ESS1.C** The History of Planet Earth
CCC Stability and Change

Math and **English Language Arts** standards and features are detailed on lesson planning pages.

	Print and Online Student Editions	Explore online. ▶
ENGAGE	**Lesson Phenomenon** pp. 224–225 **Can You Explain It?** Slow Changes to Earth's Surface	▶ Can You Explain It? Video
EXPLORE/ EXPLAIN	**Weathering by Wind** **Weathering by Water and Ice** **Weathering by Plants** **Erosion by Wind** **Erosion by Water and Ice** 🔍 **Hands-On Activity** Model Erosion pp. 237–238	**Hands-On** Worksheet
ELABORATE	**Take It Further** pp. 239–240 Careers in Science & Engineering • Farming	Take It Further How Does a Delta Form?
EVALUATE	**Lesson Check** p. 241 **Self Check** pp. 242–243	Lesson Quiz

Hands-On Activity Planning

Model Erosion

Objective Children will build a model of a stream to observe what happens to Earth's surface during erosion caused by water.

👥 small groups
🕐 1 class period

Suggested Materials
- disposable plastic gloves
- small rocks
- soil
- sand
- a foil tray or plastic tub
- a small book
- a container of water
- a plastic cup
- safety goggles

Preparation/Tip

Preassemble material bundles for small groups. Place newspaper on top of desks or tables to keep them from getting dirty or wet. Have paper towels handy.

Lesson 2 What Changes on Earth Happen Quickly? pp. 244–263

Overview

Objective Use information from several sources to provide evidence that some changes on Earth can happen quickly.

SEP Constructing Explanations and Designing Solutions
DCI **ESS1.C** The History of Planet Earth
CCC Stability and Change

Math and **English Language Arts** standards and features are detailed on lesson planning pages.

	Print and Online Student Editions	Explore online. ▶
ENGAGE	**Lesson Phenomenon** pp. 244–245 **Can You Explain It?** Quick Changes to Earth's Surface	▶ Can You Explain It? Video
EXPLORE/ EXPLAIN	**Earthquakes** **Volcanoes** **Landslides** **Hurricanes** **Floods** ◯ **Hands-On Activity** Model Quick Changes on Earth pp. 257–258	Hands-On Worksheet
ELABORATE	**Take It Further** pp. 259–260 People in Science & Engineering • Dr. Rosaly M.C. Lopes	Take It Further Earthquake Locations
EVALUATE	**Lesson Check** p. 261 **Self Check** pp. 262–263	Lesson Quiz

Hands-On Activity Planning

Model Quick Changes on Earth

Objective Children will build a model to observe what happens to Earth's surface during a flood.

👥 small groups
🕑 1 class period

Suggested Materials
• water
• a container
• rocks
• soil
• sand
• disposable plastic gloves

Preparation/Tip
Preassemble material bundles for small groups. Place newspaper on top of desks or tables to keep them from getting dirty or wet. Have paper towels handy.

3D Unit Planning, continued

Lesson 3 Engineer It • How Can We Prevent Wind and Water From Changing Land? pp. 264 - 279

Overview

Objective Compare design solutions that prevent wind and water from changing the land.

SEP Constructing Explanations and Designing Solutions
DCI ESS2.A Earth Materials and Systems
DCI ETS1.C Optimizing the Design Solution
CCC Stability and Change
CCC Influence of Engineering, Technology, and Science on Society and the Natural World
CCC Science Addresses Questions About the Natural and Material World

Math and **English Language Arts** standards and features are detailed on lesson planning pages.

	Print and Online Student Editions	Explore online.
ENGAGE	Lesson Problem pp. 264–265 **Can You Solve It?** Preventing Changes to Land	Can You Solve It? Video
EXPLORE/ EXPLAIN	**Changes Caused by Wind** **Changes Caused by Water** **Ways to Prevent Changes to Land** **Hands-On Activity** Engineer It • Prevent Water from Changing Land pp. 273–274	**Hands-On** Worksheet **You Solve It** Preventing Wind Erosion
ELABORATE	**Take It Further** pp. 275–276 **Careers in Science & Engineering •** Geotechnical Engineer	Take It Further The Dust Bowl
EVALUATE	**Lesson Check** p. 277 **Self Check** pp. 278–279	Lesson Quiz

Hands-On Activity Planning

Engineer It • Prevent Water from Changing Land

Objective Children will design, test, and redesign possible solutions that will prevent water from changing land. Children will then communicate their findings to others.	👥 small groups 🕑 1 class period

Suggested Materials
- disposable plastic gloves
- soil
- small cup or container
- foil tray or plastic tub
- water in a pitcher or other large container
- toothpicks
- craft sticks
- straws
- chenille sticks
- small rocks
- glue or tape
- clay or modeling clay

Preparation/Tip
Have children brainstorm the materials they might use the day before conducting the hands-on activity. Then preassemble the materials before conducting the hands-on activity.

You Solve It — Go online for an additional interactive activity.

Preventing Wind Erosion

This interactive activity offers practice in support of **PE 2-ESS2-1.**

SEP Constructing Explanations and Designing Solutions

DCI ESS2.A Earth Materials and Systems

DCI ETS1.C Optimizing the Design Solution

CCC Stability and Change

3D Learning Objectives

- Identify ways to prevent wind erosion from changing the land.
- Choose either a beach or farmland, and choose methods to prevent wind erosion for that type of land.

Activity Problem

- Choose between beach and farmland.
- Watch how the land changes with wind erosion, and then choose a method to try to prevent wind erosion.

Interaction Summary

- Choose the type of land: beach or farmland.
- Watch an animation of how the wind changes the land.
- Choose a method to try to prevent wind erosion.
- Watch an animation to see if the method is effective.
- Take screenshots.

Assessment

Preassessment

Assessment Guide, Unit Pretest

The Unit Pretest focuses on prerequisite knowledge and is composed of items that evaluate children's preparedness for the content covered within this unit.

Formative Assessment

Interactive Worktext, Apply What You Know, Lesson Check, and Self Check

Summative Assessment

Assessment Guide, Lesson Quiz

The Lesson Quiz provides a quick assessment of each lesson objective and of the portion of the Performance Expectation aligned to the lesson.

Interactive Worktext, Performance Task pp. 280–281

The Performance Task presents the opportunity for children to collaborate with classmates in order to complete the steps of each Performance Task. Each Performance Task provides a formal Scoring Rubric for evaluating children's work.

Interactive Worktext, Unit 5 Review, pp. 282–284

Assessment Guide, Unit Test

The Unit Test provides an in-depth assessment of the Performance Expectations aligned to the unit. This test evaluates children's ability to apply knowledge in order to explain phenomena and to solve problems. Within this test, Constructed Response items apply a three-dimensional rubric for evaluating children's mastery on all three dimensions of the Next Generation Science Standards.

 **Assessment Online** — Go online to view the complete assessment items for this unit.

Differentiate Instruction

Leveled Readers

The Science & Engineering Leveled Readers provide additional nonfiction reading practice in this unit's subject area.

On Level • Why Are Resources Important?
This reader reinforces unit concepts and includes response activities for children.

Extra Support • Why Are Resources Important?
This reader shares the title, illustrations, vocabulary, and concepts with the On-Level Reader; however, the text is linguistically accommodated to provide simplified sentence structures and comprehension aids. It also includes response activities.

Enrichment • All About Rocks
This high-interest, nonfiction reader will extend and enrich unit concepts and vocabulary and includes response activities.

Teacher Guide
The accompanying Teacher Guide provides teaching strategies and support for using all the readers.

ELL

English Language Learner support resources include a glossary and Leveled Readers in Spanish and English. ELL teaching strategies appear throughout this unit:

pp. 224B, 226, 233, 244B, 248, 264B, 271

RTI/Extra Support

Strategies for children who need extra support appear throughout this unit:

pp. 223, 223I, 224B, 228, 238, 239, 244B, 255, 259, 264B, 268, 275

Extension

Strategies for children who have mastered core content and are ready for additional challenges appear throughout this unit:

pp. 223, 223I, 224B, 228, 238, 239, 244B, 255, 259, 264B, 268, 275

▶ **Leveled Readers** All readers are available online as well as in an innovative, engaging format for use with touchscreen mobile devices. Contact your HMH Sales Representative for more information.

Connecting with NGSS

Connections to Community

Use these opportunities for informal science learning to provide local context and to extend and enhance unit concepts.

At Home

Break Water Have children experiment with objects they can use to block the spray of water from a bathtub or sink. Remind children to take care not to make a mess. Children can write their observations about the effectiveness of different objects in a log book.
Use with Lesson 3.

In the Community

Guest Speaker Invite an engineer to speak to the class about how structures are designed and built to protect Earth's surface from wind or water. Alternatively, invite a farmer to speak to the class about how they prevent soil erosion in their fields. Have children prepare questions for him or her to answer. Encourage children to ask a mix of appropriate science and engineering questions.
Use with Lesson 3.

Observe Erosion Plan a class field trip to a local park, stream, or wooded area. Have children observe the area, looking for signs of erosion. Discuss whether the erosion was caused by wind, water, or both. After returning to the classroom, have children draw pictures of the erosion they observed.
Use with Lesson 1.

Culture

Folktales Hawaii is famous for its volcanoes. There are five major volcanoes -- Loihi, Kilauea, Mauna Loa, Hualalai, and Haleakala. There are folktales associated with the volcanoes of Hawaii. Have small groups research a folktale and display their findings in a poster to share with the class.
Use with Lesson 2.

Home Letters Go online to view the Home Letters for this unit.

Collaboration

Collaboration opportunities in this unit:

Build on Prior Knowledge
pp. 225, 245, 265

Jigsaw
pp. 230, 270

Small Groups
pp. 239, 260, 276

Cultivating New Questions
pp. 241, 261, 277

Think, Pair, Share
p. 253

Connections to Science

Connections to Science opportunities in this unit:

Connection to Engineering Design
Defining and Delimiting Engineering Problems
Lesson 1, p. 232
Connection to Physical Science
Chemical Reactions Lesson 2, p. 252
Connection to Life Science
Cause and Effect Lesson 3, p. 266

Unit Project

👥 small groups 🕐 1 class period

Make a Windbreak

There are many ways to complete this Unit Project. The steps and Suggested Materials indicate one way to complete the investigation. Encourage children to come up with their own ideas of how to make a windbreak. If children decide to follow another process to complete their investigation, be sure to review each group's plans before the children begin. Provide guidance for groups that may have strayed off topic. This Unit Project supports content in Lessons 1 and 3.

3D Learning Objective

SEP Constructing Explanations and Designing Solutions

Design and test a windbreak. Make observations to use as evidence to answer a question. Construct an argument using evidence to support a claim.

Skills and Standards Focus

This project supports building children's mastery of **Performance Expectations 2-ESS1-1 and 2-ESS2-1.**

SEP Constructing Explanations and Designing Solutions
DCI **ESS2.A** Earth Materials and Systems
DCI **ETS1.C** Optimizing the Design Solution
CCC Influence of Engineering, Technology, and Science on Society and the Natural World

Suggested Materials

- 2 same-size flat boxes
- sand or loose soil
- fan or hair dryer
- cardboard, wood, clay
- safety goggles

Preparation

Have enough boxes and safety goggles available for each pair or group of children. Remind children to arrange the sand the same way in both boxes. Monitor children as they pour the sand. Children should wear safety goggles when they turn on the fan or hair dryer. Remind children to use the lowest setting possible and to hold the fan or hair dryer at least one arm's length away from the sand.

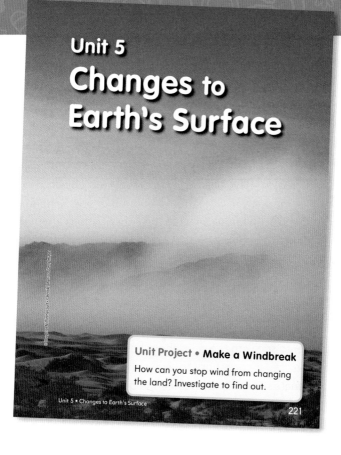

Unit 5
Changes to Earth's Surface

Unit Project • Make a Windbreak
How can you stop wind from changing the land? Investigate to find out.

Unit 5 • Changes to Earth's Surface
221

Differentiate Instruction

RTI/Extra Support Children can be provided with 2–4 ideas for making a windbreak. They can then choose their method to investigate.

Extension Challenge children to model a terrain other than a sandy beach, such as sand or soil on a hillside.

Name _____

 ## Unit 5 Project
Make a Windbreak

What is a windbreak? How can a windbreak stop wind from changing the land? Write your ideas on the lines below. Then choose two ideas to test. Plan and conduct an investigation to find out.

Children should write ideas they have for what a windbreak is and
_____
how it can stop wind from changing the land.
_____

_____

Materials
Draw and label the materials you will need.

> Children should draw and label materials. The following are possible materials children can use for this investigation: two boxes, sand or loose soil, fan or hair dryer, cardboard, wood, clay, and safety goggles

Unit 5 Project • Page 1 of 3

Unit 5 Project

Make a Windbreak

SEP **Constructing Explanations and Designing Solutions** . . . .

Pose the Unit Project question to children. Discuss what a windbreak is. **Ask: What do you think a windbreak does?** It stops the wind. Encourage children to think of different ways a windbreak can stop wind from changing the land. Discuss all of the ideas as a class. Have children use print and online resources to find out more about windbreaks.

In the sample investigation shown, children compare how the sand in two boxes changes when exposed to wind from a fan. They compare how the sand moves when cardboard is placed in front of one box and how sand moves in a box without cardboard. Then have children redesign their solution and test again.

Children will cover the bottom two shallow boxes with sand. They will place a piece of cardboard in front of one box and then point a fan at both boxes. **Ask: Which box of sand will change more? Why?** I think the box without the cardboard in front of it will change more because there is nothing blocking the wind from moving the sand.

ESSENTIAL QUESTIONS Prepare children for their project by asking the following questions.

- What are some ways that wind can change Earth's surface?
- When might wind cause Earth's surface to change quickly?
- When might wind cause Earth's surface to change slowly?

Ask: What do you think will happen when the fan blows air on the sand? I think the fan will act like wind and move the sand.

Steps

Discuss with children why it is important to list the steps in their investigation. If children need support, brainstorm the steps together as a class.

(CCC) Influence of Engineering, Technology, and Science on Society and the Natural World. . . .

Discuss with children the process by which windbreaks block wind. **Ask: How will you use your materials to model the way a windbreak works?** Sample answer: I will use cardboard to model the structure of the windbreak. I will use the fan to model the wind. **Ask: Do you think people use only one kind of windbreak? Explain.** No. There are many different kinds of land and different uses for land, so there are probably different kinds of windbreaks.

(DCI) Earth Materials and Systems . . . .

Before beginning the investigation, have children observe sand in both boxes. **Ask: How would you describe the sand?** The sand is flat and smooth and spread across the bottom of the box. Challenge children to identify the type of change they are modeling with the fan blowing on the sand. **Ask: How is the wind blowing on the sand changing the surface of the sand in the box?** The wind is blowing the sand like erosion. Refer children to Lesson 1 What Changes on Earth Happen Slowly? Have them record their observations using words and pictures.

Data

Remind children to make observations as they investigate. Observations can be used as data to determine the outcome of the investigation.

(DCI) Optimizing the Design Solution . . . .

Have children redesign their windbreaks in order to compare their solutions. **Ask: Which solution worked better?** Answers may vary.

Steps Write the steps you will do.

Answers may vary but should reflect a logical order of steps in the investigation. Sample steps listed:

1. Cover the bottom of two boxes with sand.

2. Place a piece of cardboard in front of the sand in one box.

3. Point the fan at the boxes and turn it on.

4. Observe and record how the sand in each box changes.

5. Redesign your idea and then compare the two solutions.

Data

Record your data.

> Answers and drawings may vary but should reflect how the two design solutions stopped the sand from changing.

Analyze Your Results

Look for patterns in your data.

Restate Your Question

Write the question you investigated.

Answers should identify the question children initially chose at the

beginning of the investigation.

Claims, Evidence, and Reasoning

Make a claim that answers your question.

Answers should identify how the windbreak stopped the

sand from moving and which solution worked best.

Review the data. What evidence from the investigation supports your claim?

Answers should cite evidence from the investigation to support their

claim about how the windbreak protects the sand.

Discuss your reasoning with a partner.

Analyze Your Results

 **Optimizing the Design Solution** . . . .

Have children analyze their data. Elicit from them any patterns they noticed. Encourage them to share their data with the other groups in order to compare test results. **Ask: What types of windbreaks were most effective at preventing the fan from blowing the sand?** Answers may vary.

Claims, Evidence, and Reasoning

Children should understand that the sand in the box with the windbreak moved less than the sand in the box without the windbreak. They should compare their solutions to see which worked best.

Review with children what it means to make a claim. Guide them to understand that the data they collected will be used as evidence to support their claim. **Ask: What can you use as evidence from your investigation?** I can use the data collected, such as the drawings and writings.

Ask: What claim can you make? Windbreaks protect sand from the wind. **How does your evidence support your claim?** My evidence supports this because the sand in the box with the windbreak moved less than the sand in the box without the windbreak. Encourage children to discuss their reasoning.

Scoring Rubric for Unit Project	
3	States a claim supported with evidence that the windbreak protects the sand from the wind
2	States a claim somewhat supported with evidence that the windbreak protects the sand from the wind
1	States a claim that is not supported by evidence
0	Does not state a claim and does not provide evidence

Lesson 1 # What Changes on Earth Happen Slowly?

Building to the Performance Expectation

The learning experiences in this lesson prepare children for mastery of:

2-ESS1-1 Use information from several sources to provide evidence that Earth events can occur quickly or slowly.

 Trace Tool to the NGSS
Go online to view the complete coverage of these standards across this lesson, unit, and time.

 **Science & Engineering Practices**

Constructing Explanations and Designing Solutions
Make observations from several sources to construct an evidence-based account for natural phenomena.

 VIDEO SEPs: Constructing Explanations and Designing Solutions / Engaging in Argument from Evidence

Disciplinary Core Ideas

ESS1.C: The History of Planet Earth
Some events happen very quickly; others occur very slowly, over a time period much longer than one can observe.

Crosscutting Concepts

Stability and Change
Things may change slowly or rapidly.

 VIDEO CCC: Stability and Change

CONNECTIONS TO MATH

MP.2 Reason abstractly and quantitatively.

MP.4 Model with mathematics.

2.NBT.A.1 Understand place value.

CONNECTIONS TO ENGLISH LANGUAGE ARTS

RI.2.1 Ask and answer such questions as *who, what, where, when, why,* and *how* to demonstrate understanding of key details in a text.

W.2.7 Participate in shared research and writing projects (e.g., read a number of books on a single topic to produce a report; record science observations).

W.2.8 Recall information from experiences or gather information from provided sources to answer a question.

SL.2.2 Recount or describe key ideas or details from a text read aloud or information presented orally or through other media.

Supporting All Students, All Standards

Integrating the Three Dimensions of Learning

This lesson focuses on how weathering and erosion cause slow changes to Earth. Children observe how weathering by wind, water, ice, and plants causes Earth's surface to change slowly **(SEP Constructing Explanations and Designing Solutions) (DCI The History of Planet Earth) (CCC Stability and Change)**. Then children observe how erosion by wind, water, and ice causes slow changes to Earth **(SEP Constructing Explanations and Designing Solutions) (DCI The History of Planet Earth) (CCC Stability and Change)**. Finally, children extend their exploration in a hands-on activity in which they model erosion by water **(SEP Constructing Explanations and Designing Solutions) (DCI The History of Planet Earth)**.

 Professional Development

Go online to view **Professional Development videos** with strategies to integrate CCCs and SEPs, including the ones used in this lesson.

Build on Prior Knowledge

Children should already know and be prepared to build on the following concepts:

- Observations can be used as evidence. *(Grade 2, Unit 2, Lesson 2)*
- Earth has weather patterns that may include wind and water. *(Grade K, Unit 5, Lesson 1)*
- Liquid water can change state to become solid ice. *(Grade 2, Unit 4, Lesson 1)*
- Events in nature can happen quickly or slowly.

Differentiate Instruction

Lesson Vocabulary
- erosion
- weathering

Reinforcing Vocabulary To help children remember these vocabulary words, show them different pictures of erosion or weathering. Then have children write the words and use them in a sentence. Remind children to look for these highlighted words as they proceed through the lesson.

RTI/Extra Support Place the word *weathering* on one side of a bulletin board and the word *erosion* on the other side. Ask children to look for pictures (or take pictures) where these things are happening and add them to the bulletin board next to the correct word.

Extension Challenge children to search for evidence of weathering or erosion in the area they live. Have children make a poster or slideshow to describe how the weathering or erosion takes place slowly over time.

ELL Be sure to point out all labels, pictures, captions, and headings throughout the lesson to assist children with strategies to summarize chunks of content. Discuss with children real-life connections to content, and provide hands-on examples of materials when possible to best support the needs of these learners.

Lesson Phenomenon

Build on Prior Lessons

In Unit 4, children explored bodies of water and their different states. They modeled land and water on maps to look for patterns in the natural world. Lesson 1 builds on these concepts to explore how water can cause slow changes to Earth's surface.

Lesson Objective

Use information from several sources to provide evidence that some changes to Earth happen slowly over time.

About This Image

Explain to children that this was once a solid, round piece of rock. **Ask: What do you think happened to make this rock look like an arch?** Sample answer: The wind may have blown out the center of the rock.

 The History of Planet Earth

Alternative Engage Strategy

Splashes and Gusts	👥 small groups 🕓 15–25 minutes

Place a pile of soil, rocks, and sand in the center of light-colored box tops. Show children that you have a small container of water and a fan. **Ask: What do you think will happen to the things on this table if water is splashed on them?** Allow time for children to brainstorm answers. Next, to symbolize rain, splash a small amount of water on each pile. Have children observe the box tops around each pile and discuss. **Ask: What do you think will happen to the things on this table if I point the fan in their direction?** Allow children time to brainstorm. To represent wind gusts, turn the fan so the air blows over each pile. Have children observe and discuss any changes noted.

Lesson 1 What Changes on Earth Happen Slowly?

Nature slowly changes rocks on Earth.

By the End of This Lesson
I will be able to describe some changes that happen slowly on Earth.

224

Can You Explain It?

Slow Changes to Earth's Surface Changes to Earth can be made through slow events or fast events. The rocks shown in the video make up part of Bryce Canyon and have slowly formed over time. If the video is not available, guide children in a discussion of the two pictures on the page. **Ask: What caused the changes to the rocks seen in this canyon?** Accept all reasonable answers.

Ask children to record their initial thoughts on what caused the slow changes to the rocks in the pictures. Remind children not to be concerned if they are unsure of their answers. At the end of the lesson, children will revisit these pictures as part of the Lesson Check. At this point, children should be able to explain that weathering and erosion cause slow changes to rocks.

Collaboration

Build on Prior Knowledge Allow children time to discuss places they have seen in their neighborhood where sand or soil appears to be changing. Guide children to think about a playground or ball field where there may be sand or soil, and heavy rains have caused a rut.

Support for Unit Project

The **Unit Project** Make a Windbreak supports content in this lesson.

Slow Changes to Earth's Surface

Look at these pictures to explore how Bryce Canyon has formed over time.

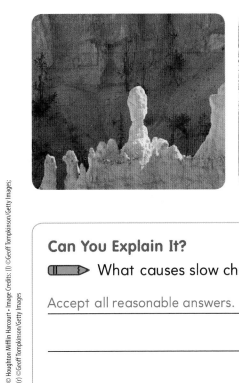

Explore online. ▶

Can You Explain It?

▭▭▷ What causes slow changes to rocks on Earth?

Accept all reasonable answers.

_____

_____

_____

_____

Lesson 1 • What Changes on Earth Happen Slowly? 225

Weathering by Wind

3D Learning Objective

Children **observe and describe** what happens during **weathering by wind**. They use their observations to identify **weathering by wind as a slow process**.

SEP **Constructing Explanations and Designing Solutions** . . . .

CCC **Stability and Change** . . . .

Ask: What happens during weathering? Wind and water break up rocks into smaller pieces. Have children observe and compare the two pictures at the top of the page. **Ask: Is weathering a slow or quick process? How do you know?** It is a slow process because it took millions of years for the mountain to change.

DCI **The History of Planet Earth** . . . .

Ask: How can wind change the shape of rocks? The wind carries bits of sand and hits the rock. When this happens for a long time, the rock becomes weak and breaks, changing its shape. **Why do you think weathering is important?** Breaking down rocks can help make soil.

Differentiate Instruction

ELL Children may be unfamiliar with the word *weathering*, and may require additional support to understand how the word is used in this context. **Ask: What is the root word in weathering?** weather **Ask: What is the suffix?** –ing. The suffix *–ing* in this case means "involved in a process". Explain that weathering occurs when something is affected by weather conditions, such as wind, rain, and snow.

Weathering by Wind

Look at these pictures to explore how weathering causes slow changes to Earth over time.

Explore online.

4 million years ago
before

Today
after

Weathering is a process that breaks rocks into smaller pieces. Wind and water smash against these mountains every day. Bits of rock break off very slowly. Over millions of years, the mountains become smoother and more rounded.

Explore online.

Weathering by wind is a slow change. Wind carries bits of sand. The sand hits the rock when the wind blows. Over time, the rock becomes weaker. Small pieces break off. Over many years, weathering from wind changes the shape of the rock.

© Houghton Mifflin Harcourt • Image Credits: ©Getty Images

226

How will wind change a rock?

Ⓐ Wind will blow a rock to a new place.

Ⓑ Wind will turn a rock into a mountain.

Ⓒ Wind will weather a rock.

Apply What You Know

Evidence Notebook • Observe a rock. Record your observations. Then rub sandpaper all over the rock for 5 minutes. Observe the rock again. Did it change? How does this relate to weathering? Use evidence to support your answer. Record it in your Evidence Notebook.

Constructing Explanations and Designing Solutions
Go to the online handbook for tips.

Lesson 1 • What Changes on Earth Happen Slowly?   227

© Houghton Mifflin Harcourt • Image Credits ©Katrina Brown/Fotolia

DCI The History of Planet Earth . . . .

Children should choose C—Wind will weather a rock. If children choose A or B, review the process of weathering and how it changes rocks. Guide them to observe the picture at the bottom of the previous page. **Ask: What is happening in the picture?** Wind is carrying bits of sand that can hit rocks and break them into smaller pieces.

SEP Constructing Explanations and Designing Solutions . . . .

Have children observe a rock and a piece of sandpaper. Discuss how each one looks and feels. **Ask: How does the sandpaper simulate weathering?** The sandpaper rubs away small pieces, changing the shape of the rock. Similarly, wind carries sand, which hits the rock and breaks it, causing its shape to change.

✋ **FORMATIVE ASSESSMENT**

Evidence Notebook

Children use sandpaper to change a rock and relate their observations to the weathering process. Guide children to make a connection between what they observe happening to the rock to what happens during the weathering process.

Scoring Guidelines

• describes what happened to the rock while it was rubbed
• makes connections to what happens to Earth's surface from weathering by wind
• provides evidence to support how the activity relates to the weathering process

💡 **Constructing Explanations and Designing Solutions** When constructing explanations and designing solutions, it is important to make observations from a variety of sources in order to gather and compare information. Guide children to use their observations as evidence when explaining phenomena.

Weathering by Water and Ice

3D Learning Objective

Children **observe and describe** what happens during **weathering by water and ice**. They use their observations to identify weathering by water and ice as a slow process.

 **The History of Planet Earth** . . . .

Ask: What do you see in the top picture? There is a rock with cracks that have filled up with water. **Ask: What changes do you see in the middle picture?** The water freezes into ice when it gets cold. **What happened to the rock in the bottom picture?** The ice melted in the spring and caused the rock to break into pieces.

Ask: What is different when we compare the top picture with the bottom picture of the same rock? The ice has made the cracks in the rock bigger. **What do you think happens when this cycle repeats year after year?** The rock will finally break apart.

Differentiate Instruction

RTI/Extra Support Make a circle of plaster of Paris and place a small crater in the center of the circle. Have children place water in the crater and set it in the freezer until the water freezes. **Ask: What do you think will happen to the water and our plaster?** It will freeze. After it is frozen, remove the circle from the freezer and observe while the water melts. Remind children that this weathering process takes place over a long period of time in real life.

Extension Have children fill a container with different rocks and clean, clear water. Close the lid and shake the container. Open the lid and observe what can be found in the water.

Weathering by Water and Ice

Look at the pictures to explore how water and ice cause slow changes to Earth's surface.

 Explore online. ▶

Water and ice can break down rocks into smaller pieces. Most rocks have small cracks. When it rains, water gets into these cracks. Some water stays in the cracks.

In winter, the water in the cracks turns to ice. Ice takes up more space than water. This causes the ice to push against the cracks and make them bigger.

In spring, the ice melts. The cracks are bigger now. This cycle repeats every year. After many years, these cracks are big enough to cause the rock to break into pieces.

© Houghton Mifflin Harcourt

228

Which actions repeat in the process of weathering by water and ice? Choose all correct answers.

Stability and Change Go to the online handbook for tips.

Ⓐ Water gets into cracks in rocks.

Ⓑ Water freezes to form ice in the cracks and pushes against them.

Ⓒ Wind blows water to a new place.

Apply What You Know

Constructing Explanations and Designing Solutions Go to the online handbook for tips.

Evidence Notebook • Work with a partner. Fill one-half of a small plastic cup with water. Mark the water line. Put the cup in a freezer overnight. Observe the cup and the mark the next day. Do you observe any changes? How does this relate to weathering? Use evidence to support your answer. Record it in your Evidence Notebook.

Lesson 1 • What Changes on Earth Happen Slowly?

229

 Stability and Change ....

Have children underline text that supports all the actions that repeat from the captions on the previous page. Children should choose both A—Water gets into cracks in rocks—and B—Water freezes to form ice in the cracks and pushes against them. If they choose C, remind them that when we see cracks like this in a rock, it is most likely the result of water freezing in the rock and pushing against it. **Ask: This is a process that constantly repeats. Do you think the process brings about a slow change or a fast change? Why or why not?** I think it is a slow change because it takes many years for the cracks to finally break the rock into pieces.

 Stability and Change Guide children to observe the changes and look for things that change slowly.

SEP Constructing Explanations and Designing Solutions ....

Ask: How does the water change as it freezes in the activity? How does this relate to weathering? Ice takes up more space than water in the cup. Similarly, as water gets into rocks and freezes, it takes up more space and enlarges the cracks in the rock.

FORMATIVE ASSESSMENT

Evidence Notebook

Guide children to connect the water freezing in the cup to what happens when water freezes in the cracks of rocks. Be sure they use evidence to support their claims.

Scoring Guidelines

- describes what happened to the water when it froze
- makes connections to what happens to Earth's surface from weathering by water and ice
- provides evidence to support how the activity relates to the weathering process

 Constructing Explanations and Designing Solutions Observations can be used to help construct explanations. Guide children to use their observations to describe what happened.

© Houghton Mifflin Harcourt

Weathering by Plants

3D Learning Objective

Children **observe and describe** what happens during **weathering by plants**. They use their observations to identify **weathering by plants as a slow process**.

DCI **The History of Planet Earth** . . . .

Guide children in a discussion about what they might find in or under the ground. **Ask: Other than wind, water, and ice, what is something found underground that can weather rocks?** Plant roots can weather rocks. **Ask: How do plants change Earth's surface?** Plants have roots that can get into the cracks of a rock. They make the cracks get bigger. Over time, the rock can break apart. This process can help make more soil.

SEP **Constructing Explanations and Designing Solutions** . . . .

Guide children to the pictures to explain how plant roots contribute to the weathering process. Compare this example to the one with water and ice in the rocks. **Ask: How is this example similar to weathering with water and ice?** Plants have roots that can get into the cracks of a rock. They make the cracks get bigger. Over time, the rock can break apart. This is similar to how water gets into cracks, freezes, and then causes the rocks to break over time.

Collaboration

Jigsaw Group children in three groups: wind, water and ice, and plants. Have them find out as much information as they can about weathering as it is related to their group title. Allow time for information to be gathered. Provide multiple modes of research opportunities for children. After research is completed, re-group children into groups of three, each representing a different weathering element. Have children share the results of their research with their new group.

Weathering by Plants

Look at the pictures to explore how plant roots cause changes to Earth's surface.

Explore online.

Plant roots grow into cracks in rock and press on it.

This plant grew through rock. As its roots and trunk grew, the pressure was too much for the rock. The rock split in half.

Look at the roots. Nearby are pebbles and soil. Over a long time, these roots have split the rock so many times that it became pebbles and soil.

© Houghton Mifflin Harcourt

230

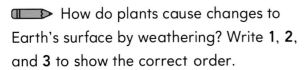 How do plants cause changes to Earth's surface by weathering? Write **1**, **2**, and **3** to show the correct order.

Explore online. ▶

3   2   1

Apply What You Know

Evidence Notebook • Have you ever seen weathering by plants? Think about what you have observed. Draw to record your observations in your Evidence Notebook. Share your picture with a classmate. Use evidence to explain how the plants caused changes by weathering to the rock.

 SEP **Constructing Explanations and Designing Solutions** . . . .

Guide children to think about the how plant roots cause changes to Earth's surface. Children should number the pictures 3, 2, 1 from left to right. If children incorrectly sequence the pictures, review how the roots of a tree grow and expand into rocks found in the soil. **Ask: Observe the three pictures. What is happening to the roots in each picture? How does this cause weathering?** The roots are growing and getting longer. They grow into rocks, causing them to break.

CCC **Stability and Change** . . . .

As a class, discuss all types of weathering that children have explored. **Ask: Think about the kinds of weathering we have talked about. Do you think weathering by plants is a slow or quick process. How do you know?** I think it is a slow process because it is similar to when water freezes into ice and cracks rocks open. The process repeats, so it takes a long time.

FORMATIVE ASSESSMENT

Evidence Notebook

Guide children to think about areas they have observed that are examples of how a plant can weather Earth's surface. Encourage children to use labels and captions to explain their drawing. Remind children to use evidence to support their observations.

Scoring Guidelines
• draws a picture representing weathering by plants
• makes connections to what happens to Earth's surface from weathering by plants
• provides evidence to support how plants cause weathering to rocks

Erosion by Wind

3D Learning Objective

Children **observe and describe** what happens during **erosion by wind**. They use their observations to identify wind erosion as a slow process.

SEP Constructing Explanations and Designing Solutions . . . .

Guide children in a discussion to determine their background knowledge of the meaning of the word *erosion*. **Ask: What is erosion?** Erosion is the movement of sand, rocks, or soil from one place to another. Have children describe what is happening in the picture. **Ask: How could erosion cause problems for people, especially those working the land?** Water can move away soil that is good for growing crops.

DCI The History of Planet Earth . . . .

Lead children in a discussion about the different elements that can cause erosion. **Ask: What causes rocks, soil, or sand to move?** Wind, water, or ice can cause erosion. **How is Earth's surface changed during erosion?** The land can be reshaped. **How is erosion different than weathering?** Erosion changes Earth's surface by the moving of sand, soil, or rocks by wind, water, or ice to another location. Weathering is the wearing or breaking away of rocks that reshapes or changes Earth's surface.

Connection to Engineering Design

Defining and Delimiting Engineering Problems
Engineering design is one way that people can discuss problems caused by natural processes such as erosion, and then work on solutions. **Ask: How could wind erosion become a problem after a long period of time?** Have children work in groups to find a problem and a possible solution to prevent or reduce the effects of wind erosion.

Erosion by Wind

Look at the picture to explore how erosion causes slow changes to Earth's surface.

Explore online. ▶

© Houghton Mifflin Harcourt • Image Credits: ©Geoff Renner/Robert Harding World Imagery/Getty Images

Erosion is the picking up and moving of rocks, soil, or sand from one place to another. Wind, water, and ice can all cause erosion. Erosion happens slowly over long periods of time. Changes from erosion may reshape a beach, a coastline, or a whole island.

232

Look at these pictures to explore how wind causes erosion.

Explore online. ▶

Erosion by wind can damage farms. Wind can blow away the rich soil used to grow crops.

Erosion by wind can reshape deserts. Wind can bury an entire area in dust, sand, or ash.

Erosion by wind moves rocks, soil, and sand from one place to another. This often happens in dry places. There, wind can easily pick up and blow around small, dry pieces of sand or dust. This causes slow changes to Earth's surface.

SEP **Constructing Explanations and Designing Solutions** . . . .

Have children observe and describe what is happening in each picture. **Ask: How does the wind cause erosion?** The wind can pick up small, dry pieces of sand or dust and carry it away. **Wind erosion can happen anywhere the wind is blowing. Why do you think it happens in mostly dry places?** The soil there is looser, and not as compact as in other places. It is easier for the wind to pick up pieces of soil, sand, and rocks and blow them to another location.

DCI **The History of Planet Earth** . . . .

Ask: What are some examples of how wind erosion can change Earth's surface? A farm could lose the rich top soil. A desert or shoreline of a beach may be reshaped. Accept other reasonable answers that may show examples of wind erosion.

CCC **Stability and Change** . . . .

Ask: Do you think erosion by wind takes place over a long or short period of time? Explain your reasoning. Erosion happens slowly over a long period of time. It takes time for the wind to blow away enough soil, sand, or rocks in order for the change to be visible.

Differentiate Instruction

ELL Some children might have difficulty in understanding the difference between the words *weathering* and *erosion*. Guide children to write each word on paper, and then draw an illustration to help them remember the difference. One example could be to write the word *weather* with *–ing* breaking off the side to symbolize the breaking away of parts. *Erosion* can be written with an arrow pointing to either side to symbolize the movement of sand, soil, or rocks.

Constructing Explanations and Designing Solutions . . . .

Guide children to think about the effects of wind erosion. Children should choose A—The wind moves sand from one place to another. If children choose B or C, review the meaning of the word *erosion*. Discuss how erosion is moving sand, not breaking it down or combining it with rocks.

 The History of Planet Earth . . . .

Ask: Some days the wind blows stronger than other days. Some days the wind does not blow at all. How does the strength of the wind play a role in erosion? The stronger the force of the wind, the more erosion will take place.

 FORMATIVE ASSESSMENT

Evidence Notebook

Guide children to set up and explore erosion through a simulation. Monitor children for safety as they blow through the straws. Discuss with children their outcomes when they use different speeds of air to simulate erosion with their sand trays. Remind children to support their claims with evidence.

Scoring Guidelines

• draws a picture of their mountain before blowing through the straw
• draws a picture of their mountain after blowing through the straw
• makes connections to what happens to Earth's surface from wind erosion
• provides evidence to support how the mountain changed and how the activity relates to erosion

🔆 **Stability and Change** Guide children to observe the changes and to look for things that change slowly.

This picture shows erosion by wind. What is happening in the picture?

Ⓐ The wind moves sand from one place to another.

Ⓑ The wind breaks sand into smaller pieces.

Ⓒ The wind pushes bits of sand together into rocks.

 Apply What You Know

Evidence Notebook • Pile sand into a small mountain on a tray. Sketch a picture of it in your Evidence Notebook. Then blow air gently through a straw toward the mountain. Observe what happens. Sketch it in your Evidence Notebook. Use evidence to explain how the mountain changed and how this relates to erosion. Repeat the activity and use different speeds of air.

Stability and Change
Go to the online handbook for tips.

© Houghton Mifflin Harcourt

234

Erosion by Water and Ice

Look at these pictures to explore how flowing water carves a canyon over many years.

Explore online. ▶

This river may look small, but its rushing water moves lots of rocks and soil.

Over many years, the river has carved away some of the rock. It has carried away bits of rock and soil. It has slowly made the canyon deeper and wider.

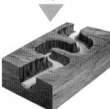

The flowing river keeps carrying away bits of rock and soil. This erosion causes the canyon to be deeper and wider. What do you think the canyon will look like a long time from now?

Do the Math! • The Grand Canyon is 277 miles long. Which is another way to write the number 277?

Stability and Change • Understand Place Value Go to the online handbook for tips.

Ⓐ 2 + 7 + 7

Ⓑ 200 + 70 + 7

Ⓒ 270 + 7 + 7

Lesson 1 • What Changes on Earth Happen Slowly?

235

Erosion by Water and Ice

3D Learning Objective

Children **make observations and use examples** to explore the slow process of **erosion by water and ice** on Earth's surface.

DCI **The History of Planet Earth** . . . .

Ask: What is the water doing to Earth's surface in the top picture? The water is moving soil and rocks to other places.

SEP **Constructing Explanations and Designing Solutions** . . . .

Ask: Look at the middle picture and compare it to the top picture. What is happening to the land as water erosion is taking place? The river has made the canyon deeper and wider.

CCC **Stability and Change** . . . .

Ask: How long do you think it would take a river to change from the first picture to the third picture? It could take the river thousands of years to carve out a canyon as deep and wide as the one in the third picture.

Do the Math! • Stability and Change • Understand Place Value

Children should choose B—200 + 70 + 7. If children choose A or C, review place value and different ways to write numbers. **Ask:** What is the value of each digit in the number 277? The 2 in the hundreds place has a value of 200. The 7 in the tens place has a value of 70. The 7 in the ones place has a value of 7.

💡 **Stability and Change • Understand Place Value • Model with Mathematics** Remind children that erosion is a slow process that can occur over thousands, or even millions, of years. Then discuss how the place of each digit in a number tells its value.

Constructing Explanations and Designing Solutions . . . .

Have children observe and describe what is happening in each picture. **Ask: What are glaciers?** Glaciers are large and powerful sheets of ice. **Ask: Where might glaciers be found?** In places that have very cold temperatures.

DCI **The History of Planet Earth** . . . .

CCC **Stability and Change** . . . .

Discuss what changes may be made to Earth's surface by glaciers. **Ask: Do glaciers change Earth's surface by weathering or by erosion?** erosion **Ask: Does this erosion take place quickly or slowly?** Erosion from glaciers takes place very slowly. **Ask: What evidence do you have that this erosion process is slow?** It takes glaciers many, many years to travel great distances.

 FORMATIVE ASSESSMENT

Guide children to apply the information they have gained from the sections on Erosion by Wind and Erosion by Water in order to help them answer the question. Encourage children to write a paragraph with a main idea, using evidence as details to support the main idea and their claim.

Scoring Guidelines
• describes the changes made to the beach over time
• provides evidence to support their claim

💡 **Stability and Change** Guide children to observe how the location and amount of sand on the beach might change over time. Remind them that this is a slow process.

A glacier is a thick sheet of moving ice. Look at the pictures to explore how a glacier causes Earth's surface to change.

Explore online. ▶

Most glaciers are very large and powerful. They can move gigantic boulders, as well as soil, sand, and rocks. Over many years they travel great distances, taking a lot of soil and rocks with them. Glaciers cause most of the erosion by ice on Earth.

 Apply What You Know

This picture shows a single moment at a beach. However, a beach is always changing. Work with a partner. Talk about how wind and water can change a beach over time. Record your answer.

Stability and Change Go to the online handbook for tips.

236

Hands-On Activity
Model Erosion

Name _____

Materials _____
_____

Ask a Question

What can I find out by modeling erosion by water? _____

Test and Record Data Explore online. ▶

Step 1

Make a model of a stream. Observe the model before adding water to it. Record your observations.

Sample answer: The model is made of soil, sand, and rocks

in a pan.

Step 2

Add water to the model. Observe the model. Record your observations.

Check children's work.	Sample answer: When I pour the water downstream, it washes some soil and sand along with it.

Lesson 1 • What Changes on Earth Happen Slowly?   237

Hands-On Activity 👥 small groups ⏱ 1 class period
Model Erosion

3D Learning Objective

 Constructing Explanations and Designing Solutions . . . .

Children build a model of a stream to observe what happens to Earth's surface during erosion by water. **Ask: How does erosion by water change Earth's surface?** Erosion by water might change the shape of the area because sand and soil are being moved.

Suggested Materials Disposable plastic gloves, small rocks, soil, sand, foil tray or plastic tub, small book, container of water, plastic cup, safety goggles

Preparation

Pre-assemble materials bundles for small groups. Place newspaper or another covering on top of desks or tables to keep them from getting dirty or wet. Have paper towels handy to clean up spills.

DCI The History of Planet Earth . . . .

Activity

Remind children what models are. **Ask: What question could we try to answer by building a model to study erosion?** Sample answer "What can I find out by modeling erosion by water?"

STEP 1 Circulate around the room as children begin making their models, and provide assistance as needed. Be sure children record their observations before adding the water.

STEP 2 Remind children not to pour the water too fast over their models. Discuss how the models look now. Be sure children record their observations now that the water has been added.

© Houghton Mifflin Harcourt

Hands-On Activity, continued

STEP 3 Encourage children to think about how their model changed once the water was added.

STEP 4 Guide children to use their observations as evidence, and explain the connection between their model and water erosion.

Differentiate Instruction

RTI/Extra Support Ask children to find more pictures of streams on the Internet or in books. Have them draw a picture that predicts how the stream will look in 1,000 years.

Extension Group children into three groups and assign one of the following topics: Cape Hatteras Lighthouse, Arches National Park, and the Great Lakes. Allow time for each group to research the changes caused by weathering or erosion in these locations. Have them share their findings with the class.

Claims, Evidence, and Reasoning

Ask: **What can we learn by building a model and simulating a stream?** We can see how the water carries away part of the soil and sand. **What evidence do you have?** We saw the water move the soil and sand, changing how the land looked.

Scoring Rubric for Hands-On Activity	
3	States a claim supported with evidence that explains how their model shows water erosion
2	States a claim somewhat supported with evidence that explains how their model shows water erosion
1	States a claim that is not supported by evidence
0	Does not state a claim and does not provide evidence

Step 3

Analyze your results. Compare the model before and after you added water to it.

Before	After
Check children's work.	

Step 4

Identify any differences you observed. How do they help you understand how water causes slow changes to Earth's surface?

Make a claim that answers the question.

Answers should reflect children's solutions regarding what

they can find out by modeling erosion.

What is your evidence?

Answers should cite evidence from children's models.

238

© Houghton Mifflin Harcourt

Explore online. ▶   **Guide children to the Interactive Online Student Edition where they can choose from and explore both paths.**

Take It Further

Careers in Science & Engineering •
Farming

Explore more online.
• How Does a Delta Form?

Explore online. ▶

Erosion can be harmful to farmland. If too much soil erodes, farmers cannot grow crops.

Farmers can slow erosion by adding plants. These plants have roots that help keep soil in place when the wind blows.

Another way farmers can slow erosion is by planting trees. The trees break up the gusts of wind. This keeps soil in place, too.

Lesson 1 • What Changes on Earth Happen Slowly?   239

Take It Further

Careers in Science and Engineering •
Farming

Children investigate how farmers try to prevent or reduce the effects of erosion. Have children describe each picture.

SEP **Constructing Explanations and Designing Solutions** . . . .

Ask: How can plants or trees help slow down erosion? Plants have roots that help keep soil in place when the wind blows. Trees break up the gusts of wind, which helps keep soil in place.

Differentiate Instruction

RTI/Extra Support Provide children with goggles. Have children place loose soil on a table and blow across the soil to simulate the wind. Then have children use clay to build a wall around the soil and blow across the soil again. Discuss how the wall of clay helped the soil stay in place.

Extension Have children research erosion-prevention methods, such as strip cropping, covering soil by leaving residue or planting winter crops, zero-tillage approaches, wet season spelling, and controlled runoff with flumes.

Collaboration

Small Groups Have children work in small groups to research crops grown in your area. Encourage group members to brainstorm and discuss what type of erosion prevention they think would work best for farms in the area. Have each group member research different methods for erosion prevention and share their findings with the group.

Take It Further, continued

Read, Write, Share! • Describe Details • Gather Information

SEP **Constructing Explanations and Designing Solutions** . . . .

Remind children to use a variety of resources in order to gather and compare information. Details should be used as evidence to support their main idea. Encourage children to add a drawing with labels or captions.

💡 **Describe Details • Gather Information • Participate in a Research and Writing Project** Guide children to look for the details about how farmers protect their farms from erosion. Describe the details in an order that helps listeners understand the topic. Children should gather and compare information from several sources.

DCI **The History of Planet Earth** . . . .

Review the components of a friendly letter. Then discuss the information presented by the class on things farmers do to protect their farms. **Ask: What are some other things you would like to know about what farmers do to help the land?** Accept all reasonable questions.

💡 **Ask Questions** Guide children to think about what they already know and then think about other questions they have about farmers and erosion.

Explore more online.

How Does a Delta Form?

Have children go online to explore more about how a delta forms.

Read, Write, Share! • Find out more about how farmers use plants to slow erosion. Do research using online and print resources. Record what you find out. Be sure to include a main idea and details. Share your findings with your classmates.

Check children's work.

_____

_____

_____

_____

> **Describe Details • Gather Information**
> Go to the online handbook for tips.

Do you still have questions about how farmers help Earth's surface? Ask a farmer. Write a friendly letter to a local farmer. Introduce yourself. Describe what you are learning in school. Then ask your questions about erosion and what farmers can do to help slow it.

> **Ask Questions**
> Go to the online handbook for tips.

240

© Houghton Mifflin Harcourt

LESSON 1   Engage • Explore/Explain • Elaborate • **Evaluate**

Explore online. ▶   Have children explore online to find out more about slow changes to Earth's surface.

Lesson Check

Lesson Check   Name _____

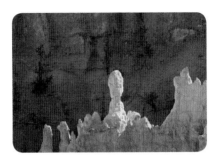 

Explore online. ▶

Can You Explain It?

✏️➤ What causes slow changes to rocks on Earth?
Be sure to
- Explain changes caused by weathering.
- Explain changes caused by erosion.
- Describe whether these changes happened slowly or quickly.

Sample answer: First, weathering changes Earth's surface in

Bryce Canyon. When the wind blows, the sand hits the rocks, and

small pieces break off. Then, erosion takes over because

the wind picks up the small pieces of rocks and blows them

around. Both changes happen very slowly.

Lesson 1 • What Changes on Earth Happen Slowly?   241

© Houghton Mifflin Harcourt • Image Credits: (l) ©Geoff Tompkinson/Getty Images; (r) ©Geoff Tompkinson/Getty Images

Lesson Check

Can You Explain It?

Have children reread their answers to the Can You Explain It? prompt at the beginning of the lesson.

DCI **The History of Planet Earth** . . . .

Have children review the two pictures and discuss weathering and erosion that have possibly occurred. **Ask: What happens to Earth's surface from weathering?** Weathering breaks up rocks into smaller pieces. **Ask: What happens to Earth's surface from erosion?** Erosion picks up and moves the smaller pieces of rock to a new location. **Ask: How fast do the changes happen from weathering and erosion?** Changes to Earth's surface from weathering and erosion normally take a very long time.

Scoring Guidelines

- Children should explain how weathering changed Earth's surface in Bryce Canyon.
- Children should explain how erosion changed Earth's surface in Bryce Canyon.
- Children should describe if these changes happened slowly or quickly.

Collaboration

Cultivating New Questions As children complete this lesson and prepare for the next lesson, ask them to identify additional questions they have about slow changes to Earth's surface. **Ask: How do you think weathering and erosion will change Earth's surface in the future?** I think wind will erode more mountains and water will cause more canyons to form. As children continue to the next lesson, they will apply concepts related to Earth's surface changing.

Lesson Check, continued

SUMMATIVE ASSESSMENT
Self Check

1. Children should choose B—weathering. If children choose A or C, review the Weathering by Water and Ice section of the lesson. Remind children that water fills in the cracks of a rock. As the water freezes, ice forms. The ice takes up more space in the rock than water so the rock's cracks get larger.

2. Children should choose all four answers. If children do not choose all four answers, ask volunteers to describe how each thing can weather rocks. Direct them to the following sections of the lesson: Weathering by Wind, Weathering by Water and Ice, and Weathering by Plants

3. Children should write *wind* under the first picture, *water* under the second picture, and *ice* under the third picture. If children do not correctly label the pictures, remind them that a glacier is ice that moves rocks and soil from one place to another. A sandstorm moves bits of sand and soil to different places. A canyon forms when water erodes bits of rock and soil.

Self Check

1. Which process do these pictures show?

Ⓐ erosion
🅑 weathering
Ⓒ wind

---

2. Which can weather rocks? Choose all correct answers.

🅐 plant roots   🅒 wind
🅑 water   🅓 ice

---

3. What does each picture show?
   Use the words in the box to label each picture.

   | ice   wind   water |

wind   water   ice

242

4. How does erosion form a canyon? Write **1**, **2**, and **3** to show the correct order.

3 _____   1 _____   2 _____

5. How do glaciers cause Earth's surface to change?
- (A) They move boulders.
- (B) They move sand.
- (C) They move soil.

4. Children should sequence the pictures as 3, 1, and 2 from left to right. If children do not sequence the pictures in the correct order, review the Erosion by Water section of the lesson and discuss how canyons are formed.

5. Children should choose all three answers: A—They move boulders. B—They move sand. C—They move soil. If children do not choose all three answers, refer them back to the section on Erosion by Water and Ice to see how glaciers can change Earth's surface.

Lesson 2 · What Changes on Earth Happen Quickly?

Building to the Performance Expectation

The learning experiences in this lesson prepare children for mastery of:

2-ESS1-1 Use information from several sources to provide evidence that Earth events can occur quickly or slowly.

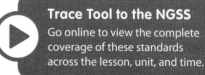

Trace Tool to the NGSS
Go online to view the complete coverage of these standards across the lesson, unit, and time.

 Science & Engineering Practices

Constructing Explanations and Designing Solutions
Make observations from several sources to construct an evidence-based account for natural phenomena.

▶ **VIDEO** SEPs: Constructing Explanations and Designing Solutions / Engaging in Argument from Evidence

---

 Disciplinary Core Ideas

ESS1.C: The History of Planet Earth
Some events happen very quickly; others occur very slowly, over a time period much longer than one can observe.

 Crosscutting Concepts

Stability and Change
Things may change slowly or rapidly.

▶ **VIDEO** CCC: Stability and Change

CONNECTIONS TO MATH

MP.2 Reason abstractly and quantitatively.

MP.4 Model with mathematics.

2.NBT.A.1 Understand place value.

CONNECTION TO ENGLISH LANGUAGE ARTS

W.2.6 With guidance and support from adults, use a variety of digital tools to produce and publish writing, including in collaboration with peers.

W.2.7 Participate in shared research and writing projects (e.g., read a number of books on a single topic to produce a report; record science observations).

Supporting All Students, All Standards

Integrating the Three Dimensions of Learning

This lesson focuses on events that cause quick changes to Earth's surface. Children explore how earthquakes, volcanoes, landslides, hurricanes, and floods cause Earth's surface to change quickly **(SEP Constructing Explanations and Designing Solutions) (DCI The History of Planet Earth) (CCC Stability and Change)**. Then children will extend their exploration by modeling how a flood can cause a quick change to Earth's surface.

Professional Development

Go online to view **Professional Development videos** with strategies to integrate CCCs and SEPs, including the ones used in this lesson.

Build on Prior Knowledge

Children should already know and be prepared to build on the following concepts:

- Observations can be used as evidence. *(Grade 2, Unit 5, Lesson 1)*
- Earth has some weather patterns that can be severe. *(Grade K, Unit 5, Lesson 3)*
- Wind and water can change Earth's surface. *(Grade 2, Unit 5, Lesson 1)*
- Events in nature can happen quickly or slowly. *(Grade 2, Unit 5, Lesson 1)*

Differentiate Instruction

Lesson Vocabulary

- earthquake
- flood
- volcano
- hurricane
- landslide

Reinforcing Vocabulary To help children remember these vocabulary words, have them draw an illustration of each of the five events. Then have them write the word for each event beneath the illustration and use it in a sentence. Remind children to look for these highlighted words as they proceed through the lesson.

RTI/Extra Support Supply children with two sets of flash cards. The first set contains a picture of the events (earthquake, flood, volcano, hurricane, and landslide). The second set contains the word for each event. Have children match the correct word with its event.

Extension Challenge children to search for information on one of the events that happened in the area they live. Have children make a poster or slideshow to present these facts about the event to the class.

ELL Be sure to point out all labels, pictures, captions, and headings throughout the lesson to assist children with strategies to summarize chunks of content. Discuss with children real-life connections to content, and provide hands-on examples of materials when possible to best support the needs of these learners.

Lesson Phenomenon

Build on Prior Lessons

In Lesson 1, children explored **slow changes to Earth's surface** by using **observations from several sources.** Lesson 2 builds on these concepts by again **using several sources to observe fast changes to Earth's surface.**

Lesson Objective

Use information from several sources to provide evidence that some changes on Earth can happen quickly.

About This Image

Ask: What do you think is happening in this picture? Lava from a volcano is moving over the ground. **What do you think this will do to Earth?** I think the lava could destroy plants and cover soil. Remind children that as they explore, they will find out about events that can quickly change Earth's surface.

SEP **Constructing Explanations and Designing Solutions**

Alternative Engage Strategy

Volcanic Eruption	👥 small groups
	🕐 15–25 minutes

Shape clay or play dough around the bottom of a plastic cup to form a mountain. Cover the area under the mountain with a vinyl tablecloth or alternative that will make clean up easy and quick. Place 60 mL water, $\frac{1}{4}$ cup vinegar, a few drops of liquid soap, and red food coloring in the plastic cup. Wrap 1 tablespoon of baking soda into a small tissue square. Drop the baking soda wrapped with tissue into the plastic cup.
Ask: What have we just made? How will this affect the land around it? We made a volcanic eruption. The lava will cover the land around it.

Lesson **2** **What Changes on Earth Happen Quickly?**

Some changes on Earth happen quickly.

By the End of This Lesson
I will be able to describe changes to Earth that happen quickly.

244

© Houghton Mifflin Harcourt • Image Credit: ©Budi Susak/Photographer's Choice/Getty Images

Explore online. ▶

Have children explore online to find out more about what causes Earth's surface to change quickly.

Can You Explain It?

Quick Changes to Earth's Surface Ash, dust, and lava come out during a volcanic eruption. Play the video to show how a volcano can quickly change the surface of Earth. If the video is not available, have children review the pictures on the page. Allow them to discuss their observations about how the volcano has changed Earth's surface. **Ask: What is happening to Earth in these pictures? What happens to the mountain when a volcano erupts? How quickly do you think this happens?** Accept all reasonable answers.

Ask children to record their initial thoughts about how volcanoes can quickly change the land. At the end of this lesson, children will revisit the video and the pictures as part of the Lesson Check. At this point, children should be able to explain that ash, dust, and lava can cover the land after a volcanic eruption.

Quick Changes to Earth's Surface

Look at the pictures to explore how a volcanic eruption caused the land to change.

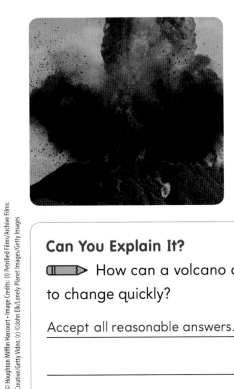

Explore online. ▶

Can You Explain It?

✏️ How can a volcano cause Earth's surface to change quickly?

Accept all reasonable answers.

_____

_____

_____

_____

Lesson 2 • What Changes on Earth Happen Quickly?   245

Collaboration

Build on Prior Knowledge Have children work with a partner to brainstorm ideas about volcanoes and what they might already know about their structure. Have partners share with the class before beginning the Volcanic Eruption Activity.

Support for Unit Performance Task

The **Unit Performance Task** Engineer It • Build an Earthquake-Proof Structure supports content in this lesson.

Earthquakes

3D Learning Objective

Children **observe and describe** what happens during **an earthquake**. They use their observations to identify **the quick changes made to Earth's surface.**

DCI The History of Planet Earth . . . .

Ask: What happens during an earthquake? Earth's surface begins to shake, causing the land to rise and fall. Earthquakes can change Earth's surface. Anything on the ground can also shake or sway. Trees and bushes can sometimes fall over.

SEP Constructing Explanations and Designing Solutions . . . .

Have children compare the before and after pictures on this page. **Ask: What did the land look like before the earthquake?** There were no cracks in the surface. **How has the land changed after the earthquake?** The ground has shifted, and a crack has appeared on the surface.

Children should choose all three answer choices. If children do not choose all three, have them return to the captions at the top of the page. Have children underline any text that will help them answer the question.

CCC Stability and Change . . . .

Earthquakes are events on Earth that happen very quickly. **Ask: How long do earthquakes last?** Most earthquakes last only a few seconds, but stronger ones can last longer.

Earthquakes

before

An earthquake happens quickly. The shaking starts suddenly. It usually lasts for only a few seconds.

after

An earthquake may cause many changes to the land. Cracks may form on Earth's surface. The ground may shift and lose some strength. When the ground shakes, everything on it shakes, too. Buildings may sway. Trees may fall over.

An **earthquake** is a sudden shaking of the ground that causes land to rise and fall. It can cause fast changes to Earth's surface.

Which changes may be caused by an earthquake? Choose all correct answers.

Ⓐ cracks on Earth's surface

Ⓑ shifting ground

Ⓒ swaying buildings

246

Apply What You Know

Evidence Notebook • Model Earth's surface during an earthquake. Observe what happens.

Step 1: Break a graham cracker in half.

Step 2: Put the two pieces back together so they touch.

Step 3: Move one piece away from you while moving the other piece towards you. Repeat two times.

Step 4: Observe what happens to the crackers. Record your observations in your Evidence Notebook. Use evidence to describe how it is similar to what happens to Earth's surface during an earthquake.

Stability and Change • Constructing Explanations Go to the online handbook for tips.

SEP Constructing Explanations and Designing Solutions . . . .

Remind children that a model shows what something looks like or how it works. **Ask: How will making a model help you understand what happens to Earth's surface during an earthquake?** It will provide evidence to explain how Earth's surface changes.

CCC Stability and Change . . . .

Have children complete the Apply What You Know activity. **Ask: How is the graham cracker similar to what happens to Earth's surface during an earthquake?** The graham cracker crumbled quickly as we moved the pieces. Some crumbs fell away from the graham cracker.

FORMATIVE ASSESSMENT

Evidence Notebook

Children complete the model earthquake activity and observe what happens to the graham cracker. Circulate around the room and make sure that children are not having trouble performing the activity. Guide them to make a connection between what they observe with the graham cracker, and what happens during an earthquake.

Scoring Guidelines

- describes what happened in the graham cracker model
- makes connections to what happens to Earth's surface during an earthquake
- provides evidence to support their answers

 Stability and Change • Constructing Explanations Guide children to observe the changes, and look for things that change slowly or rapidly. Have children observe what happens during the model earthquake, and use evidence to describe what happened.

Volcanoes

3D Learning Objective

Children **observe and describe** what happens during **a volcanic eruption**. They use their observations to identify **the quick changes made to Earth's surface**.

DCI The History of Planet Earth . . . .

Ask: What are volcanoes? mountains that have openings **Ask: What happens when a volcano erupts?** Ash and dust come out of the opening, and hot lava pours out and covers the land.

SEP Constructing Explanations and
Designing Solutions . . . .

Have children observe and describe the pictures. **Ask: What is happening in the top picture?** The volcano is quiet before it erupts. **Ask: The middle picture shows what happens during an eruption. How has the land changed in the bottom picture?** A huge chunk of the mountain has come off. There is ash, dust, and lava on the ground now.

CCC Stability and Change . . . .

Ask: Do you think a long time has passed between the middle and bottom picture? No, a volcanic eruption is a quick change made to Earth's surface.

Differentiate Instruction

ELL Children may be unfamiliar with the word *eruption* and how the term is used in this context. Discuss how the first time a carbonated beverage is opened, there is the sound of gas being released and bubbles of gas can be seen floating to the top of the bottle. **Ask: How do you think that is similar to a volcano when it has an eruption?** When a volcano has too much gas, the ash, dust, and lava need to escape, like the gas in the bottle.

Volcanoes

Explore online. ▶

Before many volcanoes erupt, they look like quiet mountains. This is Mount St. Helens just days before it erupted in 1980.

During an eruption, ash and dust burst from the opening at the top. Lava pours out from openings in the mountain. All of this happens quickly.

After the eruption, a huge chunk has blown off the mountaintop. Ash and dust cover the ground nearby. Some volcanoes gain new land at the bottom where lava cools into rock.

A **volcano** is an opening in Earth's surface where lava, gases, and bits of rock erupt. It can cause fast changes.

248

Do the Math! • Zukur Volcano is 2047 feet tall. Masaya Volcano is 2083 feet tall. Write <, >, or = to compare their heights.

Use Symbols
Go to the online handbook for tips.

2047 feet $<$ 2083 feet

✋ **Apply What You Know**

✏️▷ Draw before and after pictures of a volcano changing Earth's surface. Share your drawing with a classmate. Use evidence to explain the changes.

Check children's drawings.

© Houghton Mifflin Harcourt

Do the Math! • Use Symbols

Review with children how to compare numbers using place value. Remind them that they can find the value of a digit by its place in a number. Guide children to observe that both numbers have ones, tens, hundreds, and thousands.

Children should write "<" when comparing 2047 feet and 2083 feet.

💡 **Use Symbols** Remind children that > stands for "is greater than," < stands for "is less than," and = stands for "is equal to."

SEP **Constructing Explanations and Designing Solutions** . . . .

Volcanoes change Earth's surface quickly. Remind children of the three pictures on the previous page showing a volcanic eruption. **Ask: How do these pictures help explain how Earth's surface has changed?** The pictures show what happens to the land and the mountain before, during, and after a volcano erupts.

✋ **FORMATIVE ASSESSMENT** ━━

Guide children to think about what they have seen and read about volcanoes. Have them use this understanding to draw before and after pictures of a volcano changing Earth's surface. Have pairs work together to describe what happens when a volcano erupts. Encourage children to use labels or captions to add information to their drawings. Be sure children use evidence to support their answers.

Scoring Guidelines

• draws before and after pictures to describe what happens to Earth's surface after a volcano erupts
• provides sufficient evidence to support their claims

Landslides

3D Learning Objective

Children **observe and describe** what happens during **a landslide**. They use their observations to identify **the quick changes made to Earth's surface**.

DCI The History of Planet Earth . . . .

Direct children's attention to the top picture. **Ask: What are landslides?** Landslides are when the soil and rocks slide down the side of a hill, mountain, or slope. **Ask: What are some possible reasons landslides happen?** Heavy rains can start a landslide. When soil and rocks become too heavy, they can begin to slide.

SEP Constructing Explanations and Designing Solutions . . . .

Have children compare the before and after pictures of a landslide. **Ask: How has the land changed in the after picture?** In the after picture, a landslide has covered the area in soil and rocks. **Ask: What is another change that could happen to Earth's surface when there is a landslide?** Land could be washed out.

CCC Stability and Change . . . .

Ask: Is a landslide a fast change? Explain your reasoning. Yes, it is a fast change because landslides can move between 10 and 35 miles per hour.

Landslides

A **landslide** is when rocks and soil slide down a hill, mountain, or other slope. Once a landslide starts, it moves fast. The rushing soil, rocks, and mud can run down a slope at 10 to 35 miles per hour. Look at the pictures to explore how a landslide changes Earth's surface quickly.

Explore online.

before

A landslide starts when the soil and rocks on the side of a slope become too heavy and start to slide. Often, heavy rain triggers a landslide.

after

A landslide moves a lot of land very quickly. Both the slope and the area around it change shape. Large areas can be buried or washed out.

250

What changes do landslides make to Earth's surface? Choose all correct answers.

Ⓐ They start volcanoes and earthquakes.

🅑 They change the shape of hills.

🅒 They bury or wash out areas around a slope.

Apply What You Know

✏️ Draw a picture of how a landslide causes changes to Earth's surface. Use evidence to describe the changes.

> **Constructing Explanations**
> Go to the online handbook for tips.

Children should draw a picture of a landslide. It should show a change in Earth's surface.

DCI The History of Planet Earth . . . .

Children should choose B—They change the shape of hills; and C—They bury or wash out areas around a slope. If children choose A, refer them back to the sections of the lesson that talk about volcanoes and earthquakes. Remind children that while volcanoes and earthquakes are changes to Earth's surface, landslides do not start these fast changes. However, volcanoes and earthquakes can sometimes trigger landslides.

SEP **Constructing Explanations and Designing Solutions** . . . .

Remind children that during a landslide, rocks and soil slide down a slope. Have children observe the two bottom pictures on the previous page. **Ask: How do you think the slope affects a landslide?** I think the steeper the slope is, the faster the rocks and soil will slide down.

FORMATIVE ASSESSMENT

Guide children to think about what they have seen and read about landslides. Children can look in books or on the Internet to find pictures of a landslide for inspiration before they draw their own picture. Their pictures should show how Earth's surface has been changed. Encourage children to use labels and captions in their drawings.

Scoring Guidelines
- draws a picture of a landslide
- describes how the landslide changes Earth's surface
- provides sufficient evidence to support their answers

💡 **Constructing Explanations** Have children use observations and information they have gathered to describe what happens during a landslide.

Explore online. ▶ Have children explore online to find out more about changes to Earth's surface.

DCI The History of Planet Earth . . . .

Children should match the top picture with "The ground shakes." They should match the middle picture with "Lava, gas, and rocks erupt." They should match the bottom picture with "Rocks and soil rush down a slope." If children do not make the correct matches, have them review the sections of the lesson that talk about earthquakes, volcanoes, and landslides. **Ask: Which changes caused the results shown in the pictures?** An earthquake caused the damage to the road in the top picture. A volcanic eruption caused lava to cover the road in the middle picture. A landslide covered the road in the bottom picture.

CCC Stability and Change . . . .

Review the matching activity with children. Guide children in a discussion about the changes seen in each picture. **Ask: What is something that all three of these changes have in common?** They all bring about fast changes to Earth's surface.

💡 **Stability and Change** Remind children that some changes happen slowly, and some changes happen rapidly. Fast changes can happen in as little as a few minutes or a few days; while slow changes can take anywhere from hundreds, to thousands, to even millions, of years.

Connection to Physical Science

Chemical Reactions Heating or cooling a substance may cause changes that can be observed. When a volcano erupts, lava flows out of the volcano as a liquid. As it cools, it hardens and becomes a solid. As a class, discuss how the hardened lava changes Earth's surface.

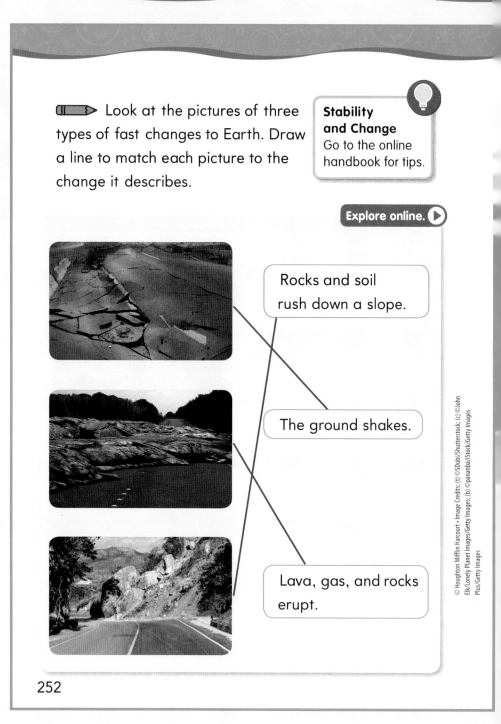

✏️ Look at the pictures of three types of fast changes to Earth. Draw a line to match each picture to the change it describes.

Stability and Change Go to the online handbook for tips.

Explore online. ▶

Rocks and soil rush down a slope.

The ground shakes.

Lava, gas, and rocks erupt.

© Houghton Mifflin Harcourt • Image Credits: (t) ©SDubi/Shutterstock; (c) ©John Elk/Lonely Planet Images/Getty Images; (b) ©pananba/iStock/Getty Images Plus/Getty Images

252

Hurricanes

Explore online. ▶

The beach looks quiet now, but a hurricane is on the way. Hurricanes form over warm water in the ocean.

The storm brings strong wind and heavy rain. The wind makes large, powerful waves that crash on the beach.

Wind, waves, and rain move sand to new places. A hurricane can uproot trees and cause flooding, too.

A **hurricane** is a tropical storm with powerful winds and heavy rain. It can cause fast changes to Earth's surface.

Lesson 2 • What Changes on Earth Happen Quickly?

253

Hurricanes

3D Learning Objective

Children **observe and describe** what happens during **a hurricane**. They use their observations to identify **the quick changes made to Earth's surface**.

DCI The History of Planet Earth . . . .

CCC Stability and Change . . . .

Ask: What are hurricanes? They are strong tropical storms that form over warm water in the ocean. **Ask:** What happens during a hurricane? There are strong winds and heavy rain. The strong winds make large, powerful waves in the ocean that can come crashing onto the shore. **Ask:** How long can a hurricane last? Hurricanes can last a few days, but the changes to Earth's surface happen quickly.

SEP Constructing Explanations and Designing Solutions . . . .

Have children observe and describe what is happening in each picture. **Ask:** Compare the top and middle pictures. How are they different? The top picture shows the beach before a hurricane appears. The middle picture shows how powerful wind from a hurricane is. **Ask:** Observe the bottom picture. How does a hurricane change Earth's surface? Hurricanes move sand on the beach to a new place. They can uproot trees and cause flooding.

Collaboration

Think, Pair, Share Have pairs of children research additional information about hurricanes, including category types and names. Provide resources to help children gather information. Have them present their findings to the class.

Constructing Explanations and Designing Solutions . . . .

Discuss with children how observing significant changes in the weather and using them as evidence can help explain what is happening. **Ask: How would you describe what this picture shows?** There are huge waves crashing over a parking lot. This is evidence of a hurricane.

 The History of Planet Earth . . . .

Discuss what changes may be made to Earth's surface because of the hurricane in this picture. **Ask: Did these changes happen slowly or quickly?** The changes happened quickly. **Can you think of any changes to Earth's surface that could happen over time if hurricanes continue to occur?** The water could erode the sand on the beach.

 FORMATIVE ASSESSMENT ——————

Evidence Notebook

Have pairs discuss the rapid changes hurricanes cause to Earth's surface before children record their answer in their Evidence Notebook. Make sure that children use evidence to support their answer.

Scoring Guidelines
- describes two events that happen during a hurricane
- provides evidence of changes to Earth's surface

💡 **Stability and Change** Remind children that hurricanes bring rapid changes to Earth's surface. Within just a few hours, land after a hurricane can be drastically different.

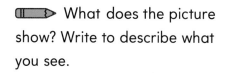 What does the picture show? Write to describe what you see.

Sample answer: Strong winds from

a hurricane caused huge waves to

crash onto the land.

_____

_____

 Apply What You Know

Evidence Notebook • Think about the changes that a hurricane causes to Earth's surface. Which two events does a hurricane bring? How do they cause Earth's surface to change? Record your answers in your Evidence Notebook. Use evidence to explain how they cause changes.

Stability and Change
Go to the online handbook for tips.

254

Floods

Look at the picture to explore how a flood changes Earth's surface.

Explore online. ▶

A **flood** occurs when a huge amount of water overflows or soaks an area that is usually dry. A flood starts quickly, often with little warning. Rain may fill a river with extra water. When the river cannot hold any more, it overflows. That triggers a flood. A flood can knock down trees and wash away land. It can bury huge areas with mud or silt. When the water goes down, the land is changed.

Lesson 2 • What Changes on Earth Happen Quickly?   255

Floods

3D Learning Objective

Children **observe and describe** what happens during **a flood**. They use their observations to identify **the quick changes made to Earth's surface**.

DCI The History of Planet Earth . . . .

CCC Stability and Change . . . .

Ask: What happens during a flood? Floods make areas that are usually dry become soaked with water. **Ask:** How does a flood change Earth's surface? Floods can knock down trees and bushes. They can wash away land and bury areas with mud. **Ask:** How long can floods last? Floods start quickly and can last a few days.

SEP Constructing Explanations and Designing Solutions . . . .
Have children turn their attention to the picture. **Ask:** What is happening in the picture? A flood has covered the land. **Ask:** What do you think the land will look like once the water goes down? I think some areas might have less land, while others might have a build-up of soil.

Differentiate Instruction

RTI/Extra Support Share with children before and after pictures of land that has been affected by a flood. Have them describe how the flood changed the land.

Extension Children who want to find out more about floods can gather information on flood zones or flood levels as they apply to the area where they live.

The History of Planet Earth . . . .

Discuss what changes may be made to Earth's surface as a result of the flood in these pictures. Children should write 3 under the first picture, 1 under the middle picture, and 2 under the last picture. If children do not put the pictures in the correct order, have them return to the previous page and underline any text that would help them sequence the pictures.

Stability and Change . . . .

Discuss the changes seen between the three pictures of Earth's surface when flooding occurs. **Ask: What changes did the flood make to the surface of Earth in these pictures?** The water level is low in the middle picture before the flood. It is much higher during the flood in the last picture. Once the water has receded, we see there are changes to the riverbank.

FORMATIVE ASSESSMENT

Read, Write, Share! • Participate in a Research Project • Use Digital Tools to Publish Writing
Children collect information from a variety of resources to use as supporting evidence for their claim. Guide children as they locate pictures, charts, and audio or video clips to go with their writing.

Scoring Guidelines
• uses a variety of resources to find information
• uses the information as evidence to support their claim

💡 **Participate in a Research Project • Use Digital Tools to Publish Writing** Children can use note cards to take notes in their own words from various sources to remember and organize information. Guide children to use a variety of digital tools to produce and publish writing as they work together to show how floods cause quick changes to Earth's surface.

✏️ What takes place during a flood? Write **1**, **2**, and **3** to show the correct order

| 3 | 1 | 2 |

 Apply What You Know

Read, Write, Share! • Work with a partner. First, state a claim: Floods cause quick changes to Earth's surface. Next, gather information to use as evidence to support your claim. Look at books and online sources. Then, use the information to write a report. Share your report with your classmates.

Participate in a Research Project • Use Digital Tools to Publish Writing
Go to the online handbook for tips.

256

© Houghton Mifflin Harcourt • Image Credits: (l) ©Nicole Duplaix/Photolibrary/Getty Images; (r) ©Jason Edwards/National Geographic Magazines/Getty Images; (l) ©Utopia_88/iStock/Getty Images Plus/Getty Images

Hands-On Activity

Model Quick Changes on Earth

Name _____

Hands-On Activity

Model Quick Changes on Earth

Materials _____

Ask a Question

What changes do floods cause on Earth's surface? _____

Test and Record Data   Explore online. ▶

Step ①

Make a model of land. Observe the model before adding water. Record your observations.

Children should draw or describe their model before pouring water.	Sample answer: The model is an area made of soil, sand, and rocks in a tub.

Step ②

Add water to the model. Observe the model. Record your observations.

Children should draw or describe their model after pouring water.	Sample answer: When water moves across the soil and sand, it moves the sand and soil. It changes the way the soil and sand look.

Lesson 2 • What Changes on Earth Happen Quickly?   257

© Houghton Mifflin Harcourt

Model Quick Changes on Earth

3D Learning Objective

SEP **Constructing Explanations and Designing Solutions** . . . .

Children build a model to observe what happens to Earth's surface during a flood. **Ask:** Have you ever seen a flood? Accept all reasonable answers.

Suggested Materials water, container, rocks, soil, sand, disposable plastic gloves

Preparation

Pre-assemble materials bundles for small groups. Lay down newspaper or another covering over the desks or tables to keep them from getting dirty or wet. Have paper towels handy to clean up spills.

DCI **The History of Planet Earth** . . . .

Activity

Remind children what models are. **Ask: What can a model flood show us?** We should be able to see changes made to our model when we make it flood. **What question can we ask before building our model?** Sample answer "What can I find out by modeling a flood?"

STEP 1 Guide children to use the soil, sand, and rocks to make a model of land. Circulate around the room and provide assistance as necessary while children are building their models. Be sure children record their observations before adding the water.

STEP 2 Guide children to pour the water into their model to simulate a flood. **Ask: What changes do you observe as you flood your model?** The water has moved the soil, the sand, and some of the rocks. Have children draw a second picture and write about what their model looks like now that it has been flooded.

Hands-On Activity, continued

STEP 3 Children should analyze and compare the before and after pictures they drew. Have each group compare their results with another group to see if they are similar.

STEP 4 Allow children to discuss how the differences they saw during Step 3 tell how water can quickly change Earth's surface. Guide children to make a claim that answers the questions using their models as evidence.

Claims, Evidence, and Reasoning

Ask: What can we learn by building a model and flooding it? We can see how the land changes by modeling a flood. **Ask:** What evidence do you have? The water covered the soil and everything became wet. The water moved the soil and changed the way it looked.

Scoring Rubric for Hands-On Activity

3	States a claim supported by evidence about what happens during a flood
2	States a claim that is somewhat supported by evidence about what happens during a flood
1	States a claim that is not supported by evidence
0	Does not state a claim and does not provide evidence

Step 3

Analyze your results. Compare the model before and after you added water to it. Draw your results.

Before	After
Children should draw a picture of their model before pouring water.	Children should draw a picture of their model after pouring water.

Step 4

What differences do you observe? How do they help you understand how water causes quick changes to Earth's surface?

Make a claim that answers your question.

Sample answer: By modeling a flood, I can see how water covers the soil and how it changes the way the land looks as it moves.

What is your evidence?

Sample answer: I observed the water covering the soil and getting everything wet when I poured it in the model. I observed the soil being moved by the water, which changed the way the land looked.

258

© Houghton Mifflin Harcourt

Explore online. ▶   Guide children to the Interactive Online Student Edition where they can choose from and explore both paths.

Take It Further

People in Science & Engineering •
Dr. Rosaly M.C. Lopes

Explore more online.
• Earthquake Locations

Dr. Lopes visited the Yasur volcano in the South Pacific Ocean.

Explore online. ▶

Dr. Rosaly Lopes is a volcanologist. A volcanologist is a scientist who studies volcanoes. Dr. Lopes studies volcanoes on Earth and on other planets. How does she do this?

Some volcanoes leave colorful mineral deposits.

Dr. Lopes takes an Explorers Club flag on many of her trips.

First, Dr. Lopes studies volcanoes on Earth. She explores volcanoes that explode like fireworks and flow like rivers. She also explores volcanoes with lava lakes. She measures how lava cools at each volcano and looks for patterns.

Take It Further

People in Science and Engineering •
Dr. Rosaly M. C. Lopes

Children investigate who Dr. Rosaly M. C. Lopes is and what a volcanologist does. Volcanologists perform a variety of tasks. They study the history of volcanoes, both active and dormant, and measure any seismic activity. Volcanologists want to understand how volcanoes work. They travel to the sites of volcanoes and collect data, which can help them try to predict future eruptions. This is extremely important for people who live around volcanoes because it helps them be better prepared.

Differentiate Instruction

RTI/Extra Support This would be a good time to introduce the suffix *–ology*. Explain that the suffix *–ology* means "one who studies." Therefore, the volcanologist is one who studies volcanoes.

Extension Children who want to find out more can do research on Dr. Lopes. She is a Senior Research Scientist at NASA and the Deputy Manager for Planetary Science. There is a wealth of information on her scientific research and publications, and she was honored in the 2006 edition of *The Guinness Book of World Records* because she has discovered the most active volcanoes around the world.

Take It Further, continued

SEP Constructing Explanations and Designing Solutions . . . .

Explanations and solutions come from observations made from several sources. **Ask: What observations does Dr. Lopes make to help her get information about volcanoes?** Dr. Lopes looks at images of volcanoes, measures lava flow, and looks for patterns to help her find new volcanoes. **Ask: How can using lava flow patterns help to find new volcanoes?** Lava flow patterns can be observed to see where the lava came from. The patterns of lava flow lead back to a volcano.

Children should choose all three answer choices. If they do not, have them go back and underline text that will help them answer the question.

Collaboration

Small Groups You may choose to have children work in small groups to research another type of scientist that studies one of the events in this unit. Encourage group members to brainstorm and discuss why we need people who study these events. Have each group member research the answer to a particular question, and then have that group member share his or her findings.

Explore more online.

Earthquake Locations

Have children go online to explore more about earthquakes.

Then, Dr. Lopes studies images from space. She looks for cooling patterns in these images to locate volcanoes on other planets and moons. Dr. Lopes has used patterns to discover more than 70 volcanoes on Io, which is one of Jupiter's moons. These patterns tell her that Io has many lava lakes. Dr. Lopes believes that Io must be very colorful due to the number of deposits from volcanoes.

© Houghton Mifflin Harcourt • Image Credits: ©NASA

How does Dr. Lopes study volcanoes?
Choose all correct answers.

Ⓐ She explores different volcanoes.

Ⓑ She measures how lava cools.

Ⓒ She looks for patterns in images from space.

260

Lesson Check

Lesson Check   Name _____

Explore online. ▶

Can You Explain It?

✏️ How can a volcano cause Earth's surface to change quickly?

Be sure to

• Describe the event.

• Explain how it causes changes to Earth's surface.

Sample answer: When a volcano erupts, lava, gases, and bits

of rock explode out of an opening in Earth's surface. When the

eruption is over, ash and dust cover the ground nearby, and

there may be new land at the bottom where lava cools into rock.

_____

Lesson 2 • What Changes on Earth Happen Quickly?   261

Can You Explain It?

Have children reread their answers to the Can You Explain It? prompt at the beginning of the lesson.

DCI **The History of Planet Earth** . . . .

Review the two pictures and discuss what happens to Earth's surface when a volcano erupts. **Ask: How would you describe what is happening in these pictures?** A volcano is erupting and lava, gases, and bits of rock are exploding out of an opening in Earth's surface. Large amounts of lava have hardened and are now blocking the road.

SEP **Constructing Explanations and Designing Solutions** . . . .

Have children identify how Earth's surface changes after a volcanic eruption. **Ask: What happens to Earth's surface after a volcano has erupted?** Ash and dust cover the ground, and there may be new land at the bottom where lava cools into rock.

Scoring Guidelines

• Children should describe the event of a volcanic eruption.
• Children should explain how Earth's surface changes after a volcanic eruption.

Collaboration

Cultivating New Questions As children complete this lesson and prepare for the next lesson, ask them to identify additional questions they have about fast changes to Earth's surface. **Ask: What are some other events that happen quickly to change Earth's surface?** Tornadoes are fast-moving storms with strong winds that can change the land. As children continue to the next lesson, they will apply concepts related to Earth's changing surface.

Lesson Check, continued

SUMMATIVE ASSESSMENT
Self Check

1. Children should write the number 3 under the first picture, the number 1 under the middle picture, and the number 2 under the last picture to show the sequence for the hurricane. If children incorrectly sequence the pictures, discuss what is happening in each picture. The middle picture shows a beach before the hurricane. The last picture shows the beach while the hurricane is happening. The first picture shows the beach after the hurricane has passed, when sand has been moved and trees have been blown over.

2. Children should choose A—a few minutes. If children choose B or C, review the Landslides section of the lesson. A landslide changes Earth's surface quickly and only lasts a few minutes.

3. Children should choose A—Beaches are reshaped; and C—Trees blow over. If children choose B, review the Volcanoes section of the lesson to show that volcanoes can cause ash and dust to cover the ground. Also review the Hurricanes section of the lesson to remind them that the powerful winds of a hurricane can cause beaches to be reshaped and trees to blow over.

Self Check

1. How does a hurricane cause changes to Earth's surface? Write **1**, **2**, and **3** to show the correct order.

<u>   3   </u>   <u>   1   </u>   <u>   2   </u>

2. How long does a landslide last?
   - Ⓐ a few minutes
   - Ⓑ a few months
   - Ⓒ a few years

3. What are some effects of a hurricane? Choose all correct answers.
   - Ⓐ Beaches are reshaped.
   - Ⓑ Farms get buried in ash and dust.
   - Ⓒ Trees blow over.

262

4. Draw a line to match the cause in each picture on the left with its effect on the right.

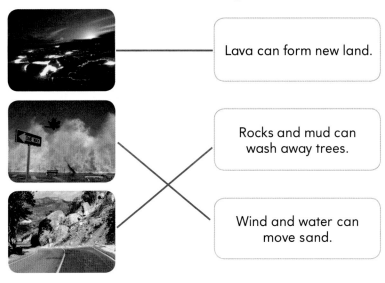

Lava can form new land.

Rocks and mud can wash away trees.

Wind and water can move sand.

5. What happens when the ground begins to shake?
Ⓐ earthquake
Ⓑ flood
Ⓒ volcano

6. How can you describe floods and hurricanes? Write **flood** or **hurricane** in each sentence.

A ____flood____ happens when waters overflow.

A ____hurricane____ brings high winds and large waves to a coastline.

4. Children should match the top picture with the top caption, Lava can form new land. If this match is incorrect, have children revisit the Volcanoes section of the lesson to review what happens when a volcano erupts. Children should match the middle picture with the bottom caption, Wind and water can move sand. If this match is incorrect, have children revisit the Hurricanes section of the lesson to review how a hurricane's strong winds can affect the land. Children should match the bottom picture with the middle caption, Rocks and mud can wash away trees. If this match is incorrect, have children revisit the Landslides section of the lesson to review how landslides can cause changes to Earth's surface.

5. Children should choose A—earthquake. If children choose B or C, have them revisit the Earthquakes section of the lesson to review what happens during an earthquake.

6. Children should write flood on the top line and hurricane on the bottom line. If children reverse the words, have them revisit the Floods section and the Hurricanes section of the lesson to review what happens during floods and hurricanes.

Engineer It • How Can We Prevent Wind and Water from Changing Land?

Building to the Performance Expectation

The learning experiences in this lesson prepare children for mastery of:

2-ESS2-1 Compare multiple solutions designed to slow or prevent wind or water from changing the shape of the land.

 Trace Tool to the NGSS
Go online to view the complete coverage of these standards across this lesson, unit, and time.

 **Science & Engineering Practices**

 **Disciplinary Core Ideas**

 **Crosscutting Concepts**

Constructing Explanations and Designing Solutions
Compare multiple solutions to a problem.

▶ **VIDEO** SEPs: Constructing Explanations and Designing Solutions / Engaging in Argument from Evidence

ESS2.A: Earth Materials and Systems
Wind and water can change the shape of the land.

ETS1.C: Optimizing the Design Solution
Because there is always more than one possible solution to a problem, it is useful to compare and test designs.

Stability and Change
Things may change slowly or rapidly.

▶ **VIDEO** CCC: Stability and Change

Influence of Engineering, Technology, and Science on Society and the Natural World
Developing and using technology has impacts on the natural world.

Science Addresses Questions About the Natural and Material World
Scientists study the natural and material world.

CONNECTIONS TO MATH

MP.2 Reason abstractly and quantitatively.

MP.4 Model with mathematics.

MP.5 Use appropriate tools strategically

2.MD.B.5 Use addition and subtraction within 100 to solve word problems involving lengths that are given in the same units, e.g., by using drawings (such as drawings of rulers) and equations with a symbol for the unknown number to represent the problem.

CONNECTION TO ENGLISH LANGUAGE ARTS

RI.2.1 Ask and answer such questions as *who*, *what*, *where*, *when*, *why*, and *how* to demonstrate understanding of key details in a text.

Integrating the Three Dimensions of Learning

This lesson focuses on ways to prevent erosion to the land caused by wind and water. Children explore how wind and water cause the land to change over time **(DCI Earth Materials and Systems) (CCC Stability and Change)**. Next, children explore ways to prevent changes to land through the use of different types of technology **(DCI Optimizing the Design Solution) (CCC Influence of Engineering, Technology, and Science on Society and the Natural World; CCC Science Addresses Questions About the Natural and Material World)**. Finally, children will design, test, and compare possible solutions that will prevent water from changing the land **(SEP Constructing Explanations and Designing Solutions)**.

Professional Development

Go online to view **Professional Development videos** with strategies to integrate CCCs and SEPs, including the ones used in this lesson.

Build on Prior Knowledge

Children should already know and be prepared to build on the following concepts:

- There is more than one way to solve a problem. *(Grade 2, Unit 1, Lesson 2)*
- Wind and water can cause changes to the surface of Earth. *(Grade 2, Unit 5, Lessons 1 and 2)*
- Engineers solve problems by asking questions, analyzing information, and using models. *(Grade 2, Unit 1, Lessons 1 and 2)*
- Technology can be used to help solve problems. *(Grade 2, Unit 1, Lessons 1 and 2)*
- Events in nature can happen quickly or slowly. *(Grade 2, Unit 5, Lessons 1 and 2)*
- Technology impacts the natural world.
- Scientists study the natural and designed world. *(Grade 2, Unit 2, Lesson 1; Grade 2, Unit 3, Lessons 3 and 4)*

Differentiate Instruction

Lesson Vocabulary
- dike
- windbreak

Reinforcing Vocabulary To help children remember each vocabulary word, have them draw to illustrate each one. When discussing *windbreak*, explain that it is a compound word. Discuss the word *wind* and how it means moving air. Explain that fast–moving air can cause damage. The word *break* means to separate. A windbreak is placed to "break the wind up" to reduce the amount of damage caused by fast–moving air, or wind.

RTI/Extra Support Children may be unfamiliar with solutions that can be used to prevent land from changing. Provide children with a variety of pictures that show different solutions. Take children on a walk around school and point out different solutions, such as a retaining wall or bushes planted on a hillside.

Extension Challenge children to research different words that can be used to describe forms of wind. For example, a derecho is a windstorm that moves with severe thunderstorms. The jet stream is an air current found in the atmosphere. Monsoons are seasonal winds normally found in Asia.

ELL Be sure to point out all labels, pictures, captions, and headings throughout the lesson to assist children with strategies to summarize chunks of content. Discuss with children real-life connections to content, and provide hands-on examples of materials when possible to best support the needs of these learners.

Lesson Problem

Build on Prior Lessons

In Lesson 2, children explored **fast changes to Earth's surface** by **using observations from several sources.** Lesson 3 builds on these concepts by exploring how **wind and water can change the shape of the land** and how **multiple solutions can help reduce or prevent these changes.**

Lesson Objective

Compare design solutions that prevent wind and water from changing the land.

About This Image

Ask: Why do you think people wanted to build this concrete wall? to block the ocean water from getting on land Remind children that as they explore, they will find out what changes wind and water make to Earth and some ways to prevent these changes.

SEP Constructing Explanations and Designing Solutions

Alternative Engage Strategy

Investigating Erosion	 small groups 🕐 15–25 minutes

Provide each small group with a cookie sheet or flat piece of thick cardboard. Guide each group to lay a pencil flat at the top of the sheet and let it go. Have them make observations about what happened to the pencil. Children should observe the pencil rolling down the cookie sheet or cardboard. Ask children to brainstorm ideas on how to prevent the pencil from rolling down the cookie sheet or cardboard. Have groups share their ideas and discuss.

Lesson 3

Engineer It • How Can We Prevent Wind and Water from Changing Land?

A sea wall can protect the shore from ocean waves.

By the End of This Lesson

I will be able to describe and evaluate different solutions to help stop wind and water from changing land.

264

Can You Solve It?

Preventing Changes to Land Allow children time to watch
the video that shows how heavy rainfall can change the
land. If the video is not available, guide children in making
observations about the two pictures on the page. **Ask: What
are some things we could do to prevent changes to Earth
by water? Have you seen any erosion or weathering in your
area? Is there something in place already to slow down this
erosion or weathering? Is there something else you can do to
slow down or prevent this erosion or weathering?** Accept all
reasonable answers.

Ask children to record their initial thoughts about how land
can be changed by wind and water. Remind them not to be
concerned if they are unsure of their answers. At the end of this
lesson, children will revisit these pictures as part of the Lesson
Check. At this point, children should be able to explain how
people can prevent water and wind from changing the land.

Preventing Changes to Land

Look at the pictures to explore how heavy
rainfall can cause changes to the land.

Explore online. ▶

© Houghton Mifflin Harcourt • Image Credits: (l) © CrackerClips Stock Media/Alamy Stock Video; (r) ©Mike Kipling Photography/Alamy

Can You Solve It?

✏️➤ What can people do to prevent water
and wind from changing the land?

Accept all reasonable answers.

_____

_____

_____

Collaboration

Build on Prior Knowledge Allow children time to
think about places where they have seen wind and/or
water erosion or weathering in the area where they
live. Allow time for children to brainstorm possible
ways to slow down or prevent erosion and weathering.
Have children plan what needs to happen to build or
complete one of their ways to slow down or prevent
erosion where they live.

Support for Unit Project

The **Unit Project** Make a Windbreak supports content in
this lesson.

Changes Caused by Wind

3D Learning Objective

Children observe how **wind erosion changes** the land.

DCI Earth Materials and Systems . . . .

Guide children in a discussion about the two top pictures on the page. Have children make comparisons between the two pictures. Explain that the photograph on the right doesn't have any plants, therefore wind is able to move the soil around. **Ask: What problems does wind cause for the farmer?** Wind erosion causes the rich top soil to blow away. The land becomes useless to farmers because the soil doesn't have enough nutrients for plants to grow.

CCC Stability and Change . . . .

Have children discuss how the sand dunes have changed in the two bottom pictures. **Ask: What problem did wind cause on this beach?** Wind erosion caused the sand on the beach to move, causing the dunes to become smaller. **Ask: Do you think these changes happened quickly, or slowly?** Accept reasonable answers as children discuss how fast or slow these changes happened.

Connection to Life Science

Cause and Effect Remind children that a cause is why something happens and an effect is what actually happens. Then discuss how wind erosion can make it very difficult for crops to grow and survive due to the loss of rich soil. Have children work in small groups to discuss how the loss of crops can effect people. Have each group share their ideas with the class.

Changes Caused by Wind

Look at these pictures to explore how erosion by wind can harm the land.

before

after

A farm has rich soil to grow crops. <u>Wind can blow the soil away.</u> The land is useless to farmers. They cannot grow crops in soil with no nutrients.

before   after

These pictures show the same beach. Once, there were tall sand dunes. Over time, wind carried away much of the sand, making the dunes smaller.

Underline the sentence that tells what caused the farm to lose its healthy soil.

266

Do the Math! • A beach is 52 feet wide. Strong winds cause a lot of the sand to be eroded. The beach now measures 37 feet. How much smaller is the beach now because of wind erosion?

Subtract Lengths Go to the online handbook for tips.

Ⓐ 25 feet

Ⓑ 89 feet

Ⓒ 15 feet

Do the Math! • Subtract Lengths

Children should choose C—15 feet. If they choose A or B, have them read the problem aloud. Then have them underline important words such as *how much smaller*. **Ask: How did you know this wasn't an addition problem?** The problem was not an addition problem because it asked how much smaller the beach was because of wind erosion. This means that there is less beach than there was at the beginning of the problem.

💡 **Subtract Lengths • Reason Abstractly and Quantitatively • Model with Mathematics • Use Appropriate Tools**
Guide children to use a number line to solve this word problem. Have them draw a line above the number line for the greater number, 52, and a line below the number line for the lesser number, 37. Then have children find the difference between the two numbers.

Apply What You Know

Evidence Notebook • Think about how wind can change the land. Why do you think it is important to stop wind erosion? Write two reasons why. Use evidence to support your answers. Record your answers in your Evidence Notebook.

© Houghton Mifflin Harcourt

 FORMATIVE ASSESSMENT

Evidence Notebook
Children first discuss how wind changes the land. Monitor children as they brainstorm at least two reasons why it is important to stop wind erosion. Guide children to record their two reasons in their Evidence Notebook.

Scoring Guidelines
• provides two reasons why it is important to stop wind erosion
• provides evidence to support their answers

Changes Caused by Water

3D Learning Objective

Children observe how **water erosion** **changes** the land.

(DCI) Earth Materials and Systems . . . .

Guide children in a discussion about the three pictures. Have children make observations and compare the pictures. Discuss with children that just like wind, water causes erosion too. **Ask: What problems does water cause to Earth?** Heavy rains can trigger a landslide. Flooding can also damage the land. Rushing water can wash away soil.

Differentiate Instruction

RTI/Extra Support Children may be unfamiliar with the word *erosion* and require additional support to understand how the word is used in this context. Explain that erosion is a kind of change that happens when wind and water move rock and soil. **Ask: What do you think the waves are doing to the sand?** The waves are carrying the sand away to another place.

Extension Children may want to find out more about flooding. Have children go online to research flood zones. **Ask:** Are there any flood zones where you live? Accept all reasonable answers.

Changes Caused by Water

Look at the pictures to explore how water can cause harmful changes to land.

Explore online. ▶

Rushing water can crash into riverbanks. It moves the soil from one place to another. It causes the edges of rivers to change shape.

Heavy rains on a mountain slope can cause a landslide. The wet soil becomes loose and muddy. It slides downhill.

Floods can damage the land. The water rises and covers large areas of land. It can knock over bushes and trees.

268

✏️➤ How can water harm the land? Match the pictures with the labels that tell how.

flood | rushing water | heavy rains

Evidence Notebook • Look at the picture. What is happening to the farmland? In your Evidence Notebook, record two ways that flooding harms farmland. Use evidence to support your answer.

Lesson 3 • Engineer It • How Can We Prevent Wind and Water from Changing Land?   269

DCI **Earth Materials and Systems** . . . .

Review the photographs of problems with the land. **Ask: What caused the problem we see in each of these pictures? Was it a flood, rushing water, or heavy rains?** Match the picture with the cause of its problem. Children should match the image on the left with flood, the middle image with heavy rains, and the last image with rushing water.

CCC **Stability and Change** . . . .

Have children discuss whether or not the changes in the pictures were fast or slow changes. Encourage children to support their thinking with evidence from the pictures.

 FORMATIVE ASSESSMENT

Evidence Notebook
Guide children to observe what is happening to the farmland in this picture. Children write their observations in their Evidence Notebooks. Make sure that children use evidence to support their answers.

Scoring Guidelines
• describes what happened to the farmland
• identifies two ways flooding harms the farmland
• provides evidence to support their claims

Ways to Prevent Changes to Land

3D Learning Objective

Children **observe** and **compare multiple solutions to erosion**. They **compare different solutions** to determine how **technology** was used to prevent erosion.

ccc **Influence of Engineering, Technology, and Science on Society and the Natural World . . . . .**

Ask: In what ways did engineers use technology to prevent erosion? Sample answer: Engineers used sandbags stacked on top of each other to build a wall. The wall stopped water from flooding the house.

ccc **Science Addresses Questions About the Natural and Material World . . . .**

Remind children that when they make observations, they should pay attention to details. Discuss with children how scientists ask questions and make observations about the world around them to better understand what they are studying. **Ask: What materials were used in each prevention method?** Sand, concrete, wood, and metal were used in the prevention methods. **Why do you think these materials were used?** Many of these materials are very strong, so they are good to use when there is a lot of erosion.

Collaboration

Jigsaw Group children as evenly as possible. Assign each group one type of erosion prevention such as sandbags, dikes, windbreaks, retaining walls, or metal wires and brackets. Allow each group time to research their type of prevention. Once research is complete, regroup children by having one member from each of the different solution groups join together. Then have children share the information they researched about their particular solution.

Ways to Prevent Changes to Land

Look at the pictures to explore how people try to prevent wind and water from changing the land.

Explore online. ▶

Farmers have ways to keep wind from blowing away rich soil. They plant trees and shrubs to help block the wind. These trees and shrubs are called **windbreaks**.

Beach grass can help keep some of the sand from blowing away. Fences help block some of the wind and keep sand from being moved.

270

Bags of sand can help prevent or slow flooding. People pour sand into water-resistant bags. Then they stack the sandbags to build a wall. The wall keeps the water from covering the land.

A **dike** is a wall by a river or another body of water. People build dikes in places where the water often rises and falls. Dikes can be made of concrete, wood, clay, or other materials.

SEP Constructing Explanations and Designing Solutions . . . .

Discuss with children the different types of erosion prevention. Have children compare the differences between sandbags and dikes as a solution to prevent erosion. **Ask: What would be another solution to prevent water from entering the home?** A small retaining wall could be built to block water if it floods.

DCI Optimizing the Design Solution . . . .

Have children discuss the highlighted word. Share with children that a dike is used predominantly around large bodies of water. A dike is a more permanent solution compared to sandbags, which are not a permanent solution. **Ask: Why is it important to have different solutions to water erosion?** Having different solutions ensures that all types of water erosion situations can be prevented. Each solution might work best for only one type of situation.

Differentiate Instruction

ELL Children may be unfamiliar with the word *prevent* and require additional support to understand how the word is used in this context. Give one child a soft ball and tell him or her to gently toss it in the air. Then instruct the child to not let the ball hit the floor. The child will instinctively catch the ball to stop it from hitting the floor. Explain that the child "prevented the ball from hitting the floor" and that the word *prevent* means to keep something from happening.

Constructing Explanations and Designing Solutions . . . .

Encourage children to make detailed observations about all three landslide solutions. Discuss and compare the designs to determine which one would prevent the most erosion. **Ask: Which of the three pictures would be the best method to prevent or slow down the damage from a landslide?** A design that uses all three methods would prevent the most erosion.

Constructing Explanations and Designing Solutions
Guide children to think of different ways to solve a problem. They can make comparisons to see how the ways are alike and different.

 FORMATIVE ASSESSMENT

Read, Write, Share! • Ask and Answer Questions
Children brainstorm two questions about ways to prevent wind and water erosion, and search for information to answer these questions. Guide children as they locate information to answer the questions. Allow children to share their findings with the class.

Scoring Guidelines
• records two questions about preventing erosion
• locates information from multiple sources
• answers each question and supports it with evidence

Ask and Answer Questions Children should ask and answer questions that begin with words such as *who, what, where, when, why,* and *how* to demonstrate understanding of key details in a text.

Look at the pictures to explore several ways to prevent landslides. Some solutions work better than others.

Constructing Explanations
Go to the online handbook for tips.

Explore online.

Plant roots hold soil in place, but heavy rain can loosen the soil.

A wall keeps mud and rocks in place, but it does not prevent a landslide.

Technology like wires and brackets hold the whole hillside in place.

 Apply What You Know

Read, Write, Share! • What are two questions you have about ways to prevent wind and water from changing the land? Look in books, magazines, or on the Internet to find answers. Share your questions and answers with your class.

Ask and Answer Questions
Go to the online handbook for tips.

© Houghton Mifflin Harcourt

272

Hands-On Activity

Engineer It • Prevent Water from Changing Land

Name _____

Materials _____
_____

Ask a Question

What are some ways to prevent water from changing the land?

Test and Record Data Explore online. ▶

Step 1

Make a model. Observe the model before adding water. Record your observations and data.

Children's pictures should show their model before adding water.	Children's descriptions should list out the details of the model.

Step 2

Add water to your model. Observe the model. Record your observations and data.

Lesson 3 • Engineer It • How Can We Prevent Wind and Water from Changing Land?   273

© Houghton Mifflin Harcourt

Hands-On Activity 👥 small groups 🕐 1 class period

Engineer It • Prevent Water from Changing Land

3D Learning Objective

SEP Constructing Explanations and Designing Solutions . . . .

Children design, test, and redesign possible solutions to prevent water from changing land. Children then communicate their findings to others.

Suggested Materials disposable plastic gloves, soil, small cup or container to transfer soil, foil tray or plastic tub, water in a pitcher or other large container, toothpicks, craft sticks, straws, chenille sticks, small rock, glue or tape, clay or modeling clay

Preparation

Have children brainstorm the materials they might use the day before conducting the hands-on activity. Then pre-assemble the materials before conducting the hands-on activity.

Activity

Guide children to read the activity title and pose a question they want to answer in the investigation based on this topic.

STEP 1 Provide children with assigned roles within the groups in order to keep all children engaged in the activity. Discuss with children what a model is and why it is important to build a model.

STEP 2 Guide children to pour the water into their model. Ask children to record their observations and data about the changes made to their model. Encourage children to make detailed observations and notes.

CCC Science Addresses Questions About the Natural and Material World . . . .

Remind children that they can record any questions they have as they observe water being added to their model. Review with children that scientists ask questions in order to better understand the topic they are studying.

Hands-On Activity, continued

STEP 3 The step will require time for children to implement their designs. Setting a timer will help children manage their designs, and work more collaboratively.

STEP 4 Guide children to pour the water into their new model with the water damage prevention design. Ask children to record their observations and data about the changes made to their new model design.

SEP **Constructing Explanations and Designing Solutions** . . . .

Have children discuss their design and the results of their test. **Ask: How do you know if your design is successful?** The changes to the model will be minimal.

STEP 5 Guide children to revise and retest their design to prevent water damage. Ask children to record their observations and data about the changes made to their revised model design.

Claims Evidence and Reasoning

Children should make a claim that states at least one solution that prevents water from changing their model. They should cite evidence to support how their design prevented the water from changing the land. Allow children to share their claims and evidence with other groups.

	Scoring Rubric for Hands-On Activity
3	States a claim supported with evidence about a solution that prevents water from changing land
2	States a claim somewhat supported with evidence about a solution that prevents water from changing land
1	States a claim that is not supported by evidence
0	Does not state a claim and does not provide evidence

Step 3
Design and build a solution to slow or prevent changes by the water. Rebuild the model. Put the design solution in place.

Step 4
Test your design. Fill the model with about the same amount of water as before. Observe your model and measure the height of its banks. Record your observations and data.

Check children's observations and data.

Step 5
Revise and retest your design. Compare your results with the results of other groups.

Make a claim that answers your question.

Children should describe what they used for their design solution.

_____

_____

What is your evidence?

Children should list specific examples of how their design solution

prevented the water from changing the land.

_____

274

© Houghton Mifflin Harcourt

Explore online. ▶   Guide children to the Interactive Online Student Edition where they can choose from and explore both paths.

Take It Further

Careers in Science & Engineering •
Geotechnical Engineer

Explore more online. ▶
• The Dust Bowl

Explore online. ▶

Geotechnical engineers study soil and rock to plan the best way to build things on land.

They also work to keep wind and water from changing the land. They build dikes to stop flooding. They plan walls to protect the shore. They design technology to stop landslides.

What do geotechnical engineers do?
Choose all correct answers.

Ⓐ They study soil and rock.

Ⓑ They plan the best way to build things on land.

Ⓒ They work to change the land.

Lesson 3 • Engineer It • How Can We Prevent Wind and Water from Changing Land?   275

© Houghton Mifflin Harcourt • Image Credits: (t) ©Image Bank Film/Getty Images

Take It Further

Careers in Science and Engineering •
Geotechnical Engineer

Children explore how geotechnical engineers work to keep wind and water from changing land. A geotechnical engineer studies soil and rock in order to design structures that remain stable on land. They design and construct a variety of structures such as dams, roadways, tunnels, and levees. Their work is to design solutions for use during earthquakes, landslides, and floods.

CCC **Influence of Engineering, Technology, and Science on Society and the Natural World . . . .**

Discuss the pictures on the page, and have children observe the one of the lady writing on the clipboard. Explain to children that writing or drawing is one way to make a plan. **Ask: What are other ways to make a plan for an investigation?** Accept all reasonable answers.

Children should choose A—They study soil and rock.; and B—They plan the best way to build things on land. If children choose C, refer them back to the pictures and text. Encourage children to underline or mark the answers as they read.

Differentiate Instruction

RTI/ Extra Support Review ways wind and water can change land. Point out that geotechnical engineers work to protect land from wind and water erosion. Have children underline the text that describes what a geotechnical engineer does.

Extension Children who want to find out more about geotechnical engineering can do research on the different areas in which geotechnical engineers work.

Take It Further, continued

Children design a structure to reduce damage from wind or water. Encourage children to use evidence to support their explanations when they share with the class.

SEP Constructing Explanations and Designing Solutions . . . .

Discuss wind or water damage in your area. **Ask: Where can we see problems from wind or water damage in our own community?** Sample answers: When it rains, the road always floods. The soccer net always blows away. The playground is always too muddy around the swings after it rains. **Ask: What are some things we could do to slow down or prevent this from happening?** Guide children to draw and label a structure that would prevent damage from the wind or water.

Collaboration

Small Groups You may choose to have children work in small groups to research different structures that could prevent or slow down the problem. Encourage group members to brainstorm and discuss how their ideas would help. Allow time for the group to finalize their structure and present it to the class.

Explore more online.

The Dust Bowl

Children explore how wind can affect land and form a dust bowl.

✏️ What would you design if you were a geotechnical engineer? Design a structure that would reduce damage from wind or water. Then draw and label your design. Explain your idea to a partner or to the class.

Drawings will vary but should reflect a structure that would reduce wind or water from damaging the land, such as a dike or a retaining wall.

276

Explore online. ▶

Lesson Check

Lesson Check   Name _____

Explore online. ▶

Can You Solve It?
✏️ What can people do to prevent water and wind from changing the land?

Be sure to
- Identify and describe ways to prevent flooding.
- Identify and describe ways to prevent wind erosion.
- Identify and describe ways to prevent landslides.

Sample answer: People can use sandbags and dikes

to prevent flooding. They can also use windbreaks,

shrubs, trees, and retaining walls to prevent erosion

and landslides.

Lesson 3 • Engineer It • How Can We Prevent Wind and Water from Changing Land?   277

© Houghton Mifflin Harcourt • Image Credits: (l) ©Medford Taylor/Getty Images; (r) ©Mike Kipling Photography/Alamy

Can You Solve It?
Have children reread their answers to the Can You Solve It? prompt at the beginning of the lesson.

DCI **Optimizing the Design Solution** . . . .

Guide children in a discussion of the problems caused by slow and fast changes to Earth's surface. Remind them about the different ways they have learned to prevent or reduce these negative effects. **Ask: What are some ways you've learned to prevent water or wind erosion?** Children should list all of the prevention methods mentioned in the lesson.

CCC **Influence of Engineering, Technology, and Science on Society and the Natural World** . . . .

Have children think about how engineers use their jobs to help people solve problems. Relate this work to the problems caused by fast and slow changes. **Ask: How do these solutions help solve problems that are caused by changes to Earth's surface?** These solutions help reduce or prevent wind and water erosion.

Scoring Guidelines
- Children should identify and describe ways to prevent flooding, wind erosion, and landslides.

Collaboration
Cultivating New Questions As children complete this lesson, ask them to identify additional questions they have about ways to prevent wind and water from changing land. **Ask: What other types of technology help keep water from changing land?** Levees are used to keep bodies of water from overflowing onto land.

Lesson Check, continued

SUMMATIVE ASSESSMENT
Lesson Check

1. Children should choose the middle picture. If children choose the first or last picture, briefly review the Ways to Prevent Changes to Land section of the lesson. Discuss how farmers prevent wind from blowing away the soil.

2. Children should choose the first and last pictures. If children choose the middle picture, briefly review the Ways to Prevent Changes to Land section of the lesson. Discuss how people prevent water damage during floods.

3. Children should choose B—keep landslides from starting. If children choose A or C, briefly review the Landslide Solutions section of the lesson. Discuss why engineers use these techniques.

Self Check

1. Which shows a way to help stop wind from blowing soil from a farm or field?

2. How can people help prevent or slow floods? Choose all correct answers.

3. What do designs to prevent landslides try to do?
   - Ⓐ slow landslides down
   - Ⓑ keep landslides from starting
   - Ⓒ make landslides smaller

278

4. What change are people trying to prevent in each picture? Use a word from the box to identify the change.

flood
landslide
wind erosion

landslide
_____

flood
_____

wind erosion
_____

5. Which country would need to build dikes? Choose the best answer.

Ⓐ Mongolia, which is high in the mountains

🅱 Netherlands, which is mostly at or below sea level

Ⓒ Chile, which is covered with a sandy desert

4. Children should write *landslide* on the top line, *flood* on the middle line, and *wind erosion* on the bottom line. If children answer incorrectly, review how the top picture shows trees on the side of a mountain, which are meant to prevent a landslide. The middle picture shows a dike along the shore of the ocean, which is meant to prevent a flood. The bottom picture shows trees close together and bending with the wind, which is a windbreaker and meant to prevent wind erosion.

5. Children should choose B—Netherlands, which is mostly at or below sea level. If children choose A or C, remind them that dikes are built to hold back water, not mountains or sand. Have them review the Ways to Prevent Changes to Land section of the lesson.

Unit 5 Performance Task

Engineer It • Build an Earthquake-Proof Structure

👥 small groups   ⏱ 2 class periods

Objective
Children plan and design a **solution to a problem** in order to **compare and test possible designs** of an earthquake-proof structure that will **impact the natural world**.

Suggested Materials
toothpicks, marshmallows, straws, rubber bands, cardstock, paper, paper clips, string, clay, paper plates

Preparation
Review Lesson 2 to provide context for this Unit Performance Task. Collect materials such as those suggested above in advance of this activity. Guide children to select two or three materials and to use a paper plate as the base of their earthquake-proof structure.

SEP Constructing Explanations and Designing Solutions . . . .
Children design, test, and redesign possible solutions for an earthquake-proof structure. **Ask: Is an earthquake an event on Earth that happens slowly or quickly?** quickly **Ask: Can a problem have more than one solution?** yes

STEPS

Step 1 • Define a Problem
Guide children in a discussion about the problem they will solve.

Step 2 • Plan and Build
Remind children that engineers think of different ways to solve a problem. **Ask: How can you build a structure that can withstand an earthquake?** Sample answer: I can build a structure that will move some without falling down. **What materials will you use, and how will you show your design?** Answers will vary.

Unit 5 Performance Task
Engineer It • Build an Earthquake-Proof Structure

Materials

_____

_____

STEPS

Step **1**

Define a Problem You want to build a structure that can survive an earthquake.

Step **2**

Plan and Build Think about the materials you will use. Come up with at least two ideas for your structure. Build your structure.

© Houghton Mifflin Harcourt

280

Step 3

Test and Improve Test your design. Shake your structure. Does it stay together? Does it fall apart?

Step 4

Redesign How can you improve your design? Change how you put the materials together to make your structure stronger.

Step 5

Communicate Explain how your structure works. Use evidence to tell how your design solves the problem.

✔ Check

_____ I built a structure that can survive an earthquake.

_____ I tested my structure.

_____ I improved the design of my structure.

_____ I shared my results.

_____ I used evidence to explain how my design solves a problem.

© Houghton Mifflin Harcourt

Step 3 • Test and Improve

CCC Stability and Change . . . .

Children may have limited ideas for improvements. Consider having the groups critique each other's designs and reasoning. Use sentence frames, such as the following, to guide their discussions:
- "Why did you choose straws instead of toothpicks?"
- "What could be the weak area in your structure?"

Step 4 • Redesign

DCI Optimizing the Design Solution . . . .

Guide children to implement one improvement discussed in Step 3. Children should retest their structures to evaluate their ability to stay intact when the paper plate is shaken to represent an earthquake. **Ask: How did the improvement help your structure work better? Did it change in the way that you thought it would?** Answers will vary.

Step 5 • Communicate

Children should communicate their results, and include an explanation for each step of a design process that they followed. Children should explain, based on their test results, which materials are best suited for a structure that can survive an earthquake.

Scoring Rubric for Performance Task		
3		Builds, tests, and redesigns an earthquake-proof structure, communicates the results, and uses evidence to explain the design
2		Builds, tests, and redesigns an earthquake-proof structure, but does not communicate results or use evidence to explain the design
1		Builds an earthquake-proof structure, but does not test or redesign it, and does not communicate results or use evidence to explain the design
0		Does not build, test, or redesign a structure that can withstand an earthquake

Unit 5 Review

SUMMATIVE ASSESSMENT

1. Children should choose C—Wind blows sand against rocks. If children choose A, reinforce that the wind does not weather rocks by moving them. If children choose B, reinforce that water makes rocks wet, not wind. By completing Weathering in Lesson 1, children explored how wind can break off small pieces from a rock over hundreds of years.

2. Children should choose C—water. If children choose A or B, reinforce that water is what caused the arch to form. By completing Erosion by Water in Lesson 1, children explored how water can wear down rock, and cause erosion over a long period of time.

3. Children should choose A—Ice makes the cracks in the rock bigger each year. If children choose B or C, reinforce how ice takes up more space than water and pushes against the rocks. By completing Weathering by Water and Ice in Lesson 1, children explored how water and ice cause weathering to rocks.

Unit 5 Review   Name _____

1. How does wind cause weathering to rocks?
   - (A) Wind moves rocks.
   - (B) Wind makes rocks wet.
   - ● Wind blows sand against rocks.

---

2. What caused this arch to form over a long period of time?
   - (A) a glacier
   - (B) a hurricane
   - ● water

---

3. Each winter, water freezes in the cracks of this rock. How does this ice cause weathering to the rock?
   - ● Ice makes the cracks in the rock bigger each year.
   - (B) Ice makes the cracks in the rock thinner each year.
   - (C) Ice makes the cracks in the rock darker each year.

© Houghton Mifflin Harcourt • Image Credits: (tr) ©Patrick Walsh/EyeEm/Getty Images; (br) © Jennifer Booher/Alamy Stock Photo

282

4. Which can cause erosion? Choose all
correct answers.
Ⓐ Wood can cause erosion.
🅑 Wind can cause erosion.
🅒 Water can cause erosion.

5. Which changes Earth's surface quickly?
Choose all correct answers.
🅐 flood
🅑 volcano
Ⓒ weathering

6. What is one effect of a volcano?
Ⓐ It causes a hurricane.
Ⓑ It floods the land with water.
🅒 It covers the ground nearby with ash and dust.

7. A farmer planted a row of trees at the end of
a field. What does this farmer hope to prevent?
Ⓐ water from flooding the field
🅑 wind from blowing away soil
Ⓒ lava from covering the field

4. Children should choose B—Wind can cause erosion; and C—Water can cause erosion. If children choose A, reinforce that wood cannot pick up and move rocks, soil, and sand. By completing the sections about erosion in Lesson 1, children explored how erosion is caused by wind, water, and ice.

5. Children should choose A—flood and B—volcano. If children choose C, remind children that weathering changes Earth over time. By completing the Volcanoes and Floods sections in Lesson 2, children explored how these two events change Earth's surface quickly.

6. Children should choose C—It covers the ground nearby with ash and dust. If children choose A or B, remind them that hurricanes and floods change Earth's surface, and they are not caused by a volcano. By completing Volcanoes in Lesson 2, children explored the effects of a volcano.

7. Children should choose B—wind from blowing away soil. If children choose A or C, reinforce that trees can't stop floods, and lava can knock down trees and burn them. By completing Ways to Prevent Changes to Land in Lesson 3, children explored different ways to prevent wind and water from changing land.

3D Item Analysis	1	2	3	4	5	6	7
SEP Constructing Explanations and Designing Solutions	•	•	•	•	•	•	•
DCI The History of Planet Earth	•	•	•	•	•	•	
DCI Earth Materials and Systems							•
CCC Stability and Change	•	•	•	•	•	•	•
CCC Influence of Engineering, Technology, and Science on Society and the Natural World							•
CCC Science Addresses Questions About the Natural and Material World							•

8. Children should choose A, B, and C. If children do not choose all three answer choices, discuss how each item could slow or stop a flood. By completing Ways to Prevent Changes to Land in Lesson 3, children explored ways people try to prevent water from changing land.

9. Children should choose B—a landslide. If children choose A or C, reinforce that a rock wall stops rocks and mud from sliding down. By completing Ways to Prevent Changes to Land in Lesson 3, children explored how a wall can help prevent a landslide.

10. Children should choose C—at least 8 feet. If children choose A or B, guide children to understand that they need to add the two given lengths. By completing Do the Math! in Lesson 3, children practiced subtracting lengths.

3D Item Analysis	8	9	10
SEP Constructing Explanations and Designing Solutions	•	•	•
DCI Earth Materials and Systems	•	•	•
DCI Optimizing the Design Solution	•		
CCC Stability and Change	•	•	
CCC Influence of Engineering, Technology, and Science on Society and the Natural World	•	•	•
CCC Science Addresses Questions About the Natural and Material World	•	•	•

8. Which items can you use to build something that will slow or stop a flood? Choose all correct answers.

Ⓐ empty sandbag   Ⓑ concrete cinder block   Ⓒ pile of builder's sand

9. Look at this wall built on the side of a mountain. What do the people who built it hope to prevent?

Ⓐ a flood
Ⓑ a landslide
Ⓒ a hurricane

10. Li-Mei is building a structure to protect a town from floods. The town has an existing structure that is 5 feet tall. But in the past, floodwaters rose 3 feet higher than that. How high should the new structure be?
Ⓐ at least 3 feet
Ⓑ at least 5 feet
Ⓒ at least 8 feet

284

© Houghton Mifflin Harcourt • Image Credits: (tc) © Jiang Zhongyan/Shutterstock; (tr) © CGIBackgrounds.com/Getty Images; (br) © Worraket/Shutterstock

Resources

Reading in the Science Content Area

Integrating Reading and Science Instruction

This listing compiles readers and trade books that align with the topical organization of the Performance Expectations and Disciplinary Core Ideas for Grade 2 of the NGSS, and the units contained within the *HMH Science Dimensions™* program. Titles are arranged according to their approximate Guided Reading Levels.

As with all materials you share with your class, we suggest you review the books first to ensure their appropriateness. While titles are available at time of publication, they may go out of print without notice.

Structure and Properties of Matter—Units 1–2

Level G

Condensation by Rice, William (Shell Educational Publishing/TCM)

Evaporation by Rice, William (Shell Educational Publishing/TCM)

Made of Wood by Rigby Staff (Rigby/Steck-Vaughn)

Solids, Liquids, and Gases by Garrett, Ginger (Grolier/Scholastic Library Publishing)

Level I

How Do You Measure Liquids? by Adamson, Thomas (Capstone Press)

States of Matter by Hutchinson, Caroline (Newmark Learning)

What Is Liquid? by Boothroyd, Jennifer (Lerner Publishing Group)

What Is Solid? by Boothroyd, Jennifer (Lerner Publishing Group)

Level J

All about Matter by Schuh, Mari (Capstone Press)

Matter Comes in All Shapes by Hansen, Amy (Rourke Publishing)

Salt by Rigby Staff (Rigby/Steck-Vaughn)

What is Matter? by Curry, Don L. (Grolier/Scholastic Library Publishing)

Level K

Changing Materials by Oxlade, Chris (Crabtree Publishing Company)

Saving Water and Energy by Rigby Staff (Rigby/Steck-Vaughn)

Solids by Greathouse, Lisa (Shell Educational Publishing/TCM)

Working with Metal by Rigby Staff (Rigby/Steck-Vaughn)

Level L

Liquids by Ryback, Carol (GarethStevens)

Solids by Mezzanotte, Jim (GarethStevens)

What Floats? What Sinks? A Look at Density by Boothroyd, Jennifer (Lerner Publishing Group)

Level M

Gases by Mezzanotte, Jim (GarethStevens)

How Big? How Heavy? How Dense? A Look at Matter by Boothroyd, Jennifer (Lerner Publishing Group)

How Do We Measure Matter? by Peppas, Lynn (Crabtree Publishing Company)

The Nature of Matter by Housel, Debra (Shell Educational Publishing/TCM)

What Is a Gas? by Peppas, Lynn (Crabtree Publishing Company)

What Is a Liquid? by Peppas, Lynn (Crabtree Publishing Company)

What Is a Solid? by Peppas, Lynn (Crabtree Publishing Company)

Level N

Matter: See It, Touch It, Taste It, Smell It by Stille, Darlene (Capstone Press)

Measuring Volume by Reinke, Beth Bence (Cherry Lake Publishing)

Melting Matter by Hansen, Amy (Rourke Publishing)

The Scoop about Measuring Matter by Maurer, Tracy (Rourke Publishing)

Interdependent Relationships in Ecosystems—Unit 3

Level G

A Butterfly's Life by Rigby Staff (Rigby/Steck-Vaughn)

Animals on the Go by Brett, Jessica (Houghton Mifflin Harcourt Publishing)

Level H

A Nest of Grass by Rigby Staff (Rigby/Steck-Vaughn)

Animal Habitats by Lundgren, Julie (Rourke Publishing)

Dinosaur Nests by Rigby Staff (Rigby/Steck-Vaughn)

Growing Peas by Rigby Staff (Rigby/Steck-Vaughn)

How Do Animals Change? by Kalman, Bobbie (Crabtree Publishing Company)

The Spider Plant by Rigby Staff (Rigby/Steck-Vaughn)

Where Do Snakes Live? by Rigby Staff (Rigby/Steck-Vaughn)

Level I

Amazing Plants by Hewitt, Sally (Crabtree Publishing Company)

Living in a Rain Forest by Fowler, Allan (Grolier/Scholastic Library Publishing)

Pine Trees by Weiss, Ellen (Grolier/Scholastic Library Publishing)

Save the Sea Turtles by Leonhardt, Alice (Rigby/Steck-Vaughn)

Seasons of the Deciduous Forest Biome by Duke, Shirley (Rourke Publishing)

Which Insects Live Here? by Pyers, Greg (Rigby/Steck-Vaughn)

Wolves by Smith, Richard G. (Rigby/Steck-Vaughn)

Level J

Desert Animals by Snyder, Jane (Rosen Publishing)

Flower Farms by Rigby Staff (Rigby/Steck-Vaughn)

Grassland Habitat by MacAulay, Kelley (Crabtree Publishing Company)

Growing Cotton by Rigby Staff (Rigby/Steck-Vaughn)

Hippos by Rigby Staff (Rigby/Steck-Vaughn)

Plants We Use by Rigby Staff (Rigby/Steck-Vaughn)

Pollination by Rice, Dona (Shell Educational Publishing/TCM)

Terrific Trees by Rigby Staff (Rigby/Steck-Vaughn)

Wonderful Worms by Rigby Staff (Rigby/Steck-Vaughn)

Level K

Fantastic Fungi by Rigby Staff (Rigby/Steck-Vaughn)

From A Tree by Rigby Staff (Rigby/Steck-Vaughn)

Ocean Animal Adaptations by Murphy, Julie (Capstone Press)

Plants That Eat Animals by Fowler, Allan (Grolier/Scholastic Library Publishing)

Rainforest Animal Adaptations by Amstuty, Lisa J. (Capstone Press)

Soil Basics by Schub, Mari (Capstone Press)

Step into the Desert by Rice, Howard (Shell Educational Publishing/TCM)

What Can Live In A Grassland? by Anderson, Sheila (Lerner Publishing Group)

What Is a Carnivore? by Kalman, Bobbie (Crabtree Publishing Company)

What Is a Herbivore? by Kalman, Bobbie (Crabtree Publishing Company)

What Is an Omnivore? by Kalman, Bobbie (Crabtree Publishing Company)

Level L

Baboon Troops by Rigby Staff (Rigby/Steck-Vaughn)

Carrots Grow Underground by Schaub, Mari (Capstone Press)

Let's Look at Soil by Conners, Cathy (Rosen Publishing)

Plants Live Everywhere! by Wade, Mary Dodson (Rosen Publishing)

Plants Make Their Own Food by Lundgren, Julie (Rourke Publishing)

Seeds Go, Seeds Grow by Weakland, Mark (Capstone Press)

Seeds, Bees and Pollen by Lundgren, Julie (Rourke Publishing)

What Can Live In The Lake? by Anderson, Sheila (Lerner Publishing Group)

What Can Live In The Mountains? by Anderson, Sheila (Lerner Publishing Group)

Level M

A Look at Snakes by Halpern, Jerald (Rigby/Steck-Vaughn)

An Encyclopedia Of Animals by Rigby Staff (Rigby/Steck-Vaughn)

Bats by Rigby Staff (Rigby/Steck-Vaughn)

Forests by Rigby Staff (Rigby/Steck-Vaughn)

Peculiar Plants by Ganeri, Anita (Capstone Press)

Photosynthesis: Changing Sunlight Into Food by Kalman, Bobbie (Crabtree Publishing Company)

Plants In Different Habitats by Kalman, Bobbie (Crabtree Publishing Company)

Soil Basics by Ditchfield, Christin (Grolier/Scholastic Library Publishing)

Superstar Plants by Spilsbury, Richard (Rosen Publishing)

Level N

Caribou by Rigby Staff (Rigby/Steck-Vaughn)

Composting by Hicks, Dwayne (Rosen Publishing)

Deserts by Rigby Staff (Rigby/Steck-Vaughn)

Endangered Mammals by Rigby Staff (Rigby/Steck-Vaughn)

How Do Plants Make and Spread Their Seeds? by Owen, Ruth (Rosen Publishing)

Living in Groups by Rigby Staff (Rigby/Steck-Vaughn)

Mammals Around the World by Rigby Staff (Rigby/Steck-Vaughn)

My Frog Log by Rigby Staff (Rigby/Steck-Vaughn)

Toothwalkers by Rigby Staff (Rigby/Steck-Vaughn)

Level O

Antarctic Seals by Rigby Staff (Rigby/Steck-Vaughn)

Waterbirds by Rigby Staff (Rigby/Steck-Vaughn)

Earth's Systems: Processes that Shape the Earth—Units 4–5

Level G

Lakes by Rigby Staff (Rigby/Steck-Vaughn)

The Land And Water Of The United States: A Dictionary by Rigby Staff (Rigby/Steck-Vaughn)

Water Cycle by Hutchinson, Caroline (Newmark Learning)

Water Cycle by Maloof, Torrey (Shell Educational Publishing/TCM)

Level H

Canals by Rigby Staff (Rigby/Steck-Vaughn)

Whatever the Weather by Wallace, Karen (DK Publishers)

When a Storm Comes Up by Fowler, Allan (Grolier/Scholastic Library Publishing)

Level I

Looking At Rocks by Dussling, Jennifer (Penguin Random House)

Where Did All The Water Go? by Rigby Staff (Rigby/Steck-Vaughn)

Wild Weather by Rigby Staff (Rigby/Steck-Vaughn)

Level J

Angel Falls: World's Highest Waterfall by Rigby Staff (Rigby/Steck-Vaughn)

Earthquakes! by Armour, Cy (Shell Educational Publishing/TCM)

Earth's Rock Cycle by Dee, Willa (Rosen Publishing)

Tornadoes and Hurricanes by Armour, Cy (Teacher Created Resources)

Unearthing Metamorphic Rocks by Dee, Willa (Rosen Publishing)

Volcanoes! by Armour, Cy (Shell Educational Publishing/TCM)

Weathering and Erosion by Maloof, Torrey (Shell Educational Publishing/TCM)

Level K

Ice on the Move by Rigby Staff (Rigby/Steck-Vaughn)

Inside Caves by Rigby Staff (Rigby/Steck-Vaughn)

Melting and Freezing by Greathouse, Lisa (Shell Educational Publishing/TCM)

Rivers by Sweney (Capstone Press)

Shaping the Earth by Rigby Staff (Rigby/Steck-Vaughn)

Unearthing Igneous Rocks by Dee, Willa (Rosen Publishing)

Level L

Canyons by Sweney (Capstone Press)

Earth's Mountains by Kalman, Bobbie (Crabtree Publishing Company)

Earth's Rivers by Kalman, Bobbie (Crabtree Publishing Company)

Igneous Rocks by Nelson, Maria (GarethStevens)

Introducing Landforms by Kalman, Bobbie (Crabtree Publishing Company)

Metamorphic Rocks by Nelson, Maria (GarethStevens)

Our Earth by Walsh, Kenneth (Shell Educational Publishing/TCM)

Rocks and Minerals by Symes, R.F. (DK Publishers)

Sedimentary Rocks by Nelson, Maria (GarethStevens)

Storms by Rigby Staff (Rigby/Steck-Vaughn)

The Wonderful Water Cycle by Rigby Staff (Rigby/Steck-Vaughn)

Volcanoes by Kalman, Bobbie (Crabtree Publishing Company)

Weathering and Erosion by Nelson, Maria (GarethStevens)

What Holds Us to Earth? A Look at Gravity by Boothroyd, Jennifer (Lerner Publishing Group)

What Shapes the Land? by Kalman, Bobbie (Crabtree Publishing Company)

Level M

Earth's Rock Cycle by Allen, Nancy Kelly (Rosen Publishing)

Fossil Fuels by Rigby Staff (Rigby/Steck-Vaughn)

Landforms by Rice, William (Shell Educational Publishing/TCM)

Mountains, Hills, and Cliffs by Rigby Staff (Rigby/Steck-Vaughn)

Oceans by Franklin, Yvonne (Shell Educational Publishing/TCM)

Oceans, Seas, and Coasts by Rigby Staff (Rigby/Steck-Vaughn)

Our Changing Earth: An Encyclopedia of Landforms by Rigby Staff (Rigby/Steck-Vaughn)

Rivers, Streams, and Lakes by Rigby Staff (Rigby/Steck-Vaughn)

Shaping Our Environment by Buchanan, Shelly (Shell Educational Publishing/TCM)

Waterfalls by Rigby Staff (Rigby/Steck-Vaughn)

Weathering and Erosion by Hoffman, Steven M. (Rosen Publishing)

Level N

Cracking Up: A Story of Erosion by Bailey, Jacqui (Capstone Press)

Glaciers by Schub, Mari (Capstone Press)

Mountains by Hutmscher (Capstone Press)

Ponds by Franklin, Yvonne (Shell Educational Publishing/TCM)

Level O

Volcanoes and Geysers by Rigby Staff (Rigby/Steck-Vaughn)

Common Core State Standards
for English Language Arts

A correlation to the Next Generation Science Standards is located in the front of this Teacher Edition. Correlations for the Common Core State Standards for English Language Arts are provided on these pages.

Grade 2	Units/Lessons
Reading Standards for Informational Text	
Key Ideas and Details	
RI.2.1 Ask and answer such questions as *who, what, where, when, why,* and *how* to demonstrate understanding of key details in a text.	Unit 1 Lesson 1 Unit 2 Lesson 3 Unit 5 Lesson 1 Unit 5 Lesson 3
Integration of Knowledge and Ideas	
RI.2.8 Describe how reasons support specific points the author makes in a text.	Unit 2 Lesson 4 Unit 2 Lesson 2
Writing Standards	
Production and Distribution of Writing	
W.2.6 With guidance and support from adults, use a variety of digital tools to produce and publish writing, including in collaboration with peers.	Unit 1 Lesson 1 Unit 1 Lesson 2
Research to Build and Present Knowledge	
W.2.7 Participate in shared research and writing projects (e.g., read a number of books on a single topic to produce a report; record science observations).	Unit 3 Lesson 1 Unit 3 Lesson 3 Unit 3 Lesson 4 Unit 5 Lesson 1 Unit 5 Lesson 2

Grade 2	Units/Lessons
W.2.8 Recall information from experiences or gather information from provided sources to answer a question.	Unit 1 Lesson 2
	Unit 2 Lesson 1
	Unit 2 Lesson 2
	Unit 3 Lesson 1
	Unit 3 Lesson 3
	Unit 3 Lesson 4
	Unit 4 Lesson 1
	Unit 4 Lesson 2
	Unit 5 Lesson 1
Speaking and Listening Standards	
Comprehension and Collaboration	
SL.2.2 Recount or describe key ideas or details from a text read aloud or information presented orally or through other media.	Unit 5 Lesson 1
Presentation of Knowledge and Ideas	
SL.2.5 Create audio recordings of stories or poems; add drawings or other visual displays to stories or recounts of experiences when appropriate to clarify ideas, thoughts, and feelings.	Unit 1 Lesson 1
	Unit 3 Lesson 2

Common Core State Standards for Mathematics

A correlation to the Next Generation Science Standards is located in the front of this Teacher Edition. Correlations to the Common Core State Standards for Mathematics are provided on these pages.

Grade 2	Units/Lessons
Operations and Algebraic Thinking	
Represent and solve problems involving addition and subtraction	
2.OA.A.1 Use addition and subtraction within 100 to solve one- and two-step word problems involving situations of adding to, taking from, putting together, taking apart, and comparing with unknowns in all positions, e.g., by using drawings and equations with a symbol for the unknown number to represent the problem.	Unit 2 Lesson 4
Work with equal groups of objects to gain foundations for multiplication	
2.OA.C.4 Use addition to find the total number of objects arranged in rectangular arrays with up to 5 rows and up to 5 columns; write an equation to express the total as a sum of equal addends.	Unit 3 Lesson 1
Number and Operations in Base Ten	
Understand place value	

2.NBT.A.1 Understand that the three digits of a three-digit number represent amounts of hundreds, tens, and ones; e.g., 706 equals 7 hundreds, 0 tens, and 6 ones. Understand the following as special cases:
 	
    2.NBT.A.1.A
 	
    100 can be thought of as a bundle of ten tens — called a "hundred."
 	
    2.NBT.A.1.B
 	
    The numbers 100, 200, 300, 400, 500, 600, 700, 800, 900 refer to one, two, three, four, five, six, seven, eight, or nine hundreds (and 0 tens and 0 ones).
	Unit 5 Lesson 1
	Unit 5 Lesson 2

2.NBT.A.3 Read and write numbers to 1000 using base-ten numerals, number names, and expanded form.	Unit 4 Lesson 2
2.NBT.A.4 Compare two three-digit numbers based on meanings of the hundreds, tens, and ones digits, using >, =, and < symbols to record the results of comparisons.	Unit 2 Lesson 3 Unit 4 Lesson 1

Grade 2	Units/Lessons
Measurement and Data	
Relate addition and subtraction to length	
2.MD.B.5 Use addition and subtraction within 100 to solve word problems involving lengths that are given in the same units, e.g., by using drawings (such as drawings of rulers) and equations with a symbol for the unknown number to represent the problem.	Unit 4 Lesson 2 Unit 5 Lesson 3
Represent and interpret data	
2.MD.D.10 Draw a picture graph and a bar graph (with single-unit scale) to represent a data set with up to four categories. Solve simple put-together, take-apart, and compare problems using information presented in a bar graph.	Unit 1 Lesson 1 Unit 1 Lesson 2 Unit 2 Lesson 1 Unit 3 Lesson 2 Unit 3 Lesson 3 Unit 3 Lesson 4 Unit 4 Lesson 1
2.G.A.2 Partition a rectangle into rows and columns of same-size squares and count to find the total number of them.	Unit 2 Lesson 2

Math Correlations

Grade 2	Units/Lessons
Mathematical Practices	
MP.2 Reason abstractly and quantitatively.	Unit 1 Lesson 1 Unit 1 Lesson 2 Unit 3 Lesson 1 Unit 3 Lesson 3 Unit 3 Lesson 4 Unit 4 Lesson 1 Unit 4 Lesson 2 Unit 5 Lesson 1 Unit 5 Lesson 2 Unit 5 Lesson 3
MP.4 Model with mathematics.	Unit 1 Lesson 1 Unit 1 Lesson 2 Unit 2 Lesson 1 Unit 3 Lesson 1 Unit 3 Lesson 2 Unit 3 Lesson 3 Unit 3 Lesson 4 Unit 4 Lesson 1 Unit 4 Lesson 2 Unit 5 Lesson 1 Unit 5 Lesson 2 Unit 5 Lesson 3
MP.5 Use appropriate tools strategically.	Unit 1 Lesson 1 Unit 1 Lesson 2 Unit 5 Lesson 3

cienceSaurus, A Student Handbook, is a "mini-encyclopedia" hildren can use to explore more about unit topics. It contains umerous resources including concise content summaries; an lmanac; many tables, charts, and graphs; a history of science and a lossary. ScienceSaurus is available from Houghton Mifflin Harcourt.

Science Dimensions Grade 2	*ScienceSaurus* Topic
Unit 1 Engineering Design Process	
Lesson 1 Engineer It · What Is a Design Process?	Doing Science, Science is Observing
	Doing Science, Doing an Investigation
	Doing Science, Engineering and Technology
Careers in Science & Engineering · Mechanical Engineer	Doing Science, Engineering and Technology
	Yellow Pages, History of Science
	Yellow Pages, Science Time Line
	Yellow Pages, Famous Scientists and Inventors
Lesson 2 Engineer It · How Can We Compare Design Solutions?	Doing Science, Science is Observing
	Doing Science, Doing an Investigation
	Doing Science, Engineering and Technology
People in Science & Engineering · Gustave Eiffel	Doing Science, Engineering and Technology
	Yellow Pages, History of Science
	Yellow Pages, Science Time Line
	Yellow Pages, Famous Scientists and Inventors
Unit 2 Matter	
Lesson 1 Engineer It · What Are Properties of Matter?	Physical Science, Matter
People in Science & Engineering · Dr. Eugene Tssui	Yellow Pages, History of Science
	Yellow Pages, Science Time Line
	Yellow Pages, Famous Scientists and Inventors
Lesson 2 How Are Objects Put Together?	Physical Science, Matter
Careers in Science & Engineering · Architect	Physical Science, Matter
	Yellow Pages, History of Science
	Yellow Pages, Science Time Line
	Yellow Pages, Famous Scientists and Inventors

Correlation to *ScienceSaurus*

Science Dimensions Grade 2	*ScienceSaurus* Topic
Unit 2 Matter (continued)	
Lesson 3 How Do Heating and Cooling Change Matter?	Physical Science, Matter
	Physical Science, Energy
Careers in Science & Engineering • Chefs at Work	Physical Science, Matter
	Physical Science, Energy
	Yellow Pages, History of Science
	Yellow Pages, Science Time Line
	Yellow Pages, Famous Scientists and Inventors
Lesson 4 How Does Matter Change?	Physical Science, Matter
	Physical Science, Energy
Unit 3 Environments for Living Things	
Lesson 1 What Do Plants Need?	Life Science, Living Things
	Life Science, Plants
	Earth Science, The Earth
Lesson 2 **Engineer It** • How Do Plants Depend on Animals?	Life Science, Living Things
	Life Science, Plants
Careers in Science & Engineering • Horticulturalist	Life Science, Plants
	Yellow Pages, History of Science
	Yellow Pages, Science Time Line
	Yellow Pages, Famous Scientists and Inventors
Lesson 3 What Plants and Animals Live in Water Habitats?	Life Science, Animals
	Life Science, Environments and Ecosystems
Careers in Science & Engineering • Marine Biologist	Life Science, Environments and Ecosystems
	Yellow Pages, History of Science
	Yellow Pages, Science Time Line
	Yellow Pages, Famous Scientists and Inventors
Lesson 4 What Plants and Animals Live in Land Habitats?	Life Science, Animals
	Life Science, Environments and Ecosystems
People in Science & Engineering • Dr. Emilio Bruna	Yellow Pages, History of Science
	Yellow Pages, Science Time Line
	Yellow Pages, Famous Scientists and Inventors

Science Dimensions Grade 2	*ScienceSaurus* Topic
Unit 4 Earth's Surface	
Lesson 1 Where Is Water Found on Earth?	Earth Science, The Earth
People in Science & Engineering • John G. Ferris	Yellow Pages, History of Science
	Yellow Pages, Science Time Line
	Yellow Pages, Famous Scientists and Inventors
Lesson 2 Engineer It • How Can We Map Land and Water?	Almanac, Maps
	Almanac, Units of Measure
Careers in Science & Engineering • Mapmakers	Almanac, Maps
	Almanac, Units of Measure
	Yellow Pages, History of Science
	Yellow Pages, Science Time Line
	Yellow Pages, Famous Scientists and Inventors
Unit 5 Changes to Earth's Surface	
Lesson 1 What Changes on Earth Happen Slowly?	Natural Resources and the Environment, Earth's Natural Resources
Careers in Science & Engineering • Farming	Natural Resources and the Environment, Earth's Natural Resources
	Yellow Pages, History of Science
	Yellow Pages, Science Time Line
	Yellow Pages, Famous Scientists and Inventors
Lesson 2 What Changes on Earth Happen Quickly?	Earth Science, The Earth
People in Science & Engineering • Dr. Rosaly M.C. Lopes	Yellow Pages, History of Science
	Yellow Pages, Science Time Line
	Yellow Pages, Famous Scientists and Inventors
Lesson 3 Engineer It • How Can We Prevent Wind and Water from Changing Land?	Earth Science, The Earth
Careers in Science & Engineering • Geotechnical Engineer	Natural Resources and the Environment, Earth's Natural Resources
	Yellow Pages, History of Science
	Yellow Pages, Science Time Line
	Yellow Pages, Famous Scientists and Inventors

Interactive Glossary

Teacher Notes

_____

_____

_____

_____

_____

_____

_____

_____

_____

_____

_____

_____

Interactive Glossary

This Interactive Glossary will help you learn how to spell and define a vocabulary term. The Glossary will give you the meaning of the term. It will also show you a picture to help you understand what the term means.

Where you see ⬛✏️▷, write your own words or draw your own picture to help you remember what the term means.

Glossary Pronunciation Key

With every glossary term, there is also a phonetic respelling. A phonetic respelling writes the word the way it sounds, which can help you pronounce new or unfamiliar words. Use this key to help you understand the respellings.

Sound	As in	Phonetic Respelling	Sound	As in	Phonetic Respelling
a	bat	(BAT)	oh	over	(OH•ver)
ah	lock	(LAHK)	oo	pool	(POOL)
air	rare	(RAIR)	ow	out	(OWT)
ar	argue	(AR•gyoo)	oy	foil	(FOYL)
aw	law	(LAW)	s	cell	(SEL)
ay	face	(FAYS)		sit	(SIT)
ch	chapel	(CHAP•uhl)	sh	sheep	(SHEEP)
e	test	(TEST)	th	that	(THAT)
	metric	(MEH•trik)		thin	(THIN)
ee	eat	(EET)	u	pull	(PUL)
	feet	(FEET)	uh	medal	(MED•uhl)
	ski	(SKEE)		talent	(TAL•uhnt)
er	paper	(PAY•per)		pencil	(PEN•suhl)
	fern	(FERN)		onion	(UHN•yuhn)
eye	idea	(eye•DEE•uh)		playful	(PLAY•fuhl)
i	bit	(BIT)		dull	(DUHL)
ing	going	(GOH•ing)	y	yes	(YES)
k	card	(KARD)		ripe	(RYP)
	kite	(KYT)	z	bags	(BAGZ)
ngk	bank	(BANGK)	zh	treasure	(TREZH•er)

R1

© Houghton Mifflin Harcourt

Interactive Glossary

compass rose (KUM·puhs ROHZ)

A part of a map that shows directions north, south, east, and west. (p. 205)

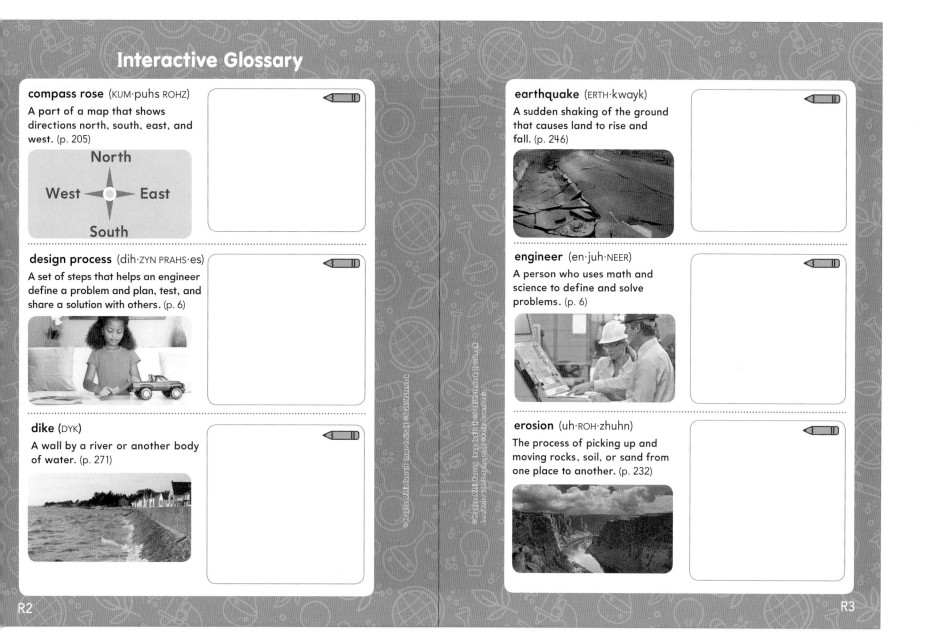

design process (dih·ZYN PRAHS·es)

A set of steps that helps an engineer define a problem and plan, test, and share a solution with others. (p. 6)

dike (DYK)

A wall by a river or another body of water. (p. 271)

earthquake (ERTH·kwayk)

A sudden shaking of the ground that causes land to rise and fall. (p. 246)

engineer (en·juh·NEER)

A person who uses math and science to define and solve problems. (p. 6)

erosion (uh·ROH·zhuhn)

The process of picking up and moving rocks, soil, or sand from one place to another. (p. 232)

R2

R3

Interactive Glossary

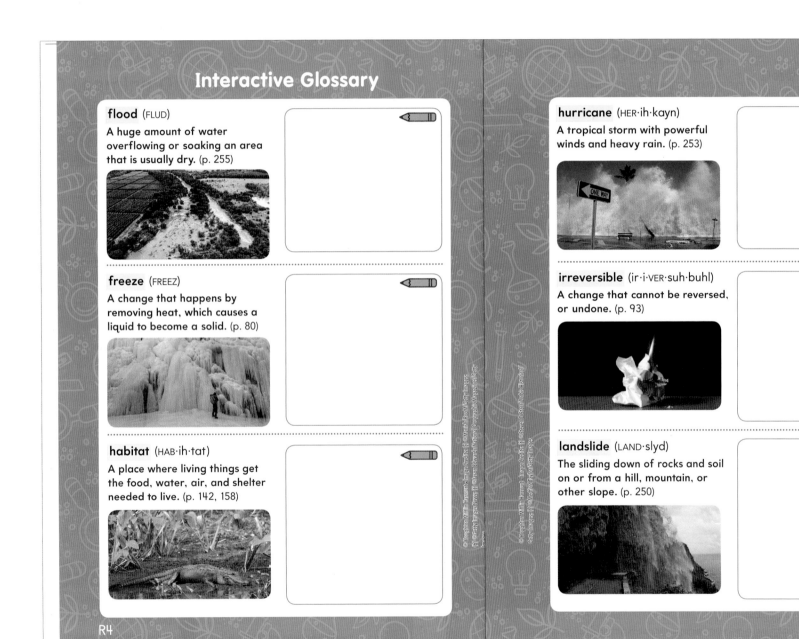

flood (FLUD)

A huge amount of water overflowing or soaking an area that is usually dry. (p. 255)

freeze (FREEZ)

A change that happens by removing heat, which causes a liquid to become a solid. (p. 80)

habitat (HAB·ih·tat)

A place where living things get the food, water, air, and shelter needed to live. (p. 142, 158)

hurricane (HER·ih·kayn)

A tropical storm with powerful winds and heavy rain. (p. 253)

irreversible (ir·i·VER·suh·buhl)

A change that cannot be reversed, or undone. (p. 93)

landslide (LAND·slyd)

The sliding down of rocks and soil on or from a hill, mountain, or other slope. (p. 250)

Interactive Glossary

liquid (LIK·wid)

A state of matter that takes the shape of its container. (p. 49)

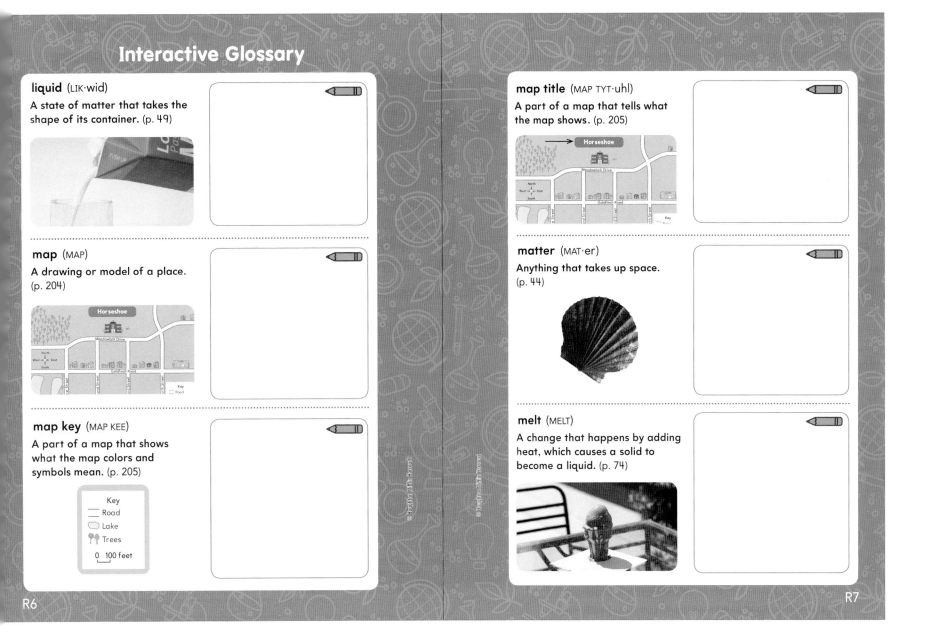

map (MAP)

A drawing or model of a place. (p. 204)

map key (MAP KEE)

A part of a map that shows what the map colors and symbols mean. (p. 205)

map title (MAP TYT·uhl)

A part of a map that tells what the map shows. (p. 205)

matter (MAT·er)

Anything that takes up space. (p. 44)

melt (MELT)

A change that happens by adding heat, which causes a solid to become a liquid. (p. 74)

Interactive Glossary

nutrient (NOO·tree·uhnt)

Anything that living things, such as plants, need as food. (p. 112)

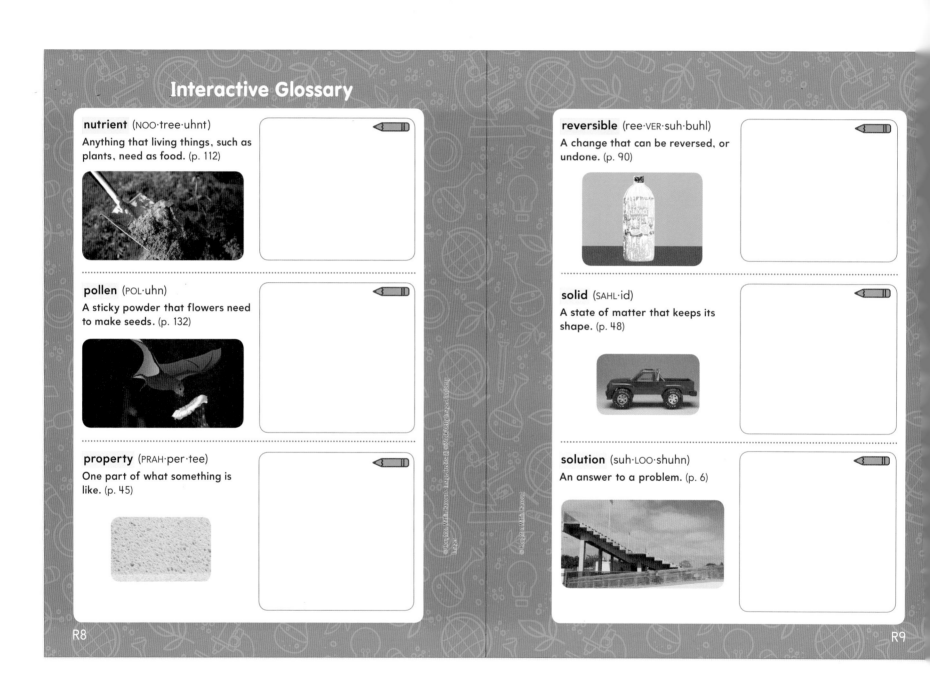

pollen (POL·uhn)

A sticky powder that flowers need to make seeds. (p. 132)

property (PRAH·per·tee)

One part of what something is like. (p. 45)

reversible (ree·VER·suh·buhl)

A change that can be reversed, or undone. (p. 90)

solid (SAHL·id)

A state of matter that keeps its shape. (p. 48)

solution (suh·LOO·shuhn)

An answer to a problem. (p. 6)

Interactive Glossary

strength (STRENGTH)

A good feature. (p. 24)

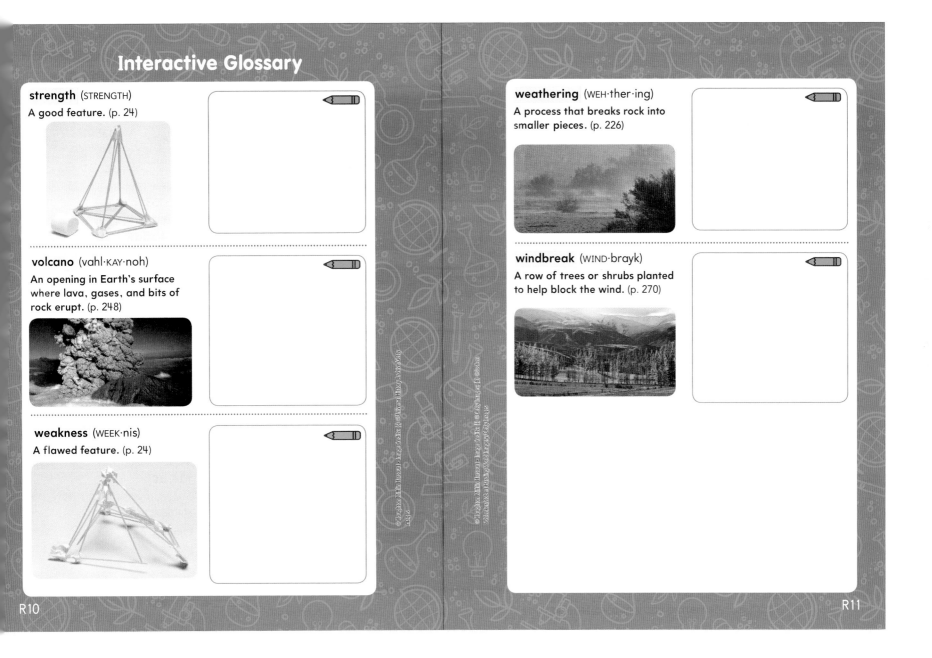

volcano (vahl·KAY·noh)

An opening in Earth's surface where lava, gases, and bits of rock erupt. (p. 248)

weakness (WEEK·nis)

A flawed feature. (p. 24)

weathering (WEH·ther·ing)

A process that breaks rock into smaller pieces. (p. 226)

windbreak (WIND·brayk)

A row of trees or shrubs planted to help block the wind. (p. 270)